S0-BMA-415

NIGER

CHAD

Lake
Chad

Kano

Fort Lamy

JOS PLATEAU

Chari

Logone

ERIA

Benue

BR. CAMEROONS

UBANGI - SHARI

CAMEROONS

CAMEROON HIGHLANDS

Bangui

Ubangi

Douala

Yaoundé

Congo

Bata

RIO
MUNI

Yangambi

Lake
Albert

Libreville

Stanleyville

Lake
Edward

GABON

MIDDLE CONGO

BELGIAN
CONGO

Lac
Kivu

Bukavu

Brazzaville

Sankuru

Léopoldville

Kasai

Lualaba

Cabinda

Congo

Lake
Tanganyika

Luanda

Lake
Mweru

Elisabethville

BIÉ PLATEAU

ANGOLA

P. L. Theimer

THE STAPLE FOOD ECONOMIES OF WESTERN TROPICAL AFRICA

Withdrawn from UF. Surveyed to Internet Archive

Publications of the Institute

CURRENT SERIES

STUDIES ON FOOD, AGRICULTURE, AND WORLD WAR II
STUDIES IN COMMODITY ECONOMICS AND AGRICULTURAL POLICY
STUDIES IN TROPICAL DEVELOPMENT
MISCELLANEOUS PUBLICATIONS

DISCONTINUED SERIES

COMMODITY POLICY STUDIES   GRAIN ECONOMICS SERIES
FATS AND OILS STUDIES   WAR-PEACE PAMPHLETS
            WHEAT STUDIES

A complete list of publications
of the Food Research Institute
will be furnished on request.

A Publication of the
FOOD RESEARCH INSTITUTE
STANFORD UNIVERSITY

One of a group of
STUDIES IN TROPICAL DEVELOPMENT

The

STAPLE FOOD ECONOMIES

of

WESTERN TROPICAL AFRICA

By

BRUCE F. JOHNSTON

Stanford University Press

STANFORD, CALIFORNIA

1958

35.3
J72s

AGRI-
CULTURAL
LIBRARY

FOOD RESEARCH INSTITUTE

Established at Stanford University, Stanford, California, in 1921, jointly by Carnegie Corporation of New York and the Trustees of the Leland Stanford Junior University, for research in the production, distribution, and consumption of food.

STAFF

MERRILL K. BENNETT
Director

KARL BRANDT
Associate Director

HOLBROOK WORKING
Associate Director

JOSEPH S. DAVIS
Consultant

VLADIMIR P. TIMOSHENKO
Consultant

WILLIAM O. JONES
Executive Secretary

HELEN C. FARNSWORTH
Economist

S. DANIEL NEUMARK
Acting Economist

VERNON D. WICKIZER
Economist

ROGER W. GRAY
Associate Economist

BORIS C. SWERLING
Economist

BRUCE F. JOHNSTON
Associate Economist

E. LOUISE PEFFER
Economist

ROSAMOND H. PEIRCE
Associate Statistician

P. STANLEY KING
Cartographer and Editorial Assistant

STANFORD UNIVERSITY PRESS, STANFORD, CALIFORNIA
LONDON: OXFORD UNIVERSITY PRESS

© 1958 BY THE BOARD OF TRUSTEES OF THE LELAND STANFORD JUNIOR UNIVERSITY
ALL RIGHTS RESERVED

PRINTED IN THE UNITED STATES OF AMERICA

The Library of Congress catalog entry for this book appears at the end of the text.

PREFACE

The purpose of this study is to present a broad picture of the staple food crops of major importance in African agriculture and diets. A huge region, here called western tropical Africa, has been considered in order to bring out similarities and contrasts in the position of the staple food crops. Particular attention is given to the physical, economic, and social factors which seem most pertinent in explaining the considerable variation in the relative importance of the staple crops, not only as among territories but also as among smaller districts. An effort has been made, although of necessity a highly tentative one, to consider prospective changes in the position of the staple food crops as well as the outlook for increasing productivity and enlarging supplies to meet the rising demand for food which is a corollary of economic development.

While the work is based primarily on published materials, a four-month trip in early 1958 to West and Central Africa, and London, Brussels, Paris, and Rome afforded opportunities to complete and verify many points and to correct a number of erroneous impressions and interpretations. It is a pleasure to express my appreciation of the extremely kind assistance given me by government officials and research workers in each of the territories that I visited. In spite of such aid, a book of this scope will inevitably be found to contain errors; and I shall be grateful to have mistakes of fact or interpretation called to my attention.

My greatest obligation is to my colleague, William O. Jones, who has helped me without stint throughout the preparation of this study. His forthcoming book, *Manioc in Africa*, has been the source of much valuable information and has suggested many useful lines of inquiry. M. K. Bennett assisted me greatly in outlining the present study, and his critical reading of the draft manuscript resulted in many improvements in style and organization. Although I have no illusions about attaining here the standard set by Bennett and V. D. Wickizer in their book, *The Rice Economy of Monsoon Asia*, I should say that the plan of this one was influenced by that valuable study as well as by Naum Jasny's *Competition Among Grains*.

I owe thanks to P. Stanley King and Mrs. Patricia Theimer for preparation of the maps and charts; the maps which portray the staple food crop zones reflect many of their ideas. Mr. King has also given valuable editorial assistance. Professor C. W. Thornthwaite kindly permitted reproduction of maps and data prepared at the Laboratory of Climatology which have been particularly valuable in considering the availability of moisture as a factor influencing the pattern of crop distribution.

Among the persons who have read and criticized portions of the manuscript, I wish to acknowledge especially the assistance of Professor W. Arthur Lewis, Mr. J. O. Torto, and Dr. F. R. Irvine, all of whom read the entire manuscript and offered helpful suggestions for revision. Miss Rosamond Peirce and Mrs. Catherine Whittemore assisted me in the preparation and checking of the statistical tables. My secretary, Mrs. Hortensia J. Butler, has given me competent and careful assistance in preparing the index and checking citations as well as in typing successive drafts of the manuscript.

Grateful acknowledgment is made to Carnegie Corporation of New York for a grant to the Food Research Institute of funds which made this study possible. The Corporation is not, however, the publisher or proprietor of this publication and is not to be understood as approving by virtue of its grant any of the statements made or views expressed herein.

BRUCE F. JOHNSTON

STANFORD, CALIFORNIA
September 1958

CONTENTS

ix

MAPS

xi

MAPS

THE STAPLE FOOD ECONOMIES OF
WESTERN TROPICAL AFRICA

CHAPTER 1

THE STAPLE FOOD CROPS IN RELATION
TO ECONOMIC DEVELOPMENT

The expansion of food production and increased productivity in agriculture are widely recognized as important aspects of the process of economic growth. Urbanization, rising incomes, and population growth[1] mean an enlarged demand for food. An increase in productivity on the farms is required in the first instance simply to satisfy this rising demand for foodstuffs, but it is also needed to release people from the land for employment in industry, mining, and commerce.

The general proposition that improvements in agricultural productivity and enlargement of food supplies are highly important features of economic development need not be labored here. A recent study of industrialization in underdeveloped countries by the United Nations Secretariat takes pains to stress the dependence of industrial development on parallel progress in agriculture, and asserts that in some areas the relative neglect of agriculture "has been the cause of serious interruptions in the course of economic development" (27, p. 3). W. A. Lewis is considerably more emphatic in his *Report on Industrialisation and the Gold Coast*. "The most certain way to promote industrialisation in the Gold Coast," he declares, "is to lay the foundation it requires by taking vigorous measures to raise food production per person in agriculture" (14, p. 2).[2] In tropical Africa

---

[1] It is not possible to infer the rate of population growth in tropical Africa by comparison of population statistics for different points of time; the margin of error in these estimates is considerable and the inclusiveness and reliability of census enumerations or estimations have varied substantially over the years. On the basis of a critical evaluation of all available evidence, the French statistical services estimate that the current rate of population growth in the French territories of tropical Africa is between one and two per cent per year. A series of sample surveys carried out in recent years has provided estimates of fertility, mortality, and natural increase for the areas studied, and for the most part these survey estimates suggest that the over-all rate of increase is close to two per cent. For a good general description of these demographic surveys and other evidence available see 4a.

[2] In Lewis' book, *The Theory of Economic Growth* (15, see especially pp. 92–93, 230–31, 276–77), the role of agriculture in economic development is analyzed with more attention to the complex interrelationships involved.

3

the rising demand for food poses special problems related to the adaptation of a primitive hand agriculture, with its reliance on shifting cultivation,[3] to this new situation which requires that increasingly large quantities of foodstuffs move through commercial channels to supply the needs of a growing nonself-supplier population.

In many parts of tropical Africa the rapid pace of industrial development and urbanization has evoked concern whether food production will increase fast enough to satisfy this rising demand of the nonfarm population. Economic growth as reflected in expanded employment in mining and manufacturing enterprises has been particularly evident in the Belgian Congo, where the number of Africans employed in European enterprises has increased from about half a million in 1940 to over a million in 1953 (10, pp. 581–82). More generally, the growth of cities in the Congo and elsewhere represents an increasingly large population to be fed, whether by local production or by imports. While urban population in western tropical Africa is still a small fraction of the total, ranging from just over one per cent of the total population residing in towns of 5,000 or larger in Liberia to 12 per cent in Ghana, the recent growth has been striking (26, p. 146). Comparison of the prewar and postwar population figures for the major cities shown in Table 1-1 gives an indication of the way food requirements of nonself-suppliers have been enlarged simply by the increase in numbers; and rising incomes have meant an increase in per-capita demand as well.

Although the general relationship between food requirements and urbanization and economic growth has been a large factor in French West Africa, the French authorities have been particularly conscious of the effect on food supplies of the loss of abundant and cheap rice from Indochina. Prior to World War II rice imports from Indochina were of particular importance in Senegal, where a high level of peanut exports depends upon adequate supplies of staple foods from outside sources, and the shortage and high level of prices for rice in the early postwar years underscored the importance of expanding local food production. Food imports from other sources, with a partial shift from rice to wheat, has been part of the answer to this problem; but measures to increase local production have been

---

[3] Shifting cultivation, or "bush fallowing" as it is often termed, is the common African practice of clearing a piece of land in the forest or bush, planting crops on the clearing for several years until the fertility is depleted, and then abandoning the field for an indefinite period. Natural regeneration of the forest or bush cover restores the fertility and humus content of the soil if sufficient time, perhaps 5 to 30 years, elapses before the same piece of land is cleared again for cropping.

regarded as the preferred solution for various reasons, particularly because of shortage of foreign exchange, a problem in the French overseas territories as well as in metropolitan France.

TABLE 1-1.—PREWAR AND POSTWAR POPULATION, SELECTED CITIES OF
WESTERN TROPICAL AFRICA*

City	Territory	Population[a] (thousand persons)	
		Prewar	Postwar
Dakar and Gorée	Senegal	54 (1931)	231 (1956)
Saint Louis	Senegal	30 (1931)	39 (1954)
Conakry	French Guinea	7 (1931)	53 (1951)
Freetown	Sierra Leone	55 (1931)	85 (1956?)
Abidjan	Ivory Coast	10 (1931)	128 (1956)
Accra	Ghana (Gold Coast)	70 (1931)	136 (1948)
Ibadan	Nigeria	387 (1931)	459 (1952)
Lagos	Nigeria	126 (1931)	267 (1952)
Leopoldville	Belgian Congo	90 (1939)	257 (1953)
Luanda	Angola	61 (1940)	142 (1950)

* Sources for city populations are as follows: DAKAR AND GORÉE, SAINT LOUIS, and ABIDJAN, Afrique Occidentale Française, Haut Commissariat, A.O.F. 1957. Tableaux économiques (November 1957); CONAKRY, France, Min. Outre-mer, Serv. Stat., Inventaire social et économique des territoires d'Outre-mer, 1950 à 1955 (Paris, 1957), p. 27; LEOPOLDVILLE (prewar), Lord Hailey, "Post-war Changes in Africa," J. Roy Soc. Arts (London), July 8, 1955, pp. 581–82; IBADAN and LAGOS (prewar), Lord Hailey, An African Survey . . . (London, 1939), p. 1426, (postwar) United Nations, Dept. Econ. and Soc. Affairs, Demographic Yearbook, 1955 (New York), p. 171; LEOPOLDVILLE (postwar), Belg., Min. Col., Dir. Études Écon., Les Investissements au Congo Belge: Perspectives et réglementation (La Louviére, 1955), p. 8; LUANDA, Adriano Moreira, "The Formation of a Middle Class in Angola and Mozambique," in Inst. Internatl. des Civilisations Differents, Développement d'une classe moyenne dans les pays tropicaux et sub-tropicaux, Compte rendu de la XXIXe session tenue à Londres du 13 au 16 septembre 1955 (Brussels, 1956), p. 238; FREETOWN, H. R. Jarrett, "Some Aspects of the Urban Geography of Freetown, Sierra Leone," Geog. Rev., July 1956, p. 351.
[a] Figures in parentheses are the year of census or estimation.

Preoccupation with rising food prices has keynoted interest in food production in Ghana (the Gold Coast)[4] and Nigeria in recent years. Food prices rose sharply in both territories in 1948–49 and again between 1950 and 1951. According to the retail price index for locally produced foodstuffs in seven cities, food prices in the Gold Coast showed a sharp rise of 45 per cent between 1948 and 1949 and a further increase of 28 per cent between 1950 and 1951,

[4] In historical references to the period prior to March 1957 when Ghana became an independent state, the term Gold Coast is used. In all other instances, including references to the geographical entity or statements in which the historical timing is not especially relevant, the new name Ghana is used.

with a 56 per cent rise in Accra (*23*, p. 23; *7*, p. 19). Price data for
Ibadan suggest an even sharper rise in Nigerian food prices between
1950 and 1951. Between January 1950 and January 1951, the price
of maize nearly doubled and the prices of yams and *gari* (manioc
meal) increased more than twofold (*16*, p. 47). In the Gold Coast
the rising food prices provoked considerable anxiety, and the Department of Agriculture's report for 1949/50 asserted that "if something were not done the country would be faced with a chronic food
shortage and greatly inflated prices" (*6*, p. 3). In reporting on
a visit to the Gold Coast in the summer of 1951, Seers and Ross
stressed the problem of inflationary increases in food prices and were
skeptical about the extent to which domestic food production would
respond to higher prices: "Rising prices have induced some increase
in output, but the production of food for market has not increased
fast enough to meet the enormous increases in demand associated
with growing population, rising money incomes and the rapid growth
in the number of people working in the towns" (*23*, p. 23).

Possibly stimulated by this type of interpretation of the situation
in the Gold Coast, the notion seems to have come in vogue that the
supply function for food in tropical Africa is particularly inelastic.
Peter Ady, for example, has asserted that "it is only to be expected
that a period of rapid growth in Africa will be characterized by a
sharp rise in local food prices, because of the inelasticity of domestic
food supplies" (*1*, p. 409; see also p. 407). Whether these assertions are accurate is unknown. Their meaning and validity are examined briefly in Chapter 10, where an attempt is also made to assess the prospects for long-run expansion of staple food supplies to
meet the growth of demand. But this study is primarily concerned
with prior questions: What are the chief staple food crops in the
various regions of western tropical Africa? And what are the factors
—climatic, economic, and cultural—underlying the existing geographical distribution of these crops?

"Western tropical Africa," as the term is used in this study, embraces West Africa,[5] French Equatorial Africa and the Cameroons,
the Belgian Congo; Spanish Guinea, and Angola. Some 80 million
persons occupy this area of about 4.7 million square miles, an area
considerably larger than the United States with its three million
square miles. Statistical limitations and lack of certain types of
data will be noted in due course, but quite apart from those prob-

[5] Comprising the eight territories of French West Africa; French Togo; Gambia,
Sierra Leone, Ghana, Nigeria; Portuguese Guinea; and Liberia.

lems the enormous size and considerable diversity of the area considered would have been sufficient to compel a broad and tentative treatment of the subject. No attempt has been made to deal with East Africa in this study for various reasons, including the complex and quite different physical features and the much greater importance of European farming there. But it should be pointed out that the major staple foods of tropical East Africa and South Africa are the same as those considered here although, of course, the relative importance of the various crops is quite different.

With regard to the picture of the present geographical distribution of the staple food crops which emerges, a number of corrections, and certainly refinements, could no doubt be made with more complete and accurate data. Nevertheless, the general pattern of crop distribution presented seems reasonably accurate, although there are a half-dozen territories where no local breakdown is possible. The examination of the factors underlying the pattern of crop distribution is a highly provisional effort to bring together information about the characteristics of the crops and the views which have been offered to explain in some measure the position of the various crops in different areas. Far more intensive analysis of the pertinent influences at work in a limited area would be needed in order to evaluate the relative importance of the various causal factors.

IMPORTANCE OF THE STARCHY STAPLES

Attention is focused in this study on a group of starchy staple foods—millets and sorghums, maize, rice, manioc,[6] yams, cocoyams,[7] sweet potatoes, and the starchy banana or plantain—that are of pre-eminent importance in African diets. Pre-eminence of starchy staples—cereals and roots and tubers—is characteristic of nearly all low-income nations or communities the world over and for essentially

---

[6] Manioc, *Manihot utilissima*, is often known as cassava or tapioca; the latter term is more properly limited to a product prepared from manioc starch.

[7] The term cocoyam is used here to include *Colocasia esculentum* and *Colocasia antiquorum*, the so-called "old" cocoyams, and *Xanthosoma sagittifolium*, the "new" cocoyams. The Polynesian name "taro" should, strictly speaking, only be applied to the genus *Colocasia* but is often used as a common name for *Xanthosoma* as well (4, p. 417). In discussing cocoyams in Nigeria, V. A. Oyenuga refers to the genus *Colocasia* as "taro" and applies the name "tania" to varieties of *Xanthosoma* (17). In the United States and the Caribbean the name "dasheen" is commonly applied to varieties of *Colocasia*; and a number of varieties of *Xanthosoma* are frequently termed "Yautias." R. Cerighelli (4, p. 418) distinguishes between *Colocasia antiquorum* and *C. esculenta*, but in Africa the two terms seem to be used interchangeably and, in fact, the difference is very slight.

the same reason. Production of the starchy staples requires less land and less labor per thousand calories than other foods. In the rain-forest zones of tropical Africa where the oil palm thrives, palm oil rivals or even surpasses the starchy staples as a cheap and easy source of calories; palm oil probably contributes something like 10 to 20 per cent of total calories in such regions. Although the contribution of cereals and roots—perhaps 60 to 80 per cent of the total —is much larger, their importance is not so great as in the savanna regions where they appear to contribute at least 85 per cent of total food calories.

The major staples considered here loom very large in the predominantly agricultural economies of tropical Africa. According to the recent national income estimates for Nigeria by Prest and Stewart, consumer expenditures for food and drink accounted for some 60 per cent of the Gross Domestic Product. The estimated value of output of the starchy staples, including production for home consumption valued at retail prices prevailing at neighboring markets, was equal to 70 per cent of total expenditures for food and drink and just over 40 per cent of the Gross Domestic Product—remarkably high figures considering that these are the cheapest foodstuffs (20, pp. 23, 26, 27, and 49).

A survey of expenditures of wage-earning families in Accra shows a lesser though considerable concentration of expenditures on starchy staple foods. Food purchases accounted for 58 per cent of total family expenditures, but this included almost 9 per cent of total outlay devoted to imported food items. Expenditures on meat, fish, and shellfish by these urban families were high for tropical Africa, accounting for nearly a third of total consumer expenditures. Nevertheless, purchases of locally produced staples, which provided the cheap calories of the diet, amounted to some 28 per cent of the average family budget (8, pp. 2, 3, 14).

For many years to come a major part of the increased demand for food resulting from population growth, urbanization, and industrial development will be satisfied by enlarged output of these starchy staples. Efforts to increase agricultural productivity and promote economic development in Africa must, if priorities are determined in an intelligent manner, be concerned in large measure with the production, distribution, and processing of these staple food crops.

Apart from the significance of the staple crops in relation to increasing agricultural productivity, these staple foods will probably have a still more direct connection with economic development in tropical Africa. As income levels rise high enough to permit a considerable increase in livestock products and other desired but expensive commodities, it may be expected that "the starchy staple ratio"—the proportion of total calories provided by cereals, roots, and starchy fruits—will decline, a familiar feature of economic growth (*2*, pp. 213–22). In the territories considered here, however, it seems likely that in an initial period rising income levels will also be associated with increased consumption of the staple foods and a shift toward "superior" staples.

THE STAPLE FOOD CROPS IN RELATION TO CHANGING AGRICULTURAL SYSTEMS

Plant breeders, agronomists, agricultural engineers, and soil scientists are currently giving a good deal of attention to means of expanding production of tropical food crops by methods which avoid serious problems of erosion or deterioration of soil structure. There has also been a mounting interest in developing improved systems of farming with greater attention to increasing yields, minimizing production costs, and enhancing farm incomes.

F. J. Pedler has recently argued that the primitive agriculture generally prevailing in West Africa, with its reliance on shifting cultivation, "is not a system of agriculture which can provide surpluses to support large urban populations" (*18*, p. 44). In their study of Nigeria, Buchanan and Pugh argue that in certain regions the traditional system of shifting cultivation or bush fallowing is becoming untenable as a result of population pressure and consequent shortening of the fallow period. This situation is said to prevail in the closely settled areas of the Jos Plateau, and more acutely in Owerri Province and parts of Calabar Province in the Eastern Region where population densities exceed 400 per square mile (*3*, p. 105). With regard to the Owerri and Calabar districts, Buchanan and Pugh assert (*3*, pp. 105–07):

Under these conditions the natural vegetation has no opportunity to regenerate, and there has been a progressive degeneration, resulting in the replacement of high forest by barren grassland over wide areas. Such grasslands are of little use except as rough grazing, and their protective value is reduced by their tussock character and by annual grass fires, which lay bare the soil to erosion by the heavy rains of summer. The beginning of large-scale gully erosion in parts of this area is an indication of the final collapse of the system of bush fallowing as a result of increasing population pressure.

Later they speak of "the growing instability of African agriculture" not only because of growth of population but also as a result of "the expansion of cash cropping" for internal and external markets (*3*, p. 159).[8]

From a different point of view, Kellogg and Davol have spoken of the need to evolve improved systems of management which will enhance the productivity of African soils. They have stressed particularly the importance of fundamental and applied research to provide "a basis for new inventions in soil management" needed to realize "the great potentialities of tropical soils" (*13*, p. 71). In a similar vein, A. L. Jolly has underscored the importance of devising improved management systems based upon knowledge which is accumulating with respect to crop rotations, fertilizer use, and mixed farming (*12*, p. 62; *11*, pp. 80–87).

Recently G. Tondeur, Director of the Soil Conservation Mission in the Belgian Congo, has spoken (*25*, p. 71) of the "huge scope for scientific agricultural research . . . to find farming methods to replace shifting cultivation. Such studies would seek to:

1. work out the agricultural techniques that would save the maximum organic matter in the soils, chiefly by preventing erosion, protecting the soil against excessive aeration, light and heat from the sun: it would be advisable in this respect to adopt a system of unbroken crop rotations and mixed crops, patterned on the native method, together with perennials;

2. work out the simplest, most efficient and cheapest methods to supply the soil with organic matter, other than by the forest fallow;

3. devise farming methods compatible with a low level of humus in the soil without endangering the conservation of the agricultural value of the latter."

Tondeur goes on to say that in the long run "the prerequisite for substantial progress along these lines is the introduction and widespread use of cattle in the rural economy" (*25*, p. 71). This will not only return manure to the soil but will also make possible a more intensive agriculture and provide an economic utilization of fallow crops. At present, however, the emphasis in the Belgian Congo is on measures to develop a more systematic system of "crop rotations and mixed crops, patterned on the native methods . . ." (*25*, p. 71). These efforts to develop a stabilized and improved version of "Bantu

---

[8] In a similar vein R. M. Prothero has stated that the problems resulting from growth of population are "vastly aggravated by the increase in the growing of export crops, the cash incentive offered by them causing land to be retained in cultivation long after it should have been returned to fallow" (*21*, p. 330).

agriculture" through the creation of *paysannats indigènes*, or "native agricultural settlements," are reviewed in Chapter 10.

Measures to introduce mixed farming were initiated as early as 1928 in northern Nigeria (*3*, p. 124),[9] and in recent years considerable attention has been given to this line of development in the Northern Territories of Ghana and in parts of French West Africa. The years since World War II have seen a number of schemes in both British and French West Africa to introduce mechanized farming. The widespread interest in measures to enlarge the production of irrigated rice will be examined later in some detail.

Quite apart from government-sponsored measures, there is evidence that African cultivators in many areas are modifying their farming practices and, in particular, modifying the pattern of crops produced and the extent to which their production is commercialized. Speaking of the Niari valley of French Equatorial Africa, Gilles Sautter has observed that (*22*, p. 75):

in this part of Africa, the systems of cultivation are much less static, much more in flux than is commonly imagined. The trade carried on by the women, the contacts with other groups, the men who returned from trips, the action of the administration and the missions, and the demands of commerce involve a continuous transformation and adaptation which have a notable influence on the crops. Certain species, certain varieties, which are being supplanted by others or are no longer attractive, are declining; the area devoted to them is being reduced steadily. In contrast, others are the object of strictly local trials.

In addition to changes stimulated by "the demands of commerce," adjustments in cropping patterns are also likely to occur in response to increasing recognition of factors such as relative yields and costs of production for alternative crops. The increasing importance of production for sale will tend to focus attention on such factors, and in all probability there are many areas in tropical Africa where, as Shantz has suggested, migrating groups continue to cultivate their traditional crops even though these may be "somewhat out of adjustment with the local soil and climatic conditions" (*24*, p. 13). Roland Portères cites the tribal groups which inhabit the Ubangi savanna region of French Equatorial Africa as a striking example of migrant peoples who have failed to achieve a satisfactory adjustment of their agriculture to a new environment (*19*, pp. 761–62).

Although changes in the pattern of staple food production are to

[9] M. Greenwood indicates that experiments with mixed farming began as early as 1922 (*9*, p. 170).

be expected in the years ahead, it seems certain that most if not all of the staple crops examined in this study will continue to bulk large as human foods, or as feed for livestock. Substantial changes in their relative importance are to be expected; and an understanding of the present pattern of crop production and some of the underlying factors may well throw light on changes which seem desirable or probable. As the late Clement Gillman observed in an admirable maxim, "To know what is, is vital for discussing what ought to be" (5, p. 7).

CITATIONS

1 Peter Ady, "Africa's Economic Potentialities," in C. Grove Haines, ed., *Africa Today* (Baltimore, 1955).

2 M. K. Bennett, *The World's Food* . . . (New York, 1954).

3 K. M. Buchanan and J. C. Pugh, *Land and People in Nigeria* . . . (London, 1955).

4 R. Cerighelli, *Cultures tropicales. I.—Plantes vivrières* (Nouvelle Encycl. Agr., Paris, 1955).

4a France, Min. Outre-mer, Serv. Stat., *Les Populations des territoires d'Outre-mer* (Paris, October 1957).

5 Clement Gillman, "A Vegetation-Types Map of Tanganyika Territory," *Geo. Rev.*, January 1949.

6 Gold Coast, Dept. Agr., *Annual Report . . . 1949–1950* (Accra, 1951)

7 ———, Min. Fin., *Economic Survey 1953* (Accra, 1954).

8 ———, Off. Govt. Stat., *1953 Accra Survey of Household Budgets* (Stat. and Econ. Papers 2, Accra, December 1953).

9 M. Greenwood, "Mixed Farming and Fertilizers in Northern Nigeria," in *Proc. First Commonwealth Conf. on Trop. and Sub-Trop. Soils, 1948* (Commonwealth Bur. Soil Sci., Tech. Communic. 46, Harpenden, 1949).

10 Lord Hailey, "Post-war Changes in Africa," *J. Roy. Soc. Arts* (London), July 8, 1955.

11 A. L. Jolly, "Small-scale Farm Management Problems," *Trop. Agr.* (London), April 1955.

12 ———, "A Third Revolution in Tropical Agriculture?" *New Commonwealth* (London), Jan. 23, 1956.

13 C. E. Kellogg and Fidelia D. Davol, *An Exploratory Study of Soil Groups in the Belgian Congo* (INÉAC Série Sci., 46, Brussels, 1949).

14 W. A. Lewis, *Report on Industrialisation and the Gold Coast* (Gold Coast Govt., Accra, 1953).

15 ———, *The Theory of Economic Growth* (Homewood, Ill., 1955).

16 Nigeria, Dept. Agr., *Annual Report . . . 1950–51* (Lagos, 1953).

17 V. A. Oyenuga, "The Composition and Nutritive Value of Certain Feedingstuffs in Nigeria . . ." *Emp. J. Exp. Agr.* (London), April 1955.

18 F. J. Pedler, *Economic Geography of West Africa* (London, 1955).

19 Roland Portères, "*L'agriculture flottante* Congolo-Tchadienne des Savanes de l'Oubangui," *J. agr. trop. et de botanique appliquée* (Paris), November 1956.

20 A. R. Prest and I. G. Stewart, *The National Income of Nigeria 1950–51* (Gr. Brit., Col. Off. Col. Res. Studies 11, 1953).

21 R. M. Prothero, "Agricultural Problems in Nigeria," *Corona* (Gr. Brit., Col. Off.), September 1953.

22 Gilles Sautter, "Notes sur l'agriculture des Bakamba de la vallée du Niari," *Bull. Inst. Études Centrafricaines* (Brazzaville-Paris), New Ser. 9, 1955.

23 Dudley Seers and C. R. Ross, *Report on Financial and Physical Problems of Development in the Gold Coast* (Gold Coast, Off. Govt. Stat., Accra, 1952).

24 H. L. Shantz, "Agricultural Regions of Africa. Part I. Basic Factors," *Econ. Geog.*, January 1940.

25 G. Tondeur, "Shifting Cultivation in the Belgian Congo," *Unasylva* (FAO, Rome), June 1955. [Translated from original French text.]

26 G. T. Trewartha and Wilbur Zelinsky, "Population Patterns in Tropical Africa," *Ann. Assn. Am. Geog.*, June 1954.

27 United Nations, Dept. Econ. Affairs, *Processes and Problems in Underdeveloped Countries* (New York, 1955).

CHAPTER 2

GENERAL VIEW OF THE STAPLE FOODS OF WESTERN TROPICAL AFRICA

In tropical Africa a great deal of regional variation is evident in the staple foods which are produced and consumed. Throughout most of Asia, rice is the staple food *par excellence*.[1] Wheat is dominant in most of Europe and North America, while maize accounts for the principal exceptions. But in tropical Africa each of a half-dozen or more different crops is by turn the dominant staple for different localities; and over a distance of a few miles the position of different staples in the diet may change drastically.

INTERNAL TRADE

Variations in the consumption of staple foods are a direct result of regional variations in staple food production. François Sorel asserts that in French West Africa 50 years ago "the native was obliged to eat solely that which was grown in his locality" (*26*, p. 155). With the improvement of transportation and the cessation of internal warfare this situation has changed, but it is difficult to generalize confidently about the importance of internal trade in staple foodstuffs today, particularly since there is a good deal of variation in the extent to which exchange has become a major factor in the food economies of tropical Africa.[2] It seems clearly an exaggeration to characterize western tropical Africa as an area of "subsistence agriculture." Local trade at the village level or among neighboring villages is common, and bulky staple foods as well as specialty items figure prominently in these local markets. In addition, certain com-

---

[1] This is notably true of the extensive areas where ample rainfall makes it possible to grow lowland (or irrigated) rice; outstanding as exceptions are northern China and northwestern India where wheat and millets and sorghums are predominant.

[2] The Department of Economic Affairs of the United Nations has attempted to estimate the portion of cultivated land "mainly under crops for market." Their estimates, admittedly very rough approximations, range from only 19 per cent of the area under cultivation in French West Africa to 75 per cent of the cultivated area in Ghana. These figures include land under crops both for domestic markets and for export, and in the case of Ghana it is estimated that export crops alone account for 45 per cent of the area under cultivation (*27*, p. 14).

modities such as kola nuts, livestock, and dried fish often move long
distances; but substantial shipments of the staple foods in excess of
50 or 100 miles appear to be the exception.

A study of the Hausa economies of Zaria in northern Nigeria,
for example, indicates that purchases of kola nuts and palm oil from
the south, of beef and manure from the pastoral Fulanis, and of manufactured or imported goods such as soap, cigarettes, salt, cloth, kero-
sene, perfume, and hardware are of some importance; but these "urban areas depend largely on imports of grain and other imports from
the surrounding area" (*25*, pp. 142–43). Further evidence on this
region is afforded by Nigerian railway statistics. Figures for 1949–
50 show arrivals in Kano and Jos of over 5,000 tons of manioc meal,
close to 2,000 tons of yams, 1,000 tons of maize, and another 1,000
tons of millets and sorghums in each city. But those are not large
shipments for staple foods; rail arrivals of kola nuts in the same year
totaled 13,000 tons and 8,000 tons in Kano and Jos respectively (*24*,
pp. 99–103, 106). Additional quantities move by truck, the famous
"Mammy wagons" of West Africa, but no data are at hand for road
shipments to northern Nigeria. The great bulk of the food supplies
for Accra in Ghana move by truck, and truck transport is also of
prime importance in the cocoa region of western Nigeria. But M. G.
Smith asserts that shipments from southern Nigeria to Zaria are
mostly by rail, and it seems likely that this is true of the other northern cities as well (*25*, p. 145).

Lagos, capital city of Nigeria, also appears to draw the bulk of its
staple food supplies from production centers nearby. With respect
to the chief staple of the city, W. O. Jones reports that some 50 to
100 tons of manioc meal are shipped to Lagos daily. But most of this
is shipped through the lagoons in large canoes from the Ijebu-Ode
region only some 40 miles away (*18*).

For Accra, capital city of Ghana, we have an analysis by H. P.
White of an unpublished survey of movements of staple foodstuffs
by road into the city carried out by the Office of the Government
Statistician (*31*). By studying the flow of traffic at various points
on the incoming roads, it was possible to determine where the shipments originated. Of chief interest here is the fact that roughly
80–85 per cent of total shipments of the order of 120,000 tons a year
seem to have originated in producing areas within 75 miles of Accra.

A survey of food supplies carried out in 1953 and 1954 in
Douala, port city of the French Cameroons, indicated that nearly all
of the domestically produced food reaching Douala (33,000 tons of

an annual 36,500 tons) came from the area just to the north, a distance of perhaps 100 miles at most (7, p. 1366). In similar fashion, it appears that the bulk of the staple food supplies for Leopoldville originates in the Moyen-Congo and Bas-Congo districts, most of it coming from farming areas near the Leopoldville-Matadi rail line and probably not more than 100 miles away. Foremost among the staples for the Congolese population of Leopoldville are large shipments of manioc roots and products, some 42,000 tons in 1944, and in addition the Moyen-Congo and Bas-Congo districts supplied nearly 8,000 tons of dried peas, beans, and peanuts, and nearly 1,500 tons of palm oil. The only other significant shipments of staple foods were, in 1944, approximately 9,000 tons of rice from regions north and east of Leopoldville—mostly from Equateur and Orientale provinces, which lie 350 to 1,000 miles or more from Leopoldville (6, pp. 46–49). Parts of French Equatorial Africa also figure as sources of supply for Leopoldville.

The statement is sometimes made that the cocoa-producing areas of Ghana and Nigeria depend largely on purchased foods. Available evidence suggests that this is indeed the case in the cocoa regions of Nigeria, but not in Ghana. H. P. White has recently reported in a study of food production in Ghana that "all but a few of the cocoa farmers produce their own food" (32, p. 40). Beckett found that in Akokoaso, the village he selected as typical of the cocoa-producing region of the Gold Coast, virtually all of the food consumed was produced in the village. Out of 277 "independent farmers" studied, only 8 produced no food and only 50 had to buy extra food. With respect to the staple foods, the purchased food was mainly from local farmers who produced a small surplus. Of the total consumption of carbohydrate foods, Beckett estimates that more than 97 per cent was produced in the village and only about 10 per cent of the total passed through the local markets. In marked contrast, however, half of the meat suply came from outside the village, and approximately four-fifths of the small quantities of meat consumed passed through the local markets (3, pp. 18–21). The situation may have changed since Beckett made his study in 1933–35, particularly as a result of the favorable cocoa prices of the postwar period. But White's appraisal suggests that Akokoaso was fairly typical in its dependence on local food production and that this condition has not changed drastically over the past two decades.

Substantial dependence on purchased food is, however, clearly indicated by the recent survey of cocoa farmers in the Western Region of Nigeria. Budget data for a sample of 187 families, drawn from various types of towns and villages of the cocoa area, indicate that purchased foods provided more than half of the total calorie intake (*12*, p. 489). The percentage contribution of purchased foods "per standardized person" was remarkably constant through the year, varying only from 61 per cent of total calories in the June–August quarter to 63 per cent in the March–May quarter. Purchases of manioc meal (gari) and other manioc products accounted for a large part of the purchased foods, but purchases of palm oil and maize products also made significant contributions to the calorie intake. Even the category of meat, fish, poultry, and eggs, which consisted almost entirely of purchased items, made a modest contribution of about 130 calories per person per day in a total equivalent to about 3,000 calories per adult male unit.

It is pointed out that the survey year, 1951/52, "was most abnormal in one respect—that the cocoa farmers enjoyed an unusual increase in cash income" (*12*, p. 460). Moreover, prices of commodities purchased by the cocoa farmers seem to have been stable or declining, so that the change in real income was probably still more favorable (*12*, p. 63). Apparently consumption patterns in the survey year were not fully adjusted to the sharp rise in incomes, with the result that some 40 per cent of the disposable income of the families surveyed was saved, a remarkably—even astonishingly—high figure (*12*, p. 462). It is possible that the extremely favorable income situation in 1951/52 encouraged greater reliance on purchased foodstuffs than is representative of the survey families or the area generally.

The most credible explanation of this substantial dependence on purchased food, however, seems to be related to certain characteristics of the rural economy of this Nigerian cocoa region. Most obvious in this regard is the fact that for many farmers it is profitable to give priority in the use of their own and hired labor to their cocoa farms. Of equal or perhaps greater importance, however, is the fact that there is also a fair degree of specialization in the production and still more in the processing of certain food crops. Thus in the Abeokuta-Ijebu area 65 per cent of the families surveyed were manufacturing gari from purchased manioc roots. Production averaged over 2,000 pounds for each family processing gari and 87 per cent of the output was sold. In the Ibadan and Ife-Ilesha areas only a handful of families were occupied with gari production, at least from purchased roots, but over a third of the families were processing purchased maize and selling 100 per cent of their output of maize products (*12*, p. 424). Finally, it needs to be mentioned that the road net and availability of truck transport in this area are unusually good for tropical Africa. Although manioc and maize are in the category of purchased foods, it seems clear that most of their production and processing takes place fairly close to the point of consumption. Much of the gari is no doubt supplied by specialized producers in Ijebu Province, and it is reported that most of the maize comes from Oyo and Ilorin provinces, which border the cocoa area. With respect to yams, only about a fifth of the sizable quantities consumed are purchased. But it would appear that a significant fraction of the quantities purchased are from production centers in Benue Province lying between 200 and 400 miles to the west of Ibadan. According to Galletti and his associates, large quantities of yams are brought by river from Benue Province and from the Eastern Region either to Lokoja, at the junction of the Benue and Niger rivers, or farther south to Onitsha (Asaba) and are then shipped by truck to towns and villages of the cocoa region and to Lagos and Ibadan. On a much smaller scale, the "growing demand for rice in the cocoa-producing areas has drawn supplies from the Jebba area and even the Birnin-Kebbi" (*12*, pp. 61–62); the former is about 135 miles north of Ibadan and the latter lies on the Sokoto River more than 300 miles north of Ibadan.

The Katanga Province of the Belgian Congo exemplifies an area where the growth of mining activities and a doubling of urban population over the past decade have given rise to food requirements which local production could not satisfy. Manioc flour, one of the two major staples, is produced mostly within the province; but over two-thirds of the 38,000 tons of maize flour consumed originated in production areas of Kasai Province, 350 miles or more away from the Katanga centers of Elisabethville and Jadotville (*29*, pp. 60–65).

In Accra approximately 15 or 20 per cent of the truck arrivals of foodstuffs travel a considerable distance. Some 6 or 7 per cent of the total appears to originate in French Togo and appreciable quantities are shipped several hundred miles south from the Northern Territories (*31*, pp. 122–23). Shipments of swamp rice from North Mamprusi, where rice is a new crop, represent an interesting development. Exports of this crop to the south amounted to only 23 tons in 1948 but exceeded 1,500 tons in 1952 (*31*, p. 119).

A development in the Gold Coast during the 1920s provides an interesting example of the effect of transport improvements on staple food production. With the completion of the highway to the Northern Territories, farmers in the town of Ejura, located on the highway 50 miles north of Kumasi, were able to take advantage of the low freight charges on southbound traffic. Within a relatively short period, shipments of yams and maize from Ejura to Kumasi and other markets had been developed to the point where three-fourths of the yam crop and one-half of the output of maize were commercialized (*15*, pp. 218, 223).

There can be no doubt that the rising demand for food in the growing urban centers is stimulating commercial production and, in some instances, giving rise to fairly lengthy shipments of staple foods. And, at least in the Western Region of Nigeria, a degree of specialization in the production of cocoa has led to considerable reliance on purchased foodstuffs. This type of development is obviously most likely to occur where economical shipment by water, truck, or rail transport is possible. Staple foods are far too bulky to support the high cost of transport by headloading, donkey, or bicycle over any considerable distance; and for much of tropical Africa those are still the prevailing modes of transportation.[3]

IMPORTS AND EXPORTS OF STAPLE FOODS

Imports of staple foods from overseas sources, although in aggregate quite small, have been of appreciable importance in supplying some of the larger cities, especially in French West Africa and Ghana (see Table 2-1). In most territories wheat flour is by far the principal food import. In Liberia and apparently Spanish Guinea most of the imports are rice. Prior to World War II, rice was the chief import of French West Africa. In recent years takings of flour have generally been somewhat larger than those of rice, but in 1955 rice imports reached 112,000 tons and exceeded shipments of wheat and flour.[4] Since 1955 flour mills in Dakar, using mainly French and Moroccan wheat, have accounted for a substantial and growing percentage of the flour consumed in French West Africa. Of total flour consumption estimated at 80,000 tons in 1955, the Dakar mills accounted for

---

[3] E. P. Hanson has reported on a demonstration program of the Foreign Economic Administration in which Liberians of the Kpoh Valley eagerly learned to use donkeys, which they had never seen before, and were impressed with the fact that a donkey could carry the load of four or five men. This modest improvement in transportation encouraged the production of grapefruit in the area, since they could now be transported economically to Monrovia (*14*, p. 64).

[4] Of this total nearly 86,000 tons went to Senegal, and the Ivory Coast and French Guinea imported close to 17,000 and 6,500 tons of rice respectively (*8*, p. 284).

TABLE 2-1.—NET IMPORTS OF CEREALS, WESTERN TROPICAL AFRICA*

(1,000 metric tons)

Territory	1934–38	1948–50	1951	1952	1953
Belgian Congo	−5.6	−15.4	−8.4	27.1	24.5
French Cameroons[a]	0.1	7.9	21.6	18.2	21.1
French Equatorial Africa[a].	4.8	7.9	13.8	12.8	10.6
French Togoland[a]	−11.2[b]	1.4	3.0	2.2[c]	1.0
French West Africa[a]	84.3	94.6	154.9	124.2	148.5
Gambia[d]	7.4	3.5	5.4	7.2	4.8
Gold Coast (Ghana)	21.6[e]	27.5[e]	45.4	48.0	43.5
Liberia[d]	...	2.4	3.8	6.8	2.4
Nigeria	14.1[a]	12.3	21.1	22.8	28.8
Sierra Leone[d]	2.5	3.5	5.3	3.9	5.1
Spanish Guinea[f]	...	2.6	2.1	2.8	4.6

* Data from FAO, *Yearbook of Food and Agricultural Statistics 1954; Part 2: Trade* (Rome, 1955). Cereals include wheat and wheat flour (as wheat), rice (milled equivalent), maize, millets, and sorghums, except as noted.

[a] Millets and sorghums not included as no estimates are available, but quantities were probably small or nil.

[b] Maize and wheat estimates only. There may have been small imports of rice.

[c] Includes gross imports of rice of 0.7.

[d] Wheat and rice only.

[e] Maize figures not available prior to 1951, and millets and sorghums not included in prewar total.

[f] Rice only.

34,000 tons. In 1957 total flour consumption was up to 97,000 tons, according to the preliminary estimate of the Office of Coordination of Economic Affairs, and of that total 70,000 tons were supplied by the Dakar mills. Sugar imports, of the order of 60,000 tons in 1953 and 1954, are also a factor in the local food supply in the territories of French West Africa (*4*, p. 18). According to a survey in Douala, from 15 to 20 per cent of the food supply of the African population is imported (*7*, p. 1366).

Trade returns for Liberia suggest a remarkably sharp rise in food imports, with rice imports rising from about 2,000 metric tons in 1953 to nearly 12,000 tons in 1954 and 9,000 tons in 1955 (*20*, p. 32). In Ghana and Nigeria a rising trend is evident in the trade returns for wheat flour. From 7,000 tons prewar, Ghana's flour imports increased to 20,000 tons in 1949, to 29,000 tons in 1953, and rose sharply in 1957 to nearly 50,000 tons. Nigerian imports of flour, not quite 3,000 tons prewar, stood at 20,000 tons in 1953 and in 1957 reached a level of about 45,000 tons. In Accra, Lagos, Abidjan, and other major coastal cities, rising imports of flour have accounted for a significant fraction of the increase in food supplies for these urban areas. Trends in flour consumption are reviewed in Chapter 9.

Apart from Angola's exports of maize—about 100,000 tons a year prewar (1934–38) and a little more than that since 1949—the territories of western tropical Africa do not figure as exporters of staple food crops. Since 1947 the Belgian Congo has exported modest quantities of maize—on the order of 20,000 tons a year except for 1952 and 1953 when only very small quantities were shipped abroad. Prior to World War II, Dahomey exported small quantities of maize, and Portuguese Guinea exported about 4,000 tons of rice prewar, but smaller quantities in recent years.

RELATIVE IMPORTANCE OF THE MAJOR STARCHY STAPLES

The geographical distribution of the staple food crops is examined in Chapter 4; maps introduced there identify the dominant and secondary staple food crops down to the smallest administrative unit for which data are available. It is useful here, however, to give a general indication of their relative importance, considering first the situation in West Africa and then noting a few of the contrasts in the position of the staple crops in the other territories of western tropical Africa as compared with West Africa.

Throughout the huge Sudan zone of the interior of West Africa the millets and sorghums stand virtually alone as the dominant staple food crops, a direct consequence of the low rainfall and long dry seasons of that region. Most of the millets are grain *Pennisetums* commonly called bulrush millet.[5] An inferior millet (*Digitaria exilis*), referred to as *fonio* in the French territories, as *fundi* in Sierra Leone, and as *acha* or "hungry rice" in Nigeria, is grown on especially poor or dry soils. It is very important in the Jos Plateau of Nigeria and in the high elevations of the Futa Jallon (Fouta Djallon) of French Guinea. In some other areas it is of considerable importance in tiding over the preharvest shortage period because of its exceptionally short growing season (*1*, p. 30). Finger millet (*Eleusine corocana*), known as *tamba* in Nigeria, is also important in some localities.

---

[5] The scientific name *Pennisetum typhoideum* is frequently attached to bulrush millet. According to J. M. Dalziel this lumps together a number of species that have now been given binomials; he lists eight distinct species cultivated in West Africa (*9*, pp. 538–39). In the United States the term cattail millet is applied to the grain *Pennisetums* (*2*, p. 16).

Although the roots and tubers occupy a considerably smaller area than millets and sorghums, they probably contribute a greater share of the total food calories consumed. On the basis of rough approximations of average yield, it appears that the calorie yield per hectare of manioc is some 3½ to 4 times as high as that of millets and sorghums. The advantage for yams in terms of "net yield" is considerably less, since something like a quarter of the output of yam tubers must be used for seed. Inasmuch as manioc is replanted with stem cuttings, there is no comparable deduction to be made.

In West Africa, manioc and yams each occupy less than a fifth as much land as millets and sorghums, but it is possible that manioc contributes around 80 per cent as many food calories, and yams close to 50 per cent as many. Cocoyams probably contribute 5 or 6 per cent as many calories as millets and sorghums, sweet potatoes only 3 or 4 per cent. Plantains, a starchy fruit which sometimes replaces the roots and tubers as a major staple food, must also be mentioned. Crop estimates, almost invariably poor for the starchy roots[6] and fruits, are simply not available for plantains in a number of areas where they are of considerable importance. On the basis of the incomplete data available, it appears that plantains account for roughly 10 per cent as many calories as millets and sorghums.

For West Africa as a whole, maize and rice together appear to provide roughly half as many food calories as the millets and sorghums. The cereals as a group may account for a slightly larger share of total food calories than the starchy roots and fruits, although the margin of error in the data, and especially the incomplete statistics for plantain, leave the question in doubt.

In the remaining territories of western tropical Africa—the Cameroons, French Equatorial Africa, Spanish Guinea, the Belgian Congo, and Angola—these same starchy staples hold sway. The great importance of manioc is a conspicuous feature of the Belgian Congo; roughly 40 per cent of the total area in food crops is given over to manioc, whereas yams are of slight importance. Another notable contrast between the Belgian Congo and West Africa is that in the former millets and sorghums are of comparatively small importance. Maize, on the other hand, ranks second only to manioc in terms of area in the Belgian Congo, though plantains outrank maize in production and even in terms of food calories produced. The

---

[6] The general terms "roots" or "root crops" will often be used for convenience to refer both to true roots such as manioc and to tubers such as yams and sweet potatoes.

woefully inadequate statistics available for Angola suggest that maize is the leading crop in terms of area, and quite likely outranks manioc in production of food calories as well. Since Angola's exports of maize are considerable, averaging about 115,000 tons for the 5-year period 1949–53, domestic consumption is appreciably less than the production, which has been variously estimated at 150,000 to 700,000 tons.[7]

SOME DISTINCTIVE FEATURES OF THE AFRICAN STAPLE FOOD ECONOMY

Limited cultivation of rice.—Considering tropical Africa as a whole, rice is a crop of limited importance, especially in comparison with its all-important role in Monsoon Asia. Only within a coastal zone of West Africa stretching from Gambia south to the Bandama River in the center of the Ivory Coast does rice assume a truly dominant position. It has become a major crop, however, in several provinces of the Belgian Congo, and is of local importance in a number of other territories.

The limited development of rice culture in tropical Africa, in contrast with tropical Asia, is related to many factors. Social and cultural factors are of great, perhaps predominant importance. Pierre Gourou, who knows both regions well, is emphatic on this point: "It is due not to physical, but to cultural conditions and arises through man's different reactions to similar physical conditions" (*13*, p. 99).[8] Gourou considers the limited development of rice culture in Africa "a mark of backward civilization, for the flooded ricefield offers mankind in the tropics the best chance of a yearly production of a sufficiency of carbohydrates with a minimum of manure, and without fallow periods or risk of erosion or exhaustion of the soil" (*13*, pp. 93–94).

[7] D. O. Fynes-Clinton speaks of Angola's maize production as being "estimated normally at from 150–200,000 tons, of which rather more than half is exported" (*11*, p. 8). G. Lefebvre lists a figure of 305,000 tons, whereas the United States Department of Agriculture has used an estimate of 700,000 tons (*19*, p. 88; *28*).

[8] Later Gourou raises a question about a possible physical advantage of the Far East: "Are the alluvial plains built up in the sea at the mouth of Asiatic rivers not more fertile than those due to African or American rivers?" He considers this likely because the great rivers of Asia get a good deal of their water and alluvium from headwaters outside the tropics; and he suggests that the relatively light load of nutrient-bearing silt carried by African rivers such as the Niger may be due to the fact that their watersheds lie within the tropics (*13*, p. 105n.) In any event it seems true that tropical Africa does not have any river deltas comparable to the delta plains of the Ganges, the Red River, the Irawaddy, and other great rivers of Asia.

Certainly it can be said that the comparative lack of long-established civilization and of political stability have been adverse factors. The reliance on shifting cultivation and a long bush fallow to compensate for the rapid decline in fertility when rain-forest soils are cropped must have worked in the same direction. Much labor is required to develop permanent paddy fields for lowland rice even without facilities for controlled irrigation. And this is the type of rice culture which has the important advantage of high or at least satisfactory yields year after year on the same land. Presence of tsetse fly and the virtual absence of draft animals in most of the areas wet enough for rice with natural irrigation are also significant since thorough preparation of the seedbed—essential for satisfactory rice yields—is made more difficult. Probably most important of all, Africa's population is sparse. Hence, shifting cultivation with a long bush fallow could be practiced without difficulty, and population pressure has not provided incentive or abundant labor for constructing permanent paddy fields.

Exceptional importance of roots and tubers.—The dominant role of root crops and plantains as staple foods in western tropical Africa is unusual. In Ireland and Germany, European countries noted for their high consumption of potatoes, root crops represent only about one-fourth to one-third as many calories as cereals. Perusal of the *Food Balance Sheets* (*10*) published by the Food and Agriculture Organization of the United Nations (FAO) suggests that only in Brazil and in Java and Madura does the calorie contribution of roots and tubers reach 40 per cent of the calorie intake from cereals. Jamaica and perhaps other islands in the West Indies, the state of Travancore in India, and some of the islands of the Pacific should be mentioned as localities where calories from roots and tubers exceed the calorie contribution of cereals. In East Africa roots and tubers are far less important than in West Africa and the Congo; but in certain areas, notably Uganda, plantains are perhaps even more important.

The natural factors favorable to the cultivation of roots and tubers in the rain-forest regions will be considered later, but an economic characteristic of these crops is appropriately mentioned at this point. Because of their bulky and perishable nature, roots and tubers do not lend themselves to long-distance transport. When they become the object of long-distance shipments from specialized production centers they lose their price advantage. Sweet and white potatoes in the United States are typically 2, 3, or 4 times as expensive per 1,000 calories as wheat flour; the difference is much larger than it was 50 years ago, when the root crops were produced locally in far larger proportion. Up to the present time, this factor has not been of much importance in tropical Africa, owing to the limited development of specialized centers of production and long distance shipment to consuming centers. Nevertheless, gari (manioc meal) has acquired special importance largely because it compares not unfavorably with grain as a transportable and storable commodity.[9] The calorie value of a pound of gari is about the same as flour; its protein content, however, is exceptionally low (see Table 6-9, p. 161) and the same is true for vitamins of the B complex. It appears that the storage qualities of gari do not equal those of wheat flour but are nonetheless quite good; a storage period of two or three months is reported (*22*, p. 26). Regular availability of gari is enhanced by the fact that manioc is harvested and gari is produced throughout the year with a fairly small seasonal variation in output.

For reasons which are not clear, gari seems to be virtually unknown in the Belgian Congo, where manioc flour plays a role similar to that of gari in West Africa. The relative advantages of these two products is a question of some interest. One aspect that deserves to be mentioned is the superior, in fact quite exceptional ease with which gari can be prepared. It can be mixed with hot or cold water, sprinkled into other dishes, or simply eaten as is. In addition to manioc flour, the sliced and dried roots known as *cosettes* in the French-speaking territories, and as *kokonte* in Ghana, are a commercial product of considerable importance in the Belgian Congo and other parts of Africa, and these also lend themselves to storage and transport. It is reported that dried roots were of considerable importance in Nigeria 15 or 20 years ago, but they have now given way to gari.

RECENT INTRODUCTION OF SOME OF THE STAPLE CROPS

Another interesting feature of the African staple food economy is the extent to which the important crops have been introduced from other continents. Manioc, maize, and sweet potatoes were introduced

---

[9] Gari is approximately the same as the *farinha de mandioca* of Brazil. The manioc roots are first cleaned, peeled, and grated. The pulp is then placed in a large cloth bag and set in the sun to drain and ferment, sometimes under pressure of heavy stones or logs. After 3 or 4 days when the pulp is fairly dry, it is passed through a sieve and then dried over a low fire. A slight amount of palm oil may be added to prevent burning (*18*).

from the Americas early in the sixteenth century by Portuguese traders as foodstuffs for slaves awaiting shipment.[10] It is reported that the so-called "new cocoyam" (*Xanthosoma sagittifolium*) was brought to the Gold Coast by missionaries in the middle of the nineteenth century (*16*, p. 137). The Asiatic varieties of rice (*Oryza sativa*) are another important and recent introduction. The native African rice, *Oryza glaberrima*, has been cultivated since ancient times, but the *Oryza sativa* varieties are another Portuguese introduction. According to A. Chevalier, these varieties began to penetrate the interior only about 150 years ago, but they have now supplanted the native varieties to a large extent (*21*, p. 48).

CITATIONS

1 Jean Adam, "Cultures vivrières," in *Encycl. Col. et Mar: Afrique Occidentale Française*, II (2 vols., Paris, 1949).

2 Elna Anderson, *World Production and Consumption of Millet and Sorghum* (U.S. Dept. Agr., Bur. Agr. Econ., 1946).

3 W. H. Beckett, *Akokoaso: A Survey of a Gold Coast Village* (London Sch. of Econ. and Pol. Sci., Monograph on Soc. Anth. 10, London, 1944).

4 *Bull. mensuel stat. Outre-mer* (France, Min. Outre-mer), Jan.–Feb. 1955.

5 R. Cerighelli, *Cultures tropicales. I.—Plantes vivrières* (Nouvelle Encycl. Agr., Paris, 1955).

6 Suzanne Comhaire-Sylvain, *Food and Leisure Among the African Youth of Leopoldville (Belgian Congo)* (Communications from Sch. Afr. Studies, New Ser. 25, Univ. of Capetown, 1950).

7 "La Consommation africaine de produits alimentaires à Douala," *Marchés col. du monde* (Paris), May 14, 1955.

8 Yves Coyaud, "La Culture du riz à l'Office du Niger," *Riz et riziculture* (Paris), 2ᵉ année, 4ᵉ trimestre 1956.

9 J. M. Dalziel, *The Useful Plants of West Tropical Africa* (London, 1955).

10 Food and Agriculture Organization of the United Nations (FAO), *Food Balance Sheets* (Washington, 1949).

11 D. O. Fynes-Clinton, *Portuguese West Africa* (Gr. Brit. Bd. of Trade, Overseas Econ. Surv., 1949).

[10] The introduction of maize has been the subject of a lively controversy. Roland Portères argues persuasively that maize reached Africa from the New World by two routes—across the Atlantic to the Guinea Coast and also by way of Spain, the Mediterranean, Egypt, and thence south and west to the West African Sudan (*23*, pp. 221–31). Detailed arguments supporting the American origin of maize are given by Paul Weatherwax and L. F. Randolph in their article, "History and Origin of Corn," (*30*). M. D. W. Jeffreys argues that maize reached the Guinea Coast from the north via the Arab world before 1492 and was being cultivated there at the time of the first Portuguese contacts (*17*).

12 R. Galletti, K. D. S. Baldwin, and I. O. Dina, *Nigerian Cocoa Farmers* ... (Nigeria Cocoa Mkt. Bd., London, 1956).

13 Pierre Gourou, *The Tropical World* ... (London, 1953).

14 E. P. Hanson, "An Economic Survey of the Western Province of Liberia," *Geog. Rev.*, January 1947.

15 T. Hunter and T. V. Danso, "Notes on Food Farming at Ejura," in Gold Coast, Dept. Agr., *Year-Book, 1930* (Accra, n.d.).

16 F. R. Irvine, *A Text-book of West African Agriculture, Soils and Crops* (London, 1953).

17 M. D. W. Jeffreys, "The Origin of the Portuguese Word Zaburro as Their Name for Maize," *Bull. Inst. Français Afr. Noire* (Dakar), Ser. B., Jan.-Apr. 1957.

18 W. O. Jones, *Manioc in Africa* (to be published in 1959).

19 Gabriel Lefebvre, *L'Angola: Son histoire, son économie* (Liège, 1947).

20 Liberia, Dept. Agr. and Comm., *Foreign Trade Supplement of the Republic of Liberia*, Apr. 20, 1956, III.

21 Jacques Miège, "Les Cultures vivrières en Afrique Occidentale...," *Cahiers Outre-mer* (Bordeaux), Jan.-Mar. 1954.

22. S. D. Onabamiro, *Food and Health* (London, 1953).

23 Roland Portères, "L'Introduction du maïs en Afrique," *J. agr. trop. et de botanique appliquée* (Paris), May-June 1955.

24 A. R. Prest and I. G. Stewart, *The National Income of Nigeria 1950-51* (Gr. Brit., Col. Off., Col. Res. Studies 11, 1953).

25 M. G. Smith, *The Economy of Hausa Communities of Zaria* (Gr. Brit., Col. Off., Col. Res. Studies 16, 1955).

26 François Sorel, "L'Alimentation des indigènes en Afrique Occidentale Française," in G. Hardy and Ch. Richet, eds., *L'Alimentation indigène dans les colonies françaises, protectorats et territoires sous mandat* (Paris, 1933).

27 United Nations, Dept. Econ. Affairs, *Enlargement of the Exchange Economy of Tropical Africa* (New York, 1954).

28 U.S. Dept. Agr., For. Agr. Serv., *Food Balances, 1953, for Angola, Belgian Congo, Kenya and Nigeria* (1955, mimeo.).

29 R. Wauthion, "L'Avenir agricole de la Province du Katanga," extr. from the *Société Belge d'Études et Expansion*, Aug.-Sept.-Oct. 1954, No. 162, in the *Bull. de doc. et tech. agr.* (Belg. Congo, Comité Natl. du Kivu et l'Office des Produits Agricoles de Costermansville, Bukavu), 1er trimestre 1955.

30 Paul Weatherwax and L. F. Randolph, "History and Origin of Corn," in G. F. Sprague, ed., *Corn and Corn Improvement* (New York, 1955).

31 H. P. White, "Internal Exchange of Staple Foods in the Gold Coast," *Econ. Geog.*, April 1956.

32 ———, "Some Aspects of Food Crop Production in the Gold Coast," in L. D. Stamp, ed., *Natural Resources, Food and Population in Inter-Tropical Africa* (Rept. of a Symposium held at Makerere Coll., September 1955, London, 1956).

CHAPTER 3

THE PHYSICAL ENVIRONMENT

The present chapter describes the climatic and other physical factors which appear to be particularly relevant to the distribution of staple food crops in western tropical Africa. Following Klages, the most important of these influences may be classified as (*13*, pp. 73–82):

1. Climatic factors
    a) Moisture
    b) Temperature
    c) Light
2. Physiographic factors
    a) Nature of the geologic strata
    b) Topography
    c) Altitude
3. Edaphic factors
    a) Soil conditions (texture, structure, aeration, reaction, etc.)
    b) Chemical make-up of the soil

Other physiological factors considered by Klages include the effects of other plants or animals on the crop being studied; man-made changes in the plant environment; the effect of "pyric factors," such as grass fires; and the timing and duration of various environmental influences, notably whether unfavorable conditions occur at a vulnerable period in the growth cycle of a plant.

The purpose of the two following chapters is to describe and explain the distribution of the staple crops insofar as this appears to be determined by physical features of the environment or characteristics of the various crops, such as their water need, soil requirement, or yield. The attempt at explanation, however, is extremely tentative; the various causal factors which seem pertinent are described, but only rarely is it possible to assess their relative importance in influencing the pattern of crop distribution.

MOISTURE CONDITIONS

Particular attention is given to the distribution of rainfall and factors affecting the "efficiency" or agricultural value of the precipitation received. The moisture factor, always important for agriculture, is all-important in the areas considered in this study. "Since the pattern of climate in the tropics is one of marked temperature uniformity," as C. W. Thornthwaite observes with regard to the tropics in general, "it has been realized for many years that the more important subject of investigation is variation in moisture" (24, p. 166).

Frost is nowhere a problem in western tropical Africa although frosts do occur on the higher elevations of Cameroon Mountain which rises 13,350 feet above sea level; and the peaks of the Ruwenzori Mountains in the eastern highlands of the Belgian Congo reach 16,800 feet and are snow-covered and have glaciers. On clear winter nights there may be ground frost in West Africa as the fringe of the Sahara is approached, and frost is frequent in the higher and southern portions of the interior plateau of Angola (12, pp. 82 and 103). But those areas are exceptional. Virtually the whole of western tropical Africa, apart from Angola and a few of the higher elevations, is hot, or "megathermal" in Thornthwaite's classification of thermal efficiency. There are significant differences between the temperature regimes of the coastal belt and the interior regions, but these relate mainly to the seasonal and diurnal variations. Coastal areas show a very small temperature range through the year and between day and night, and the discomfort from heat "is due to the combination of excessive humidity and considerable heat, not to excessive heat . . ." (12, p. 62).

In the interior, where the continental influence is marked, seasonal and daily temperature ranges are much greater.[1] Although the January mean in Kano at 12° N is above 70 degrees F, the nights are uncomfortably cold; maximum temperatures in the north are reached in April and May, just prior to the monsoonal rains, with monthly means above 90 degrees and daily maxima of 110 degrees or more. Somewhat surprisingly, the minimum temperatures in a coastal city such as Lagos occur in July and August, when the humid monsoonal winds reduce temperatures, but there is only a difference of some five degrees between the monthly means for the coolest and hottest month in Lagos. In connection with this extreme uniformity of the coastal climate, mention may be made of Hildebrand's view,

[1] The very low concentration of water vapor in the atmosphere in the savanna regions during the dry season, which reduces the heating effect of the solar radiation received, should be mentioned as a particularly significant factor accounting for the much greater variation in such regions.

cited with approval by Klages, that uniform climates are favorable
to the growth of perennial plants while climates with periodic changes,
including changes in the relative length of night and day, favor
annual plants (*13*, p. 77).

MAP 3-1

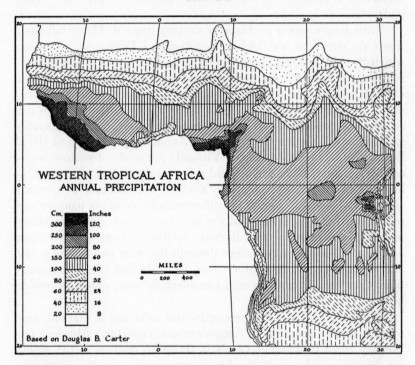

WESTERN TROPICAL AFRICA
ANNUAL PRECIPITATION

Cm.	Inches
300	120
250	100
200	80
150	60
100	40
80	32
60	24
40	16
20	8

MILES

0   200   400

Based on Douglas B. Carter

Based on Douglas B. Carter, *Climates of Africa and India According to Thornthwaite's
1948 Classification* (Johns Hopkins University, Laboratory of Climatology, Publications in
Climatology, Vol. VII, No. 4, Final Report, Centerton, N.J., 1954), p. 463.

Annual rainfall data, shown in Map 3-1, although of key importance in determining the availability of moisture, are insufficient as
an indicator of moisture conditions for crop production. For agriculture, the seasonal pattern of precipitation is also highly important
and varies greatly within western tropical Africa; there are zones
with abundant rain through 10 or 11 months, areas with 7 or 8 rainy
months and two maxima of rainfall, and other areas with a single
rainy season which may be as short as three months or less. Since

crop production in the drier regions is almost entirely confined to the rainy season, it is the availability of moisture during those months which is most significant. Even as between areas of high rainfall, differences in the seasonal distribution may be important. Thus Hiernaux calls attention to the fact that Conakry, in French Guinea, has a relatively long dry season of five months although it receives the very high annual total of some 420 cm (*11*, p. 2). Though the annual total in Abidjan (Ivory Coast) is not quite half as high as at Conakry, there is virtually no dry season, and the Abidjan area is therefore more favorable for plantains and certain other crops which require not only ample but well-distributed rainfall.

Of more fundamental importance than variations in the seasonal distribution of rainfall is the fact that the efficiency of a given volume of precipitation will vary substantially depending on temperature, length of day, atmospheric humidity, wind movement, and other factors which determine the return movement of moisture into the air by way of evaporation and transpiration of plants. In stressing the significance of this factor, H. O. Walker has pointed out "that although Accra and Manchester receive much the same annual rainfall, Accra receives between one-half and one-third of the amount required to balance evaporation while Manchester receives about twice the amount required to achieve balance" (*28*, p. 108). Rough estimates of the variation in water requirements of perennial crops also underscore the wide difference in the efficiency of precipitation in different regions. While the water demands of these crops are not well known, it has been suggested that perennial crops need approximately 15–20 inches in the United Kingdom, 40–50 inches in subtropical regions, and on the order of 60 inches in tropical regions (*8*, p. VII).

Various efforts have been made to adjust rainfall data in order to obtain a more meaningful index of precipitation. In 1951, G. Mangenot suggested a formula (reproduced in *14*, p. 39) which incorporates, in addition to the annual rainfall, the average precipitation of the dry months, the number of months of the dry season, and the annual maximum and minimum figures for relative humidity. A somewhat similar approach has been suggested by C. R. Hiernaux (*11*, pp. 1–6 and insert map). The distinctive feature of the index he has used as the basis for a map of the moisture regions in West Africa is the inclusion of the difference between the annual average maximum and minimum temperatures as a factor which reflects the

MAP 3-2

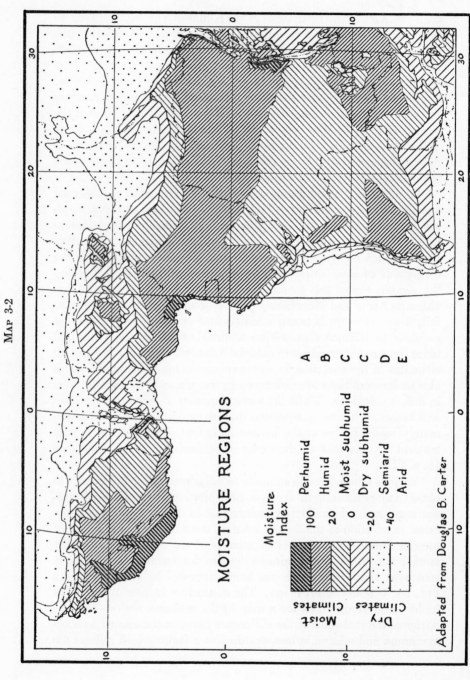

MOISTURE REGIONS

Moisture
Index

100	Perhumid	A
20	Humid	B
0	Moist subhumid	C
-20	Dry subhumid	C
-40	Semiarid	D
	Arid	E

Moist
Climates

Dry
Climates

Adapted from Douglas B. Carter

Douglas B. Carter (after the 1948 System of C. W. Thornthwaite) Climatic Maps of Africa, Plate I (Lab. of Climatology, Centerton, N.J. ...)

importance of the continental influence at a station. Harroy has offered a classification of climate and vegetation in Africa which utilizes E. de Martonne's formula for an "index of aridity" in which annual rainfall (in millimeters) is divided by annual mean temperature (in degrees centigrade) plus 10 (*10*, p. 65).

Étienne Bernard's 1945 monograph on the climate of the Congo basin gave considerable attention to factors influencing the efficiency of the precipitation received. In calling attention to the low efficiency of rainfall in a tropical region, he recalls the remark by Szymkiewicz that "in a country such as Java, the air is very humid for man, but fairly dry for the vegetation" (*2*, p. 119). Bernard first considers this problem of "water need," as influenced by the rate of evaporation, by computing the saturation deficit for forest, forest border, and savanna stations. He finds that the saturation deficit (the difference between the maximum or saturation vapor pressure for the temperature of the air at the moment of observation and the actual vapor pressure) is much higher in the Congo than in Belgium. This is, of course, the result of the high average temperatures in the Congo which means that the saturation or maximum pressure averages so much higher that this factor more than offsets the fact that the actual vapor pressure is much higher in the Congo than in Belgium. Thus for a savanna station, Luluabourg, he calculates that the annual average saturation deficit as measured during the middle of the day is 13.3 mm as compared with 8.0 mm at a forest station (Yangambi) and only 3.4 mm at Uccle, in Belgium (*2*, pp. 110, 114–18). Bernard also makes interesting use of a "hygrometric quotient" which he defines as monthly precipitation divided by monthly evaporation as determined by Piche evaporation pans (*2*, pp. 197–99). On the basis of this quotient, which he uses essentially as an index of potential evapotranspiration, he concludes, for example, that the savanna station of Gandajika has a water deficit (*rupture d'équilibre bilan en eau*) of six months' duration, whereas the "dry season," defined simply as the period of absence or virtual absence of rainfall, is only three months. Bultot's 1954 monograph on the seasonal pattern of rainfall in the Congo (*7*), which will be considered presently, utilizes still another approach in measuring the "dessicating power" of the climate in different regions of the Congo.

The moisture regions as shown in Map 3-2 are based on a highly interesting approach to the classification of climate outlined by Thornthwaite in 1948 (*21*). Although similar to his earlier classification (*22* and *23*) in its stress on the moisture factor, the 1948 classifica-

MAP 3-3

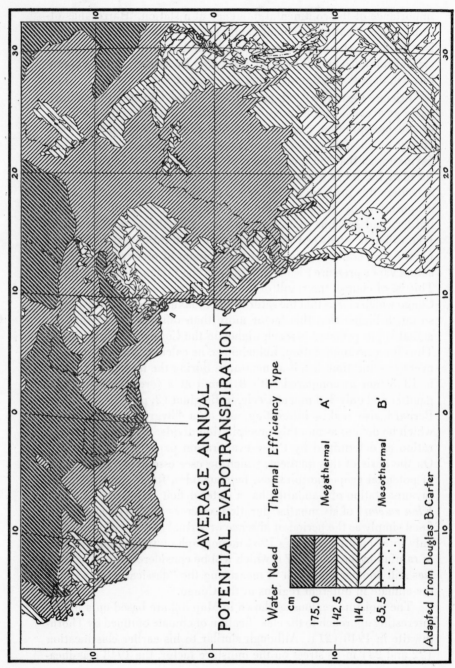

AVERAGE ANNUAL
POTENTIAL EVAPOTRANSPIRATION

Water Need   Thermal Efficiency Type
cm

175.0   Megathermal   A'

142.5

114.0   Mesothermal   B'

85.5

Adapted from Douglas B. Carter

Douglas B. Carter (after the 1948 System of C. W. Thornthwaite), *Climatic Maps of Africa*, Plate I (Lab. of Climatology, Centerton, N.J., n.d.).

tion is based fundamentally on the concept of "potential evapotranspiration."[2] Potential evapotranspiration is defined as "the evapotranspiration which would occur from a vegetation covered surface if soil moisture conditions were adaquate for unrestricted transpiration" (25, p. 56). The external supply of energy to the evaporating surface, principally by solar radiation, is considered the principal factor determining potential evapotranspiration. Wind speed and certain other factors are also relevant, although Thornthwaite and Hare emphasize that one of these factors—the nature of the vegetation—is not nearly so important as some statements suggest. It is true that when the soil is partially dried out, forests may have much higher rates of transpiration because their deep roots can continue to draw moisture from lower levels. But when soil moisture is ample, the availability of the heat required to bring about the evaporation is the critical factor: "A grassland may easily consume 80 per cent of the incoming net radiation for evapotranspiration when the soil is moist, and mature high forest cannot transpire much more" (25, p. 54).[3]

Evapotranspiration is not easy to measure, and the data available concerning the geographical distribution of evapotranspiration are limited. Thornthwaite has found, however, that with adjustment for variations in day length, there is a close relation between mean temperature and potential evapotranspiration; and he has developed an empirical formula which makes it possible to compute potential evapotranspiration for any place for which temperature records are available.

Potential evapotranspiration in western tropical Africa is shown in Map 3-3, which is reproduced from a report on Africa and India prepared by Douglas B. Carter. The zones shown are based on categories of "water need" which is the average annual potential evapo-

[2] In addition to Thornthwaite's 1948 article in the *Geog. Rev.*, the following are especially useful: C. W. Thornthwaite and F. K. Hare, "Climatic Classification in Forestry," *Unasylva* (FAO, Rome), June 1955, pp. 50–59; Thornthwaite and J. R. Mather, "The Water Budget and Its Use in Irrigation," in U.S. Dept. Agr., *The Yearbook of Agriculture, 1955: Water*, pp. 346–58; and Thornthwaite and Mather, *The Water Balance* (Pub. in Climatology, VIII, No. 1, Centerton, New Jersey, 1955), which includes an extensive bibliography.

[3] Recent investigations by Bernard at Yangambi confirm the validity of the "energy balance" view of evapotranspiration. The evapotranspiration from a luxuriant cover of *Paspalum* (grown with fertilizer) was only 10 per cent greater than in an unfertilized plot with a sparse cover, though the foliar development was 2.75 times greater in the first plot. Only in the relatively unimportant case of plants growing in isolated pots was transpiration found to be proportional to foliar surface. See 3.

Table 3-1.—Water Balance for Two Stations of West Africa*

(Centimeters)

KAYES, FRENCH WEST AFRICA

		Jan.	Feb.	March	Apr.	May	June	July	Aug.	Sept.	Oct.	Nov.	Dec.	Annual
Mean temperature	°C	25.0	27.4	31.3	34.3	35.7	32.3	28.8	27.8	28.7	30.1	28.8	24.9	29.6
Potential evapotranspiration	PE	9.6	13.0	17.4	18.9	20.2	18.8	17.1	15.8	15.6	16.4	14.8	9.3	186.9
Precipitation	P	0	0	0.1	0.3	1.7	9.5	18.4	21.4	14.0	4.0	0.1	0.2	69.7
Difference	Δ	−9.6	−13.0	−17.3	−18.6	−18.5	−9.3	+1.3	+5.6	−1.6	−12.4	−14.7	−9.1	−117.2
Storage change	ΔST	−0.6	−0.5	−0.4	−0.2	−0.2	0	+1.3	+5.6	−0.4	−2.2	−1.7	−0.7	—
Soil-moisture storage	ST	1.4	0.9	0.5	0.3	0.1	0.1	1.4	7.0	6.6	4.4	2.7	2.0	—
Actual evapotranspiration	AE	0.6	0.5	0.5	0.5	1.9	9.5	17.1	15.8	14.4	6.2	1.8	0.9	69.7
Water deficiency	D	9.0	12.5	16.9	18.4	18.3	9.3	0	0	1.2	10.2	13.0	8.4	117.2
Water surplus	S	0	0	0	0	0	0	0	0	0	0	0	0	0

FREETOWN, SIERRA LEONE

		Jan.	Feb.	March	Apr.	May	June	July	Aug.	Sept.	Oct.	Nov.	Dec.	Annual
Mean temperature	°C	26.7	27.2	27.5	27.8	27.5	26.8	25.7	25.3	25.8	26.3	26.9	26.8	26.7
Potential evapotranspiration	PE	13.8	13.0	14.8	15.1	15.4	14.5	12.8	12.1	12.4	13.6	13.6	13.8	164.9
Precipitation	P	0.5	0.1	1.5	6.3	14.9	31.4	95.5	91.3	64.9	26.8	13.6	4.1	350.9
Difference	Δ	−13.3	−12.9	−13.3	−8.8	−0.5	+16.9	+82.7	+79.2	+52.5	+13.2	0	−9.7	186.0
Storage change	ΔST	−7.8	−4.9	−3.2	−1.5	−0.1	+16.9	+9.0	0	0	0	0	−8.4	—
Soil-moisture storage	ST	13.8	8.9	5.7	4.2	4.1	21.0	30.0	30.0	30.0	30.0	30.0	21.6	—
Actual evapotranspiration	AE	8.3	5.0	4.7	7.8	15.0	14.5	12.8	12.1	12.4	13.6	13.6	12.5	132.3
Water deficiency	D	5.5	8.0	10.1	7.3	0.4	0	0	0	0	0	0	1.3	32.6
Water surplus	S	0	0	0	0	0	0	73.7	79.2	52.5	13.2	0	0	218.6

* Data made available by Dr. C. W. Thornthwaite, The Laboratory of Climatology, Centerton, New Jersey.

transpiration expressed in centimeters. Since the potential evapotranspiration is estimated as a function of mean monthly temperature
adjusted for latitude, it also serves as an index of "thermal efficiency."

The moisture regions in Map 3-2, also reproduced from the report
by Carter, portray a relationship between annual rainfall and an annual value for potential evapotranspiration. The moisture index used
as a basis for classifying the moisture regions is derived from monthly
figures showing the estimated "water surplus" and "water deficit" at
a station through the year. These values represent the balance between water need in a month (potential evapotranspiration) and
water available. When precipitation exceeds water need a moisture
surplus exists and water is stored in the ground. When precipitation
is less than water need a water deficit results unless this difference is entirely offset by drawing on stored soil moisture. The basis
used for estimating the monthly change in soil-moisture storage has
been explained by Thornthwaite and Mather (26). During periods
when soil moisture is at field capacity, potential and actual evapotranspiration are the same, and the moisture surplus is the excess of
precipitation over evapotranspiration, less whatever amount is used
for recharging soil moisture. When there is water deficit its amount
shows the difference between actual and potential evapotranspiration.
The moisture index for a station is then derived from a formula which
relates the difference between the total water surplus and total water
deficit during the year to the annual total of potential evapotranspiration.

The monthly values for water surplus or deficit, potential and
actual evapotranspiration, precipitation, and other components of
Thornthwaite's system provide valuable insight into the seasonal
march of the water balance. In a more intensive study of crop distribution, it might be interesting to examine the crop pattern in relation
to seasonal profiles of the water balance at a number of stations. For
present purposes it is useful to examine the monthly water balance
for a few stations to illustrate some of the strikingly different rainfall
regimes which characterize West Africa, and these examples also
serve to clarify the concepts underlying Maps 3-2 and 3-3. Table 3-1
presents monthly values for water deficiency, water surplus, and the
other elements of the water balance for Kayes, a station at 14° 26′ N
in a semiarid region in the French Sudan, and for Freetown on the
west coast of Sierra Leone. Chart 3-1 shows the seasonal profile of
the water balance for these two stations and for Kano at 12° N in

CHART 3-1.—WATER BALANCES OF SELECTED STATIONS IN AFRICA*
(Centimeters)

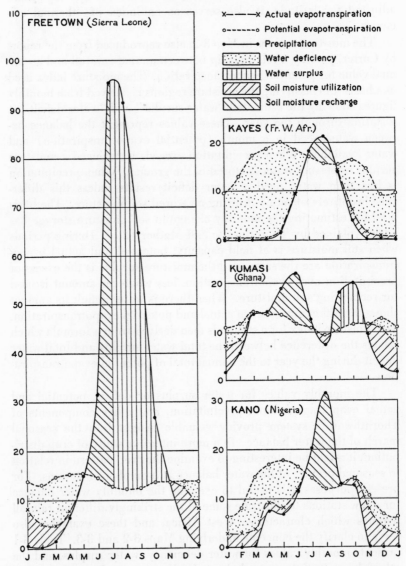

x——x Actual evapotranspiration
o------o Potential evapotranspiration
•——• Precipitation
Water deficiency
Water surplus
Soil moisture utilization
Soil moisture recharge

FREETOWN (Sierra Leone)

KAYES (Fr. W. Afr.)

KUMASI (Ghana)

KANO (Nigeria)

* Data from Douglas B. Carter, *Climates of Africa and India According to Thornthwaite's 1948 Classification* (Johns Hopkins University, Laboratory of Climatology, Publications in Climatology, Vol. VII, No. 4, Final Report, Centerton, N.J., 1954), p. 456, and material provided directly by Dr. C. W. Thornthwaite.

northern Nigeria and Kumasi at 6° 43′ N in the forest zone of Ghana. Kano and Kayes are both characterized by a single and short rainy season, but with the considerably larger water deficit at Kayes distinguishing its "semiarid" climate from the "dry subhumid" region at Kano.[4] Kumasi's seasonal pattern shows the characteristic double maximum of an "equatorial-type" rainfall regime, and Freetown is representative of a "perhumid" region with a huge water surplus during July to November. To an overwhelming extent the alternation of periods of deficit and of soil recharge or water surplus are related to the seasonal variation in rainfall. Potential evapotranspiration at Freetown is never much above or below 15 cm (6 inches) per month throughout the year, but at Kayes it increases from about 10 cm (4 inches) a month in midwinter to a May maximum of 20 cm (8 inches), reflecting the substantial seasonal increase in temperature and, to a small extent, the increase in the length of day.

The decision to use the Thornthwaite classification of moisture regions in considering the correlation between the pattern of distribution of the staple food crops and moisture conditions was influenced by the availability of Carter's maps of Africa showing moisture regions, potential evapotranspiration, water deficiency, and water surplus according to Thornthwaite's 1948 system. Moreover, the concepts on which the system is based seem very appropriate for the present study. But it is necessary to call attention to questions which have been raised with regard to its validity in relation to tropical Africa. Thornthwaite himself has observed that "there is no assurance that the empirical relations derived from the data of middle latitudes will apply in the tropics" (24, p. 171). Recent investigations in the Belgian Congo and in Nigeria seem to indicate quite clearly that the Thornthwaite empirical formula does understate po-

---

[4] Computation of the moisture indexes used in Map 3-2 can be illustrated for these two stations. The moisture index is defined as

$$I_m = \frac{100s - 60d}{n}$$

where s is the total water surplus during the year, d is the water deficit, and n is the water need as indicated by the annual total of potential evapotranspiration. For Kayes, $s = 6.9$ cm, $d = 124.1$ cm, and $n = 186.9$ cm, giving $I_m = -36$ which is near the arid limit of the "semiarid" region (defined as -20 to -40). The comparable figures for Kano are: $s = 25.8$ cm, $d = 73.3$ cm, $n = 151.1$ cm, and $I_m = -12$, thus placing Kano in the "dry subhumid" region (defined as 0 to -20). The moisture indices for Kumasi and Freetown are 11 (moist subhumid) and 127 (perhumid).

tential evapotranspiration in tropical savanna regions such as the southern Congo or northern Nigeria.

F. Bultot, director of the Bureau of Climatology of the Institut National pour l'Étude Agronomique du Congo Belge (INÉAC), has concluded that estimating potential evapotranspiration from monthly temperature alone gives a misleading picture in areas such as the Kasai or Katanga provinces which are characterized by a long dry season. Under these conditions a marked decline in nocturnal minimum temperatures may obscure the effect of increased insolation during the day or of other factors tending to increase evapotranspiration. He summarizes the difficulty in these terms (6):

Since the average monthly temperature varies little during the course of the year, one obtains a value for potential evapotranspiration which is nearly constant from one month to another even in the regions characterized by a dry season. In the course of the dry season the dry winds (southeast or northeast trade winds) gather strength, the saturation deficit increases, often the short-wave radiation from sun and sky increases because of an increase in direct insolation; one would therefore expect the potential evapotranspiration to increase as well, sometimes considerably. If the monthly average air temperature remains constant or, as is common, declines during the dry season it is because the nocturnal minimum is lowered substantially as a result of the reduced cloudiness.

For eight Congo stations Bultot has calculated monthly averages of the daily evaporation to be expected from an open water surface or from a surface saturated with water, using the energy-balance approach devised by H. L. Penman.[5] Apart from the southeastern region, the estimates of annual evaporation by Bultot on the basis of Penman's approach seem reasonably in accord with Carter's estimates of potential evapotranspiration using Thornthwaite's empirical formula. But the value obtained by Bultot for Elisabethville points up a very considerable discrepancy. Carter's map shows this portion of the Katanga as having potential evapotranspiration of only 85.5 to 114.0 cm, considerably less than the bulk of the Congo which falls in the category with potential evapotranspiration between 142.5 and 175.0 cm, whereas Bultot's estimate of evaporation at Elisabethville, 181 cm, is considerably higher than for any other station he considered. Comparison of Bultot's estimates for Luluabourg in Ka-

---

[5] Penman's formula, first published in the *Proceedings of the Royal Society*, Vol. 193 (1948), pp. 120–45, is given in 7, pp. 33–34. It includes as parameters several measures of radiation, effective insolation compared with the possible insolation, values for vapor pressure and saturation deficit of the air, average wind speed, and several other factors.

sai Province and Carter's figures for Gandajika, not much over a hundred miles southeast of Luluabourg, reveals a marked discrepancy in the seasonal pattern although the annual values do not differ very much. The figure for evaporation in June, in the early part of the dry season, is the annual maximum according to Bultot's estimates, whereas Carter shows it as virtually the annual minimum.

Somewhat similar conclusions are reached by B. J. Garnier on the basis of measurements of potential evapotranspiration by evapotranspirometers in Nigeria. For Ibadan he finds a very good correlation between measured potential evapotranspiration and values computed according to the Thornthwaite formula. But for Samaru in the savanna zone of northern Nigeria, he found that during the dry season months, the measured values are considerably higher than the computed values (9, Fig. 2 following p. 11). Garnier has examined several possible adjustments of the Thornthwaite formula aimed at obtaining a better fit with the measured values for potential evapotranspiration in Nigeria. Most promising is an adjustment based on the mean daytime saturation deficit. Values computed by a formula incorporating this parameter give a good fit with measured potential evapotranspiration at Ibadan and Samaru in Nigeria (and also Hong Kong). Garnier finds it reasonable that taking account of the mean daytime saturation deficit would improve the estimates, since this is a measure of the "degree of attraction exercised by the atmosphere," an important factor influencing evapotranspiration which does not seem to be adequately reflected in the Thornthwaite formula (9, pp. 12–18).

Reference should also be made to the view expressed by E. C. J. Mohr and F. A. Van Baren that the "influence of the general properties of the most common tropical soils on the intake, storage and loss of water" is an additional element which should be considered in applying the concept of potential evapotranspiration to tropical areas (15, p. 60). The present writer has no basis for judging how important or feasible it might be to take account of this factor.

Despite the evidence considered above, which indicates that the values for potential evapotranspiration are probably underestimated for the savanna areas with a strongly marked dry season, the moisture regions and zones of thermal efficiency shown in Maps 3-2 and 3-3 appear to be of considerable value. For West Africa the effect of appropriate adjustments of the maps would probably not be very great since it would simply be a matter of moving certain of the boundaries for the arid, semiarid, and dry subhumid regions somewhat closer to the coast. Actually, even with the degree of understatement believed to exist, nearly all of West Africa and the Congo basin are of either the highest or second highest category of potential evapotranspiration. The exceptions evident in the higher elevations of the Cameroon Highlands, the Jos Plateau of Nigeria, and the Futa Jallon of French Guinea pose no particular problem. Complications do arise, however, in the southern savanna regions of the Belgian Congo, which is one of the reasons that major reliance is placed on an alternative climatic classification in describing moisture conditions in the Congo.

WEST AFRICA[6]

Apart from a few of the areas of higher elevation, the pattern of moisture regions in West Africa as shown in Map 3-2 seems to be influenced primarily by the variations in rainfall (see Map 3-1). The huge semiarid and arid region north of 12 or 13° N reflects not only low annual rainfall but maximum values of potential evapotranspiration as well. But in the areas to the south there is much greater variation in climatic conditions.

Along the Guinea coast, with the exception of a coastal strip stretching some 300 miles east from Cape Three Points in Ghana, there is a zone of "abundant rain throughout the year and constant moist heat . . ." (12, p. 51). This general pattern of heavy coastal rainfall declining northward to the interior is mainly to be explained in terms of the movement of moisture-laden, monsoonal-type winds coming from the southwest across the South Atlantic. Inland penetration of these moist southwest winds depends on the position of the Intertropical Front where these winds meet the dry northeast winds coming off the Sahara.[7] In midwinter this Intertropical Front lies only a short distance from the Guinea coast, and the dry Harmattan winds from the Saharan high-pressure belt reach almost to the coast and for a brief period may actually continue for a distance over the sea.

The belt of maximum rainfall, according to Kendrew, extends from about 100 miles to about 400 miles south of the Intertropical Front. Thus in January, when the Intertropical Front is in its southernmost position, even the coastal areas of extremely heavy annual

---

[6] The grouping of territories referred to here and in the following chapters as "West Africa" comprises French West Africa and French Togo and the French Cameroons, the Gambia, Sierra Leone, Ghana, Nigeria, Liberia, and Portuguese Guinea.

[7] Maps depicting the pattern of air movements and the position of the Intertropical Front in January, April, and July, based on the pioneering 1932 article by Brooks and Mirrlees, are presented in Stamp (20, pp. 65–67).

rainfall have little or relatively little precipitation. Buchanan and Pugh cite the example of Debundscha on the western side of Cameroon Mountain as having less than five inches of rainfall in January, although its annual average of over 425 inches (for the five years 1944–48) probably makes it the second wettest place in the world (4, pp. 23–24).[8] With the warming of the continental interior as the summer solstice is approached, the Intertropical Front and the rainbelt move northward. Two rainy seasons, typically May–June and September–October, characterize most parts of an area which Kendrew (12, p. 56) depicts as running inland in a northeasterly direction from Monrovia to nearly 10° N and then dipping gently southward to cross Nigeria just south of the confluence of the Niger and Benue rivers. Examination of Nigerian precipitation data for individual years, however, leads Buchanan and Pugh to draw the northern limit of the zone typically marked by a double rainfall maximum a good deal farther to the north (4, pp. 26–28). North of the area characterized by an "equatorial" type of rainfall regime, reflecting the influence of the northward and southward migration of the Intertropical Front and the rain-belt, is the region of a single rainy season limited to a few months of late spring and summer. Year-to-year variation in the timing and extent of the northward migration of the Intertropical Front is said to be an important factor underlying the extreme variability of rainfall in the Sudan zone (20, p. 71). Kendrew has summarized in the following schematic table the increasingly dry zones encountered as one moves northward from the Guinea coast (12, p. 56):

Zone	Number of rainy months (2" or more)	Number of rain-days in a rainy month	Mean annual rainfall (inches)
Coast to 9° N	8–7	20–15	>50
9° to 15° N	7–4	15–10	50–10
Beyond 15° N	<3	<10	<10

Significant exceptions occur, however, in this general tendency toward East-West belts of increasing dryness in moving from the coast northward to the Sahara. The most striking departure from the pattern is the semiarid coastal strip more or less centering on Accra in Ghana. Over a distance of perhaps 300 miles eastward from Cape Three Points and extending in a wedge that widens in the eastern portion to a depth of 50 miles, the mean annual rainfall is below

---

[8] The map in 4 (p. 27) of "The Dry Winter" shows that in western Nigeria the zone characterized by two months with less than one inch of rain reaches to within a few miles of the coast.

MAP 3-4

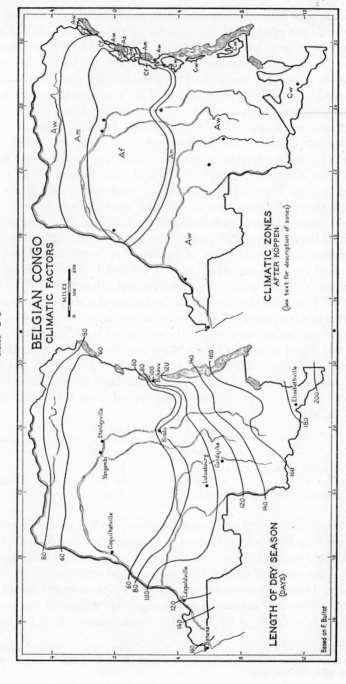

BELGIAN CONGO
CLIMATIC FACTORS

MILES
0   100   200

CLIMATIC ZONES
AFTER KÖPPEN
(See text for description of zones)

LENGTH OF DRY SEASON
(DAYS)

Based on F. Bultot

40 inches; and in the center of this strip is a small area with less than 20 inches of annual precipitation. Kendrew attributes the low rainfall in this area to a summer upwelling of cool water off the coast caused by the pull of the Guinea Current and the fact that the prevailing wind is parallel to the coast in this stretch.

To the west, centering on Sierra Leone and Liberia, is a very rainy belt with the 120-inch isohyet extending approximately a hundred miles inland. Here the southwest winds, blowing directly toward the coastline, are cooled on scaling the rising elevations inland and so contribute to the high rainfall. These same two factors are pronounced in the high-rainfall areas of the western and southwestern slopes of Cameroon Mountain and the Cameroon Highlands.

THE CONGO REGION[9]

Major features of the moisture regime of the Belgian Congo can best be described in relation to the map of climatic conditions prepared by Bultot which is reproduced here, with some simplification, as Map 3-4. It is based on Köppen's (1936) system of classification but also includes isopleths showing the length of the dry season; in Bultot's original map (5) isohyets of annual rainfall are also shown.

A dominating feature of the Congo is the huge *Af* zone (see Map 3-4) extending approximately from 1° 30′ N to 3° S, to cover an area which corresponds rather well with the equatorial rain-forest region of the Congo basin. This *Af* classification of Köppen defines a zone in which the average temperature of the coldest month is about 18 degrees C and the average annual rainfall expressed in centimeters exceeds a level defined as twice the annual mean temperature (in degrees centigrade) plus 14; and *f* specifies that the rainfall of the driest month is at least 60 mm. The *Am* climate, which appears as a narrow band south and a wider band north of the *Af* region, is a transitional zone, giving way both in the south and the north to the *Aw* climate which has at least one month with average rainfall below 60 mm.[10] More limited areas located in the higher elevations east of

[9] The term Congo Region is used in a very broad sense to embrace the Belgian Congo, French Equatorial Africa, Spanish Guinea, and Angola.

[10] The *w* indicates that the dry season occurs during the winter (the southern hemisphere winter, of course, for the zone lying to the south of the equator). The transition zone *Am* is defined by the formula $m = a/25$ in which a is the annual average rainfall expressed in millimeters and m is a factor to be compared with the mean monthly rainfall of the driest month. If the value m so obtained exceeds the mean rainfall of the driest month (expressed in millimeters), the climate is classed as *Am*.

the Congo basin and in Katanga Province are classed as *Cf* or *Cw*. The *C* climate of Köppen signifies that the mean temperature of the coldest month falls below 18 degrees C but is above 3 degrees C. The *Cf* subclass defines a climate in which the average rainfall of the driest month is at least one-tenth as high as the precipitation received during the wettest month. In the *Cw* zones the rainfall of the driest month is less than one-tenth as heavy as during the month of greatest rainfall, and *w* indicates that the driest month occurs during the winter (of the hemisphere in which the region is located).

Examination of the isopleths indicating the length of the dry season (Map 3-4) reveals the manner in which the dry season becomes increasingly long in moving south and north from the zone of the equatorial rain forest. At the boundary between the *Am* and *Aw* zones the dry season is of about two months' duration, but in the savanna regions of the most southerly portions of the Congo are dry seasons of 5, 6, and nearly 7 months' duration. Bultot's approach is to define a "dry season as a series of days without precipitation (or nearly without precipitation) occurring each year at approximately the same period . . ." (7, p. 9).

Annual rainfall follows a similar pattern, declining from a maximum in the *Af* zone where it is above 1,800 mm. It falls to 1,600 mm at about 4° N, coinciding roughly with the northern border of the Belgian Congo, and to considerably lower levels south of the equator. In speaking of the southern region, however, it is essential to call attention to the manner in which the isohyets of annual rainfall and the isopleths indicating the duration of the dry season curve toward the equator in moving west (or, in lesser degree, east) from the central Congo. Thus the 1,600 mm isohyet nearly reaches 5° S at the 23d meridian, which roughly bisects the Congo, but lies at only 1° S at the point where it reaches the Congo's western boundary with French Equatorial Africa. Similarly, in the Bas Congo in approaching the coast the annual precipitation declines to about 1,000 mm and the dry season exceeds 5 months. The occurrence of such a relatively dry climate within 5° to 6° of the equator reflects the influence of the cool Benguela Current which is responsible for the very dry coastal zone of Angola. In the Katanga Province, in the southeast, the 1,000 mm isohyet encloses an area extending from 7° S to 11° S. Rainfall then shows a slight increase in moving further to the south, but the duration of the dry season continues to increase, reaching nearly 7 months at 13° S.

The great bulk of the moisture ultimately precipitated over the

Congo basin is carried by the southeast trade winds off the Atlantic, so deflected as to have become southwest winds of monsoonal type. Convectional rains account for the major part of the annual rainfall throughout the Congo basin. Although the rain-forest zone is characterized by fairly high rainfall throughout the year, maxima occur and coincide fairly closely with the equinoxes. The maximum at the autumnal equinox is in general the greater because it coincides with the period when the Intertropical Front is farthest inland over the Congo basin, permitting greater penetration of the moisture-bearing monsoonal winds from the Atlantic.[11] Bernard suggests that trade winds originating in the east over the Indian Ocean provide some of the moisture precipitated in the Congo, especially in the Katanga region. He emphasizes, however, that these easterly and southeasterly winds encounter a formidable obstacle in crossing the Rift highlands whereas the winds from the Atlantic encounter much less important obstacles (the Kwango Plateau and the Crystal Mountains).

In the Belgian Congo, as in West Africa, the availability of moisture for plants stands out as the key limiting factor. Only in the high elevations found in parts of the relatively small *Cw* and *Cf* zones of Map 3-4 do temperatures fall low enough to be a significant adverse factor. But in moving south and north from the rain forest *Af* zone, conditions gradually become less favorable for agriculture because of factors influencing the availability of moisture. Most obvious, of course, is the effect of declining rainfall and the lengthening of the dry season evident in moving south and north from the equator. Moreover, throughout most of these huge *Aw* zones and in the *Cw* zone of Katanga Province as well, the effects of the dry season are accentuated because the rate of evaporation, rather high throughout the year, reaches its maximum values at that season. It must be emphasized, however, that nowhere in the Congo do moisture conditions become as unfavorable as in the Sudan zone of West Africa. Thus the isohyet of 1,500 mm of rainfall embraces by far the greater part of the Congo, whereas much less than half of West Africa receives as much as 1,500 mm of annual precipitation. And a large part of West Africa lies to the north of the 1,000 mm isohyet, whereas all of the Belgian Congo appears to receive average annual rainfall of at

[11] See Bernard (2, pp. 104, 148, 151). The atmospheric circulation and position of the Intertropical Front as mapped by Brooks and Mirrlees is shown by Bernard for the Congo basin on pp. 96–97. He also presents charts (pp. 63–65) for nine stations representative of forest, forest border, and savanna zones, showing monthly precipitation and the annual march of temperature.

least that amount. For the rain-forest zone of the Congo, Bernard goes so far as to conclude that "the conditions of temperature and the humidity of the air and soil appear to be on the average rather close to those which characterize the ecological optimum of plants" (*2*, p. 202).

French Equatorial Africa, which is similar to West Africa in the transition from a humid southern region to increasingly arid zones in the north, covers an immense span of latitude—from nearly 5° S to beyond 20° N. The Chad, the Federation's northernmost territory, lies wholly within the arid and semiarid zones as shown in Map 3-2, apart from very limited areas bordering Lake Chad. Ubangi Chari is a transitional zone, most of it being either dry subhumid or moist subhumid. Virtually all of the southern territories of Gabon and Moyen Congo are humid or moist subhumid. The enclave, Spanish Guinea (Río Muni), is entirely humid.

A striking feature of the climate of Angola is its coastal strip of arid or semiarid climate. As a result of the cold Benguela Current off the coast of Angola, the southeast trade winds, which have been deflected to blow across Angola from the southwest or south, bring cool, damp air, but very little precipitation. Somewhat heavier precipitation occurs inland where the winds encounter higher elevations; the plateau and subplateau regions of central Angola receive some 60 to 80 inches of rainfall and are "humid" by the Thornthwaite classification of Map 3-2. Elsewhere the territory is mainly "moist subhumid," but in the south this zone gives way to sizable "dry subhumid" and "semiarid" regions. In this drier southern area, the precipitation inland declines to only 16 to 24 inches, and it averages less than four inches on the southern coast.

OTHER PHYSICAL FACTORS

Temperature and light.—Apart from the availability of moisture, temperature and light are probably the principal climatic factors influencing crop distribution in western tropical Africa. It was noted above that virtually the entire area is warm or "megathermal" in the classification of Map 3-3. For at least one crop, however, temperatures are high enough to be optimum in only limited areas. According to Jacques Miège, in West Africa it is only in the Niger delta and the northern Cameroons that wet rice finds its optimum temperature of 30–34 degrees C —86–93 degrees F (*14*, p. 34). In those areas the water in the paddy fields is warm, and it is desirable to leave the plants in water during the growth period which is not the case with rice culture in the forest zone where the temperature of the water is only 25–26 degrees C (77–79 degrees F). Miège also observes that exposed slopes are the preferred sites for upland rice because of the greater warmth and exposure to sunlight.

Although generally less critical than moisture or temperature, light is an additional factor which "may influence plant behavior by its intensity, its composition, and by its continuity or duration for any 24-hour period" (*13*, p. 277). This factor is probably of greatest importance in high-rainfall regions where insolation is often reduced by cloudiness or fog. Bultot reports that relative insolation (the ratio of actual insolation to the insolation astronomically possible) is uniformly low at Leopoldville and at Banana (on the coast) because of the cloudiness engendered by the cool Benguela Current. Relative insolation is also uniformly low at Kindu, and Bultot regards this as typical of rain forest stations (*7*, pp. 35–38). For stations of the interior savanna and in the highlands of the eastern Congo, the relative insolation shows very marked seasonal variation. Thus at Luluabourg the relative insolation, which is only .31 and .36 in the rainy season months of December and January, rises to .73 during June. (Bultot stresses this seasonal increase in relative insolation as one of the key factors accounting for the fact that, according to his computations, evaporation reaches a distinct maximum during the dry season.)

Bernard regards fairly weak solar radiation as the principal unfavorable climatic factor influencing agriculture in the Congo rainforest region. He attibutes this mainly to the cloudiness which is so prevalent, but particles in the air reducing radiation are probably of some importance. This last factor would be especially important in or near savanna areas where grass fires are common. Bernard suggests that this factor of relatively weak insolation has a distinct bearing on the low yields of certain cereal crops in the equatorial zone as compared with yields in regions receiving more sunlight (*2*, pp. 202–03). The frequency of overcast and the fact that summer brings relatively little lengthening of the hours of daylight is perhaps of particular importance in limiting the yield potential for rice in these low latitudes.

Soils.—Among the other physical factors influencing crop distribution, variation in soils and soil requirements of the various plants is clearly of great importance. It appears, however, that soil conditions are important chiefly as a micro-factor influencing the location of particular crops within the rather broad crop zones considered in this study. Thus it is pointed out by Miège that in some areas of the Ivory Coast where plantains are important, they are found only in bottom land where alluvial soil has accumulated. But in regions where the soils were formed by decomposition of schists and have a better capacity for holding water, plantains are found on the slopes as well as in low-lying areas.

One soil relationship of particular importance is the contrast between manioc and yams in their ability to adapt to mediocre soils. Whereas yams are quite demanding in their soil requirements, manioc is extremely tolerant and will often give at least tolerable yields on poor or depleted soils. It is emphasized in the next chapter that this ability of manioc to adapt itself to inferior soils or land whose fertility has been reduced by undue shortening of the fallow period is unquestionably a significant factor in the spread of manioc cultivation in recent decades.

H. Vine's classification of soil groups provides valuable insight into the soil factor in Nigeria. The principal distinction he makes is between the high-rainfall zones of intensely leached soils and the light, sandy soils of the north. The soils in the north are generally deficient in phosphate, but there is no marked deficiency of nitrogen, and fertility can usually be well maintained when the land is cropped 2 to 4 years and then left as bush fallow for several years. Southern Nigeria appears to be better supplied with phosphate but frequently deficient in nitrogen and "fertility appears to be lost rapidly under cultivation . . ." (27, p. 4). Detailed study of the Nigerian soil maps in relation to the distribution of the staple crops would no doubt reveal interrelationships more specific than the general characteristics of the staple crops with respect to soil requirements which are considered in Chapter 5.

Vegetation.—The value of natural vegetation as an indicator of climate has long been recognized. Köppen, the most distinguished advocate of this approach, held the view that "the plant is a meteorological instrument which integrates the various factors of a climate . . ." (21, p. 88). The climax vegetation of a region is, of course, influenced by soil as well as by climate, but for some purposes this enhances the value of knowledge of natural vegetation as an indicator of the potential capabilities of land for agriculture. Descriptions of African agriculture frequently note the way in which native cultivators are guided by the character of the vegetation, usually secondary growth, in deciding when to clear land and in choosing the crops to be sown.

There is little uniformity in the vegetation classifications which have been used in tropical Africa; also there has been considerable controversy concerning the limits of the zones even with comparable definitions of the vegetation types.[12] A highly generalized picture of the distribution of vegetation in western tropical Africa is presented in Map 3-5, reproduced from a map prepared by G. Delevoy (*18*, p. 386). Of the 15 vegetation zones shown on the original map, which includes the entire continent, only four are important in West Africa and the French Cameroons.[13]

(1) *Rain forest (Forêt équatoriale)*.—The forest included in this zone shows considerable variation and several subzones are commonly distinguished. Coastal areas of brackish swamp invaded by the tides are generally mangrove forest and are frequently not classed as Rain forest at all. Richards divides the Rain forest (Closed forest or High forest) into "Tropical Rain forest proper" consisting mainly of evergreens, and the "Mixed Deciduous forest" found as the outer edge of the forest is approached (*17*, pp. 336–38). Furthermore, local maps for Nigeria show extensive areas classed as "oil palm bush" and "derived savana." These are areas where it is believed the climatically determined climax vegetation would be Rain forest were it not for the influence of man (*4*, p. 35).

But on poorer soils and under less humid conditions abandoned fields tend, especially if over-cultivated, to be invaded by grasses; the inevitable grass fires kill off the younger trees which may attempt to establish themselves and high forest is replaced by "derived savana" dominated by grasses and fire-tolerant

---

[12] At a specialist meeting at Yangambi in 1956, organized by the Scientific Council for Africa South of the Sahara (CSA), recommendations were made concerning standard terms to be used in the preparation of types of vegetation maps. In addition, it was recommended that A. Aubréville of the Centre Technique Forestier, Nogent-sur-Marne, assemble materials for an atlas of the principal types of vegetation. As a longer range project, it was recommended that a scientific correspondent be appointed to organize the preparation of a *Botanical Atlas of Africa*. This *Atlas*, the preparation of which is expected to take five years, should offer valuable insights with regard to the distribution of staple food crops. Building on the *Climatological Atlas*, being prepared under the direction of Dr. S. P. Jackson and which is soon to be published, the *Botanical Atlas* is to include vegetation maps (at a scale of 1:5,000,000), and "maps of analogous eco-climates allowing for the extension of certain cultivated plants or of types of agricultural, pastoral or forest activities . . ." (*19*, p. 26).

[13] A good description of the vegetation zones, with photographs and sketches, is given by Robert in *18* (pp. 384–98). A. Aubréville gives an interesting series of "schematic profiles" depicting the succession of vegetation types from rain forest to the thorn land of the desert fringes in *1* (pp. 310 ff). Sketches illustrating 10 of the standard vegetation types recommended by the CSA specialist meeting at Yangambi are presented in *16*.

savana trees. In appearance this derived savana is very similar to the savanas of the Guinea zone farther N., though patches of relict forest on the poorer and agriculturally unattractive soils of the hills and on the humid soils of valley bottoms provide a clue to the character of the climax vegetation. Elsewhere in the heart of the rain forest belt, in the Provinces of Owerri and Calabar, human interference has destroyed the original forest and replaced it over hundreds of square miles by oil-palm bush.[14]

MAP 3-5

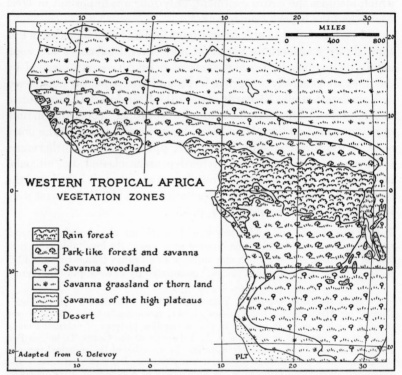

WESTERN TROPICAL AFRICA
VEGETATION ZONES

Rain forest
Park-like forest and savanna
Savanna woodland
Savanna grassland or thorn land
Savannas of the high plateaus
Desert

Adapted from G. Delevoy

(2) *Park-like forest and Guinea Savanna (Forêt-parcs et savanes guinéennes).*—Park-like forest is a term used to describe what is essentially a transition between the Rain forest and Savanna woodland. It is characterized by gallery forests along watercourses and other outliers of Rain forest, where soils contain moisture above the

---

[14] In connection with this statement, however, Buchanan and Pugh call attention to a view advanced by Leo Waibel that the original climax in semihumid tropical areas such as those classed as "derived savana" was "a vegetation type intermediate between forest and grassland . . ." (*4*, p. 35).

average, and tall-grass savanna is apt to occupy the open spaces which separate the forest clusters. Many of the trees, including the oil palm, are species which are characteristic of the Rain forest. Clusters of trees also characterize the Savanna woodland, but their foliage is light and the intervening grass is likely to be short. Richards describes this Guinea zone as varying from open savanna with scattered, mainly deciduous, fire-resistant trees to Savanna woodland with grassy undergrowth. He stresses that most of this zone is subject to frequent fires and suggests that the vegetation is a fire-climax rather than a climatic climax (*17*, pp. 336–38).

(3) *Savanna woodland of the Sudan Zone* (*Savanes boisées soudanaises*).—Here again the characteristic vegetation is open savanna with scattered trees. In addition, however, to the broad-leaved species which are also found in the Guinea zone, there are fine-leaved, thorny species such as are dominant in the next zone. Huge baobab trees are a common feature of the landscapes of this zone.

(4) *Savanna grassland or Sahel thorn land* (*Savanes herbeuses ou steppes à épineux sahéliennes*).—This region, often termed the Sahel zone, reflects the scanty rainfall of 600 mm (24 inches) or less which prevails. The woodland is dominated by spiny trees such as species of acacia, and the grass cover when present grows in scattered tufts rather than as a solid cover.

CITATIONS

1 André Aubréville, *Climats, forêts et désertification de l'Afrique tropicale* (Paris, 1949).

2 E. A. Bernard, *Le Climat écologique de la cuvette centrale* (Inst. Natl. pour l'Étude Agronomique du Congo Belge—INÉAC—Brussels, 1945).

3 ——, "On Various Consequences of the Energy Balance Method for the Study of Evapo-Transpiration from Crops of Natural Vegetal Covers," *Afr. Soils* (Inter-Afr. Bur. Soils and Rural Econ., CCTA [London]), IV, No. 1, 1956.

4 K. M. Buchanan and J. C. Pugh, *Land and People in Nigeria . . .* (London, 1955).

5 F. Bultot, "Notice de la carte des zones climatiques du Congo Belge et du Ruanda Urundi," *Atlas Général du Congo*, No. 33 (Acad. Royale Sci. Col., Brussels, 1954).

6 F. Bultot, personal communication, June 25, 1956.

7 ——, *Saisons et périodes sèches et pluvieuses au Congo Belge et au Ruanda-Urundi* (INÉAC, Bur. Climatology Communication 9, Brussels, 1954).

8 Econ. Intelligence Unit and Cartographic Dept. of Clarendon Press, *Oxford Economic Atlas of the World* (Oxford, 1954).

9 B. J. Garnier, "Report on Experiments to Measure Potential Evapo-

transpiration in Nigeria," *Res. Notes, No. 8* (Dept. Geog., Univ. Coll., Ibadan), January 1956.

10 J. P. Harroy, *Afrique, terre qui meurt* . . . (Brussels, 1949).

11 C. R. Hiernaux, "Sur un nouvel indice climatique d'humidité proposé pour l'Afrique Occidentale," *Bull. Inst. Français Afr. Noire* (Dakar), January 1955.

12 W. G. Kendrew, *The Climates of the Continents* (4th ed., London, 1953).

13 K. H. W. Klages, *Ecological Crop Geography* (New York, 1942).

14 Jacques Miège, "Les Cultures vivrières en Afrique Occidentale . . . ," *Cahiers Outre-mer* (Bordeaux), Jan.–Mar., 1954.

15 E. C. J. Mohr and F. A. Van Baren, *Tropical Soils* . . . (Royal Trop. Inst., Amsterdam, 1954).

16 "Nomenclature des types de végétation de l'Afrique tropicale," *Agronomie trop.* (France, Min. Outre-mer), Mar.–Apr. 1957.

17 P. W. Richards, *The Tropical Rain Forest: An Ecological Study* (Cambridge, Eng., 1952).

18 Maurice Robert, *Le Congo physique* (3d ed., Liége, 1946).

19 Sci. Coun. Afr. South of the Sahara (CSA), *C.S.A. Specialist Meeting on Phyto-Geography, Yangambi 28 July–8 August 1956* (Pub. 22, CCTA, London, 1956).

20 L. D. Stamp, *Africa: A Study in Tropical Development* (New York and London, 1953).

21 C. W. Thornthwaite, "An Approach Toward a Rational Classification of Climate," *Geog. Rev.*, January 1948.

22 ———, "The Climates of the Earth," *Geog. Rev.*, July 1933.

23 ———, "The Climates of North America According to a New Classification," *Geog. Rev.*, October 1931.

24 ———, "The Water Balance in Tropical Climates," *Bull. Am. Meteorological Soc.*, May 1951.

25 C. W. Thornthwaite and F. K. Hare, "Climatic Classification in Forestry," *Unasylva* (FAO, Rome), June 1955.

26 C. W. Thornthwaite and J. R. Mather, "The Water Budget and its Use in Irrigation," in U.S. Dept. Agr., *Yearbook of Agriculture, 1955: Water.*

27 H. Vine, *Notes on the Main Types of Nigerian Soils* (Nigeria, Agr. Dept., Special Bull. 5, Lagos, 1953).

28 H. O. Walker, "Evaporation," *J. W. Afr. Sci. Assn.* (Achimota), August 1956.

CHAPTER 4

GEOGRAPHICAL DISTRIBUTION OF THE STAPLE CROPS

The rather complex pattern of distribution of dominant and secondary staple food crops in western tropical Africa is shown here in a series of maps based on relatives computed from official statistics of crop area. West Africa, defined as in the preceding chapter to include the French Cameroons, and the Belgian Congo are considered in the first two sections of this Chapter. In the subsequent sections, the distribution of crops in French Equatorial Africa, Spanish Guinea (Río Muni), and Angola is described rather briefly, the lack of statistical data being especially acute for those territories.

Agricultural statistics for tropical Africa do not inspire much confidence. Discrepancies between various published estimates are common and sometimes disconcertingly large.[1] Certain characteristics of African agriculture have been cited by the Inter-African Committee on Statistics as giving rise to special difficulties compounding the customary problem of inadequate statistical services in an underdeveloped area (15, pp. 18–19):

1. The irregularity of the plots. "Fields tend to be small, highly irregular in shape and it is frequently difficult to decide where a field begins and uncultivated land ends."

2. The predominantly subsistence basis of African agriculture; limited commercialization of most crops; and the common practice of harvesting in small quantities for immediate consumption.

3. The prevalence of mixed and succession crops which complicates the problem of obtaining and presenting a satisfactory statistical picture.

4. Communal ownership of land.

[1] An extreme example of a discrepancy between different published statistics is provided in the manioc figures for Ubangi-Shari in French Equatorial Africa. The *Annuaire statistique de l'Afrique Équatoriale Française, Vol. I, 1936–1950*, p. 100, gives a figure of 364,000 tons whereas the *Annuaire statistique de l'Union Française Outre-mer, 1939–1949*, Tome Premier, p. F-360, gives an estimate of 1,278,000 tons, both presumably for a recent "average year." The former has been used, since it seems more reasonable in relation to the estimated population, but it is uncomfortable to make such a drastic choice.

These special problems give rise to formidable difficulties even with the most careful sample survey techniques, but the data for most of the territories considered are based on rough approximations by agricultural or district officers. The authorities are frank in warning the reader of the large degree of approximation involved. The *Annuaire statistique de l'Afrique Occidentale Française,* for example, explains that the estimates for these territories are essentially extrapolations made by field personnel of the Department of Agriculture "on the basis of observations in a few villages typical of the area under consideration." In arriving at the estimates, use is made of "demographic information about the region, estimates of the area cleared, annual household consumption (data which are more or less known by ethnic group and by region)" (5, p. 174).

Similar explanations have been offered with regard to agricultural statistics for several of the British territories of West Africa. For Gambia we are told: "The main estimates of food acreage and production are derived from assumed per capita consumption figures." Essentially the same explanation is offered for Ghana and British Togoland except that in the "Northern Territories acreages and production have been extrapolated from agricultural surveys conducted between 1931 and 1936 in different limited areas." And with regard to Sierra Leone, some of the data pertaining to swamp rice are based on eye estimates, but otherwise the figures "are merely intelligent guesses, cross-checked by reference to other sources of information" (24).

Obviously no precision can be claimed for the agricultural statistics used in this study, but there is some reason to believe that the area figures give a fairly good indication of the relative importance of the different crops as measured by the amount of land they claim. The sample survey of Bouaké *cercle* in the Ivory Coast, for example, produced results which coincide rather closely with the official statistics of crop area, but the yield figures obtained in the sample survey point to a very substantial underestimation in the official statistics (33a, pp. 9–11). The situation in Bouaké cercle also points up the way in which "prevalence of mixed and succession crops . . . complicates the problem of obtaining and presenting a satisfactory statistical picture." The general practice in this district is to grow manioc as a mixed crop, with a relatively small number of plants per acre, and to treat it as a reserve crop to offset a poor harvest of other staples with the result that manioc is only partially harvested. Hence, the production of manioc and its importance in local diets is much less than is suggested by the area statistics; and its classification in Map 4-2 as co-dominant with yams in Bouaké cercle is distinctly misleading. In general, however, the calorie contribution of roots, tubers, and plantains is greater than is suggested by their planted area since these crops are usually characterized by very high per-acre yields. In Chapter 6 an attempt is made to indicate the relative importance of the staple crops in terms of food calories produced.

Distribution by Territory

The relative importance of the various staple foods in West Africa as a whole was given in Chapter 2. But it is of interest to note how the position of the eight major staples varies from territory to territory. This is shown in Table 4-1 in terms of crop-area relatives, taking the area of the leading crop as 100; relatives for the other staples thus indicate the crop area they occupy as a percentage of the area devoted to the leading staple. This device is used rather than the more conventional "percentage of crop area" because it is not possible to obtain figures of comparable completeness for total cultivated area or area in food crops. In particular, the absence of data for plantains in several territories where they are of considerable importance would distort comparisons with "per cent of total" figures which included plantains.

Viewing the distribution of staple crops by territory, the dominant position of the millets and sorghums is conspicuous. They rank as the leading crop in nine territories and are of substantial importance in others. Rice is the leading crop in five territories and maize in one. Somewhat surprisingly a root crop does not appear as the leading crop in any territory and only in the Ivory Coast do the roots and tubers as a group rank as the dominant crop. Examination of Map 4-1, based on data for smaller administrative subdivisions, reveals that the root crops are of very great importance through a broad coastal band stretching from the Ivory Coast across the French Cameroons. Furthermore, as noted above, the importance of the root crops as a source of food calories is considerably greater than the ranking by crop area suggests.

Staple Food Crop Zones

The picture of staple food crop zones in West Africa and the French Cameroons in Map 4-1 is in as great detail as is possible with the data

Table 4.1.—West Africa and the French Cameroons, Staple Food Crops Areas Expressed as Relatives, about 1950*

(Staple with largest area in each territory—100)

Territory	Maize	Millets and sorghums	Rice	Manioc	Yams	Coco-yams	Plan-tains	Sweet potatoes	Area of crop taken as 100 (1,000 ha.)
French West Africa									
Sudan	8	100	17	1	—	…	…	1	1,270
Upper Volta	14	100	1	…	…	…	…	…	1,293
Niger	—	100	—	…	…	…	…	…	1,342
Senegal	2	100	6	4	…	…	…	1	774
Guinea	12	67	100	16	…	12	…	13	353
Ivory Coast	49	45	100	72	67	8	43	2	220
Dahomey	100	33	2	57	26	—	…	2	311
French Togo	74	100	6	25	26	—	1	1	169
Gambia	2	100	20	2	—	…	…	…	52
Sierra Leone	3	6	100	4	1	…	…	—	316
Gold Coast (Ghana)	46	100	6	27	20	26	41	…	309
Nigeria	26	100	5	32	40	10	[a]	2	3,121
Portuguese Guinea[b]	…	…	(100)[b]	…	…	…	…	…	
Liberia	…	…	100	21	…	…	…	…	260
Total (excluding Portuguese Guinea)[c]	*21*	*100*	*19*	*19*	*18*	*5*	*3*	*2*	*8,789[c]*
French Cameroons	22	100	1	9	4	8	5	1	672

* Data from Appendix Table I.

[a] Plantains were not included in the Nigerian sample census of agriculture and no area or production estimates are available; but they are of considerable importance in parts of southern Nigeria.

[b] No area data available but rice is clearly the major staple. The *Anuario da Guiné Portuguesa 1948* (Publicação do Governo da Colónia, Lisbon), p. 126, gives production estimates for rice (30,000 tons), peanuts, coconuts, and palm oil but none for secondary staple crops.

[c] Millet and sorghum total.

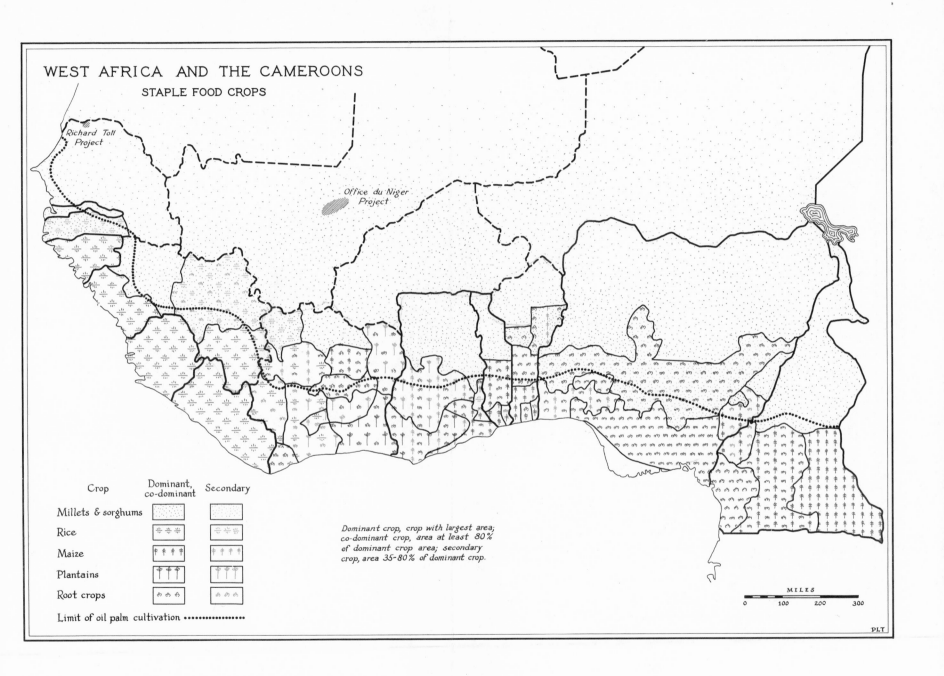

WEST AFRICA AND THE CAMEROONS
STAPLE FOOD CROPS

Richard Toll
Project

Office du Niger
Project

Crop	Dominant, co-dominant	Secondary
Millets & sorghums		
Rice		
Maize		
Plantains		
Root crops		

Limit of oil palm cultivation ••••••••••••

Dominant crop, crop with largest area;
co-dominant crop, area at least 80%
of dominant crop area; secondary
crop, area 35-80% of dominant crop.

MILES
0   100   200   300

PLT

currently available. Symbols identify the areas where millets and sorghums, maize, rice, plantains, or root crops are dominant or secondary crops. Roots and tubers, here lumped together as a group, are shown separately in Map 4-2 for the areas where they are of major importance. Dominant crops, those occupying the largest area in any district, and "co-dominant" crops, with an area not less than 80 per cent of the area of the dominant crop, appear as green symbols; secondary crops, with 35–80 per cent of the area of the dominant, are depicted by orange symbols.[2]

Millets and sorghums.—The huge expanse of the millet-sorghum zone is readily apparent from Map 4-1. These crops hold almost undisputed sway in the arid inland territories of French West Africa and in the northern regions of the territories of the Guinea coast. Only in the Casamance region of southern Senegal (Ziguinchor cercle) and the Upper Guinea district of French Guinea, where rice occupies over half as much land as the millets and sorghums, does a secondary crop appear. In areas with favorable moisture conditions, such as river valleys which flood periodically, maize, rice, and root crops are also cultivated, but apart from rice production in the inland delta of the Niger, the quantities are very small. In a detailed survey of the North Mamprusi District of Ghana, it was found that over 90 per cent of the cultivated land was planted to early millet, late millet, and sorghum (*40*, p. 19); and in areas farther to the north the dominance of millets and sorghums would tend to be even more pronounced.

Climate is obviously the key factor determining the distribution of millet and sorghum production. The area in which these crops are dominant begins in the "dry subhumid" region (see Map 3-2) and extends through the "semiarid" and "arid" zones to the limit of cultivation at the southern fringe of the Sahara. Small quantities of wheat and barley are grown under irrigation as cool season crops in oases of the Sahara, and in similar fashion irrigated maize and millets are cultivated in the hot season. But where annual rainfall reaches 200 to 300 mm (8 to 12 inches), millet begins to be cultivated without irrigation. Continuing south until approximately the 600-mm isohyet, millets continue as virtually the only grain crop cultivated. Where annual rainfall is between 600 and 1,000 mm, millets and sorghums are both of major importance, but as the 1,000-mm isohyet is reached

[2] With a few exceptions, the classification of crop regions in Map 4-1 is based on area relatives by administrative subdivision computed from official statistics as of about 1950. The relatives and sources used are shown in Appendix Table I.

ms largely supplant millet.[3] For both crops the chief source
r competitive power is the ability to withstand very high tem-
pᵤᵣᵤₜᵤres and to remain dormant through prolonged dry spells and
then resume growth with the recurrence of rain.

The "millet and sorghum" grouping is used broadly to include
the inferior millet, *Digitaria exilis,* and finger millet (*Eleusine coracana*). *Digitaria exilis,* or *fonio* as it is known in the French territories, accounts for nearly all of the millet-sorghum area in French
Guinea (an estimated 209,000 hectares out of 235,000). Owing to
its ability to grow on very poor and thin soils, it is particularly important on the Futa Jallon Plateau where degraded soils with lateritic
crusts are common. *Digitaria exilis,* or *acha* as it is known locally, also
assumes considerable importance in parts of northern Nigeria, notably in the vicinity of Zaria, Nasarawa, and in the Jos Plateau.[4] A
closely related species, *Digitaria Iburua,* is also grown in a few districts of northern Nigeria (*17,* p. 526). *Eleusine coracana* or finger
millet is of substantial importance in East Africa, but it does not extend westward beyond Nigeria. The eastern limit of cultivation of
fonio is roughly the same as the western limit for *Eleusine;* this fact
and other considerations suggest that there has been a supplanting of
fonio by *Eleusine* as the latter crop has migrated westward (*50,*
p. 481).

Rice.—The millet-sorghum zone just considered and the rice region, which stretches south along the coast from Portuguese Guinea
to the middle of the Ivory Coast, are the only large, continuous crop
zones in West Africa. The rice-dominant zone corresponds closely
with the perhumid and humid regions which center on Sierra Leone
and Liberia. The northern limit of this humid-perhumid region is
approximately the Casamance River, at which point the wet belt
extends inland some 400 miles, while toward the south it narrows to
a coastal band extending a little east of the boundary between the
Ivory Coast and Ghana (Map 3-2).

The limit of the rice region is not so far to the east, being a fairly
sharp line coinciding with the Bandama River, which reaches the sea

[3] This follows a chart presented by Jean Adrian illustrating the shift from millets
to sorghums in the French Sudan with increasing rainfall (see *4,* p. 27). Jacques
Miège places the northern limit of cultivation of sorghums at approximately the
400-mm isohyet with millets continuing to the limit where nonirrigated cultivation
is possible, roughly the 275-mm isohyet (*42,* p. 41). See also *3, 30, 60,* p. 78, and *1,*
pp. 175; 180–81.

[4] Roland Portères (*50,* p. 481) presents a map of West Africa showing areas of
"dense," "important," "sparse," and "very slight" cultivation of *Digitaria.*

in the middle of the Ivory Coast. Detailed study of the food crops of the Ivory Coast has led Jacques Miège to the conclusion, considered in some detail in Chapter 7, that historical and cultural factors are responsible for this shift from the rice culture of the western to the yam culture of the eastern Guinea coast. The limit of rice cultivation in the north, however, seems to be chiefly a climatic phenomenon. Despite a distinctly drier climate, rice is of appreciable importance in the Gambia where it is extensively grown on bottom land near the river and claims about a fifth as large an area as the dominant millets and sorghums. The region watered by the Casamance in the southern extension of Senegal receives somewhat more rainfall, and the rice area is nearly 60 per cent as large as the area devoted to millets and sorghums. Despite a lack of statistics, it seems clear that rice emerges as the major staple in Portuguese Guinea with its humid and perhumid climate and continues as such through Lower Guinea, and the Forest Region of French Guinea (and is virtually co-dominant in Upper Guinea); in Sierra Leone; in Liberia; and in a large part of the Ivory Coast.

It is important to distinguish between upland and wet rice since there are important differences between the two types of cultivation.[5] In the regions where rice is the traditional and dominant staple food, it is cultivated primarily as an upland crop. The predominance of upland rice in West Africa and the Congo contrasts with rice production in Asia and other major producing areas because, as V. D. Wickizer and M. K. Bennett observe, "rice grown under artificial systems of irrigation is the outstandingly important type of rice in the world economy" (65, p. 11). But in western tropical Africa cultivation of rice with controlled irrigation is limited to the Office du Niger project and a few other areas in the inland delta of the Niger, the Richard-Toll project on the Senegal River, and a few smaller projects in other territories. Considerably more important, however, are various modes of production of "wet rice" with natural irrigation.

---

[5] "Upland rice" refers to all varieties which are not grown in surface water. The term "wet rice" is used here to describe all varieties grown in standing water, at least during part of the growing season, whether the flooding is natural or by artificial irrigation, and embraces: "swamp rice" grown in the bottom of swampy valleys, "lowland" or "paddy" rice grown on land seasonally flooded by rivers or artificially irrigated, and "floating" rice with a stem which lengthens as the floodwaters slowly rise, floating on the surface while its roots are anchored to the bottom. According to Wickizer and Bennett, the floating rice roots at the nodes of the stems and starts growing and tillering as it rests on the surface of the ground after the water has subsided (65, p. 21n.). Dalziel (17, p. 533) speaks of floating rice in the central delta of the Nile growing in over 3 meters of water and being harvested from canoes.

ticularly important is the cultivation of rice in tidal swamps,
ice of long-standing but obscure origin. Until the latter part
.. ..e nineteenth century practically all of the rice grown in Sierra
Leone was upland, but around 1880 farmers began to develop tidal
mangrove swamps near the mouth of the Little Scarcies River for rice
production (*35*, p. 27; *33*, p. 90; and *18*). The fairly complex cultural practices used in this swamp cultivation were introduced from
French Guinea, and at the present time similar techniques are used
throughout the littoral regions of Sierra Leone, French and Portuguese Guinea, and the Casamance district of Senegal. In speaking of
the Baga of French Guinea, Church observes that it is not certain
whether they developed the techniques of reclaiming mangrove
swamps and cultivating rice themselves, or whether they learned this
skill from the Mande Kingdom of the Middle Niger, directly or in-
directly from the early Portuguese, or received it from Portuguese
Guinea (*14*, p. 291).

A distinction should be made between the cultivation of transplanted rice on tidal swamps and the growing of rice on nontidal
sedge or grass swamps. The growing of rice on tidal swamps is particularly important on the lowlands adjacent to the Great and Little
Scarcies rivers in Sierra Leone and the Konkouré River in French
Guinea. The rice to be planted on this type of swampland, which is
flooded when high tides cause the rivers to overflow their banks, is
started in seedbeds on higher ground. Transplanting is necessary to
allow time for the salinity of the fields to be reduced sufficiently following the onset of the rainy season, and also because the plants need
a start to withstand the submergence and water movement on these
tidal swamps. Although the initial clearing of these mangrove swamps
is arduous work their subsequent cultivation is a very profitable operation. The fields require little preparation for transplanting since
the brackish water with which they are flooded prior to the rainy
season limits the growth of weeds, although the salt-resistant *Paspalum
vaginatum* may be a problem; yields are said to average some 1,500
to 2,000 pounds of paddy per acre. On the sedge or grass swamps
preparation of the land for planting is more difficult owing to heavy
growth of weeds, but the rice is planted directly in the fields once they
have been hoed. In these coastal areas a certain amount of rice is
also planted in fields surrounded by small earth dikes or bunds to
hold out the sea water and to retain the rain. But the soils in fields
established in this way have often become excessively acid due to the
oxidation of sulphur compounds, possibly deposited by the brack-

ish water which periodically flooded the fields before they were empoldered. This problem is currently under study, but for the present this type of development is not looked upon with favor, at least in Sierra Leone (*62a*, pp. 29–34).

It also appears that within the rice zone there are significant differences in the extent to which rice holds sway as the dominant crop. Although rice is by far the dominant crop in French Guinea considered as a whole, it is of very limited importance in Middle Guinea where fonio is the dominant crop on the thin soils of the Futa Jallon. On the other hand, the Kissi, the "people of rice," who live in the Forest Region of French Guinea and adjacent districts of Sierra Leone and Liberia, seem exceptional in the degree to which "Life, not only material but emotional, is here dominated by the care of rice" (*48*, p. 23). Denise Paulme also notes that whereas the Kissi scorn millets and sorghum, those crops are extensively cultivated by neighboring peoples.

"Floating rice" is extremely important in the vicinity of Mopti and in other districts of the central delta of the Niger where the seasonal flooding is so deep that ordinary varieties would drown. Where the flooding is particularly deep or irregular, varieties of the indigenous African rice, *Oryza glaberrima* are grown, but elsewhere varieties of *Oryza sativa* from Indochina tend to predominate. The promising program for developing rice production in the tidal swamps of the Bonthe grasslands along the southern coast of Sierra Leone is based on strains of floating rice from Indochina.

During the past two decades there has been an important expansion of wet rice (referred to as *riz dressé* by the local agricultural officials) in the Upper Valley of the Niger, a zone upstream from Segou extending some distance beyond Bamako. The Agricultural Service in the French Sudan has actively pushed this development by construction of many small dams to provide some control of the extent and timing of the annual flooding of low-lying areas with the rise in the level of the Niger. The water control made possible by these rather inexpensive land improvement measures is, of course, only partial, and no attempt is made to level the land in order to achieve a uniform water level. In the lowest areas where the flooding is especially deep, floating rice is planted, but for the most part varieties of ordinary wet rice are grown. Expansion of this type of rice culture has also been encouraged by distributing plows and teaching local farmers how to use animal draft power. At present the rice area in the French Sudan, including something over 25,000 hectares in the

Office du Niger, amounts to approximately 180,000 hectares, and the major part of the cultivation is now done with plows drawn by oxen. A similar development has been encouraged by the Agricultural Service of French Guinea in the riverine plains of Upper Guinea.

In recent years there has also been an expansion of swamp rice in interior districts of Sierra Leone, Liberia, and Nigeria. Although rice accounts for only two or three per cent of the area in staple food crops in Nigeria, total production is of the order of 250,000 tons, comparable to production in Sierra Leone, French Guinea, and Liberia, the major producing territories of the rice zone. By far the largest part of the rice production in Nigeria is located in the Northern Region, especially in Sokoto and Niger provinces. In Sokoto Province alone, roughly 35,000 hectares are under wet rice along the Sokoto River and in other valleys draining to the Niger (11, p. 116). Considerable rice is also grown in swampy areas along the Niger, Kaduna, and Gbako rivers. In Kano, somewhat less important for rice than Benue and Ilorin provinces and much less so than Sokoto and Niger, rice is grown as an upland crop in areas with impervious soil prone to waterlogging (46, p. 521). The Western and Eastern regions each account for some 15,000 hectares of rice. Interest in developing rice cultivation in coastal swamps in Nigeria has been stimulated by the successful efforts in the Scarcies area of Sierra Leone. Despite soil conditions which are reported to be less favorable in Nigeria, considerable development of this production has occurred in recent years. In the southern regions the chief production districts are in the Onitsha and Ogoja provinces in the east, and in Delta, Benin, and Abeokuta provinces in the Western Region. In Abeokuta the rice is mainly upland, much of it interplanted with maize, but in the other provinces wet rice probably predominates (11, p. 117).

Encouragement of rice production has been singled out for such special attention in government agricultural programs that the efforts to expand rice cultivation in British and French West Africa, in Liberia, and in the Belgian Congo, and the reasons advanced for the special emphasis on rice are examined at some length in Chapter 9. Of interest, here, however, is the fact that in West Africa the policy in all territories seems to be one of encouraging production of wet rice while trying to bring about a reduction in the cultivation of upland rice, a crop widely condemned as leading to the destruction of forest cover and inducing erosion. This is, of course, particularly true when rice is grown on steep slopes, *riz de montagne* in French te.... nology; where the rice is grown on fairly level land (*riz de plaine*) the erosion problem is not nearly so serious. The Soils Conference held at Goma in 1948 adopted a recommendation that "cultivation of upland rice be forbidden and that the cultivation of irrigated rice be promoted or extended" (*28*, p. 1398). Most of the recent expansion seems to have been in irrigated rice production, usually with only the natural irrigation of seasonal flooding. As will be seen later, many writers hold that there are tremendous possibilities for expanding production of irrigated rice in West Africa. The potential danger of *Schistosomiasis* (*Bilharzia*) infection to which farmers are exposed by cultivation of swamp rice is sometimes cited as an unfavorable factor. Roger Jaspar has enthusiastically recommended that cultivation of wet rice in the Belgian Congo be greatly expanded; but he advocates that this irrigated production be completely mechanized and that transplanting of seedlings should not be practiced so that cultivators would not be obliged to work in the water of the rice fields and thus avoid the danger of *Schistosomiasis* infection (*34*, p. 92). It has also been pointed out that the tree *Balanites aegyptiaca* can be planted near streams as a control measure, since its fruit carries a solution fatal to the water snails which carry the infection (*54*, p. 76). There is considerable room for doubt, however, whether this really represents an effective control measure. There has also been resistance to abandoning the cultivation of upland rice. Miège reports that the notables and chiefs of several Baoulé villages have acted to "prohibit the cultivation of lowland rice, although it is perfectly adapted to the eastern provinces of the Ivory Coast" (*42*, p. 49). Speaking of the interior region of French Guinea, Portères observes that the "cultivation of upland rice clearly has been declining for two decades" (*50*, p. 487); and one gains an impression that this tendency has prevailed in much of the rice region of West Africa.

Maize.—Maize most commonly takes the role of a secondary or minor crop but is of widespread importance in both forest and savanna regions of West Africa. Owing to its more exacting soil requirements and greater need for moisture, maize cultivation is very limited in the drier portions of the millet-sorghum region. In the French Sudan it occupies a little less, and in Upper Volta a little more, than a tenth as large an area as the millets and sorghums. It is of negligible importance in Senegal and Niger. Within the coastal territories of the rice zone, maize is a minor crop as far east as the Ivory

Coast, where it attains considerable importance. While it is the leading crop only in Katiola District, the maize area in Seguela is exceeded
only by rice and is nearly as large as the combined yam-manioc area.
In Gagnoa District maize figures as a secondary crop, and it is of considerable importance in a half-dozen other districts. For the Ivory
Coast as a whole only rice, manioc, and yams take a larger area. The
importance of maize is very similar in Ghana. Although it is the dominant crop only in South Togo and the nonforest portion of the Colony
District, it is an important secondary crop in Ashanti and the Colony
forest zone.

The maize belt which begins in the southeast corner of Ghana continues through the southern districts of French Togo and Dahomey.
It is the dominant crop throughout the southern half of the latter territories except for the root-dominant Savalou District of Dahomey,
where not quite a third as much land is planted to maize as to manioc
and yams combined. Thus it corresponds with the drier coastal zone
of semiarid and dry subhumid climate. There does not seem to be
any very satisfactory explanation for the dominance of maize in this
area. Perhaps the soils are somewhat better suited to maize than the
light soils typical of the millet-sorghum area. It is probably significant
that, although the annual rainfall is comparable to much of the millet-
sorghum region, the humidity of the air is higher in this coastal dry
strip. Hence maize is not subject to the dry heat that is injurious to
that crop, whereas rust problems for the millets and sorghums are
aggravated.

In the Western Region of Nigeria maize continues to be of considerable importance, particularly so in Ilaro division in Abeokuta
Province, in Ijebu Province, and in southern Ondo Province (55,
p. 34). Although widely grown in the Eastern Region, maize is
dwarfed in importance by the root crops. In the southern portion of
the British Cameroons maize occupies close to a third as large an
area as the root crops combined and a larger area than any crop
except cocoyams. Immediately to the north in the Bamenda grasslands of the British Cameroons maize emerges as the dominant crop
in a region where soil and climate appear to be admirably suited to
this cereal. Apart from the Maritime District with its extremely high
rainfall, the southern half of the French Cameroons constitutes another area where maize is a dominant crop.

The effect of climatic factors in determining the distribution of
maize is not at all clear. It seems to attain its greatest importance in

transition zones between the wet regions of rain-forest climate and the dry savanna lands where the millets and sorghums take over. This is probably related to the fact that maize requires more sunlight than the root crops or plantains. H. P. White has noted, for example, that in the forest zone of Ghana the principal crops are plantains, coco-yams, manioc, and water yams; and that maize is grown where the trees have been cleared enough to admit sufficient sunlight (64, p. 38). Most of the areas where maize is a dominant or important secondary crop are characterized by an equatorial type of climate with double maxima of rainfall. This usually permits cultivation of an early and a late crop, and the possibility of double-cropping is sometimes mentioned as giving an advantage to maize in competition with other crops. Miège suggests that in the Ivory Coast maize, like yams, is favored in the southern and relatively humid savanna areas, with the zone of maize concentration lying to the north of the yam area (42, p. 35).

The most characteristic feature of maize cultivation in West Africa seems to be the fact that it is grown, though frequently as a minor crop, in such a wide range of climatic zones. It appears that maize very commonly holds a place in local cropping patterns because of its role as a "hunger breaker"; roasting ears frequently are available during the pre-harvest shortage period before other staple crops are ready to be harvested.

When grown in forest clearings maize is commonly interplanted with yams, cowpeas, pumpkins or gourds, or various other crops. In savanna bush, as in the Western Region of Nigeria or the inland region of Sierra Leone, maize is likely to be interplanted with rice—although in the latter territory maize is of very limited importance (54, p. 31; 11, p. 117). Maize production within the millet-sorghum region is confined to areas where conditions of moisture and soil fertility are especially favorable. In the French Sudan, maize, like millets and sorghums, is cultivated either during the rainy season on land not reached by the flooding of the Niger, or during the dry season on soils retaining moisture after the receding of the Niger (3, p. 30). Here and elsewhere in the north the fact that maize is more exacting in its soil requirements than millets and sorghums is reflected in the tendency to confine maize production to small plots close to village compounds where it receives animal manure and village waste.

Plantains.—The term plantain is used somewhat loosely in this study to describe varieties of plantains (*Musa paradisiaca*)[6] or banana (*Musa sapientum*) used as a staple food. French-language sources often use the term "banane" to apply to both bananas and plantains, although sometimes the latter is distinguished as the "banane plantain" or "banane à farine." R. P. Ch. Tisserant reports that in Ubangi-Shari in French Equatorial Africa virtually all of the bananas grown were of the plantain type before the arrival of Europeans; only one variety of sweet banana was grown and that was of poor quality. But since the introduction of other varieties of bananas, in about 1911, they have spread rapidly and are frequently cultivated alongside the local plantain varieties (*59*, pp. 228–29). In general it may be said that the plantain plant is somewhat larger, bears fewer and larger fruits, and its fruit is generally used before it is fully ripe, when it has a very high starch content, and is either cooked immediately, or dried preliminary to grinding into a meal or flour (*33*, pp. 220–21). A. S. Thomas has reported, however, that in a study of banana and plantain varieties in Uganda it was found that the botanical characters which are commonly cited as distinguishing plantains and bananas are not constant; and consequently a local classification into four groups of varieties according to their uses is employed (*58*, pp. 118–19).

Centers of plantain production are found in humid coastal areas between the Ivory Coast and the French Cameroons. Plantains and root crops are co-dominant in the coastal forest region extending east from the Bandama River in the Ivory Coast into Ghana, but terminating short of the semiarid Accra plain. It is an important secondary crop in Ivory Coast districts lying to the west and north of the zone where it is a dominant crop, and also in the Ashanti District of Ghana. French Togo and Dahomey are apparently too dry for plantains to be of much importance. No statistics of plantain production in Nigeria are available, but the *Report on the Sample Census of Agriculture* notes that "Bananas and plantains exist in most villages in the south. They form a useful addition to the diet and are relatively simple to produce; in Cameroons Province plantains constitute with cocoyams the staple diet of the people . . ." (*45*, p. 8). It seems likely that the heaviest concentration of plantains is in the humid Eastern Region and in the adjacent provinces of Delta and Benin with similar climate, but there is evidence that they are of modest importance in most of the Western Region with its subhumid

---

[6] Dalziel (*17*, p. 468) identifies the plantain as *Musa sapientum* var. *paradisiaca*.

climate. The economic survey of the cocoa-producing areas of Nigeria observes (27, p. 182):

> The principal fruit of the cocoa-growing areas is the banana and its cousin the plantain. These plants seem to grow well with the least possible attention in almost every part of the Western Region. They appear as boundary plants and as scattered plants in food and cocoa farms as well as in regular small plantations. . . .

Data from food consumption surveys of several groups of cocoa farmers, however, suggest that in the Abeokuta and Ibadan areas plantains are of small importance whereas in the Ife-Ilesha and Ondo areas plantains occupy a fairly important position (27, pp. 657–60).

Plantains continue as an important staple through the moister portions of the French Cameroons. In Maritime District they occupy three-fifths as large an area as the leading crop—cocoyams—but only about 35 per cent as much land as the root crops combined. In Ouest, the district just to the north of Maritime, plantains claim almost a third as large an area as the dominant maize crop, and in the large Centre District close to a fifth as large an area as maize.

For the areas just considered, a close correlation seems to exist between the distribution of plantain production and the occurrence of wet rain forest (forêt hygrophile and forêt mésophile humide) (42, p. 35). Also conspicuous is the association between plantain production and the cultivation of cocoyams, reflecting the fact that both plants require and tolerate a great deal of moisture. A question arises as to why, apart from the Ivory Coast, plantains do not appear in the humid rice zone of the western Guinea Coast. Descriptions of typical diets in Liberia indicate that plantains are of considerable importance in that country although no statistics of area or production are available. In Sierra Leone and French Guinea, however, plantains are of slight importance despite the fact that there has been a considerable development of banana production for export in the latter territory. The limited importance of plantains beyond Liberia is no doubt related to the limited extent of closed forest in those territories and the somewhat longer dry season which prevails despite high annual rainfall (as in the contrast between Conakry and Abidjan noted in Chapter 3).

Roots and tubers (manioc, yams, cocoyams, and sweet potatoes). —A generalized picture of the distribution of "root crops" is given in Map 4-1; the relative importance of the three principal crops — manioc, yams, and cocoyams—is shown on Map 4-2 for those areas

MAP 4-2

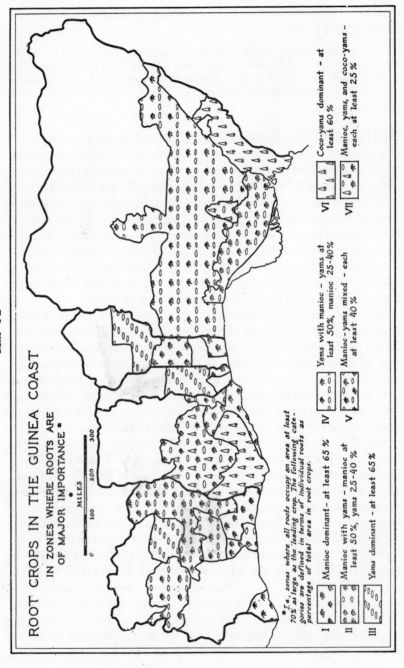

ROOT CROPS IN THE GUINEA COAST
IN ZONES WHERE ROOTS ARE
OF MAJOR IMPORTANCE *

MILES
0   100   200   300

*I.e, zones where all roots occupy an area at least
70% as large as the leading crop. The following categories are defined in terms of individual roots as
percentage of total area in root crops.

I   Manioc dominant - at least 65 %

II Manioc with yams - manioc at
    least 50%, yams 25-40 %

III Yams dominant - at least 65%

IV Yams with manioc - yams at
    least 50%, manioc 25-40%

V   Manioc-yams mixed - each
    at least 40%

VI Coco-yams dominant - at
    least 60 %

VII Manioc, yams, and coco-yams -
    each at least 25 %

of the Guinea Coast where roots and tubers rank as dominant or co-dominant crops.[7] Nowhere in West Africa do sweet potatoes rank as a dominant or even a secondary crop; and for that reason they are not represented in Map 4-2. They are, however, widely grown on a limited scale.

The root crops hold sway in more or less the southern half of the territories from the Ivory Coast through Nigeria. Exceptions are most of the Ivory Coast west of the Bandama River, which is part of the rice zone, and three districts in French Togo and Dahomey where the dominance of maize is not seriously challenged by roots or tubers. Roots are also dominant or co-dominant in the southern half of the French Cameroons (not shown on Map 4-2). In the Ouest District, where they appear only as a secondary crop, they claim 76 per cent as large an area as maize, the dominant staple.

It will be noted that areas in which a single root or tuber is dominant are much less common than mixed regions where two, or occasionally three, root crops are of substantial importance. In a few districts manioc accounts for 65 per cent or more of the root crop area, but much more extensive are the regions (categories II, IV, and V) where manioc and yams both figure prominently; and in the Ashanti District of Ghana the land in roots and tubers is quite evenly divided between yams, manioc, and cocoyams.

Competition between manioc and yams seems to be related to many factors, and no very satisfactory explanation can be offered for the complex pattern of distribution of those two crops. Manioc is preeminently a forest crop, but it differs from cocoyams and plantains in that it is by no means confined to forest regions and it thrives in rain forest of medium high moisture (*forêt mésophile moyenne*) rather than the humid rain forest (*forêt hygrophile* and *forêt mésophile humide*) which favors plantains and cocoyams. Miège indicates that in the Ivory Coast, where manioc is dominant in areas surrounding the coastal lagoons and through the forest zone of medium high moisture, it tends to give way to yams as the northern edge of the forest is reached and in the more southerly and humid savanna zone (*42*, pp. 32–35). This is related to the fact that manioc yields decline toward the north from something like 8–10 tons in the forest zone

---

[7] Three districts are included—Anecho District in French Togo, Porto Novo District in Dahomey, and agricultural zone 12 in Nigeria—where the area devoted to root crops is a little less than 80 per cent of the area planted to the dominant crop and which are accordingly not shown in the "dominant–co-dominant" category of Map 4-1.

to 2–4 tons in the Sudan zone (and even less when it is grown in mixed culture as a reserve crop). Thus in most northern areas manioc is only a stopgap food to satisfy food requirements between the planting of yams in May and their harvest which begins in August (*43*, p. 86).

A similar tendency to shift emphasis away from manioc toward yams in moving from more to less humid zones is also discernible in Nigeria and Dahomey. Other factors may be involved, however; and in any event it would be erroneous to conclude that yams resist drought better than manioc. It may well be that the optimum moisture level for yams, at least for certain species, is lower than the optimum water regime for manioc. But owing to the adaptability of manioc to a wide range of moisture conditions, including long periods of drought, manioc is grown in dry subhumid and semiarid regions where yams are not found at all. Admittedly, yields are poor and total production of manioc in such areas is small, but nonetheless it is widely grown in the millet-sorghum regions, in large part because of its ability to resist locust attacks and its general suitability as a famine reserve crop. It would perhaps be even more common in the northern regions were it not for the damage that unfenced fields of manioc suffer from grazing stock. In the North Mamprusi District of Ghana it is reported that although manioc would be a very desirable crop, its cultivation is "impracticable on native farms at present because of damage by livestock, principally goats during the dry season" (*40*, p. 48). But in the French Sudan and Senegal it is widely cultivated in small plots, generally so enclosed as to shield the plants from damage by livestock (*3*, p. 30). In French Niger, where manioc has been encouraged as a famine crop by distribution of planting material, production of manioc has shown a striking increase—from less than 8,000 tons in 1946 to nearly 120,000 tons in 1954 (*6*, p. 3075). In the semiarid Accra Plains manioc and maize are the co-dominant crops, and it is in the areas with less favorable moisture conditions that manioc is most important (*63*, p. 55).

The distribution of cocoyams has in effect been described in the earlier discussion of plantains, the pattern of distribution being similar for the two crops. Cocoyams as shown on Map 4-2 include both the "old" and "new" cocoyams (*Colocasia esculentum* and *Xanthosoma sagittifolium*). In Ghana, one of the major centers of cocoyam production, the more recently introduced varieties of *Xanthosoma* have largely replaced *Colocasia*, the "old cocoyams" which reached West Africa in the distant past. In southern Nigeria, where cocoyams

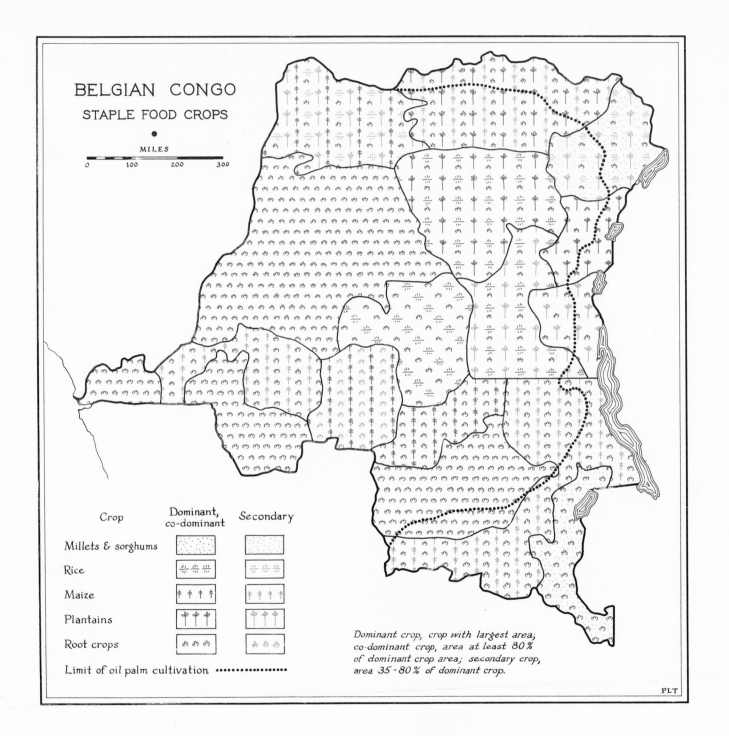

BELGIAN CONGO
STAPLE FOOD CROPS

MILES
0   100   200   300

Crop	Dominant, co-dominant	Secondary
Millets & sorghums		
Rice		
Maize		
Plantains		
Root crops		

Limit of oil palm cultivation ●●●●●●●●●●●●

Dominant crop, crop with largest area;
co-dominant crop, area at least 80%
of dominant crop area; secondary crop,
area 35-80% of dominant crop.

PLT

are widely cultivated, it seems that *Colocasia* is still the more important, although it is gradually giving way to *Xanthosoma* (*66*, pp. 198–201; *33*, p. 135). In Cameroons Province in the southern portion of the British Cameroons and in the adjacent Maritime District of the French Cameroons cocoyams are the dominant staple. Qualitative material makes it quite clear that they rank next to maize as the dominant crop in Bamenda Province (*36*, p. 20); and they are also of considerable importance in the Ouest and Centre districts of the French Cameroons. Thus cocoyams like plantains are found as an important crop only in hot and humid forest regions.

Although sweet potatoes do not rank as a dominant or even secondary crop in West Africa, Church states that they are "important in the southern French Sudan—Upper Volta—Ivory Coast borderlands, in the curious coastal savannah of the Ivory Coast, in the Volta Delta, in southern Senegal and in Northern Nigeria" (*14*, p. 119). The available estimates of crop area seem to suggest, however, that sweet potatoes reach their greatest importance in French Guinea where they occupy close to 15 per cent as large an area as the dominant rice crop and are slightly more important than cocoyams and only slightly less important than manioc.

BELGIAN CONGO

The distinctive feature of the distribution of food crops in the Belgian Congo (as shown in Map 4-3) is the paramount position of manioc. In 20 of the Congo's 22 administrative districts, root crops rank as a dominant or co-dominant crop.[8] To a large extent the "root crop" category in the Congo means manioc. The one clear-cut exception is Nord Kivu, where sweet potatoes occupy almost twice as large an area as manioc; and "other roots and tubers"—yams and cocoyams—claim an appreciable area but are less important than manioc.

Plantains rank as a co-dominant crop in three districts in the northeast—Uele, Stanleyville, and Nord Kivu. They are also an important secondary crop in Kibali-Ituri, Sud Kivu, and Maniema in the eastern Congo and also in Congo-Ubangi District in the northwest. Apart from these districts, however, plantains are of substantial im-

---

[8] Dominant, co-dominant, and secondary crops are defined as explained above for Map 4–1. Map 4–3 is based on area relatives computed from crop estimates for 1952 from *10* except that classification of Kwango and Kwilu was based on 1954 data in *Bull. agr. du Congo Belge*, Aug. 1955, XLVI, ff. p. 984.

portance only in the Bas-Congo (where they claim 34 per cent as large an area as the dominant root crops) and in Equateur District.

Rice is also a co-dominant crop in three districts—Sankuru, Maniema, and Stanleyville. Rice does not appear as a secondary crop, although it is actually of great importance in parts of the Congo-Ubangi, Tshuapa, Uele, and Kibali-Ituri districts.

Maize is co-dominant with manioc in two districts — Congo-Ubangi in the northwest and Kabinda in the southern savanna. It also has the distinction of standing alone as a dominant crop in Kasai District where manioc, with some 70 per cent as large an area, is a highly important secondary crop. In addition, maize appears as a secondary crop in five districts, and in one of these—Uele District—it falls only a point short of being classed as a co-dominant crop with roots and plantains. In several other districts—Bas Congo, Maniema, Haut Lomami, and Sankuru—maize comes very close to qualifying as a secondary crop.

The small importance of millets and sorghums is the most marked contrast with the crop pattern in West Africa. Only in the northeastern district of Kibali-Ituri and in Haut Katanga in the southeast do millets and sorghums appear on Map 4-3 and their role is as a secondary crop. In Nord and Sud Kivu millets and sorghums come close to ranking as a secondary crop, but elsewhere they do not occupy more than about a tenth as large an area as the dominant crop.

Correlations between climatic influences and the distribution of staple crops are far more difficult to discern in the Belgian Congo than in West Africa. The effect of the availability of moisture seems quite evident for rice and for millets and sorghums. Since rice is grown only as an upland crop in the Congo, it requires fairly high and well-distributed rainfall, and the districts where it is important lie pretty well within the more humid *Af* and *Am* zones shown in Map 3-4; the rice-producing areas lying outside the 1,600-mm isohyet are of limited extent (*61*, pp. 9–11). On the other hand, the two districts where millets and sorghums appear as a secondary crop are in the relatively dry districts of the northeastern and southeastern Congo. The negligible importance of millets and sorghums in the Bas Congo, also marked by comparatively low rainfall and a long dry season, may be related to the persistent cloudiness and the fairly humid air which characterize that region. Historical factors related to the introduction and spread of manioc may, however, be more important. Manioc is so ubiquitous that the principal problem posed in the Congo is to try to explain variations in its relative importance, and on that question climatic factors do not shed much light. Manioc is such a flexible crop and the Congo so generally favorable to its cultivation, that climate appears to be a limiting factor only in parts of the eastern highlands, where temperatures fall too low, and in limited fringe areas of the savanna where a long dry season gives millets and sorghums a competitive advantage.

Two of the regions that place exceptionally heavy reliance on manioc contain large areas of the so-called "Kalahari sands." These are soils of very low fertility, and the ability of manioc to produce a tolerable yield on such soils is a major reason why manioc occupies more than 75 per cent of the area in staple food crops in large parts of two administrative districts—Lac Léopold II (the *plateaux batéke*) and Kwango (Feshi Territory) (*31*, pp. 52–53, 57, 100). Another possible relationship between soils and crop distribution concerns the fertile volcanic soils which are common in Kivu Province (*51*, p. 350). Plantains thrive on volcanic soils, and this probably has a bearing on the importance of plantains in Nord and Sud Kivu.

Climatic and soil conditions are, of course, the limiting factors that determine the range of crops grown in the Congo. But the influence of those physical factors on the relative importance of the staple food crops grown appears to be fairly weak. Hence it seems likely that the influence of various social, economic, and historical factors on the pattern of crop distribution has been substantial. The influence of historical factors, on the one hand, and the physical environment and ecological characteristics of the various crops, on the other hand, are naturally closely related. A good illustration is offered by the adoption of manioc by one of the Baluba groups of Katanga Province, described in Chapter 7. The role of a famous chief in introducing manioc among his people—who are now known as the Bena Kalundwe or "people of manioc"—was of great importance. But equally important was the fact that manioc was very well received because it could be harvested at the end of the dry season when the risk of seasonal hunger was most acute (*62*, p. 232).

Historical factors may also be more important than the soil influence mentioned above in explaining the location of plantain production. Examination of Maps 4-4A and 4-4B, which show the percentage of total area devoted to staple food crops occupied by manioc and plantains, brings out the fact that manioc is of greatest importance in the southern and western Congo, whereas plaintains are of greatest importance in the northeast. The plantain map, as Gourou aptly expresses it, is very nearly the negative of the map of manioc

MAP 4.4.—BELGIAN CONGO: AREA OF MANIOC AND PLANTAINS AS PER CENT
OF TOTAL AREA OF STARCHY STAPLES IN NATIVE AGRICULTURE

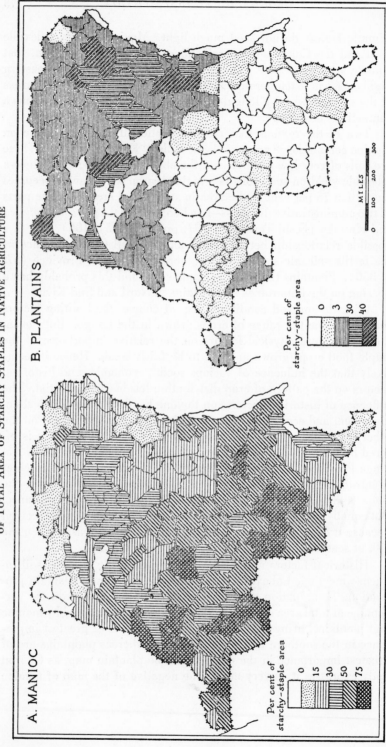

A. MANIOC

B. PLANTAINS

Per cent of
starchy-staple area

0
15
30
50
75

Per cent of
starchy-staple area

0
3
30
40

MILES
0   100   200   300

Reproduced from P. Gourou, *La Densité de la population rurale au Congo Belge* (Brussels, 1955), pp. 142, 144.

distribution. This relationship seems to reflect, in large part at least, the way in which manioc was introduced and spread through the Congo. Maps 4-4A and 4-4B, which were prepared by Gourou and his associates at the Université Libre de Bruxelles, not only are established on a different basis than Map 4-3—percentage of total area in starchy staple (carbohydrate) crops rather than area relatives—but also show a more detailed breakdown based on unpublished data by territory. Consequently, these maps and Maps 4-5A and 4-5B for maize and rice add a good deal to the more generalized picture of staple food crop zones shown in Map 4-3.

The role of certain economic factors, particularly the storability and cost of transporting different staples is probably more important in the Congo than in any of the other territories considered in this study. A specific indication of this is the way in which the centers of production of maize in Kasai Province, where it is of great importance, "are echelonned along the rail line which goes from Port-Francqui to Elisabethville . . ." (*10*, p. 51). Part of the production from this area is shipped to Elisabethville and other centers of the food-deficit Katanga region, and some of it is exported, chiefly to Belgium. More general evidence of the probable importance of transport costs, storability, and other economic factors is offered by data concerning the substantial and increasing volume of staple foods which moves into commercial channels in the Congo.

A very marked increase in the total quantities commercialized and in the percentage of production moving through commercial channels has occurred in recent years according to data published by the Banque Centrale du Congo Belge et du Ruanda-Urundi (*23*, pp. 464–65; see also *56*, Table B ff., p. 786). For the four major staples—manioc, plantains, maize, and rice—the quantities moving in commercial channels increased from 10 to 20 per cent of total consumption between 1948 and 1955.[9] Rice far exceeds any other crop in percentage produced for sale; in 1955 close to 65 per cent of all rice consumed was reported as having moved through commercial channels, and this proportion was already 60 per cent in 1948. Somewhat surprisingly, there is little difference between maize, manioc, and plantains, according to the estimates of commercialization for 1955. Maize at 23 per cent of total consumption ranked first, followed by plantains and manioc with 20 and 19 per cent respectively. For maize

---

[9] A report of the Agricultural Department of the Ministry of Colonies for the years 1948 through 1952 gives considerably higher estimates of the quantities of manioc and maize commercialized in 1948 (*10*, pp. 47, 51).

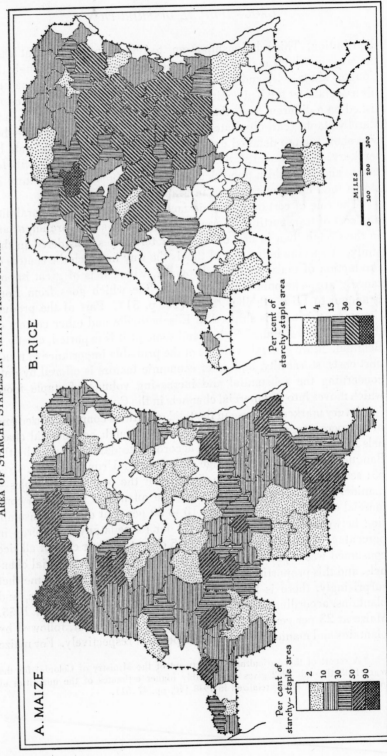

MAP 4-5.—BELGIAN CONGO: AREA OF MAIZE AND RICE AS PER CENT OF TOTAL
AREA OF STARCHY STAPLES IN NATIVE AGRICULTURE

A. MAIZE

Per cent of
starchy-staple area

2
10
30
50
90

B. RICE

Per cent of
starchy-staple area

1
4
15
30
70

MILES

0   100   200   300

Reproduced from P. Gourou, *La Densité de la population rurale au Congo Belge* (Brussels, 1955), pp. 145, 146.

and plantains these figures represented twofold increases over 1948, whereas for manioc the percentage of crop commercialized was up nearly two and one-half times (23, pp. 464–65). Of sweet potatoes, not included among the commercial crops examined in the Banque Centrale study, less than 5 per cent of the crop was commercialized in 1952, according to a Department of Agriculture estimate (10, p. 61). Rice, maize, and dried manioc seem to be particularly important in supplying the more remote consumption centers; hence demand trends in urban areas, mining centers, and among plantation workers must have a significant influence on the extent to which those crops are grown.

But in addition to the economic effects of a rising demand on the part of city-dwellers and other nonself-suppliers expressing itself through changing price relationships, food production in the Belgian Congo has been influenced by direct government action. In order to secure enlarged production of certain crops to meet the problem of provisioning urban and mining centers, the authorities in the Congo have assigned compulsory quotas for the production of a few crops as "Travaux d'ordre educatif." The introduction of this device during World War I has been described by Edm. Leplae who comments on the underlying rationale as follows (39, p. 58): "Many other methods can be used for introducing crops or teaching new agricultural methods to a native population; but only obligation makes it possible to obtain the rapid application of progress by the mass of the population." According to 1928 data for Orientale Province cited by Leplae, compulsory acreage quotas were imposed covering rice, maize, manioc, bananas, and sweet potatoes in addition to cotton, peanuts, and other export crops. In a number of areas compulsory acreage quotas have been imposed on local food crops for the purpose of insuring that sufficient food is produced for the subsistence requirements of the local farm population, a measure which is particularly evident in agriculturally poor districts such as Feshi Territory in Kwango Province.

Expansion of rice and maize, food crops which are well suited to provisioning the populations of urban areas or mining centers, seems to have been influenced particularly by the imposition of compulsory quotas. Thus G. Geortay has pointed out that between 1925 and 1928 the area planted to rice increased from 17,000 hectares to nearly 75,000 under the stimulus of the Service d'Agriculture (29, p. 309). Edgar Pauquet's report on rice cultivation in the important Itimbiri region indicates that compulsory quotas for rice were still in effect in

1954, and it seems probable that the abrupt increases in rice area which occurred periodically have been in response to changes in these acreage quotas (*49*, p. 1002). Thus in 1943 the area planted to rice rose sharply to nearly 122,000 hectares after oscillating about the 1928 level of 75,000 hectares for a decade and a half. The work which has been carried out since 1936 to make available improved, higher-yielding seed should also be mentioned, however, as an additional factor which has probably given stimulus to the recent enlargement of the rice area (*29*, pp. 309–14).

Maize production has also been influenced significantly by government action to insure the availability of increased supplies to meet the rising demand in urban and mining centers. Lord Hailey states that the compulsory acreage for maize under the "educative" system was increased from 85,000 hectares in 1935 to 135,000 hectares in 1936 (*32*, p. 893).

FRENCH EQUATORIAL AFRICA

The pattern of distribution of the staple food crops observed in moving from south to north, which is apparent in the territories of West Africa, is repeated on an enlarged scale in French Equatorial Africa. In Map 4-6 showing the crop zones in French Equatorial Africa, we find once again the characteristic transition from dominance of root crops and plantains in a humid southern region to a millet-sorghum zone in the north.[10] In both Gabon and the Middle Congo plantains and manioc are the chief crops. Cocoyams appear to be of modest importance, probably more important than yams and sweet potatoes.[11] Rice and maize are mentioned as minor crops in both territories.

It appears that in Gabon and the Middle Congo plantains are a little more important than manioc in terms of area, much more so in terms of production. But the crop statistics for French Equatorial

---

[10] The area relatives underlying Map 4-6 and referred to in the text were derived from production estimates by territory and estimates of crop area for French Equatorial Africa as a whole.

[11] The United Nations report, *Non-Self-Governing Territories: Summaries and Analyses of Information Transmitted to the Secretary-General During 1952. Vol. II* (New York, 1953), p. 30, shows a fairly high figure for yams, while cocoyams are not mentioned. The *Annuaire statistique de l'Afrique Équatoriale Française, Vol. I, 1936–1950* and the *Annuaire statistique de l'Union Française Outre-mer, 1939–49* do not list yams and show very small production of sweet potatoes, whereas the output of cocoyams is some 2 or 3 per cent of the combined production of plantains and manioc.

Africa are such rough approximations that it is perhaps unwise to go beyond the statement that the two crops are co-dominant.

MAP 4-6

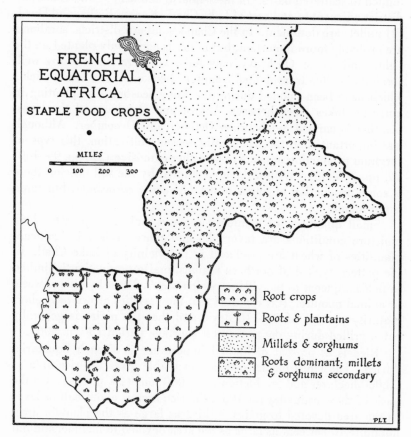

FRENCH
EQUATORIAL
AFRICA
STAPLE FOOD CROPS

MILES

| 0 | 100 | 200 | 300 |

Root crops

Roots & plantains

Millets & sorghums

Roots dominant; millets
& sorghums secondary

Ubangi-Shari is to be classed as manioc-dominant with millets and sorghums as secondary crops. Actually the territory seems to be divided into a southern zone where manioc is all-important and a northern region where the millets and sorghums take over. On the basis of descriptive material and climatic classifications, it appears that the dividing line lies somewhere between 7° and 8° N (*20*, pp. 85, 164, 170). The production of manioc continues to be of appreciable though reduced importance in the northern part of the territory.

In the Chad territory to the north, millets and sorghums are the only important staple crops. The most northern district of the Chad territory lies above 16° N; its climate is Saharan and agriculture is limited to scattered oases. In the semiarid and arid "Sahel-Saharan" district adjacent to and east of Lake Chad (Kanen, Batha, and Ouaddi) millets are dominant. In the Chad's southern districts, sorghums are probably more important, but millet is commonly planted on the light, sandy soils. On heavy, clay soils, which retain moisture well, sorghum is often transplanted from seed beds on higher land to fields which have been flooded during the rainy season. The planting in nurseries takes place between August and October and the transplanting is carried out between October and December. Although less important than the usual rainy-season cultivation, this type of sorghum production appears to be rather extensive (*22*, pp. 99–100; *30*, pp. 305–06). Within the area studied by the soil mission there is some production of finger millet (*Eleusine corocana*), but fonio is not found.

Small quantities of manioc, rice, and maize are grown where moisture conditions are favorable, and more or less insignificant quantities of wheat are produced in the vicinity of Lake Chad. In the pattern typical of northern regions, maize production is limited to fields adjacent to the villages which are enriched by village waste or animal manure. It is reported that the varieties grown have short maturity periods of 85–110 days, and that the maize is generally eaten grilled during the preharvest shortage period (*30*, p. 306).

Rice is at present of limited importance in French Equatorial Africa. The latest official estimate available gives the rice area as 23,000 hectares and production at 17,000 tons (*25*, p. 114). On the basis of these estimates for 1954, the rice area is about half as large as the area devoted to maize, a third as large as the plantain area, not quite 10 per cent as large as the area devoted to manioc, and but a slight fraction of the millet-sorghum area.[12] Prior to 1940 rice production in French Equatorial Africa was virtually nil, but in recent years it has been expanding in all four territories. Possibilities for expansion are seen in the delta region of the Mosaka River and in the valleys of the Sangha and Niari rivers. Prospects for expan-

_____

[12] The official data show an increase in the area planted to manioc from 54,000 hectares in 1949 to 253,000 in 1954, and for the same period a change from 800,000 to 1,600,000 hectares for millets and sorghums (*25*, p. 115). Such drastic changes undoubtedly represent a revised basis of estimation, and presumably the estimate for the later year is somewhat more soundly based.

sion, however, are considered to be most promising in the valleys of the Logone and Chari rivers. The 1950 reports on agriculture in French Equatorial Africa by Aimé Drogué and Kellermann attach much importance to the prospects for rice expansion, and Pierre Chauleur reports that the second Four-Year Plan called for the drainage and irrigation of several hundred thousand hectares in districts to the south of Fort Lamy (*19*, pp. 292–93; *37*, pp. 301–03; and *13*, p. 314). The report by Erhart, Pias, and Leneuf of a soil survey of the Chad districts watered by the Logone and Chari rivers seems somewhat more cautious in its assessment of the prospects for large-scale production of rice but affirms that extensive areas south of Fort Lamy appear to be well suited for rice. Additional land on the right bank of the Chari-Logone between Fort Lamy and Lake Chad is potentially suited for large-scale rice production but would require amelioration of the soil structure by green manure crops, which would pose some difficult problems. Furthermore, a double system of irrigation and drainage canals would be needed in order to avoid excessive salinity (*22*, pp. 161–62, 223–25).

In a recent study of rice culture in the valleys of the Middle Logone (in the southwestern and northwestern portions, respectively, of the Chad and Ubangi-Shari territories), Jean Cabot estimates that some 22,000 hectares are planted to rice in this region with production in 1954 of 36,000 tons, considerably higher than the published figure for the entire Federation (*12*, pp. 162–63, 168). According to Cabot, the development of production in the valleys of the Middle Logone was chiefly a result of the imposition of obligatory cultivation of the crop by the administration to secure supplies for urban areas deprived of normal imports of rice during and immediately following World War II. Commercialization of rice produced in this region apparently reached a peak in 1950/51, but since that time it has not been able to compete with imported rice owing to the high cost of transporting the crop to the urban centers in the south. High milling costs have apparently been another obstacle. In any event, the producer price of rice has been relatively low: 8.5 francs C.F.A. per kilo in 1955 compared to 28 francs for cotton, whereas in 1946 and 1947 the price of rice was approximately 3 francs C.F.A. compared with a cotton price of 5 francs C.F.A. per kilo. This has no doubt had a discouraging effect on further rice expansion, but the crop continues to be grown in substantial quantities for local consumption; in many districts there are lands subject to annual flooding which appear to be better suited to rice than any alternative crop.

SPANISH GUINEA (RÍO MUNI)

In Spanish Guinea manioc is the overwhelmingly important crop. The production of cocoyams, the only other crop for which estimates are available, is estimated at something less than a tenth of the manioc output. No local breakdown of the production estimates is at hand, and estimates of planted area are lacking even on a territorial basis. It is reported, however, that the agriculture of Spanish Guinea is rather uniform with respect to methods and crops produced, and this is not surprising since it lies almost entirely within a humid forest zone (9, p. 89). In addition to the two major crops, reference is made to yams, sweet potatoes, and maize as minor crops. Yams are said to be more important on the island of Fernando Po than on the mainland (47, pp. 69, 72). Production of plantains and bananas is said to be widespread. One authority observes that "plantains play a very important role in the native diet," as would be expected considering the territory's rain-forest climate and the importance of plantains in the adjacent coastal districts of French Equatorial Africa and the French Cameroons (47, p. 79). It seems likely that the absence of a production estimate for plantains simply reflects the great difficulty of estimating output of this crop, and that in fact plantains rank with cocoyams as an important secondary crop in Spanish Guinea.

ANGOLA

Relatively little can be said about the distribution of staple food crops in Angola. Maize and manioc are, by a wide margin, the most important food crops. The comparison of unofficial estimates in Table 4-2 (no official figures are available) gives some notion of the position of various crops; and the large discrepancies between the two sets of figures provide an eloquent reminder of how meager is our knowledge of crop area and production data for Angola.[13]

There is little basis for choosing between these two estimates of staple food production in Angola. The U.S. Department of Agriculture obtained its approximations of agricultural output by working backward from population data, assuming a per capita food intake of 2,315 calories and "utilizing such evidence as was available as to the pattern of production and consumption in Angola." Presumably Lefebvre's estimates were based on the opinions of informed people

---

[13] In a recent study of rainfall in Angola, the Meteorological Service describes, with a frankness that is refreshing but nonetheless disconcerting, a sizeable portion of southeastern Angola as a "region without information" (38).

in Angola, and I am inclined to give credence to his higher figure for manioc and lower estimate for maize.[14] On the other hand, descriptions of Angolan agriculture do not seem inconsistent with the higher Department of Agriculture figures for sweet potatoes and yams.

TABLE 4-2.—ANGOLA: ESTIMATES OF STAPLE FOOD PRODUCTION*

(*Thousand metric tons*)

Commodity	Lefebvre's "Estimates" (for 1942)	U.S. Dept. Agr. "Estimates" (for 1953)
Maize	305	700
Manioc	961	700
Millets and sorghums	49	200
Sweet potatoes and yams	71	300
Rice	20	30
Wheat	16	8
Potatoes	18	30

* Data from Gabriel Lefebvre, *L'Angola: Son histoire, son économie* (Liège, 1947), p. 88; and U.S. Dept Agr., For. Agr. Serv., *Food Balances, 1953, for Angola, Belgian Congo, Kenya, and Nigeria* (January 1955, mimeo).

The geographical distribution of the staple food crops in Angola is shown in Map 4-7, which is based on maps presented by H. L. G. Abreu Velho (*2*, pp. 1566, 1575).[15] The Portuguese enclave of Cabinda, north of the mouth of the Congo, and a large region in northern Angola adjacent to the Belgian Congo, appear to lie in a zone where root crops are distinctly dominant. Manioc is by far the principal root crop. Sweet potatoes and yams are also mentioned as being of appreciable importance in this region, although J. J. Monteiro remarks in his 1876 account that "the common yam . . . is very rarely seen, and I am quite unable to give a reason for its not being more commonly cultivated . . ." (*44*, pp. 162–63). Maize is fairly important as a secondary crop in this zone; and McCulloch reports that in the Luena tribal areas in eastern Angola bulrush millet

[14] Miss Lois Bacon, U.S. Dept. Agr., FAS, states that Lefebvre's estimates were not at hand when the U.S. Department of Agriculture balance sheet was prepared (personal communication). A recent publication of the Bank of Angola gives a figure of 300,000 tons for maize and 800,000 tons as an average figure for manioc production (*Relatorio e contas do Banco de Angola, Exercicio de 1956*, pp. 110, 120–21). Reports by D. O. Fynes-Clinton (1949) and Taylor (1935) give considerably lower figures for maize production (*26*, p. 8; *57*, p. 326).

[15] Identical maps are presented in *67*.

MAP 4-7

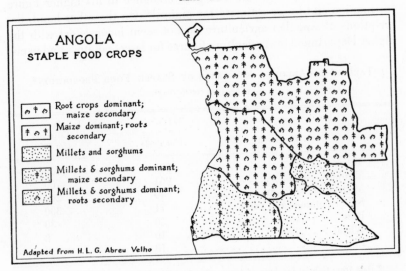

ANGOLA
STAPLE FOOD CROPS

Root crops dominant;
maize secondary

Maize dominant; roots
secondary

Millets and sorghums

Millets & sorghums dominant;
maize secondary

Millets & sorghums dominant;
roots secondary

Adapted from H. L. G. Abreu Velho

is the staple crop although there is a tendency to change to manioc (*41*, pp. 36, 59–61; *2*, pp. 1566, 1568). Maize is the dominant staple in west central Angola.[16] Most of the commercial production of maize is centered in the Bihé Plateau, much of it in a zone straddling the Benguela railroad as it passes through the plateau, beginning something like 100 miles east of Benguela and continuing for another 100 to 150 miles (*7*, pp. 88–89). It seems that millets and sorghums are dominant in the sparsely populated southern portion of Angola, with maize figuring as a secondary crop in the southwest, and roots and tubers—manioc and sweet potatoes—appearing as secondary crops in an east-central zone.[17]

[16] On the basis "of many years of travel in and exploration of" the coastal region of Angola, Monteiro reported that he found maize to be "sparingly cultivated" and far less important than manioc and seemingly somewhat less important than plantains (*44*, p. 162). It appears that the production of maize has increased substantially in response to the development of maize exports. During the period 1911–15, maize exports averaged only 1,500 tons annually; exports rose to an average of 12,000 tons during the next five years, and, after continuing to rise during the next decade and a half, reached 100,000 tons in 1936.

[17] This is on the authority of Abreu Velho (*2*, pp. 1566–68, 1575). The *Anuário Estatístico, 1954* (*8*, pp. 219–20) for Angola does not include millets and sorghums in its listing of "principal agricultural products," by province and district. But this is presumably because no information is given for any crops grown in these southern and southeastern districts (Cunene, Cuando-Cubanzo, and Moxico) which have sparse population and which are not well known.

Although the factual basis for the pattern of crop distribution shown in Map 4-7 is slim, it seems to be consistent with the physical features of Angola and with Shaw's description of its natural vegetation (53, pp. 23–48). Agriculture in the arid strip of coastal lowlands appears to be limited to a few irrigated crops; the generalized crop zones of Map 4-7 are therefore not applicable to this zone. The region of maize dominance, which embraces the subplateau and plateau regions of central Angola, receives some 60–80 inches rainfall. The root crop zone of northern Angola is for the most part a little drier, with annual precipitation of 40–60 inches; and the millet-sorghum region of the south corresponds, as usual, with a still drier area, ranging from "dry subhumid" to "arid."

CITATIONS

1 Marcel van den Abeele and René Vandenput, Les Principales cultures du Congo Belge (Belg., Min. Col., 3d ed., 1956).

2 Homero de Liz Grilo Abreu Velho, "Composição química de alguns produtos de origem vegetal utilizados na alimentação dos indígenas," Anais do Inst. de Med. Trop. (Lisbon), X, No. 3, Fasc. II, September 1953.

3 Jean Adam, "Cultures vivrières," in 21, II.

4 Jean Adrian, Les Plantes alimentaires de l'Ouest Africain, I, Les mils et les sorghos (Orgn. de Recherches sur l'Alimentation et la Nutr. Afr.—ORANA—Dakar, 1954).

5 L'Afrique Occidentale Française, Haut Commissariat, Annuaire statistique . . . , Édition 1951, II (Paris, 1951).

6 "L'Alimentation en outre-mer. Niger," Marchés trop. du monde (Paris), Nov. 24, 1956.

7 Angola Inst., Angola: Portuguese Province in Africa (Luanda, 1953).

8 Angola, Repartição Técnica de Estatística Geral, Anuário Estatístico, 1954 (Luanda, 1956).

9 Luis Baguena Corella, Manuales del Africa Española. I. Guinea (Inst. de Estudios Afr., Madrid, 1950).

10 Belg. Min. Col., L'Agriculture au Congo Belge et au Ruanda-Urundi de 1948 à 1952 (1954).

11 K. M. Buchanan and J. C. Pugh, Land and People in Nigeria . . . (London, 1955).

12 Jean Cabot, "Un domaine nouveau de riziculture inondée: Les Plaines du Moyen Logone," Cahiers Outre-mer (Bordeaux), Apr.–June 1957.

13 Pierre Chauleur, "Problemes économiques du Tchad," Encycl. mens. Outre-mer (Paris), July 1955.

14 R. J. Harrison Church, West Africa: A Study of the Environment and Man's Use of It (London, 1957).

15 Commis. for Tech. Co-op. Afr. South of the Sahara (CCTA), Inter-Afr. Com. Stat., Boletim No. 3 (Lisbon), Aug.–Sept. 1954.

16 "Cultures vivrières," in *Encycl. Col. et Mar: Cameroun, Togo* (Paris, 1951).

17 J. M. Dalziel, *The Useful Plants of West Tropical Africa* (London, 1955).

18 Jean Dresch, "La Riziculture en Afrique Occidentale," *Annales de géographie* (Paris), Oct.–Dec. 1949.

19 Aimé Drogué, "Le Développement agricole de l'A.E.F. dans le cadre du plan décennal," in *20*.

20 *Encycl. Col. et Mar: Afrique Équatoriale Française* (Paris, 1950).

21 *Encycl. Col. et Mar: Afrique Occidentale Française* (2 vols., Paris, 1949).

22 M. H. Erhart, J. Pias and N. Leneuf, *Étude pédologique du bassin alluvionnaire du Logone-Chari* (Off. de la Recherche Sci. et Tech. Outre-Mer, Commis. Sci. du Logone et du Tchad, Paris, 1954).

23 "L'Évolution de la consommation indigène au Congo Belge," *Bull. Banque Centrale du Congo Belge et du Ruanda-Urundi* (Brussels and Leopoldville), December 1956.

24 Food and Agriculture Organization of the United Nations (FAO), *Report on the 1950 World Census of Agriculture, Vol. I, Census Results by Countries* (Rome, 1955).

25 France, Min. Outre-mer, *Inventaire social et économique des territoires d'Outre-mer 1950 à 1955* (Paris, 1957).

26 D. O. Fynes-Clinton, *Portuguese West Africa* (Gr. Brit. Bd. Trade, Overseas Econ. Surv., 1949).

27 R. Galletti, K. D. S. Baldwin and I. O. Dina, *Nigerian Cocoa Farmers* . . . (Nigeria Cocoa Mkt. Bd., London, 1956).

28 "General Report of the Second Session: Conclusions and Recommendations," in *Comptes rendus de la Conférence Africaine des Sols, Goma* . . . *1948* (pub. as June 1949 issue of *Bull. agr. du Congo Belge*, Belg., Min. Col.).

29 G. Geortay, "Variétés de riz diffusées par l'INÉAC," *Bull. inf. de l'INÉAC* (Belg., Min. Col.), October 1955.

30 Ch. Godard, "Les Cultures vivrières du Tchad," in *20*.

31 Pierre Gourou, *La Densité de la population rurale au Congo Belge* (Acad. Roy. des Sci. Col., Classe des Sci. Naturelles et Med., Me. in-8°, Nouvelle ser., Tome I, fasc. 2, Brussels, 1955).

32 Lord Hailey, *An African Survey* . . . (London, 1938).

33 F. R. Irvine, *A Text-book of West African Agriculture, Soils and Crops* (London, 1953).

33a Ivory Coast, Service de la Stat., *Enquête agricole par sondage dans le cercle de Bouaké, juillet 1954–janvier 1955* (Abidjan, n.d.).

34 Roger Jaspar, "Du rôle de la nutrition dans l'économie indigène: Le riz," in *Vers la promotion de l'économie indigène* (Compte Rendu du Colloque Colonial sur l'Économie Indigène, January 1956, Inst. Soc. Solvay, Brussels, 1956).

35 H. D. Jordan, "The Development of Rice Research in Sierra Leone," *Trop. Agr.* (London), January 1954.

36 Phyllis M. Kaberry, *Women of the Grassfields* . . . (Gr. Brit. Col. Off., Col. Res. Pub. 14, 1952).

37 Kellermann, "Les Cultures vivrières des régions forestières et guinéennes et la riziculture," in *20.*

38 F. A. Leal and D. X. Queiroz, *Distribuição da Precipitação na Província de Angola. Esboço da Carta Udométrica* (Angola, Serv. Meteorológico, Luanda, 1952).

39 Edm. Leplae, "Méthode suivie pour développer l'agriculture indigène du Congo Belge," in *Ve Congrès International d'Agriculture Tropicale (Anvers, 28–31 Juillet 1930)*, organized by L'Association Belge d'Agriculture Tropicale et Subtropicale (Brussels, 1930?).

40 C. W. Lynn, *Agriculture in North Mamprusi* (Gold Coast Dept. Agr. Bull. 34, 1937).

41 Merran McCulloch, *The Southern Lunda and Related Peoples (Northern Rhodesia, Angola, Belgian Congo)* (Internatl. Afr. Inst., Ethnographic Surv. of Africa, Daryll Forde, ed., West Central Africa, Part I, London, 1951).

42 Jacques Miège, "Les Cultures vivrières en Afrique Occidentale . . ." *Cahiers Outre-mer*, Jan.–Mar. 1954.

43 Jacques Miège and M. Lefort, "Le Manioc en Côte d'Ivoire," *Congres du manioc et des plantes féculantes tropicales des territories de l'Union Française . . . 24 et 26 Septembre 1949* (Inst. Col. de Marseilles, 1949).

44 J. J. Monteiro, *Angola and the River Congo* (New York, 1876).

45 Nigeria, Dept. Stat., *Report on the Sample Census of Agriculture, 1950–51* (Lagos, 1952).

46 Nigeria, Northern Region Dept. Agr., "Farming Systems in Kano Province," *Af. Soils* (Inter-Afr. Bur. Soils and Rural Econ., CCTA [London]), Oct.–Dec. 1955.

47 Jaime Nosti, *Notas geográficas, físicas y económicas sobre los territorios españoles del Golfo de Guinea* (Dirección Gen. de Marruecos y Col., Madrid, 1942).

48 Denise Paulme, *Les Gens du riz . . .* (Paris, 1954).

49 Edgar Pauquet, "La Culture du riz en région Itimbiri," *Bull. agr. du Congo Belge*, October 1955.

50 Roland Portères, "Les Céréales mineures du genre *Digitaria* en Afrique et en Europe," *J. agr. trop. et de botanique appliquée* (Paris), July–Aug. 1955, Oct.–Nov. 1955, and December 1955.

51 Maurice Robert, *Le Congo physique* (3d ed., Liége, 1946).

52 G. Sagot, "Le Riz," in *21,* II.

53 H. K. Shaw, "The Vegetation of Angola," *J. of Ecology* (Cambridge, Eng.), December 1947.

54 Sierra Leone, Soil Conservation Com., *Soil Conservation and Land Use in Sierra Leone* (Freetown, 1951).

55 W. R. Stanton, "Factors Affecting the Yield of Maize in West Africa," in W. Afr. Maize Rust Res. Unit, *First Annual Report, 1953* (London, 1954).

56 "Statistiques 1955. Agriculture au Congo Belge," *Bull agr. du Congo Belge*, June 1956.

57 C. C. Taylor, *Agriculture in Southern Africa* (U.S. Dept. Agr., Tech. Bull. 466, 1935).

58 A. S. Thomas, "Uganda Banana Varieties and Their Uses," in J. D. Tothill, ed., *Agriculture in Uganda* (London, 1940).

59 R. P. Ch. Tisserant, "L'Agriculture dans les savanes de l'Oubangui,"

Bull. Inst. d'Études Centrafricaines (Brazzaville-Paris), New Series, No. 6, 1953.

60 William Van Royen in co-operation with U.S. Dept. Agr., Bur. Agr. Econ., *The Agricultural Resources of the World,* Vol. I of *Atlas of the World's Resources* (New York, 1954).

61 A. Vandenplas, "Le Climat des régions rizicoles," in J. E. Opsomer, ed., *La Culture du riz au Congo Belge* (Belg., Min. Col., 1950).

62 Edmond Verhulpen, *Baluba et Balubaïsés du Katanga* (Antwerp, 1936).

62a W. Afr. Rice Research Sta., *Annual Report . . . 1956* (Crown Agents for Overseas Govts. and Adminis., London, 1958).

63 H. P. White, "Environment and Land Utilization on the Accra Plains," *J. W. Afr. Sci. Assn.* (Achimota), October 1954.

64 ———, "Some Aspects of Food Crop Production in the Gold Coast," in L. D. Stamp, ed., *Natural Resources, Food and Population in Inter-Tropical Africa* (Rept. of a Symposium held at Makerere Coll., September 1955. London, 1956).

65 V. D. Wickizer and M. K. Bennett, *The Rice Economy of Monsoon Asia* (Stanford, 1941).

66 J. Wright, "Coco-yam Varieties in the Gold Coast," in Gold Coast Dept. Agr., *Year-Book, 1930* (Accra, n.d.).

67 Joaquim Xabregas, "Problemas Alimentares Africanos," *Actividade Económica de Angola* (Governo-Geral de Angola, Direcção dos Serviços de Economia), Jan.–Apr. 1956.

CHAPTER 5

CHARACTERISTICS OF THE MAJOR
STAPLE FOOD CROPS

The purpose of the present chapter is to describe those physical characteristics of the staple crops which seem most pertinent to an understanding of the relative importance and geographical distribution of these crops. Attention is given to their moisture, temperature, and soil requirements, growth period, storage characteristics, relative ease or difficulty of cultivation, and their yielding qualities. An attempt has been made to draw on all of the most useful information available, but the material at hand for some of the crops is far from complete. On certain points, the views of the authorities do not coincide and in such instances the contradictions are noted.

MILLETS AND SORGHUMS

Requirements.—The relationship between the physical or ecological characteristics of the millets and sorghums and their pattern of distribution is exceptionally clear. Both crops are characterized by a low water requirement and the ability to withstand drought by remaining dormant through prolonged dry spells and then resuming growth when moisture is available again. Another quality of the millets and sorghums which contributes to their strong competitive position in the hot, dry Sudan region of West Africa is their ability to withstand intense heat and dry air.

Closely related to the capacity for drought resistance is the fact that the sorghums and millets have short growing seasons which make their cultivation possible during a rainy season that would be too short to mature other crops. There is, however, considerable variation in the growth period of different varieties. Early varieties of sorghum mature in 110–115 days, perhaps in as few as 90 days. Medium varieties require from 130 to 170 days, while late-maturing varieties have a growth period of approximately 180 days. The adaptability of millets to sparse rainfall confined to a short rainy season

91

is apparent in their short growing seasons of 85–95 days; one variety matures in as little as 60 days but yields poorly and is especially subject to damage by birds (*43*, p. 41).

It is also noteworthy that the millets and sorghums are very tolerant in their soil requirements. R. Cerighelli, in his important study of tropical food crops, states that most varieties of sorghum require a permeable soil with not more than 20 per cent clay, although certain late-maturing varieties can resist flooding for a fairly long period. Best results are obtained on sandy-clay soils with some humus, and testing neutral or slightly acid. Light soils which dry out too quickly are not favorable. Although sorghums can withstand a little salinity, they are less resistant to it than rice. The sorghums tolerate soils of mediocre fertility, but they are a little more demanding in their soil requirements than are the millets. Cerighelli points out that in the dry areas where sorghums are commonly cultivated, moisture rather than soil nutrients is likely to be the limiting factor. But when the water supply is ample, a good supply of nutrients is required for high yields. Under those conditions its requirements, especially for nitrogen and potash, are similar to the requirements of maize (*11*, pp. 195–97). Millets are not at all demanding in their soil requirements. The only condition they will not tolerate is an impermeable soil. They do well in light soils, although the best yields are obtained on deep, fertile soils with good humus content (*11*, p. 261).

According to Church, millets are a crop which "benefits from clear skies, low humidity and considerable diurnal temperature variation" (*13*, p. 122). This probably has considerable bearing on the fact that millets and sorghums are so unimportant in the dry coastal strip of West Africa centering on Accra.

Particularly outstanding for its tolerance of poor soils is *Digitaria exilis*, the inferior grain known as fonio in the French territories and as acha (or *achcha*) in Nigeria. Fonio is typically grown on soils too poor to support other crops, or at the end of a rotation when fertility of a plot has been reduced to a low level (*49*, pp. 487–88).[1] In his comprehensive study of the *Digitaria*, Portères stresses even more the role of fonio in providing an early crop to relieve preharvest hunger. Despite its meager yields and the way in which it commonly contributes to soil erosion, Portères believes that it will continue to be of

_____

[1] Aug. Chevalier states that in much of the Futa Jallon soils have become so thin owing to the extension of lateritic crusts (*bovals*) that fonio is the only crop which can be grown (*12*, p. 1080).

considerable importance for many years because of its role as a "hunger breaker" (*49*, pp. 349–86).[2]

In the Belgian Congo, where *Eleusine* is more important than in West Africa, it is described as "the cereal of high plateaus with poor soil where the cultivation of other cereals would be totally impossible" (*1*, p. 205). Although per-hectare yields for *Eleusine* are low —600–800 kgs per hectare is regarded as typical (*1*, p. 205)—they appear to be somewhat higher than yields of fonio, which are low indeed (*49*, pp. 653–54). Two other characteristics of *Eleusine* are its outstandingly good storage qualities and the fact that its calcium content is remarkably high for a grain (*1*, p. 205; *3*, p. 52).

Yields.—Yields of the millets and sorghums are characteristically low, and their competitive position is weak where moisture and soil fertility are satisfactory for other crops. According to Abeele and Vandenput, sorghum was formerly the principal cereal in the Belgian Congo, but since the introduction of maize it has been largely supplanted except on soils of poor fertility or in regions too arid for maize.[3] Typical yields of sorghum in western tropical Africa appear to lie between 750 and 1,200 kgs per hectare: Abeele and Vandenput (*1*, p. 177) suggest a range of 750–1,000 kgs; A. Davesne (*18*, p. 126) gives the range as 1,000–1,200 kgs per hectare. In giving an indication of typical yields in the French Sudan, Cerighelli suggests that average yields are 500–700 kgs for early-maturing varieties and 1,000–1,200 kgs for late varieties (*11*, pp. 227–28). Although the principal strength of sorghum seems to be its ability to produce a fair crop under difficult conditions, exceptionally high yields are obtainable. It is reported, for example, that sorghum yields in the Belgian Congo reach 3,000 kgs with special care; and yields of the order of 6,000 kgs have been grown under irrigation in Texas, California, and Arizona, although the average sorghum yield in the United States is only about 1,000 kgs per hectare (*1*, p. 177; *28*, p. 2). Millet in general yields appreciably less than sorghum; a range of from 400

[2] According to the report *Soil Conservation and Land Use in Sierra Leone* (*53*, p. 30), it is the growing of two consecutive crops of fonio, one harvested in August and a second in December or January, which aggravates erosion. The crop itself is not "erosion inducing," the report declares, and it "will inevitably become a major grain crop in future systems of upland farming."

[3] Abeele and Vandenput (*1*, p. 177) observe that sorghum will outyield maize on mediocre soils; and L. F. Locke and O. R. Mathews have pointed out that in the hot, dry climate of southern Oklahoma corn yields are very low and uncertain compared with sorghums (*41*, p. 33).

to 600 kgs per hectare is probably typical, although a yield of 1,000 kgs may be obtained on good soil (*18*, p. 126; *1*, p. 182).

RICE

Requirements.—A vast literature exists concerning the cultivation of rice. The characteristics of the plant vary a great deal as between the upland crop, ordinary wet rice, or floating rice.[4] Even among varieties grown as irrigated rice there are great differences, the most marked being between *indica* and *japonica* varieties of *Oryza sativa*. The highest yields are obtained with the *japonica* varieties, which are grown in warm temperate regions characterized by lower temperatures, longer summer days, and more sunlight than the tropical regions where the *indica* varieties generally grown "perform better under conditions of greater warmth and less sunlight" (*50*, p. 7).

Although varieties of *Oryza sativa* introduced from Asia have spread rapidly, native varieties of *Oryza glaberrima* are still widespread, and many native groups prefer the red-skinned native varieties.[5] As between upland and wet rice, the upland crop is much more widely cultivated in West Africa and the Congo, although wet rice is gaining in importance. Rice grown as an upland crop generally matures in 90–100 days, but does not yield as well as wet rice. Most varieties of wet rice have a growing period of 150–180 days, but floating rice has a still longer growth period—228 days is the figure given for the Indochina floating rice grown in Upper Guinea (*19*, p. 250).

Cultivation of wet rice is most important in tidal swamps along the

---

[4] As explained in Chapter 4, the term "wet rice" is used in this study to describe all types of cultivation in which the rice plant is in standing water during a considerable part of the growing season, whether the flooding is natural or by artificial irrigation.

[5] Varieties of *O. glaberrima* are very important in the floating rice of the Niger's central delta, but elsewhere varieties of floating rice introduced from Indochina have become widespread (*51*, p. 35). Experience in the French Sudan indicates that the *O. glaberrima* varieties of floating rice are more tolerant of deep and irregular flooding (M. Bouchy, Service d'Agriculture, Segou, personal communication). Mr. H. D. Jordan, Officer in Charge, West African Rice Research Station at Rokupr, states that in Sierra Leone appropriate varieties of Indochina floating rice seem to yield as well with deep flooding as varieties of *O. glaberrima* provided the water does not rise too rapidly. A deep tank recently installed at the station will permit controlled experimentation on the effect of water depth on rice yields. A preference for red-skinned upland varieties of *O. glaberrima*, particularly marked among the Mendes, is cited as one of the reasons Sierra Leone farmers are reluctant to shift to swamp rice (*53*, p. 15).

western Guinea coast, but it is also practiced to a considerable extent in fresh-water swamps in inland regions and in other low-lying areas subject to annual flooding but where the maximum depth of water is not too deep for ordinary varieties of wet rice. On fields where the depth of flooding never exceeds about 0.8 meter ordinary varieties will normally be planted. *O. sativa* varieties of floating rice will tolerate a maximum depth of about 1.8 meters, though of course the rise of the water to that maximum depth must not exceed the rate of growth of the rice plant; the best yields with Indochina varieties of floating rice are obtained where the water level does not exceed 1.0 to 1.2 meters. As mentioned earlier, the indigenous varieties of floating rice (*O. glaberrima*) can tolerate up to 3.0 meters of water, but yields are very low when the flooding is that deep (see footnote 5). Denise Paulme's description of the agriculture of the Kissi, an ethnic group numbering about 140,000 persons located in the Forest Region of French Guinea and across the border in Sierra Leone and Liberia, indicates not only a distinction between wet and upland rice but also considerable variety in the techniques of producing the upland crop. These people, known by their neighbors as "the people of rice," make use of "at least four different cultural methods: continuous cultivation of flooded rice fields; continuous cultivation of garden plots, of necessarily limited extent, accompanied by application of animal manures; cultivation of savanna or forest clearings for 5 or 6 years which are then left fallow for at least an equal period; and finally, though much less extensive, cultivation after burning (*sur brûli*) in which the soil should rest 2 years out of 3" (*47*, p. 37). The Kissi do not practice transplanting, no dikes are built around the fields, and only rarely do they dig a canal to facilitate irrigation.

Jean Dresch's account of rice cultivation in West Africa contains a wealth of information concerning differences in the techniques employed by different ethnic groups (*20*, pp. 295–312). Among groups specializing in the production of swamp rice, some practice transplanting and some do not; varieties used may be of short, medium, or long maturity. Transplanting appears to be the usual practice, however, in the rice culture of the tidal swamps of Sierra Leone, French Guinea, and probably in Portuguese Guinea as well. The practice of transplanting seedlings from seedbeds to the fields proper is dictated particularly by the fact that at the beginning of the rainy season rice planted directly in the swamps would encounter salinity greater than the rice plant can tolerate. Moreover the transplanted seedlings are better able to withstand submergence and water movement on these swamps and the practice also facilitates weed control. Usually the rice is planted in ridges, but under different soil conditions it may be planted on the flat; construction of dikes or polders to control water supplies and the salinity of the fields may be a conspicuous feature of rice cultivation or it may receive little attention.

In the swampy areas along the Niger, Kaduna, and Gbako rivers in northern Nigeria, a considerable part of the rice crop is apparently sown broadcast on wet bottom land after the floods recede (*50*, p. 40). Some rice is also grown in this fashion in the valley of the Senegal, but production of millets and sorghums as "culture de décrue," as the technique is termed, is much more important there.

All varieties of rice require high temperatures and abundant moisture during the growing season. Minimum temperatures for germination vary with the variety, but are higher than for other cereals. Wet rice characteristically requires at least two and preferably three months of temperature of 20 degrees C (68 degrees F) or higher, but upland varieties will tolerate somewhat less warmth (*62*, p. 18). According to Van Royen, wet rice does best when the plant stands in about a foot of water during about four-fifths of the growing season, but with periodic drying to improve aeration of the soil (*59*, p. 83). In California, however, maximum yields are obtained with continuous flooding of the fields with about six inches of irrigation water until shortly before harvest. Occasionally a field will be drained to delay growth when the plants are maturing too fast, but normally continuous submergence is preferred in California because it affords better weed control. Rice yields are also improved if the irrigation water is warm; as noted earlier, the irrigation water on rice in forest zones of West Africa is generally only 25–26 degrees C, somewhat below the optimum range found in inland areas such as the Niger delta where the insolation is higher (*43*, p. 43).

Where rice is dependent on rainfall, wet rice requires some 40–60 inches during the growing season. Early-maturing upland varieties require approximately 24–30 inches and late-maturing upland varieties need something like 40 inches; but it is essential for the rainfall to be well distributed during the growth period (*1*, p. 160). Dresch suggests that for West Africa the limit of rice cultivation is at about the 1,000-mm isohyet compared with 600 mm for sorghum and 400 mm for millets (*20*, p. 298). Requirements vary, of course, not only with the variety grown but also with temperature and the factors governing the rate of evapotranspiration and the capacity of a particular soil to hold water. Wickizer and Bennett state that water requirements for rice "seem to run from 15 to about 35 inches per month . . ." (*62*, p. 19). The most successful production of rice takes place where there is a concentration of the annual rainfall during the growing season but with a relatively dry season at the time the crop matures. This facilitates the maturing of the rice grain and harvesting.

For wet rice the physical structure of the soil is likely to be more significant than its natural fertility. In Japan and on some of the rice land of the United States excellent yields are obtained on infertile soils through the application of fertilizers (*50*, p. 9). But a heavy soil, preferably with 40 per cent or more of clay, and an impermeable hardpan that causes water to be well retained in and on the soil are important for rice culture (*62*, pp. 17, 21). On permeable soils the water requirements would be too high for rice production. Otherwise rice is not especially demanding in its soil requirements. In Sierra Leone, where the amount and distribution of rainfall are satisfactory for rice, lack of soil fertility appears to be the principal factor limiting rice culture and leading to a shift to other crops—especially manioc—as fertility declines. Although neutral to slightly acid soils are most favorable, E. B. Copeland points out that rice "thrives on some decidedly alkaline soils, which are improved for other crops by rice culture, as the water removes some of the alkali. Some varieties endure a very considerable concentration of common salt" (quoted in *62*, pp. 21–22).

Several other factors influencing rice yields may be noted briefly. Not only does the rice plant require a warm temperature, but for satisfactory growth it must also have ample sunlight. The cloudiness of the coastal regions of West Africa reduces insolation considerably, especially during the rainy seasons, and undoubtedly has an unfavorable influence on yields. This is also a factor in the Congo basin where the average monthly insolation is only about half the possible level (*60*, p. 10). Interference with sunlight is cited as one of the reasons why weeds are particularly injurious to rice (*62*, p. 20n). Owing in part to the general lack of draft power in African agriculture, adequate weed control is commonly not attained; the fields are not puddled before planting and subsequent weeding is sketchy. The importance of careful seedbed preparation and puddling for rice is commonly stressed, but it is of interest to note that in the California rice area a very coarse seedbed with 2- to 3-inch clods is used. Planting is by airplane after the fields have been flooded, and the coarse seedbed reduces drifting of seed and seedlings.

It is not clear whether there is a specific effect of altitude on rice cultivation apart from its influence on temperature. Miège suggests that in West Africa there is a tendency for rice to give way to fonio or other minor cereals at about 800 meters, but in some tropical areas upland rice is grown as high as 2,500 meters (*43*, p. 43; *62*, p. 18). Finally, it may be mentioned that rice possesses a storage advantage in the humid tropics since the rice grain does not absorb moisture as readily as wheat and many other cereals (*40*, pp. 148–49).

Yields.—Average yield figures for rice have little meaning even if we are to regard the available statistics as trustworthy. In general, yields of wet rice can be expected to be considerably better than for upland or floating rice. The "Indo-China" floating rice being grown in the tidal swamps of the Bonthe grasslands in southern Sierra Leone, however, has given yields of over 2,000 kgs per hectare in terms of unhulled ("paddy") rice, very good yields for any type of rice culture. But this is an area of rich alluvial soil replenished by annual flooding, and rice is produced here with mechanical cultivation that permits thorough preparation of the seedbed. Even with irrigated rice grown under similar climatic conditions, large differences in yield are likely to occur because of varietal differences, the use of fertilizers, and the level of cultural practice. In Japan, for example, rice yields appear to have increased by 61 per cent between 1878 and 1901 and by another 24 per cent between 1901–10 and the decade 1931–40, when the national average yield stood at nearly 3,200 kgs of unhulled rice per hectare. That striking increase of yield seems to have been attained through the joint and interacting effect of the use of improved varieties, a large increase in the rate of application of chemical and organic fertilizers, better control of irrigation water, and improved cultural techniques (*39*, pp. 27–30).

The average rice yield for the territories of West Africa, according to the available statistics of production and area, is only a little over 700 kgs of paddy per hectare, a low yield corresponding to only about 500 kgs or less of milled rice. This is, of course, the average of upland and wet crops. Material made available to the Food and Agriculture Organization of the United Nations (FAO) brings out the substantial differences in typical yields for these two types of cultivation. In the Gambia, for example, the range for upland yields is given as 400–800 kgs of unhusked rice per hectare, whereas the range for wet rice is placed at 1,000–1,400 kgs. Comparable estimates for Nigeria are 750–1,000 kgs of unhusked rice for upland cultivation, 800–1,500 kgs per hectare for wet rice. In the case of French West Africa the estimate is 500 kgs per hectare for upland, 800 kgs for wet rice, but 2,000 kgs for irrigated rice with application of ammonium sulphate (50, p. 31). In the Belgian Congo, where virtually all of the rice is upland, typical yields, again in terms of unhusked rice, range from 500 to 1,000 kgs, although with R 66 and other improved varieties average yields of 2,500 kgs per hectare can be obtained. The R 66, the most promising of the Yangambi selections to date, is mainly grown as an upland crop, but its heredity is largely of irrigated varieties (American and Indian varieties crossed with a local variety). According to M. Pelerents of the Division of Food Crops at Yangambi, yields of as high as 6,000 kgs have been recorded in trials with R 66 grown under irrigation.

MAIZE

Requirements. — Maize has been the object of much research, owing to the fact that it is cultivated in temperate as well as tropical regions, and a mass of data is available concerning the physiological requirements of the maize plant. For the central portion of the Corn Belt in the United States "an ideal corn season" has been defined in terms of the following monthly pattern:

Month	Mean temperature (degrees Fahrenheit)	Rainfall (inches)
May	65	3.5
June	71	3.5
July	73	4.5
August	73	4.5
September	"warmer and drier than average"	

This ideal pattern, defined by Wallace and Bressman in 1937, was closely approximated in 1948 and 1952 when corn yields for the state of Iowa reached record levels of 60.5 and 62.2 bushels per acre, not much short of 4,000 kgs per hectare (52, pp. 334–35).

More pertinent to conditions in tropical Africa is the fact that maize comes close to being the cereal crop which needs the smallest amount of water per weight unit of dry matter. It probably needs slightly more water than the millets and sorghums, but even that is not certain (38, pp. 283–84). Maize also shares with the millets and sorghums the capacity of "drought resistance" in the strict sense of being able to enter a dormant state when soil moisture is unavailable and then resuming growth when the supply of water in the soil is replenished. But the millets and sorghums, especially the former, far exceed maize in this ability to withstand and recover from a period of drought, and they are superior in other respects in adapting to a

dry climate. In the first place maize is quite vulnerable to water shortage during the 10 days before and 20 days following tasseling. Second, for heavy yields maize "needs moisture not only in the soil but
also in the air" (38, p. 333). Thus dry heat is injurious to maize
whereas moist heat is beneficial. Finally, maize characteristically has
limited ability to extract moisture when the supply of soil moisture is
low—above but near the wilting point. Under such conditions maize
does not make satisfactory progress and produces relatively large
amounts of stover.[6]

As would be expected, considering its capacity to produce very
high yields, maize is highly efficient in utilizing water above its minimum requirement. Jasny reports that it is superior to all of the other
temperate zone grains, but it may be surpassed in this respect by
sorghum and rice (38, pp. 282, 334). Although maize does well with
water supplies above the minimum, yields suffer from an excessive
supply of water in the soil. It appears that the optimum saturation of
the soil for maize is about 70 per cent, a fairly low figure reflected in
the fact that maize does not do well in soils which are prone to waterlogging.

With regard to rainfall requirements in West Africa, Irvine observes that maize "does best in regions of 30–60 inches rainfall, in
sandy loam or loamy soils, rich in humus" (35, p. 83). Jean Adam
speaks of 600 mm (24 inches) as the minimum rainfall requirement
for maize in the valleys of the Niger and Senegal (2, p. 30). But the
soils must be very retentive of moisture to produce a satisfactory maize
crop under those conditions.

Soil requirements for maize have been put concisely by G. H.
Stringfield (55, p. 344):

> A good soil takes in water readily with a minimum of surface runoff. It
> retains a good supply of available moisture without becoming water-logged.
> After being saturated with water it readmits air readily for roots and soil or-
> ganisms. It is deep enough for root penetration, well supplied with available
> nutrients, and neither strongly acid nor strongly alkaline.

While noting that the dark, deep, loamy prairie soils of the American
Corn Belt are exceptionally well suited to corn, Stringfield goes on to
point out that "through good management many other soils ranging
in color through greys, browns, reds, and black and ranging in texture

---

[6] Jasny cites tests at Mandan, North Dakota, in which the water available in the
first six feet of soil, above the normal point of field reduction of moisture at harvest
time, ranged from 2.95 to 3.85 inches following maize, whereas moisture remaining
after wheat ranged from —0.24 to 1.77 inches (38, pp. 282, 289).

from sandy to clay loam have been built into corn soils that compete favorably with the best of the prairie lands" (*55*, p. 345).

Discussions of maize in Africa invariably stress the fact that it is fairly demanding in its soil requirements, especially by comparison with millets and sorghums. The tendency to confine maize production in northern regions to compound farms because of their higher fertility, has already been noted. In speaking of the Belgian Congo, Abeele and Vandenput stress the importance of soils with good physical structure and rich in humus, and note that forest and alluvial soils suit maize especially well (*1*, p. 142). Although a soil well supplied with nutrients is essential for good yields, Jasny points out that in contrast with wheat and barley "corn can utilize to advantage plant food not in readily accessible form" (*38*, pp. 232–33). He cites yield figures for maize and wheat grown on three groups of experimental fields of low fertility showing maize with a yield advantage ranging from 2 to 1 to 8 to 1.

Maize is one of the most soil-depleting of the grain crops. To some extent this is associated with its commonly high yields; its nutrient requirement per unit of grain produced does not differ much from other cereals. But it is mainly because "the waste of nutrients— especially of nitrogen — through leaching, excessive aeration, and erosion is materially larger with corn, a crop grown in widely spaced rows, than with small grains" (*38*, p. 233). The problem of leaching is, of course, a major one in tropical areas where rainfall and soil temperatures are frequently high. But the common African practice of planting maize as a mixed or succession crop is valuable in mitigating the erosion problem resulting from planting a widely spaced row crop such as maize.

Temperature and length of the frost-free season are not significant as factors limiting maize production in Africa as they are in the United States and Europe. More relevant to its position in tropical areas is its "ability to withstand high temperature of the air in the presence of sufficient moisture" (*38*, p. 261). But, as noted above, maize is distinctly inferior to sorghums and millets in its ability to withstand dry heat. Jasny cites as an example of the superior yielding power of sorghum under conditions of dry heat the following yield figures (converted to kilograms per hectare) for continuous cropping of maize and sorghum at two American localities (*38*, p. 272):

Station	Maize	Sorghum
Hays, Kansas	351	884–903
Woodward, Oklahoma	439	1,047–1,342

Rice also seems to be distinctly superior to maize in withstanding hot, dry air provided that soil moisture is maintained at high levels by irrigation.

In addition to warm temperatures, strong sunlight is favorable to the development of maize. "It is a sun-loving plant and will not thrive so well under shade" (35, p. 83; see also 1, p. 142).

The growth period for different varieties of maize varies a great deal. For varieties producing high yields in the temperate zone the minimum seems to be something like 120–125 days, although a growing period as long as 180 days is by no means unusual. In West Africa, according to Stanton, the growth period varies from 60 to 110 days; and he reports that maize varieties imported from temperate zones may have their growth period shortened by as much as 30 days (54, p. 32).

Maize is easy to cultivate and, like the sorghums and millets, does fairly well when grown under quite primitive conditions. Geortay observes that in the Belgian Congo maize is likely to be a good crop to plant on forest land which has just been cleared. It will give an economic though below-average yield on a plot not yet in condition for other crops, and it minimizes the period that newly cleared land is without a protective cover (24, p. 221). While it is true that maize does not require such a carefully prepared seedbed as rice or wheat, the high yield potential for maize means that the increase of yield amply repays thorough preparation. In temperate zones it is the usual practice to control weed growth by several cultivations during the growing season, maize being susceptible to weed damage owing to the fact that it is a slow starter and is planted in widely spaced rows (38, pp. 312–13). Under tropical conditions this type of clean cultivation obviously entails a serious risk of erosion. The prevailing mixed cultivation is of value in discouraging weed growth, but weeding, at least while the maize plants are young, is advocated (35, p. 83).[7] Stanton observes that in the savanna zone of Nigeria "the weed problem is serious in that maize must compete with a dense grass mat which is not destroyed by the primitive methods of cultivation" (54, p. 33).

Storage of maize is something of a problem under tropical con-

---

[7] D. G. Ashby and R. K. Pfieffer suggest that, in general, weed control is even more important under tropical conditions than in the temperate zones. They claim that whereas weed control in temperate zones may be expected to increase crop yields by something like 25 per cent "in the tropics/sub-tropics yield increases of 100%, or even more, result very frequently from weed control by proper methods" (4, p. 227).

ditions. It is liable to attack by insects and rodents, and storage losses are likely to be high unless the ears are dried before storage and if the place of storage is not dry and well ventilated—desiderata that are not easily realized in tropical Africa (1, p. 150). African cultivators often store corn on the cob without removing the shucks, a practice that seems to reduce damage by weevils (35, p. 85). Davesne has recommended the substitution of yellow or red maize for the white maize common in West Africa as being easier to store and transport (18, p. 121). An unusually efficient method of storage is applied to maize and other grains by the Bornu farmers of northern Nigeria. They employ pits 6–16 feet in diameter and 4–10 feet deep, lined with a woven grass matting. Millet chaff is used to line the bottom and fill the space between the mat and the wall of the pit. After the pit is filled to about a foot above ground, the top is covered with a six-inch layer of chaff and about a foot of earth. Maize so stored is said to keep for three years without deterioration in quality. This presumably applies to grain which has been kept covered throughout that period, as with this type of underground storage it is considered advisable to empty a pit completely once it has been opened. Native farmers, who sometimes store grain in pits for as long as seven years, claim that millet has better keeping qualities than either maize or sorghum (31, pp. 4–5).

Yields.—Several references have already been made to the high yielding power of maize among the world's grain crops. The world average yield of maize in relation to several other grain crops is of interest even though world averages do not give a reliable indication of yielding capacity because of the diverse combinations of climate, soil, and cultural practices applying to the different crops. Average yields of maize and four other grains in 1953 are given below for the world (ex-USSR) in kgs per hectare (21a, p. 22):

Commodity	Yield
Maize	1,670
Rice (paddy)	1,710
Millets	640
Sorghums	770
Wheat	1,200

The maize yield of approximately 2,500 kgs per hectare in the United States, where more than a third of the world's crop (ex-USSR) is produced, rather distorts the world average since maize is grown in the United States under very favorable natural conditions and with a high level of agricultural practice. Similarly, the average yield figure for rice is high in part because much of the world crop is produced with irrigation. Data available for West Africa and the French Cameroons show an average yield of maize of only a little over 700 kgs per hectare, greatly below the world average. Considerably higher yields are certainly not uncommon in tropical Africa. In the Belgian Congo yields of 1,500–2,000 kgs or higher are obtained on European farms in the higher elevations to the east of the Congo basin, and Davesne suggests that in West Africa a yield of 2,000 kgs per hectare is a reasonable expectation for maize grown on good soil. In experimental cultivation of maize in the Bas-Congo with improved varieties yields reached 4,200 kgs and average yields of 3,500 kgs are considered a feasible goal for the rich soils of Mawunzi (1, p. 148; 18, p. 123; 30, pp. 1173–74).

A number of considerations suggest themselves as possible explanations for the low level of maize yield indicated for West Africa—aside from the usual reservations about the underlying statistical data. The prevalence of interplanting of maize probably lowers the average level of yield even though reported yield figures are supposed to be corrected for intercropping. Particularly when maize is interplanted with yams it is likely that the yams are regarded as the more important crop, and in addition to competition for moisture and soil nutrients the maize plants are often spaced too far apart for satisfactory yields. Experimental yields for maize intercropped with cowpeas in Nigeria were nearly as high as for maize in pure stand, and yields for cowpeas were as good or even better when grown as an intercrop (45, p. 8). But these results must be regarded as exceptional. More generally, maize yields suffer from the low level of agricultural practice as reflected in the failure to use selected or improved seed, casual preparation of the seedbed and scant attention to weeding, and nonuse of fertilizers. The value of improved seed is borne out by experimental production of American hybrids and open-pollinated varieties in Nigeria. O. J. Webster reported yields of better than 2,000 kgs per hectare with a number of United States hybrids, and A. J. Vernon found that a dozen American varieties, half of them hybrids and half open-pollinated, "gave from 25% to 90% higher yields than the 1,000 pounds per acre average of the twelve local varieties under trial" (44, pp. 21, 45). Use of fertilizers is pretty much confined to the application of limited quantities of animal manure and compost on the small compound farms in the north; and maize is a crop which often shows a strong response to nitrogen and other fertilizers. G. A. W. Van de Goor cites the use of short-maturing varieties and nonuse of fertilizers as principal reasons for the low yields of maize in Indonesia as compared with the United States (*58*, pp. 66–67). Still another factor which may tend to depress average yields in West Africa is the common practice of growing an early and a late crop of maize during the two rainy seasons which characterize most of the centers of maize production, with a first crop planted in April or May and a second in August or September (*16*, p. 482; *56*, p. 122; *18*, p. 121). Although the aggregate yield is undoubtedly increased by such double-cropping, it is probable that varieties of fairly short maturity are required and that the yields of the individual crops are reduced. It is not suggested, however, that there is a consistent correlation between length of growing period and yield. In the southern United States the varieties grown require 180 days or more to mature, but "the best yields are obtained near the coldward limits" of maize growing with varieties requiring 120 to 130 days to ripen (*38*, p. 253).

Since 1950, damage from rust (*Puccinia polysora*) has significantly reduced maize yields in Ghana, French Togo, Dahomey, and Nigeria. The decline in production in some of the important producing areas was very sharp in 1950/51 and, as noted earlier, accentuated the inflationary increase in food prices in Nigeria and the Gold Coast. It has been estimated that losses in the coastal belt of Nigeria were of the order of 40 per cent in 1950 and approached 50 per cent in 1951 (*9*, p. 20). Good results have been obtained with early planting to escape rust damage, and since 1952–53 production has recovered substantially (*25*, p. 23). Considerable attention has been given to developing rust resistant varieties of maize, and the West African Maize Research Unit at Moor Plantation in Nigeria has reported good progress utilizing material originating in Central America and the Caribbean area (*27*, p. 158).

PLANTAINS[8]

Requirements. — Bananas and plantains are exacting in their moisture and soil requirements. On the basis of intensive study of banana and plantain soils, J. Baeyens stresses the high nutrient requirements of these plants and the interrelationship between the availability of soil nutrients and of moisture. On the rich volcanic soils of the Cameroons, plantains and bananas thrive in zones showing considerable variation in rainfall. Elsewhere the water regime must be excellent—ample and well-distributed rainfall—in order to

---

[8] As explained in Chapter 4, the term plantains is used broadly here to refer to varieties of plantains or bananas used as a starchy staple food.

get maximum value from such nutrients as are available. In this regard he points out that yields are apt to be better in an area with rainfall in excess of 1,700 mm than in one with 1,200–1,500 mm even if the soil is better in the second region. Good yields may also be possible where there is natural irrigation provided by a spring or river near by. Despite their need for an ample supply of water, plantain and banana roots can be damaged by an excess of it (5, p. 204). Much the same considerations are reflected in Van Royen's observation that soils for bananas and plantains should be "rich, deep, well-drained, preferably alluvial sandy loams, well provided with humus" (59, p. 139). He further states that they need a minimum of 2,000 mm (80 inches) of rainfall well distributed throughout the year, but it is apparent from Maps 3-1 and 4-1 that plantains are of substantial importance where rainfall is somewhat less. The precipitation requirements for plantains are naturally influenced by the fertility of a soil and its capacity for retaining moisture.

At the Goma Soil Conference in 1948, F.-L. Hendrickx and J. Henderickx advanced an interesting proposal for planting bananas or plantains on newly cleared land. Their studies indicate that because of the protection from insolation and the humus returned to the soil, plantains or bananas are very effective in protecting and restoring soil fertility. They report that with plantains spaced two meters apart other crops can be interplanted successfully for 18 months to two years by which time the plantains themselves are in production (32).

Yields.—Plantains are planted as suckers from mature trees and take from 12 to 15 months to bear. They then continue to bear for 4–6 years or longer, depending on the fertility of the soils and whether mulching is practiced. Plantain yields, although difficult to estimate because of the piecemeal way in which the crop is harvested, appear to be very high—something over eight tons per hectare as an average for the French Cameroons and the territories of West Africa for which data are available. Yields of up to 20 tons or more are sometimes obtained on good soils. It is to be borne in mind, however, that the energy value per pound of plantain is only a little more than one-fifth the calorie value of a food grain such as rice or maize, and is somewhat less than the calorie value of roots and tubers.

MANIOC (CASSAVA)

Requirements.—The chief characteristics of the manioc plant are well summarized by Van Royen (59, p. 99):

The manioc is a tropical plant and requires a completely frost-free growing season. It prefers regions with a moderate temperature range, ample rainfall, fairly high humidity, and considerable sunshine. It does not flourish at
altitudes above 4,000 feet . . . Too little rainfall results in woody tubers,
while too much moisture in the soils may result in rotting. Manioc, however,
has the merit of being able to withstand drought periods of considerable duration and intensity. As a tuberous plant, it needs a fairly deep soil. Although
it thrives best on fertile soils, rich in potash, it will still produce fairly well on
some of the more leached tropical soils.

Apart from its inability to withstand frost or water-logged soils,
manioc will tolerate a wide range of growing conditions. Particularly
outstanding is its ability to produce tolerable yields on soils of low
fertility. Many examples could be cited of the way in which African
culitvators turn to manioc on soils too poor for other crops. In describing the cropping pattern of the Accra Plains, White observes that
manioc "becomes the sole crop when the fertility of the unmanured
plot has declined" (61, p. 55). Similarly, Denise Paulme speaks of
the fact that following the rice harvest the Kissi of French Guinea
plant manioc in fields whose fertility is almost exhausted and which
could not support a more demanding plant (47, p. 25). The Report
on Soil Conservation and Land Use in Sierra Leone, in calling attention to variations in the fertility of soil in that territory, points out
that certain soils such as the coastal sands in the extreme south de-
teriorate very rapidly "until only cassava can be grown" (53, p. 25).
And speaking more generally, the Groupe d'Économie Rurale in the
Bas-Congo notes: "Manioc grows on nearly all types of land and gives
a certain yield even in soils unsuitable for all other crops" (30,
p. 1181).

The competitive position of manioc is also favored by the ease of
cultivating this remarkable crop. The Farmer's Guide prepared by
the Jamaica Agricultural Society describes approved techniques of
manioc cultivation in some detail (37, pp. 433–35). The ground
should be deeply forked or ploughed and leaves worked into the soil.
Cuttings used for planting should be from green stems with close, hard
leaf scars, and should be taken from the middle and lower portions
of sound and mature stems of branches. The bottom ends should be
dipped into ashes before planting. Weeding should be carried out
during the first three months and cultivation for a longer period, although disturbance of the soil near the base of the plants is to be
avoided. Common practice in tropical Africa appears to be much
more casual. Manioc is propagated by inserting stem cuttings, 6 or 8
inches long, into the soil which has often been loosened only by fire-

clearing or by cultivation of previous crops. Irvine remarks that manioc "is one of the easiest of crops to grow and propagate," although he also suggests that frequent weeding and surface cultivation favor high yields (35, p. 114). The Groupe d'Économie Rurale in the Bas-Congo indicates that "only one or two weedings are necessary," a prescription which seems to be in accord with common practice (30, p. 1182). A. Drogué in speaking of the importance of manioc in French Equatorial Africa, asserts that it "has won over the African by the ease with which it can be cultivated, its high yield, the possibility of storing its roots in the ground as a natural food reserve . . ." (21, p. 299).

Manioc is not only resistant to attack of locusts and drought, it is also in general "little troubled by insect pests or diseases" (35, p. 114). A mosaic virus, however, attacks the manioc leaves in a good many areas and efforts have been made to develop mosaic resistant varieties, so far with only limited success. Mosaic has become rather serious in Madagascar (11, p. 320) and parts of East Africa. It has attracted less attention in the Belgian Congo and West Africa but often results in a considerable reduction in yield (1, p. 104).

Although planting of manioc and care during its growth period make modest demands on African farmers, harvesting the crop and processing the roots involve much labor. Digging the roots is particularly hard work during the dry season; and preparation of the familiar manioc products such as gari, manioc flour, and *chickwangues* are time-consuming operations.

The growth period of manioc varies a good deal as between varieties, and there is also considerable leeway in the time of digging because the edible roots may be stored quite well in the ground. Miège mentions a range of 8–15 months while Irvine indicates that growth periods of 5–15 months are common and that roots may be left in the ground two years or occasionally as long as three years (43, p. 39; 35, p. 112). The so-called "sweet" manioc, which is frequently eaten boiled as a vegetable, may be dug in 6–8 months, although the yield is better after a growth period of about 12 months, whereas "bitter" varieties used for gari, flour, or chickwangue are dug only after a year or longer.

The designation of manioc varieties as "sweet" or "bitter" refers to the fact that manioc roots contain a substance which is converted by hydrolysis into glucose, acetone, and hydrocyanic (prussic) acid. The hydrocyanic acid is often present in sufficient quantity to be poisonous if it is not eliminated by suitable processing. This distinction between "bitter" and "sweet" varieties according to their poisonous properties is a common one. G. G. Bolhuis states, however, that "authorities are fairly unanimous in agreeing that no clear dividing line can be drawn between poisonous and non-poisonous cassava roots . . ." (7, p. 176). He has found that "a gradual transition takes place in the toxicity values, from completely innocuous to highly poisonous," and he argues that the terms "sweet" and "bitter" cassava should be abolished. Varieties found to be harmless in one locality may be very dangerous in another area mainly, it seems, because of the effect of soil and climate on prussic acid content. Various methods are used to render manioc safe: eliminating the prussic acid by a leaching action through soaking the roots for 3 or 4 days, by grating the roots to facilitate the release of the toxic substances, and sometimes by cooking—although heat may also have the effect of destroying the enzyme which assists in freeing the prussic acid (39a, Ch. 1). The spread of manioc, to be considered in Chapter 8, appears to have been influenced significantly by the spread of knowledge concerning suitable processing techniques.

It is suggested by Abeele and Vandenput that the possibility of extending the harvest period for manioc is especially significant because "fresh manioc is very difficult to store" (1, p. 106). But, as noted earlier, gari and manioc flour store moderately well as do the dried, sliced roots commonly termed cosettes or kokonte.

Of interest also is the place of manioc in some of the common crop rotations in tropical Africa. On land that has been newly cleared, it is common to interplant other crops with manioc and sometimes a more demanding crop such as yams or maize will replace it altogether. R. de Coene has called attention to the fact that most annual crops do not yield well when planted immediately after clearing heavy forest, and that perennial crops such as manioc and plantains are well suited to these conditions because "they loosen the soil with their roots, favour its aeration, and promote the accumulation of water reserves (especially in heavy clay soils); the pH, acid in forest soils, rises considerably; the enormous mass of organic residues of the fallow decomposes and mineralizes in part" (14, p. 9).[9] Despite these considerations, which are not so important after clearing young fallows of 12–15 years, manioc does not seem to appear very frequently at the head of a rotation, whereas it is commonly the last crop before a field is allowed to revert to fallow. This is related to its ability to

[9] Alfredo Hernaez observed that in the Philippines "newly opened lands are exceptionally good for cassava" (33, p. 47).

produce a fair yield even when fertility has been much depleted, and there is the further advantage that manioc planted at the end of a cultural cycle can be regarded as a reserve crop and only harvested if needed. Some writers have suggested that manioc has the further advantage of promoting forest regeneration (*48*, p. 219; *26*, p. 70); but in the Belgian Congo it has been found that manioc at the end of the rotation has an unfavorable effect on regeneration of the forest fallow (*5a*, p. 4).

Yields.—It seems especially difficult to suggest typical yield figures for manioc owing to the enormous range in the yields obtained. Under experimental conditions at Yangambi in the Belgian Congo yields have reached 65 tons of fresh roots per hectare (*1*, p. 106). A yield of 75 tons per hectare has been reported for manioc grown on the Achimota College Farm in Ghana (*57*, p. 85). Cerighelli mentions a report of manioc yielding an astounding 150 tons per hectare under exceptional conditions in Brazil and states that G. Cours, director of agronomic research in Madagascar, believes it will be possible to reach yields of close to 100 tons. Cerighelli also reports that whereas manioc yields on native farms in Madagascar rarely exceed 5–8 tons per hectare, the yields on European plantations have been increased from 12 to 40 tons per hectare over a period of 15 years by the introduction of improved varieties and better cultural methods (*11*, p. 347). At the opposite extreme, it is reported that yields of manioc grown as a pure crop on overfarmed land of poor fertility in Sierra Leone average only 2–5 tons per hectare (*53*, p. 28).

A further complication in indicating the typical yield for manioc arises from the fact that there may be a substantial discrepancy between the "biological" or "potential" yield and the "economic" yield. It is fairly common practice for farmers to leave a substantial part of the manioc crop unharvested if the price that can be obtained, or their need for the crop as food, does not seem to justify the cost or labor of lifting the roots. Cocoa farmers of western Nigeria are said to "harvest what they need for their own consumption and a little more if they think the trouble of taking it to market worthwhile: but, unless a purchaser buys the roots in the big heaps and harvests them himself (as he often will do), many roots are left unharvested—cassava roots perhaps for two or three years" (*23*, p. 292).

Published estimates of manioc area and output in West Africa suggest an average yield of nearly eight tons per hectare, very high as an average figure even when allowance is made for the fact that the calorie value per pound for manioc is less than a third the calorie value of a food grain. As noted above, yields in a particular locality may depart from the average by a large margin depending on the moisture regime, soil conditions, and other factors. In Sierra Leone, although yields obtained from exhausted fields are at a level of only 2–5 tons per hectare, when manioc is grown as a pure crop on good land, production of 35 tons per hectare seems to be a reasonable expectation and 5–10 tons are reported for manioc interplanted on rice farms (53, p. 28). Experimental data for Nigeria show yields declining from 37 tons per hectare in 1946 to 17 tons in 1950 for the top yielding variety, and from 21 tons to 13 tons for the second highest yielding variety. The decline with continuous cropping over this 5-year period was, of course, related to the decline in fertility of the plots but is also said to have been related to some extent to less favorable weather and to loss of mosaic resistance in the first variety (44, p. 46).

Conflicting views are expressed as to the soil-depleting nature of the manioc plant. Irvine speaks of it as "an exhausting crop" and a similar comment is made by Davesne (35, p. 113; 18, p. 141). Gourou asserts, however, that: "Contrary to what has too often been stated cassava is not particularly exhausting to the soil" (26, p. 70). More light is thrown on this question by citing an estimate of the quantities of soil nutrients removed from the soil by a crop of manioc. G. Cours has calculated that a manioc crop yielding 50 tons of roots and 40 tons of wood per hectare could be expected to remove approximately the following amounts of nutrients in kilograms per hectare (15, p. 367):

Nutrient	Roots	Wood	Total
Nitrogen	85	200	285
Phosphoric acid	62	70	132
Potash	280	180	460
Lime	75	150	225

Cours explains that he does not show uptake of nutrients into the leaves because in Madagascar these are always returned to the soil. The significance of such data is of course a function of the economic value of the crop and the cost and feasibility of maintaining soil nutrients at a satisfactory level. For Madagascar, Cours advocates (a) returning the wood from the manioc to the soil, (b) plowing in a green manure crop, (c) applying animal manure, and (d) application of natural phosphates since the organic fertilizers are not rich in this nutrient (15, pp. 368–70). Variations in the nutrient uptake of different varieties of manioc appear to be very large. Bonnefoy's analysis of unimproved local varieties in Madagascar differs first of all in showing a production of 40 tons of wood with a root yield of only 20 tons, whereas Cours based his calculations on a root yield of 50 tons with 40 tons of wood. Owing to the large quantities of nitrogen in the wood, the total uptake of nitrogen for the plants analyzed by Bonnefoy was nearly as high as reported by Cours for the much heavier output of roots. The uptake of phosphorus, calcium, and especially potash was, however, much lower (*11*, p. 373).

YAMS

Requirements.—Before examining the physical characteristics of the yams, it is necessary to stress the marked differences between the various species which are cultivated. Dalziel lists 10 cultivated species and several wild ones (*17*, pp. 488–93). At least four species appear to be of considerable importance in West Africa, and these differ not only in appearance but in their requirements. Unfortunately there is a certain confusion in the popular names applied and even with regard to some of the characteristics of different species.

Dioscorea alata, known variously as "water yam," "winged yam," or "greater yam," is perhaps the most widely cultivated of the African species.[10] It produces very large tubers which sometimes weigh as much as a hundred pounds. The yam most appreciated for its quality is the *D. rotundata,* known as the "white yam" or "white Guinea yam," which produces tubers ranging up to six pounds. Somewhat similar is the *D. cayenensis,* termed the "yellow yam" because of the color of its flesh. Finally, mention should be made of *D. esculenta,* commonly known as the "Chinese yam" or "lesser yam." In contrast with the huge tubers of *D. alata,* the greater yam, the tubers of *D. esculenta* weigh only a pound or two.[11]

Yams require a warm and humid climate. There is, however, great variation in the amount of precipitation where yams are grown. Brown notes that in West Africa they are cultivated in localities with annual rainfall as high as 412 inches and as low as 46 inches. He also points out: "The yam is definitely a drought resister, but it must be remembered that although tolerant of dry conditions it nevertheless re-

[10] Robert Figuères (*22*, pp. 201–06) so states, although there appear to be no estimates of production by species available. According to Miège, *D. alata* and *D. cayenensis* are easily the two most important species in the Ivory Coast, and he suspects that this may be true for all of West Africa.

[11] In addition to Dalziel (*17*) see Irvine (*35*, pp. 119–34), Thillard (*56*, pp. 201–06), and Young (*64*).

quires a heavy rainfall to reach maximum production" (8, p. 201). It is not the equal of manioc in withstanding prolonged or intense drought. But in the transitional areas often known as Guinea savanna, where the rainfall is below the optimum for manioc, yams often do very well. Bouaké cercle in the Ivory Coast, with yam yields which average from 9 to 12 tons per hectare and are often considerably higher, is a case in point. The yields obtained in that district also seem to suggest that the adverse effect on yam yields is less important than the reduction in yields of manioc grown in mixed culture.

Distinctions must be made between different varieties with regard to their ability to thrive under drier conditions. Miège, for example, points out that although yams of the *D. alata* and *D. esculenta* species flourish in the southern portion of the Ivory Coast with annual rainfall in excess of 1,800 mm, the "yellow yam," *D. cayenensis*, takes over in the drier yam regions. The latter species matures in 7–8 months compared to 8–10 months for *D. alata* and *D. esculenta.*[12]

Of the important roots and tubers, the yam is the most particular in its soil requirements both as to fertility and soil structure. Speaking of the cultivation of yams in eastern Nigeria, Irving remarks that "yams require a fertile soil and the farmers usually reserve their best land for the crop . . ." (36, p. 68).

Yams are easiest to grow in sandy loams, but yields will not be good on such soils unless they contain plenty of organic matter. Brown asserts that the best yields are obtained on deep, fertile clay

[12] Precisely the opposite contrast is noted by Irvine, who indicates that *D. alata* and *D. esculenta* do better under drier conditions than either yellow or white yams (43, p. 40; 35, pp. 130–31). It is also to be noted that whereas Miège speaks of *D. cayenensis* as being a precocious or semiprecocious species maturing in 7 or 8 months, Young indicates that it takes about 12 months to mature (64, p. 2). Dalziel lists "Twelve months Guinea yam" as one of the common names for *D. cayenensis* and speaks of it as growing "throughout the year in the moister regions . . ." Dalziel ascribes a growth period of eight months to *D. rotundata*, the White Guinea yam, and observes that it "is probably well suited for cultivation in the north with a short growing season" (17, pp. 490, 493). In a survey of the relative importance of *D. alata* and *D. cayenensis* in the Ivory Coast, Miège found a distinct shift from the former to the latter in moving north from Abidjan to Banfora in Upper Volta. In the south the ratio was about 90–10 in favor of *D. alata* in the vicinity of Abidjan, about 80–20 in the N'Douci District some 85 miles north, but toward the northern boundary of the Ivory Coast the ratio reversed and *D. cayenensis* accounted for virtually all of the yam area (personal communication, March 14, 1958). Irvine's statement that *D. alata* and *D. esculenta* outyield *D. cayenensis* under drier conditions was based on field trials that he carried out at Achimota College; he points out that although Achimota is in a relatively dry zone (25–30 inches annual rainfall), the climate there differs from the savanna regions of comparable rainfall owing to its double rainfall maxima and the rather high humidity of the air (personal communication, July 14, 1958).

soils, but cautions that "unless they are properly managed the result will be a failure" (*8*, p. 202). The essence of proper management is to maintain good drainage, since "compacted and wet soils hinder root development and too much water in a heavy soil may cause the sets to rot instead of growing" (*8*, p. 202). Irvine stresses the value of "good rich loamy soil" and of digging deep holes to be filled with "decaying leaves or manure and rich black surface soil" (*35*, p. 120). In similar vein Abeele and Vandenput observe that yams "like a loamy ('sablo-argileux') soil, rich in potash, deep and permeable; in soils which are too heavy development of the tubers is mediocre" (*1*, p. 134). Miège also mentions the importance of soils rich in potash, but states that an ample supply of nitrogen is even more important (*43*, p. 46).

Differences are sometimes noted in the soil requirements of yams according to the species. Irvine states that *D. alata,* the "greater yam" or "water yam," will generally tolerate poorer soil than the white or yellow yams (*35*, p. 130). Young indicates that *D. alata* does best "in a deep, mellow, somewhat sandy soil," whereas the white yam, *D. rotundata,* grows best in a heavier soil with higher clay content. The optimum soil for *D. esculenta,* the "lesser" or "Chinese yam," is intermediate, a rich, loamy soil being indicated (*64*, pp. 3–6).

Just as yams are rather exacting in their soil requirements, so are they fairly demanding in the care needed for their production. In order to insure a friable soil favorable to the development of large tubers, yam cultivators generally prepare large hills or mounds 18 inches to 3 feet high in which they plant their sets.[13] The Yoruba farmers "cap" their hills with a thick layer of dried grass or weeds; this helps to hold moisture in the hills and has a strongly favorable effect on yields. After heavy rain storms these "caps" often have to be replaced and the mounds "hilled up" with fresh soil to prevent the tubers from being exposed to air or light. Considerable labor is also involved in preparing poles, which ideally should be some 12 feet long and buried 2 or 3 feet in the soil, for it is necessary to stake yam plants to obtained satisfactory yields (*35*, pp. 124–25). It will be seen in Chapter 6 that owing to the special care which yams require they are a good deal more costly to produce than other roots and tubers.

Yams being stored also require careful handling, for bruised tubers

---

[13] The economic survey of the Nigerian cocoa area notes that Yoruba farmers stick to hill cultivation although the Agricultural Department has advocated the use of ridges following the contour in order to reduce the loss of top soil (*23*, p. 215).

rot easily. They should not be piled high and the storage place should be dry and well ventilated. Brown states that under favorable conditions they can be held over until the next year's crop is harvested. He also declares that during the dry season the "most effective method of storage is to leave the crop in the ground until required" (*8*, p. 203). This practice, however, greatly increases the cost of harvesting the tubers if they are left until the soil is baked hard by the sun. Consequently, yams, unlike manioc roots, are not commonly stored in the ground. In Jamaica, farmers are advised to "cure" their yams prior to storage by rubbing sifted ash or lime into all cut surfaces and then exposing the tubers to the sun for a day or two (*37*, p. 444), and this technique is used to some extent in West Africa.

Storage characteristics of the different varieties of yams are said to vary a good deal, although the ranking of the major varieties in this respect is not entirely clear. There appears to be general agreement that the "white yam," *D. rotundata,* stores particularly well. Dalziel indicates that the "water yam," *D. alata,* stores well and that the "yellow yam," *D. cayenensis,* does not keep well. Young also declares that the "yellow yam" does not store well, whereas Irvine ranks it ahead of the "water yam" in this respect. The small tubers of the "Chinese yam," *D. esculenta,* generally keep well, according to Young (*17*, pp. 489–93; *64*, pp. 2–3; and *35*, p. 130).

Yield.—Uncertainty with regard to the level of yield for yams is compounded by the wide range of estimates as to the appropriate deduction to be made for seed requirements in order to arrive at the "net yield." Galletti and his associates speak of yam yields in the cocoa region of Nigeria varying from 2 tons per acre gross or 1 ton net to 7 tons per acre gross and 5 tons net; and on the basis of rather limited data concerning seed requirements, they estimate that on the average 37 per cent of the yam output was used for seed (*23*, pp. 180, 418). In describing fertilizer experiments with yams in eastern Nigeria, Irving refers to seed requirements varying between 1,000 pounds and one ton per acre (*36*, pp. 69, 72). Considerable variation in seeding rate is to be expected according to the variety grown and the type of set used. With "white yams," for example, a farmer may plant either large or small uncut yams as sets or, more commonly, he may cut his seed yams into two, three, or more pieces in order to obtain his sets.

For West Africa as a whole the average gross yield for yams appears to be about eight tons per hectare. Assuming that close to a third of the output is required for seed use, the net yield would be between 5 and 6 tons per hectare. Under favorable conditions much higher yields are attained; Davesne suggests that yields of 12–20 tons per hectare are a reasonable expectation. The average yield for manioc in West Africa appears to exceed the "net yield" of yams by approximately the amount of the deduction for seed use, that is by two tons or a little more per hectare. But it is by no means unusual for yams to outyield manioc, even on a net basis. In the eight localities studied by the cocoa survey group the average "net yield" for yams seems to have been about the same as the yield for manioc; but the manioc yield figures shown in the survey returns were depressed by the fact that considerable quantities of manioc were left unharvested (*23*, pp. 330–31).

Although fertilizers are rarely applied to yams in West Africa, experimental data suggest that yields could often be increased by their use, particularly of nitrogen. Irving's trials in four provinces of the Eastern Region of Nigeria showed responses ranging from 750 to 1,500 pounds per acre with the application of 150 pounds of ammonium sulphate. Only one provincial farm showed a clear response to phosphate. Potash gave a favorable response at the lower levels of application, but a strong response was obtained only on provincial farms which do not use a bush fallow (*36*, pp. 57–78). With the limited data currently available, generalization about the relative ability of yams and manioc to respond to the application of fertilizers is insecurely based.

COCOYAMS (TARO)

Requirements.—As explained in earlier chapters, the term cocoyam is used in this study to refer to both the "old" cocoyams (*Colocasia esculentum*) and "new" cocoyams (*Xanthosoma sagittifolium*). Cocoyams, and more particularly varieties of *Colocasia*, are frequently referred to by the Polynesian name, taro. Cocoyams, which are found as an important crop only in hot and humid forest regions, require a high annual rainfall and a long wet season, though their need for abundant rainfall is less when they are grown on a fairly heavy and somewhat poorly drained soil. In fact, one of the distinctive features of the cocoyam is this ability to "thrive on imperfectly drained soils . . ." (*10*, p. 66). In Jamaica "the plant thrives best in moist, well-matured soil, preferring low-lying ground or shady glades in the mountains . . ." (*37*, p. 446). Pockets of rich alluvial soil are said to be especially favorable, but good results are also obtained on clay soils "provided the slope is sufficient to afford good drainage" (*37*, p. 447). Soils that are too poorly drained produce cocoyams of inferior quality, although they are not much damaged by occasional flooding. In fact, to produce good yields cocoyams should be grown on soils which are quite retentive of moisture because of their need for abundant ground water (*34*, p. 9).

Reference has been made to growing cocoyams in "shady glades," and the ability of the plant to grow in shade is an important characteristic. Hodge reports that the dasheen, a Trinidad variety of *Colocasia esculentum*, needs a "fairly moist atmosphere" (*34*, p. 8). In some parts of the cocoa region of Nigeria "cocoyams are frequently planted under cocoa" and are apparently the only food crop which is grown under mature cocoa trees (*23*, p. 180). Irvine indicates, however, that cocoyams may be affected adversely by excessive shade, noting that "if they are thoroughly smothered by luxuriant vegetation they may disappear from view for years . . ." but will reappear if the land is cleared again (*35*, p. 140).

It is also important to mention the common practice of planting cocoyams as a shade crop for young cocoa trees. Irvine points out that their large leaves give off abundant water vapor "which provides the shade and the moist atmosphere which the young cacao trees require" (*35*, p. 139). Wright also stresses the value of cocoyams as a shade plant and even declares that the "rapid spread of the cocoyams through the forest belt of the Gold Coast is without doubt associated with the planting up of cacao" (*63*, p. 200).

The growth period for cocoyams appears to be roughly the same as for yams. Abeele and Vandenput state that in the Congo cocoyams mature in 6 to 13 months depending on the variety, and Hodge speaks of a growing season of seven months for the dasheen variety of *Colocasia* grown in the American South (*1*, p. 132; *34*, p. 8). But Wright, speaking of Ghana, and Irvine, considering West Africa generally, report a longer growth period of from 12 to 18 months (*63*, p. 198; *35*, p. 139).

Little information is at hand concerning the storage characteristics of cocoyams. Hodge reports that the variety of *Colocasia* grown in the southern United States can be held up to about six months when stored with good ventilation at 50° F. This applies to the small tubers or "cormels," but the corms, the large central roots, do not store as well (*34*, p. 18). In Sierra Leone it is reported that cocoyams are preferred to sweet potatoes as a cash crop owing to their superior keeping qualities (*53*, p. 32). A disadvantage of the cocoyam is that the tubers must be lifted shortly after they reach maturity as they will quickly rot if left in the ground too long.

Yields.—It appears that the average yield for cocoyams in West Africa is something less than four tons per hectare. As with the yams, the "net yield" is considerably less, owing to the large seed requirement which one source puts as high as two tons per hectare (*23*, p. 180). Speaking of the Belgian Congo, where cocoyams are of small importance, Abeele and Vandenput mention yields ranging from 8 to 35 tons per hectare (*1*, p. 132). Hodge cites even higher yields for dasheen grown in the United States (*34*, p. 15). In Puerto Rico, yields of 10–12 tons per hectare are apparently obtained on the best soils, but only about two tons per hectare are produced on shallow soils. Some conspicuous differences in yields are reported for different territories of West Africa. The average yield in Ghana, according to the very rough estimates available, is six tons per hectare, just twice the average yield reported for Nigeria. This discrepancy may be a statistical illusion, but it seems possible that the forest region of Ghana, where cocoyams are such an important crop, is particularly well suited to their cultivation.

SWEET POTATOES

Requirements.—Sweet potatoes like a long and warm growing season, but their moisture requirement is lower than those of the other roots and tubers just considered. They grow best where annual rainfall is between 30 and 50 inches, according to Irvine, although they can be grown with less (*35*, p. 142). Their water need is greatest in the early part of the growing season, and after they are well established they can withstand drought moderately well.

A well-drained soil is especially important, but apart from this sweet potatoes are not very demanding in soil requirements. Fairly deep sandy loam, silty loam, or alluvial soils are considered best for quantity and quality of production. Too much organic matter in the soil, too much rain, or too much nitrogen stimulate excessive growth of vines and leaves at the cost of a reduced yield of tubers. Excessive rainfall or poor drainage are likely to cause the tubers to rot. Sweet potatoes are a sun-loving plant, similar to yams in this respect, but unlike cocoyams (*1*, p. 115; *33*, p. 50; *10*, p. 65; *35*, p. 142).

Of the roots and tubers considered here, sweet potatoes have the shortest growth period. Abeele and Vandenput indicate that their usual growing season is from 5 to 6 months, while Irvine states that in West Africa they generally mature in 3–4 months (*1*, p. 120; *35*, p. 144).

One of the major disadvantages of sweet potatoes as an African crop is apparently the difficulty of storing them. The preference for cocoyams over sweet potatoes on this count in Sierra Leone has already been mentioned. Unlike the other roots and tubers, and in particular manioc, sweet potatoes cannot be stored in the ground beyond maturity as they sprout easily and are subject to insect attacks. The harvested tubers are also difficult to store, so much so that Davesne advises that sweet potatoes should be eaten as soon as they are lifted (*18*, p. 139). In some areas where the crop is highly important, for example Japan, sweet potato tubers are stored with fair success for a few months, but in a temperate region this is easier since the harvest of the crop coincides with the beginning of a cool season. In Africa as elsewhere—notably Taiwan—there is some storage of sweet potatoes which have been sliced and dried.

The fact that sweet potatoes are vulnerable to locust attacks has been mentioned along with the storage problem as factors which have caused sweet potatoes to lose ground to manioc in Kivu Province in the Belgian Congo (*6*, p. 82). Cerighelli calls attention to the fact that sweet potatoes are likely to suffer serious damage from diseases such as stem rot, black rot, and foot rot unless they are planted in rotation with other crops (*11*, p. 406).

Yields.—As a rough average for the territories of West Africa that report production of sweet potatoes, the yield is not quite four tons per hectare—about the same as for cocoyams. Since sweet potatoes are generally propagated by planting slips or soft wood cuttings, no deduction to arrive at a "net yield" figure is needed.

There is a great range in the yield figures reported for sweet potatoes. According to the *Note Book of Southern Nigerian Agriculture*, yields of about 7½–15 tons per hectare are reported as normal, but the average yield in Nigeria as indicated by the Sample Census was only about 6½ tons (*23*, p. 181). Experimental production of sweet potatoes in North Mamprusi in Ghana gave yields of about 5–7½ tons per hectare; but this was not considered a satisfactory yield owing to a lack of planting material of good quality, and in any event this area is somewhat dry for high yields from roots or tubers (*42*, p. 48). In the Belgian Congo, it is reported that sweet potato yields average 10 tons on European farms and 5–10 tons under native cultivation, and that experiment station yields with selected varieties sometimes exceed 20 tons (*1*, p. 121). In the portion of Kivu Province inhabited by the Mumosho-Mugabo, a region of fairly high altitude, yields for sweet potatoes on "very good land" are given as 25–30 tons per hectare, higher than is indicated for manioc on "very good land" in the same area. With land rated as "good" and "fair," yields fall off to 10–12 and 5 tons per hectare respectively, about the same levels as are indicated for manioc (6, pp. 81–82). In Japan, where sweet potatoes are a highly important crop ranking next to rice as a source of calories, countrywide yields have averaged 15 tons per hectare in recent years.

CITATIONS

1 Marcel van den Abeele and René Vandenput, *Les Principales cultures du Congo Belge* (Belg. Min. Col., 3d ed., 1956).

2 Jean Adam, "Cultures vivrières," *Encycl. Col. et Mar: Afrique Occidentale Française*, II (2 vols., Paris, 1949).

3 Jean Adrian, *Les Plantes alimentaires de l'Ouest Africain, I, Les Mils et les sorghos* (Orgn. de Recherches sur l'Alimentation et la Nutr. Afr.—ORANA—Dakar, 1954).

4 D. G. Ashby and R. K. Pfieffer, "Weeds: A Limiting Factor in Tropical Agriculture," *World Crops* (London), June 1956.

5 J. Baeyens, "Classifying Banana Soils in Tropical West Africa," in *Proc. First Commonwealth Conf. on Trop. and Sub-Trop. Soils, 1948* (Commonwealth Bur. Soil Sci., Harpenden, Eng., 1949).

5a Belg. Inst. Natl. pour l'Étude Agronomique du Congo Belge, Div. des Plantes Vivrières, *Notice relatant les activités de la Division de 1933 à 1953* (Yangambi, n.d., mimeo.).

6 Belg. Min. Col., *Monographie des groupements Mumosho-Mugabo* (par la Mission Anti-Erosive, 1952).

7 G. G. Bolhuis, "The Toxicity of Cassava Roots," *Neth. J. Agr. Sci.* (Wageningen), August 1954.

8 D. H. Brown, "The Cultivation of Yams," *Trop. Agr.* (London), August and September 1931.

9 R. H. Cammack, "Observations on *Puccinia Polysora* Underw. in West Africa," W. Afr. Maize Rust Res. Unit, *First Annual Report, 1953* (London, 1954).

10 Caribbean Commis., *Root Crops and Legumes in the Caribbean* (Crop Inquiry Ser. 4, Washington, D.C., 1947) quoting "Soil Survey of Porto Rico."

11 R. Cerighelli, *Cultures tropicales. I.-Plantes Vivrières* (Nouvelle Encycl. Agr., Paris, 1955).

12 Aug. Chevalier, "Points de vue nouveaux sur les sols d'Afrique tropicale . . ." in *Comptes rendus de la Conférence Africaine des Sols, Goma . . . 1948*, II, (pub. as June 1949 issue of *Bull agr. du Congo Belge*, Belg. Min. Col.).

13 R. J. Harrison Church, *West Africa: A Study of the Environment and Man's Use of It* (London, 1957).

14 R. de Coene, "Agricultural Settlement Schemes in the Belgian Congo," *Trop. Agr.*, January 1956.

15 Gilbert Cours, *Le Manioc à Madagascar* (Mém. Inst. Sci. de Madagascar, Ser. B. III, Fasc. 2, Tananarive, 1951).

16 "Cultures vivrières," *Encycl. Col. et Mar: Cameroun, Togo* (Paris, 1951).

17 J. M. Dalziel, *The Useful Plants of West Tropical Africa* (London, 1955).

18 A. Davesne, *Manuel d'agriculture* (Paris, 1950).

19 M. Degras,"Etat actuel et perspective des recherches concernant les séries variétales en riziculture de Haute Guinée," *Riz et riziculture* (Paris), 2e année, 2e trimestre, 1956.

20 Jean Dresch, "La Riziculture en Afrique Occidentale," *Ann. de géog.* (Paris), Oct.–Dec. 1949.

21 A. Drogué, "Les Cultures vivrières des régions forestières et Guinéennes et la riziculture," in *Encycl. Col. et Mar: Afrique Équatoriale Française* (Paris, 1950).

21a FAO, *Yearbook of Food and Agricultural Statistics, 1954. Part 2: Trade* (Rome, 1955).

22 Robert Figuères, *Culture potagère en Afrique tropicale* (Lyon and Grenoble, 1943).

23 R. Galletti, K. D. S. Baldwin, and I. O. Dina, *Nigerian Cocoa Farmers* . . . (Nigeria Cocoa Mkt. Bd., London, 1956).

24 G. Geortay, "Données de base pour la gestion de paysannats de cultures vivrières en région équatoriale forestière," *Bull. inf. l'INÉAC* (Belg. Min. Col.), August 1956.

25 Gold Coast, Min. Fin., *Economic Survey, 1954* (Accra, 1955).

26 Pierre Gourou, *The Tropical World* . . . (London, 1953).

27 Gr. Brit. Col. Off., *Colonial Research, 1954–1955* [Cmd. 9626].

28 Gr. Brit. Col. Off., *Report of the Sorghum Mission to Certain British African Territories* by A. H. Savile and N. C. Thorpe (Col. Advisory Counc. Agr. . . . Pub. 2, 1951).

29 Gr. Brit. Col. Off., Col. Repts., *Sierra Leone, 1952* (1953).

30 Groupe d'Économie Rurale, "L'évolution de l'agriculture indigène dans la zone de Léopoldville," *Bull. agr. du Congo Belge*, October 1954.

31 D. W. Hall, G. A. Haswell, and T. A. Oxley, *Underground Storage of Grain* (Gr. Brit. Col. Off., Col. Res. Studies 21, 1956).

32 F.-L. Hendrickx and J. Henderickx, "La Jachère à bananiers," in *Comptes rendus de la Conférence Africaine des Sols. Goma* . . . *1948, II* (pub. as June 1949 issue of *Bull. agr. du Congo Belge*).

33 Alfredo Hernaez, "The Root Crops in the Philippines with Specific Reference to Cassava and Camote," *Philippine J. Agr.* (Manila), Vol. 19, 1954.

34 W. H. Hodge, *The Dasheen: A Tropical Root Crop for the South* (U.S. Dept. Agr., Circ. 950, November 1954).

35 F. R. Irvine, *A Text-book of West African Agriculture, Soils and Crops* (London, 1953).

36 H. Irving, "Fertilizer Experiments with Yams in Eastern Nigeria, 1947–51," *Trop. Agr.*, January 1956.

37 Jamaica Agr. Soc., *The Farmer's Guide* (Glasgow, 1954).

38 N. Jasny, *Competition Among Grains* (Stanford, 1940).

39 B. F. Johnston, Mosaburo Hosoda, and Yoshio Kusumi, *Japanese Food Management in World War II* (Stanford, 1953).

39a W. O. Jones, *Manioc in Africa* (to be published in 1959).

40 K. H. W. Klages, *Ecological Crop Geography* (New York, 1942).

41 L. F. Locke and O. R. Mathews, *Cultural Practices for Sorghums and Miscellaneous Field Crops . . . Woodward, Oklahoma* (U.S. Dept. Agr., Circ. 959, 1955).

42 C. W. Lynn, *Agriculture in North Mamprusi* (Gold Coast Dept. Agr. Bull. 34, 1937).

43 Jacques Miège, "Cultures vivrières en Afrique Occidentale . . . ," *Cahiers Outre-mer* (Bordeaux), Jan.–Mar. 1954.

44 Nigeria, Dept. Agr., *Annual Report . . . 1951–52* (Insp. Gen. Agr., no place, 1954).

45 ———, *Annual Report . . . (Central), 1952–53, Part I* (Lagos, 1955).

46 ———, *Annual Report . . . Western Region, 1951–52* (Ibadan, 1954).

47 Denise Paulme, *Les Gens du riz . . .* (Paris, 1954).

48 R. L. Pendleton, "The Place of Tropical Soils in Feeding the World," *CEIBA* (issued by the Escuela Agricola Panamericana), Nov. 15, 1954.

49 R. Portères, "Les Céréales mineures du genre *Digitaria* en Afrique et en Europe," *J. agr. trop. et de botanique appliquée* (Paris), July–Aug.–Sept. 1955; Oct.–Nov. 1955; December 1955.

50 K. Ramiah, *Factors Affecting Rice Production . . .* (FAO Agr. Devel. Paper 45, December 1954).

51 G. Sagot, "Le Riz," *Encycl. Col. et Mar: Afrique Occidentale Française*, II (2 vols., Paris, 1949).

52 R. H. Shaw, "Climatic Requirement" in G. F. Sprague, ed., *Corn and Corn Improvement* (New York, 1955).

53 Sierra Leone, Soil Conservation Com., *Soil Conservation and Land Use in Sierra Leone* (Sess. Paper 1, Freetown, 1951).

54 W. R. Stanton, "Factors Affecting the Yield of Maize in West Africa," in W. Afr. Maize Rust Res. Unit, *First Annual Report, 1953* (London, 1954).

55 G. H. Stringfield, "Corn Culture," in G. F. Sprague, ed., *Corn and Corn Improvement* (New York, 1955).

56 Robert Thillard, *Agriculture et l'élevage au Cameroun* (Paris, 1920).

57 F. W. Thompson, "The Use of Cassava in the Feeding of Pigs on Achimota College Farm," *Farm and Forest* (Nigerian Govt., Forest Dept.), VII, No. 2, 1946.

58 G. A. Van de Goor, *Agronomic Research on Maize in Indonesia* (No. 135, Contributions of the Gen. Agr. Res. Sta., Bogor, Indonesia, September 1953).

59 William Van Royen, in cooperation with U.S. Dept. Agr., Bur. Agr. Econ., *The Agricultural Resources of the World*, Vol. I of *Atlas of the World's Resources* (New York, 1954).

60 A. Vandenplas, "Le Climat des régions rizicoles," in J. E. Opsomer, ed., *La Culture du riz au Congo Belge* (Belg. Min. Col., 1950).

61 H. P. White, "Environment and Land Utilization on the Accra Plains," *J. W. Afr. Sci. Assn.* (Achimota), October 1954.

62 V. D. Wickizer and M. K. Bennett, *The Rice Economy of Monsoon Asia* (Stanford, 1941).

63 J. Wright, "Coco-yam Varieties in the Gold Coast," in Gold Coast Dept. Agr., *Year-Book, 1930* (Accra, n.d.).

64 R. A. Young, *Cultivation of the True Yams in the Gulf Region* (U.S. Dept. Agr., Bull. 1167, August 1923).

CHAPTER 6

ECONOMIC FACTORS INFLUENCING DISTRIBUTION OF THE STAPLE CROPS

The economic and social factors influencing the distribution of the major food crops in an area as large and diverse as "western tropical Africa" are so numerous and so complex that a brief over-all treatment must be woefully incomplete. In his study of competition among the grain crops of temperate regions, Jasny was able to concentrate almost entirely on price and cost relationships as the factors determining the position of the crops he studied—wheat, maize, rye, barley, and oats (24, especially Ch. XVII). The relative costs of production were evaluated in relation to such factors as the inherent yielding properties of the different grains, their adaptability to particular soil and climatic conditions, the variations in cultural practices and harvesting costs, and the suitability of a particular crop in a rotation system. Relative prices were viewed as a reflection of consumer preference for the various grains for food and feed uses, modified in its impact on producers by marketing costs and, frequently, by protectionist measures.

Owing to the inadequacy of available data and other limitations the present chapter is merely a preliminary survey of some of the economic factors which seem to bear significantly on the distribution of the staple food crops in tropical Africa. A comprehensive review of relevant price and cost information such as Jasny has presented for the temperate-zone grains must await more intensive study of prices and production costs in particular localities and regions. Since African farmers typically cultivate a combination of crops in mixed culture and in succession, a practice which often has distinct advantages under tropical soil conditions, the study of competition among crops poses special problems. The competitive position of a staple food may depend as much on the way it fits into a pattern of mixed or succession cropping as upon the yield and other characteristics of the individual crop.

There appears to have been relatively little economic analysis of the profitability of alternative crops or crop combinations, and the

124

reasons for the limited attention to this type of study are not hard to find. E. S. Clayton has commented on the fact that agricultural research in the British colonies has been very largely confined to the "physical factors relating to land use and family nutrition." And in his view this has been justified to a considerable extent (*10*, pp. 28, 30):

Subsistence agriculture like a siege economy is more concerned with physical factors, in this case, how to support life with minimum soil depletion. Economic inquiry is unlikely to be fruitful until cultivators have a minimal knowledge of husbandry, an awareness of economic incentives, and ability to act.

Clayton goes on to suggest that analysis of economic factors will come into its own only as cash crops become an important element in the farming system. It is unquestionably true that predominance of subsistence production obscures the operation of price and cost relationships. Whereas Jasny could concentrate almost entirely on cost-price relationships because of their predominant and relatively clear-cut influence in the production regions with which he was concerned, it is necessary in studying the distribution of the staple crops in tropical Africa to consider various noneconomic factors which have had an important influence on the existing crop pattern.

A few of the social, cultural, and historical factors which appear to have influenced crop distribution are examined in Chapter 7. The present chapter is an attempt to bring together available information concerning the economic factors influencing the supply of, and demand for, the staple food crops. Considerable attention is given to the relative yield of the staple crops as an indicator of the relative costliness of producing the different staples. For the grain crops of the temperate zone, comparison of per-acre yields give a fairly good indication of the relative cost of producing different crops since production costs per acre do not differ greatly. With the marked differences which characterize, for example, the production of manioc and sorghum, yield figures are a much less reliable indicator but are nonetheless one of the most valuable types of information available. Estimates of the costs of production of the staple crops, mainly in terms of their comparative labor requirements, are also presented, but the lack of data on this important aspect of the problem seems especially acute. The treatment of demand factors focuses on data on relative prices of the staple foods, although some fragments of information bearing directly on consumer preferences are also considered. A final section reviews the nutritional characteristics of the major staple foods. The bearing of those factors on consumer demand and producers' decisions is, for the present at least, no doubt slight; but government programs for promoting individual crops are probably influenced somewhat by notions concerning their nutritional value.

FACTORS INFLUENCING SUPPLY

Relative yields: Food calories.—A first indication of the relative yields of the staple food crops in West Africa is provided by Table 6-1. It cannot be stressed too strongly that the yield estimates are

TABLE 6-1.—APPROXIMATION OF STAPLE FOOD CROP YIELDS, CALORIE VALUES, AND INDEX OF CALORIE YIELD PER HECTARE, WEST AFRICA

Crop	(a) Approximate yield[a] (*metric tons per hectare*)	(b) Growth period (*months*)	(c) Calories[b] per 100 grams	(d) Index of calorie yield per hectare	(e) "Area relative"[c]	(f) "Production relative"[d] (*calorie basis*)
Millet-sorghum	.6	2–6	345	100	100	100
Maize	.7	2–5[e]	360	122	21	26
Rice	.7	2–6[e]	359	121	19	23
Manioc	8.0	7–24	109	421	19	80
Yams	6.0	7–12	90	261	18	47
Cocoyams	3.0	6–18	86	125	5	6
Sweet potatoes	4.0	3–6	97	187	2	4
Plantains	8.0	8–18	75	290	3	9

[a] Crude approximations by the writer based on available statistics of production and area for West African territories as of about 1950. The yam and cocoyam yield figures have been adjusted to a "net" basis by a deduction for seed requirements. No attempt has been made to adjust any of the yield figures for milling loss or a waste factor.

[b] See Table 6-9 for source.

[c] Millet-sorghum area of 9.8 million hectares taken as 100.

[d] Area relatives multiplied by Index of Calorie Yield.

[e] Under comparable conditions, the growth period for maize would be shorter than for rice. For the Itimbiri region of the Belgian Congo, Edgar Pauquet indicates a growing period of 3½–4 months for maize and 4½–5 months for rice ("La Culture du riz en region Itimbiri," *Bull. Agr. du Congo Belge*, Belg., Min. Col., October 1955, p. 993). The growth period for floating rice may be in excess of six months.

subject to a wide margin of error; and at least in the case of manioc the yield figures often correspond more closely to "potential" production than to the quantities actually harvested. Direct comparison of yields of root crops and grains in terms of product weight have little meaning. Hence, the fourth or *d* column of the table—giving an "index of calorie yield per hectare"—is of primary interest. On the basis of these rough approximations, the average calorie yield per hectare of manioc in West Africa is something like four times as high as for millets and sorghums; and yam and plantain yields are between two-and-a-half and three times as high on a calorie basis. On the same basis, sweet potato yields are nearly twice as high, whereas cocoyams, rice, and maize average only about one-fifth to a quarter higher than millets and sorghums. The last two columns of Table 6-1 show area and production relatives, the "area relatives" being the same as were presented in Chapter 4 in considering the relative importance of the staple foods as measured by the area devoted to the various crops. The "production relatives" are presented here as a crude indication of the relative importance of the different staple crops in West Africa in terms of food calories produced.

Comparable data for the Belgian Congo are presented in Table 6-2, although there the manioc yield and area have been used as a

TABLE 6-2.—APPROXIMATION OF STAPLE FOOD CROP YIELDS, CALORIE VALUES, AND INDEX OF CALORIE YIELD PER HECTARE, BELGIAN CONGO*

Crop	Approximate yield[a] (Metric tons per hectare)	Calories per 100 gm	Index of calorie yield per hectare	Area relative	Production relative
Manioc	11.54	109	100	100	100
Millets and sorghum[b]	.25	345	6.9	14	1
Maize	.87	360	24.5	60	15
Rice	1.04	359	29.6	28	8
Yams } Cocoyams	4.43	88	30.9	9	3
Sweet potatoes	6.09	97	46.9	10	5
Plantains	9.24	75	55.1	34	19

* Computed from 1952 data in Belg., Min. Col., *L'Agriculture au Congo Belge et au Ruanda-Urundi de 1948 à 1952* (1954), tables following p. 155.
[a] European production has been included in calculating yields but does not exceed 2 per cent of total production for any of these crops.
[b] Includes other small grains.

base for computing the "index of calorie yield" and "production relatives." Not only is the millet-sorghum area small in the Congo, but in addition the yield is exceptionally low, being less than half of the average yield that appears to be realized in West Africa. On the other hand, the yield figures for manioc, sweet potatoes, rice, maize, and plantains reported for the Congo all appear to be somewhat higher than my approximations for West Africa. But the relative calorie yields are roughly the same except that in the Congo manioc appears to have an astounding fifteen-fold calorie yield advantage over millets and sorghums.

This attempt to give an indication of the relative yields of the staple food crops is obviously crude and subject to important qualifications. The average yield figures for the root crops mainly reflect the high yields obtained in areas of ample rainfall, whereas the millets and sorghums are grown only in regions where rainfall is deficient. Crop yields for roots and tubers grown in the drier areas, where they are in direct competition with millets and sorghums, are considerably below the average yields shown in Tables 6-1 and 6-2. And the exceedingly low average yield for millets and sorghums in the Congo probably means that they are cultivated only in areas where the moisture is insufficient for other crops and that manioc and maize have replaced the millets and sorghums in the sort of "dry subhumid" regions where comparatively good yields of sorghums are obtained in West Africa.

The competitive advantage accruing to manioc, yams, and plantains because of their high yield is also offset to some extent by their long growth period. The extent to which a long growth period puts a crop at a competitive disadvantage is difficult to assess and must vary a great deal as between regions. Where land is abundant and its cost is essentially the labor cost of clearing a plot for cultivation, the length of time during which a crop occupies the land may not have much influence on its competitive position. Whereas the food grains generally mature in 3–6 months, manioc, yams, and plantains require a minimum of 6 months and frequently 18 months or more before they are ready for harvest (see column b of Table 6-1). Moreover, it is common to produce an early and late crop of maize, and with irrigation rice could also be double-cropped in many parts of West Africa and the Congo. And rice, when cultivated as "wet rice," has the further advantage that it can be grown on the same land almost continuously, whereas roots, maize, and most other crops can be grown in high rainfall regions for only, say, two or three years out of ten without serious risk of degrading the soil.

In addition to the qualifications that must be made concerning the margin of error which characterizes the estimates of crop yield, it should also be stressed that the average yield figures gloss over large variations resulting from differences in the level of skill of individual farmers and the intensiveness of the cultivation practiced as well as the differences in climate and soil already mentioned. With regard to the influence of the soil on crop yields, the level of yield in tropical Africa depends not only on the inherent fertility of different soil types but also on the timing of a crop in the rotation cycle. Thus C. Bonnefoy has reported that, in a coastal district of the Ivory Coast which he studied intensively, yam yields average about 8 tons the first year but then decline to 5 or 6 tons, and after three years the land must be rested. These yields relate to land which is fallowed for six years between periods of cultivation, but it is not uncommon for the Aizi cultivators of this district to put land back into cultivation after a three-year fallow, which entails a lower level of yield (7, p. 79). But planting a crop immediately after clearing forest land may also result in a below-average yield. In the Congo the typical yield for maize planted as the initial crop on forest land is only one ton per hectare, whereas maize planted later in the rotation or after secondary bush (*recru*) can be expected to give a yield of the order of two tons (*18*, p. 227).

A still more important factor giving rise to yield variations is whether a crop is grown as a pure stand or in mixed culture. In tropical Africa it is often advantageous to plant a mixture of crops in order to maintain continuous plant cover and thus minimize the loss of soil nutrients through leaching. Also mixed and succession plantings make it posible to draw on nutrients at various levels by planting both shallow- and deep-rooted plants. This type of culture also discourages weed growth, and mixed planting of rice with manioc helps to prevent lodging of the rice plants (*37*, pp. 992–93). Although the yield of individual crops is almost always lower, the aggregate yield may be better under a rotation with a suitable combination of mixed and succession crops. G. Geortay has recommended the following sequence as suitable for cultivation following forest land with good soil under conditions likely to be found in the Congo (*18*, p. 222):

    1st season..................Maize (*"avant-culture"*)
    2d season..................Rice, manioc, and plantains
    3d season..................Manioc and plantains
    4th season..................Plantains in manioc regrowth
    5th season..................Regrowth of manioc
    6th season..................Maize
    7th season..................Peanuts

Although all crops yield less in mixed culture, the unfavorable effect on the yield of plantains seems to be particularly marked (see Table

6-3 below). Geortay suggests that it would be preferable to use, for example, 40 per cent of the total area available for plantains in pure stand, giving a yield (when growing a mixture of varieties) nearly four times as high as in mixed culture, and plant the other crops on the remaining 60 per cent of the land. The advantage in planting in pure stand in rows, preferably on the edges of the clearing bordering the forest corridors, is that the better shade and more humid micro-climate favors high plantain yields. There is also an advantage for rice and certain other crops in the rotation since they benefit from increased sunlight when the plantains are placed in separate bands rather than being interplanted. More generally, it may be noted that weeding and other field operations may be more difficult with mixed cropping. The relative advantages and disadvantages of various patterns of mixed and succession cropping is an important problem on which, it would appear, relatively little research has been done.

The extent of variations in crop yield owing to differences in levels of skill is difficult to assess. It is virtually impossible to isolate the effect of skill differences from economic decisions relative to the intensity of cultivation and the extent to which the physical environment is decisive in determining the level of yield. Galletti and his associates have pointed out that levels of technique may vary appreciably not only between individual farmers but perhaps even more between villages. Miss Haswell has called attention to the large yield variations in a Gambia village. Most families, for example, had millet yields averaging only 100–200 pounds per acre, but a few obtained yields of 500–600 pounds. And whereas most compounds had swamp-rice yields of between 700 and 1,100 pounds per acre, two compounds obtained 1,400 pounds to the acre and one compound reached 1,700 pounds. While Miss Haswell recognizes that local differences in soil fertility no doubt account for a good deal of this variation, she points to differences in farming techniques between compounds as an important additional factor.

Variations in the intensiveness of cultivation must be distinguished as a separate factor even though it is difficult to isolate from the effect of differences in skill. Miss Haswell's analysis of yield variations for fields planted to late millet showed the considerable importance of density of seeding and amount of weeding in influencing yields. Whereas fields with a low plant population and little weeding gave an average yield of only about 100 pounds per acre, the fields with high plant population and much weeding reached

385 pounds. Intermediate treatments gave intermediate yields. As would be expected, the economic advantage of the more intensive practices, taking into consideration the higher labor costs, was considerably less than the increase in physical yields (*22*, pp. 46–47, 52). Considerable variation in the intensity of cultivation was also noted in the economic survey of cocoa and food-crop production in western Nigeria. It was found that the labor applied to food farms in eight villages ranged from 237 hours per acre as an average of farms in one village to 948 hours in another. The differences were no doubt due in part to differences in the physical environment and the growing of different combinations of food crops in the various localities, but variations in the intensity of cultivation appear to have been the principal explanation. Analysis of the results achieved by 84 families in these villages indicates that "production per acre tends to vary with labour per acre in a rather definite fashion," increasing with additional "doses" of labor but "at a slower rate than the hours of work per acre: in short, there are diminishing marginal returns to labour when applied to a given extent of land" (*17*, pp. 325–26). Galletti, Baldwin, and Dina also point out that there is a clear tendency for smaller holdings to be more intensively cultivated than the larger holdings. The factors which determine how intensively these Nigerian farmers cultivate their food farms are complex, but significant restraints on the intensity of cultivation on the larger holdings are imposed by a certain inelasticity in the supply of hired labor and the attractiveness of applying labor to the cocoa farms instead of the food farms.

Since average yield figures are influenced by the variations in climate, soil, and farming techniques, they are of limited value as an indication of the inherent yielding power of the various crops. It is therefore desirable to supplement the review of data on average yields by considering a few estimates that have been made by persons with an intimate knowledge of agriculture in tropical Africa concerning yields of the different staple food crops to be expected under comparable conditions. Considerable information of this character has already been presented in discussing the ecological characteristics of the individual crops in Chapter 5. Of particular value for present purposes, however, are the estimates by G. Geortay presented in Table 6-3. These estimates represent his appraisal of yields to be expected in the forest region of the Belgian Congo under several different conditions—mixed or pure culture and with extensive or semi-intensive cultivation. By "semi-intensive" cultivation, Geortay means that a crop is suited to the land where it is planted, that selected seed or cuttings are used, that the time of planting and the density of the plant population is in accordance with good practice, and that the fields are well tended (*18*, p. 225).

TABLE 6-3.—APPROXIMATION OF FOOD CROP YIELD IN THE RAIN FOREST REGION, BELGIAN CONGO*

(*Metric tons per hectare*)

		Yield[a]	
Crop	Type of cultivation	Extensive culture	Semi-intensive culture[a]
Rice (paddy) ......Mixed		1.0	1.5
Pure		1.8	2.5
Maize ....Initial crop on forest soil		1.0	1.5
Initial crop after parasol forest .		2.0	2.0
At end of rotation		2.0	2.0
Manioc ....Mixed		10.0	15.0
Pure		20.0	25.0
Plantain ....Mixed			
Mixture of varieties		4.0	4.0
Selected varieties		—	8.0
Pure			
Mixture of varieties		—	15.0
Selected varieties		—	20.0

* G. Geortay, "Données de base pour la gestion de paysannats de cultures vivrières en région équatoriale forestière," *Bull. inf. de l'INÉAC* (Belg., Min. Col.), August 1956, p. 226.
[a] See text for explanation of basis for yield estimates and definition of semi-intensive.

Cerighelli, in his appraisal of the relative yield of manioc as compared with rice and sorghum, concludes that the yield advantage of manioc is likely to be much less than is suggested in Tables 6-1 and 6-2. He takes a manioc yield of seven tons as a basis for comparison, noting that such a yield can easily be obtained even though cultural practices are not at a high level. He then suggests that under comparable conditions of cultural practice, rice would yield about 1.3 tons of paddy per hectare, equivalent to 1.0 tons of milled rice. A corresponding yield for sorghum would be approximately 1.0 ton per hectare with a negligible loss in pounding. Hence, rice and sorghum, with similar calorie values, would each yield about 3.5 million calories per hectare compared to some seven million calories per hectare from manioc (*9*, p. 373).

Despite the uncertainty about the size of the differences between level of yield of the different staple food crops, it is possible to establish a hierarchy based on relative yield in calorie terms applicable to much of western tropical Africa. Listing the crops in descending order of yield we have:

1)	Manioc	6)	Wet Rice
2)	Plantains	7)	Maize
3)	Yams	8)	Upland Rice
4)	Sweet potatoes	9)	Sorghum
5)	Cocoyams	10)	Millet

Needless to say, many instances could be cited in which this order is upset, but it appears to be broadly true for the area considered here.

Relative yields: Calories, nutrients, and value.—Since much of the output of food crops in tropical Africa is for a family's own subsistence, it is reasonable to expect that many farmers are "aiming at the highest return, per acre and per hour of work in food value . . ." (*17*, p. 322).[1] Hence the emphasis on relative yields in terms of food calories in the preceding section. Clearly, a farmer does not consciously evaluate alternative crops in relation to their calorie yields. Nonetheless, in the case of the staple food crops which account for some 65–85 per cent of the calories in the diet, it may be assumed that the quantities that cultivators seek to produce for their own consumption depend rather directly on calories—that a pound of maize or rice is regarded as roughly equivalent in "food value" to, say, three pounds of manioc root or yam tubers. Obviously, this "food value" of different staples also depends upon their content of protein and other essential nutrients, and in the final section of this chapter it is noted that certain of the staple food crops that rank high in yield of calories per hectare are rather poor sources of some of the essential nutrients (see Table 6-9 below). Also the subjective attitude of consumers with respect to the properties of different staples in giving a satisfied, "full" feeling would not correspond exactly to their relative calorie values. Phyllis Kaberry comments, in describing the diet in the Bamenda District of the British Cameroons: "Bulk is important, and a stuffed belly is equated with an adequate satisfaction of hunger" (*26*, p. 84). But the correspondence between "food value" in this subjective sense and energy value measured in calories must be close. And what better yardstick is at hand?

[1] While strictly speaking it is not possible, of course, to maximize simultaneously yield per acre and return per hour of work, in practice it seems reasonable to suppose that many cultivators pay heed to both objectives.

Insofar as a farmer's production is oriented toward the sale of cash crops, it will tend to be aimed at securing the highest net return in money value rather than the highest return in food value. Hence, the two following sections review the data available concerning the relative cost of producing the various staple crops and their relative prices. But before undertaking that chore, a difficult one owing to the inadequacy and lack of comparability of the available data, it is of interest to supplement the discussion of physical yields with a brief examination of returns in value terms.

On the basis of the survey data collected in western Nigeria in 1951/52, Galletti and his associates have calculated "indices of relative efficiency of production" in calorie and value terms for yams, maize, and manioc, reproduced here in Table 6-4. The indices were

TABLE 6-4.—RELATIVE EFFICIENCY OF ACREAGE IN YAMS, MAIZE, AND MANIOC IN PRODUCING CALORIES AND MONEY VALUES*

Locality	Calorie efficiency			Money value efficiency		
	Yams	Manioc	Maize[a]	Yams	Manioc	Maize[a]
Ibesse	0.7	1.2	0.3	1.1	1.1	0.4
Mamu	0.2	1.2	0.2	1.0	0.9	0.7
Ajia	1.7	0.4	1.0	1.8	0.4	0.7
Olosun	1.5	0.7	0.9	1.8	0.4	0.6
Gbongan	1.1	2.1	0.6	1.2	1.7	0.5
Oshu	1.1	0.2	0.8	1.6	0.1	0.6
Owena	1.6	0.4	0.4	2.2	0.2	0.2
Isho	2.0	0.5	0.8	2.4	0.2	0.4
All	1.2	1.1	0.5	1.9	0.7	0.5
All, with deduction for seed	0.7	1.1	0.5	1.1	0.7	0.5

* Data from R. Galletti, K. D. S. Baldwin, and I. O. Dina, *Nigerian Cocoa Farmers* . . . (Nigeria Cocoa Mkt. Bd., London, 1956), p. 324.
[a] Based on the aggregate yield of an early and late crop wherever second-cropping was practiced.

calculated by dividing the proportion of production of each of these crops, in calories and money values respectively, by the proportion of the total area in food crops which it claims. It is apparent from Table 6-4 that comparative yields of these three staples vary a good deal from village to village. The particularly sharp variations in the relative yield of manioc are attributed to the fact that in the four villages where the "calorie efficiency" of manioc is very low "most of the cassava appears to remain unharvested: it is treated as a reserve which may be gathered if other crops fail" (*17*, pp. 323–24). As an average for the 93 families studied in these villages, the calorie efficiency for manioc is appreciably higher than for yams when allowance is made for the rather large deduction necessary for seed-yams. As a result of the higher prices for yams, however, the "money value efficiency" of yams outranks manioc. For maize the average "calorie efficiency" and "money value efficiency" work out to be the same and are less favorable than for manioc and yams in both instances.

Relative costs of production.—We may next attempt to assess the relative costliness of producing the various staple food crops. Many of the difficulties encountered in comparing yield estimates are compounded in trying to compare labor requirements of crops produced in different regions and with different cultural practices. No attempt will be made to consider production costs under mechanized cultivation owing to the small extent of such production at present and the meagerness of the data available.

Probably the most valuable indication of comparative costs of production of the staple foods is provided by Geortay's assessment of labor requirements for maize, rice, manioc, and plantains (and also peanuts, not considered here). These represent his estimates of typical labor requirements under conditions found in the forest region of the Belgian Congo. Table 6-5, summarizing Geortay's evaluations, gives the number of man-days required per hectare and per ton of product with cultivation in forest clearings and following secondary bush (*recru*). (Geortay also gives estimates for cultivation following parasol forest, but those figures differ only slightly from the requirements for cultivation following secondary bush.)

These data bring into sharp relief the relatively low cost of production for manioc, but under the forest conditions which Geortay is considering plantains are even less costly. This difference is entirely due to the more extensive processing which manioc roots require; well over half of the labor time for manioc is related to transporting the roots and peeling, soaking, and drying them. The higher labor requirements for rice and maize result from fairly high labor demands per hectare for cultivation, combined with much lower tonnage yields than manioc and plantain. If the yields were all expressed in calories, however, the labor requirements for manioc would be a little less than for plantains, and the maize requirement only a little above, but rice would remain a good deal more costly than plantains. As to rice, a somewhat higher labor requirement per

TABLE 6-5.—ESTIMATED LABOR REQUIREMENTS FOR STAPLE FOOD CROPS, FOREST ZONE, BELGIAN CONGO*

(In man-days per hectare except as noted)

	Maize (as initial crop)		Maize (following manioc regrowth)		Rice		Manioc		Plantain	
	A[a]	B[b]	A[a]	B[b]	A[a]	B[b]	A[a]	B[b]	A[a]	B[b]
Preparation of the field[c]	25	16	25	16	25	16	25	16	25	16
Weeding after the harvest of maize					4	4	4	4	4	4
Weeding after the regrowth of manioc			20	20					10	10
Planting (including preparation of stem cuttings for manioc)	20	20	40	40	30	30	35	35	15	15
Weeding	10	10	20	20	6	6	6	6	6	6
Harvest	24	24	24	24	40	40	50	50	20	20
Subtotal (Field Operations)	(79)	(70)	(129)	(120)	(105)	(96)	(120)	(111)	(80)[d]	(71)[d]
Transporting the crop	8	16	16	16	4	4	40	40		
Building supports for drying	8	16	16	16						
Husking	3	6	6	6	30	30				
Grinding and storage (sacking for rice)	20	40	40	40	23	23				
Winnowing	2	4	4	4						
Sacking	2	4	4	4						
Peeling							50	50		
Soaking and drying							100	100		
Total man-days per hectare	122	156	215	206	162	153	310	301	80	71
Yield per hectare in tons	(1)	(2)	(2)	(2)	(1)	(1)	(10)	(10)	(4)	(4)
Total man-days per ton	122	78	107	103	162	153	31	30	20	18

* Data from G. Geortay, "Données de base pour la gestion de paysannats de cultures vivrières en région équatoriale forestière," Bull. inf. de l'INÉAC (Belg., Min. Col.), August 1956, pp. 227–29.

[a] A columns refer to production following forest.

[b] B columns refer to production following secondary bush (sur recru).

[c] Total time for preparing field for cultivation divided equally between the five cultures shown here and peanuts.

[d] Included in time required for harvesting.

hectare for planting and harvesting and a much higher requirement for winnowing the grain after threshing account for its disadvantage in relation to maize.

Reporting on a study of continuous cultivation of food crops at the Nioka experiment station in Orientale Province in the northeastern Congo, A. Van Parys has given labor requirements for sweet potatoes, finger millet (*Eleusine*), maize, and manioc grown in mixed culture with beans. He gives the following values for labor required (in man-days per hectare) under the traditional method and under intensive (continuous) cultivation (*45*, pp. 97–98):

Crop	Intensive method	Traditional method
Sweet potatoes	69	75
Finger millet (*Eleusine*)	37	40
Manioc and beans	56	50
Maize	27	32

Except for manioc and beans, the additional labor time required to apply farm manure in the intensive system is more than offset by reduction in the time required for preparing the land and for weeding. Heavy fertilization was required to sustain yields on the fields under continuous cultivation, although the author notes that the quantities required were not greatly in excess of the usage in Belgium. Good, though highly variable, yields were obtained. Sweet potato yields seem to have ranged from 4,200 to 29,570 kgs per hectare, maize from 560 to 3,560 kgs, and manioc from 2,000 to 23,660 kgs, and finger millet from 325 to nearly 1,300 kgs per hectare. Van Parys indicates that yields under the intensive, continuous cultivation tend to be about 10 per cent higher than under the traditional methods, but he does not present any estimates of average yield so it is impossible to relate these data on labor requirements to quantities produced.

An interesting report by P. de Schlippe on the native agriculture of the Logo tribe in northern Ituri in the northeastern savanna region of the Congo provides data on labor requirements for four grain crops as well as various oilseed and legume crops (*42*). Several features of the estimates of labor requirements as summarized in Table 6-6 need to be mentioned. First, the yields underlying the calculations in Table 6-6 are surprisingly high, owing in part to the fact that de Schlippe has used an average of the "three best yields" of each crop as he preferred to exclude certain plots where late planting or

TABLE 6-6.—ESTIMATED LABOR REQUIREMENTS FOR STAPLE
FOOD CROPS, NORTHERN ITURI, BELGIAN CONGO*

A. MAN-DAYS PER HECTARE

Crop	Preparation of the land	Sowing	Care of the crop	Total (prior to harvest)
Finger millet (*Eleusine*)	60	60	15	135
Sorghum	60	15	300	375
Maize	60	10	154	224
Rice	60	25	60	145

B. MAN-DAYS PER TON OF PROCESSED PRODUCT (READY TO BE COOKED)

Crop	Preparation of the land	Sowing	Care of the crop	Harvest	Processing immediately after harvest	Additional processing prior to cooking	Total
Finger millet (*Eleusine*) .	27.5	27.5	7	119	77	120	360
Sorghum	20.5	5	102.5	16	47	143	334
Maize	33.5	5.5	86	18	43	166	352
Rice	38	16	38	130	42	136	400

* Data from P. de Schlippe, "Sous-station d'essais de l'I.N.E.A.C. à Kurukwata (Extraits du premier rapport annuel)," *Bull. agr. du Congo Belge* (Belg., Min. Col.), June 1948, pp. 388–93.

other factors resulted in poor yields.[2] Second, a large proportion of the total labor time is devoted to the processing of the grain into products ready to be cooked. As an average for the four cereal crops, the field operations prior to harvest, including the time spent in clearing fields for planting, accounted for only 28 per cent of the total labor time. Some 34 per cent of the total was required for harvesting, movement of the crop from the field into storage, and such drying, threshing, and winnowing as is carried out immediately after harvest. But 38 per cent of the total labor time was spent on the final operations of threshing, grinding, winnowing, and screening carried

[2] The per-hectare yields expressed as kilos of "gross product" were: finger millet, 2,594; sorghum, 3,083; maize, 1,939; and rice, 2,214. In terms of net yield, allowing for seed requirements and processing losses, the yields were: finger millet, 2,180; sorghum, 2,926; maize, 1,792; and rice, 1,580. The hulling (*décortication*) losses were put at 5 per cent for sorghum and maize, 6.5 per cent for finger millet, and 28.7 per cent for rice.

out shortly before the grain is to be consumed. Finally, the more detailed data reported by de Schlippe point up some striking differences between the crops with regard to labor required for particular operations. A noteworthy example is the fact that some 264 man-days per hectare were devoted to protecting the sorghum crop from damage by birds and 114 man-days for protecting maize from the depredations of monkeys whereas no time was charged to "protection" for the other crops. Similarly, it is to be noted that on the order of 100 man-days per ton were required to harvest finger millet and rice, whereas only about 15 man-days per ton were needed for the harvest of maize and sorghum. For the grinding operations carried out to prepare the grain for cooking, something like 160 man-days per ton were required for maize compared to about 100 man-days for finger millet and intermediate values for sorghum and rice.

De Schlippe emphasizes that such calculations based on experience during a single season are subject to important qualifications even in relation to the Logo group which he studied. Nonetheless, they are interesting as an indication of labor requirements in a savanna region and, particularly, in underscoring the great importance of the time required for threshing, hulling, grinding, and other processing as opposed to strictly agricultural operations.

On the basis of her studies of Genieri in Gambia, Miss Haswell calculated the labor required for producing the staple crops in that savanna village. Her estimates of the grain produced in 1949 per hour of work are as follows (22, p. 57):

Crop	Return per hour of labor (*in pounds of grain*)
Late millet	1.04
Early millet	1.07
Sorghum	2.36
Fonio (*Digitaria*)	2.19
Maize	2.00
Rice (as paddy):	
Swamp	1.42
Upland	.37

The labor requirements here appear to include harvesting and transporting the crop but not the subsequent processing operations. The scant attention given to threshing (considered only for peanuts), pounding, and similar operations contrasts sharply with de Schlippe's study, but a possible explanation is the stress which Miss Haswell places on the importance of proper timing of the field operations, whereas subsequent processing does not have to compete with the operations which must be performed during busy seasons—notably the planting period immediately following the first rains. It is worth emphasizing that the "true" labor cost of certain operations is very high if they must be performed at periods of peak labor requirements; whereas the "true" or opportunity cost of labor in other operations is low since they can be carried out when labor demands are light.

When de Schlippe's estimates are expressed in terms of "gross product" per man-hour exclusive of the final processing operations, they work out to roughly 1.7 pounds for sorghum and rice and 1.8 pounds for maize, figures that do not differ greatly from those presented by Miss Haswell except that this return for upland rice in Ituri is much superior to that obtained with upland in Genieri, though only a little above the yield per hour for swamp rice. In Genieri the men cultivate the late millet crop as well as peanuts, the cash crop. The other crops are mainly worked by women, who devoted a little over 1,000 hours per head to farming in 1949, 64 per cent of the total being applied to swamp rice. The favorable position of sorghum and maize in this comparison is misleading as these crops are grown almost entirely within the compounds and thus have the advantage that little time is required going to and from the fields, and yields are favored by the use of household refuse. It is also pointed out that the yield of rice in 1949 was poor, for rainfall was low and badly distributed. Miss Haswell is emphatic in asserting that enlarged output of food crops in this locality should be achieved mainly through greater concentration on swamp rice. She emphasizes that not only is the return per hour of work higher, but also the fact that concentration on swamp rice will help prevent further loss of soil fertility. If the yield of rice is expressed as milled rice rather than paddy, however, its advantage disappears in 1949 when the per-acre yield of paddy was only about 980 pounds, but in a year of good rainfall such as 1948, when the yield for swamp rice was 1,600 pounds for eight recorded compounds, its advantage would probably be marked (22, pp. 9, 39, 57).

Rough approximations of labor requirements presented by E. S. Clayton are worth noting even though they are presumably a good deal more relevant to the conditions in Kenya, with which Clayton is familiar, than to western tropical Africa. Clayton's estimates, which he describes as "purely illustrative though not largely in error," are as follows (10, p. 29):

Crop	Labor requirement (man-days per acre)	Yield (bags per acre)	Value of output per acre (shillings)	Return per man-day in money value (shillings)
Sorghum	7	5	80	11.43
Millet (on ridges)	15	6	120	8.00
Maize (on ridges)	18	6	137	7.61
Rice	62	12.5	400	6.45

It would be of interest to know to what extent the advantage sorghum appears to enjoy in terms of labor cost is offset by a relatively higher cost of land resulting from the low per-acre yield for that crop. None of the cost estimates available attempts to evaluate the cost of land, and indeed it would be exceedingly difficult to assess the cost of the land factor because of the type of tenure arrangements prevailing in tropical Africa. Nor is any attempt made to estimate the cost of tools and other equipment used, but it would appear that this item would be too small relative to the cost of labor (essentially the value of the family labor since hired labor is of slight importance for food crops) to have appreciable effect on the comparative cost of producing different crops.

In the preceding section, Galletti's findings with regard to the "calorie efficiency" and "money value efficiency" of producing food crops in eight villages of western Nigeria were examined. Unfortunately Galletti and his associates were not able to analyze costs of production in terms of individual food crops because their acreage data were not sufficiently precise, and for many localities they obtained no record of the hours spent on individual crops. However, on the basis of their observations and such data as were assembled, they reached the following conclusion: "Paddy demands more labour per acre and per unit of production than yams, yams than maize, and maize than cassava" (17, pp. 354, 356). (Although the Galletti study speaks here of "paddy," most of the rice in the area of their survey is upland.)

Approximations of yield and labor requirements given by T. A. Phillips seem in general to bear out the ranking of the crops in the Galletti study.[3] Phillips' data and other material seem to make quite clear, however, that the labor requirements per acre for yams are higher than for rice, although not so high in terms of the labor re-

[3] The "Groupe d'Économie Rurale" which has been studying agriculture in the Bas-Congo region south of Leopoldville speaks of "the cultivation of rice being less costly than that of maize" (21, p. 1177). But conditions where production costs for maize (per acre or per pound) are higher than for rice must be exceptional.

quired per pound of product. On the basis of the estimates given by Phillips, which are summarized in Table 6-7, it would appear that the average labor requirement for yams is on the order of 200 man-days per acre compared to perhaps 125 for swamp rice and 85 for upland rice. But in terms of product per man-day, the return would appear to average roughly 40 pounds for yams, 20 for swamp rice, and less than 15 for upland rice (*38*, pp. 11–34).

TABLE 6-7.—APPROXIMATIONS BY PHILLIPS OF TYPICAL
YIELDS AND LABOR REQUIREMENTS*

Crop		Yield per acre	Labor requirement (man-days per acre)
Yams		2– 7 tons	150–240
Manioc		5–10 tons	80–90[a]
Sweet potatoes		3– 6 tons	70–80
Cocoyams		2– 4 tons	no estimate
Maize	Early crop:	1,200–2,000 lbs.	45–50
	Late crop:	650–1,000 lbs.	
Rice	Upland:	800–1,500 lbs.	85
	Swamp:	2,000 up to 4,000 lbs. "in ideal conditions"	
Millet		400–600 lbs.	no estimate
Sorghum		700–800 lbs.	60–90[b]

* Data from T. A. Phillips, *An Agricultural Note Book* (*With Special Reference to Nigeria*), London, 1956, pp. 11, 14, 18, 21, 23, 26, and 33–34.
[a] With clean cultivation; but "in native practice labour rates are much less as the crop is not cleaned."
[b] Lower figure is for sorghum following cotton; higher includes "preparatory green manure crop."

The special care required and consequent costliness of producing yams are commonly stressed; the characteristics of yam cultivation that account for this have been well summarized by Young: "On account of the deep preparation of the soil required for the best results in the field cultivation of yams, the need of the vines for support, and the labor and care necessary in the proper harvesting, curing, and packing of the tubers for shipment, the cost per pound to the producer must be greater than for the commoner root crops" (*46*, p. 8). A study of food farming in Ejura, a village in Ghana, gives the following comparison of labor requirements for yams and maize, bringing out clearly the time-consuming character of yam cultivation, especially in the additional time needed to provide stakes for supporting the vines (*23*, p. 226):

			Labor required per acre (*man-days*)				
Crop	Prepa-ration	Plant-ing	After culti-vation	Collect-ing stakes	Stak-ing	Har-vest	Total
Yams	33	8	15	22	8	18	104
Maize	23	2	10	—	–	6	41

Ejura is an area well suited to yams, and owing to the good yields obtained the situation is sharply reversed when the two crops are compared in terms of physical and monetary return per man-day (*23*, p. 226):

Production costs and monetary return (as of 1930)

	Yams	Maize
Labor requirement (*man-days per acre*)	104	41
Average yield (*pounds per acre*)	8,785	636
Physical returns (*pounds per man-day*)	84	16
Value (*per pound*)	.429*d*	.643*d*
Value of product (*per acre*)	£15 14*s*	£1 14*s*
Monetary return (*per man-day*)	36.2*d*	10.0*d*

No data on labor requirements of cocoyams have come to hand, but Ch. Godard quotes estimates of labor requirements for millets and sorghum made by Gautier, the Director General of the Institut de Recherches du Coton et des Textiles Exotiques. Gautier reports that in Chad Territory in French Equatorial Africa, 137 man-days per hectare are required for sorghum and 121 man-days for millet. The labor required on both crops for cultural operations is assessed at 60 man-days per hectare, so that the higher figure for sorghum is entirely owing to the fact that more labor is required for harvesting, pounding, and winnowing the sorghum crop with a per-hectare yield of some 700 kgs than for the millet crop yielding 550 kgs per hectare. According to these approximations by Gautier the labor requirement per pound of product would be slightly less for sorghum than for millet (*19*, p. 306).

These data on production costs are so incomplete and so lacking in comparability that it is difficult to perceive a hierarchy of the staple food crops according to their relative costliness. Moreover, local and regional variations in the conditions of production are so marked that the relative as well as the absolute costs must vary a good deal. Owing to the large differences in yields and in calorie values of the staple crops, their relative position will change, depending on whether the cost hierarchy is defined in terms of cost per acre, per pound of product, or per thousand calories. It has seemed desirable to hazard a ranking of the costliness of the staple food crops according to those three factors, but it cannot be emphasized too strongly that the tentative hierarchy given below is merely a guess guided by the fragmentary data reviewed above. It will have served its purpose if it stimulates others to correct this ordering according to cost conditions prevailing in particular localities or territories or perhaps for the region as a whole.

Costliness of producing the staple crops (highest to lowest):

Per acre	Per pound	Per thousand calories
Yams	Rice	Yams
Sweet potatoes	Millet	Rice
(Cocoyams)	Sorghum	Millet
Manioc	Maize	Sorghum
Rice	Yams	(Cocoyams)
Sorghum	(Cocoyams)	Maize
Maize	Sweet potatoes	Sweet potatoes
Millet	Manioc	Manioc
Plantains	Plantains	Plantains

DEMAND RELATIONSHIPS

Consumer preferences.—The information at hand bearing directly on consumer preferences for different staple foods is sketchy, necessarily subjective, and sometimes contradictory. There are important variations in patterns of consumer food preferences in different regions and even as between nearby districts, particularly where villagers have only slight familiarity with foods other than the staples traditionally grown and consumed in their own locality. In some instances preferences for a local staple food seem to persist strongly even after villagers have moved to the city and are obliged to buy their food in urban markets.

Interesting as an example of local variation in taste preferences, in this case as between forest and savanna peoples, is Phyllis Kaberry's report on the attitude of certain Bamenda tribes toward various staple foods (*26*, p. 83):

In many of the Widekum tribes [mainly forest peoples] cocoyam and plantain are frequently cited as preferred foods, but among the Tikar and Mbembe groups [grasslands peoples] maize or guinea corn porridge ranks high, and is considered as particularly appropriate for an honoured guest or for a feast.

Reference has already been made (Chapter 4) to the strong preference for rice of the Kissi peoples of French Guinea and adjacent districts of Sierra Leone and Liberia, a preference so marked that the Kissi are referred to by their neighbors as "the people of rice." Similarly, D. P. Gamble has called attention to the great importance of rice among the Mandinka group in the Gambia, a position that seems to be based in considerable part at least on preference since the neighboring Wolof, Fula, and Jola districts depend much more on millet and Guinea corn. Within the West African rice complex lying between the Casamance and Bandama rivers, however, preference for rice seems to be quite general. Thus the official report on *Soil Conservation and Land Use in Sierra Leone* observes: "Every tribe would, if able, use rice as the staple food throughout the year" (*44*, p. 14). The important position of manioc in coastal areas of Sierra Leone illustrates, however, that consumer preferences are subordinated (or modified) when conditions—in this case the sandy soils of areas such as the chiefdoms of Shenge and Krim—are unfavorable to production of the generally preferred staple.

Some students of Africa or of the tropics generally have expressed views concerning the consumer ranking of staple foods in relation, it would seem, to long-run tendencies to modify diets as knowledge of alternative foods becomes available and as income and other circumstances permit a range of choice. Pierre Gourou has generalized his view relative to the preference for rice to the point of asserting that among "all the natives in the hot belt" rice is "preferred above all tubers" (*20*, p. 69). Kellermann confines himself to Africa and seems to be thinking mainly of a comparison with maize when he observes: "Rice is a cereal acceptable for consumption by the great majority of Africans, which is not the case with maize, for example" (*27*, p. 301).

Two other commonly held views with regard to consumer ranking of African staples are illustrated by the statement by Galletti and his associates that consumers, at least in the cocoa region of Nigeria, "rate yams highest, maize next, and cassava and its products as an inferior food" (*17*, p. 324). The idea that yams are a preferred staple, and a prestige crop, seems to be encountered most commonly with reference to Nigeria, but it also seems to apply in greater or lesser degree to much of the Guinea Coast east of the rice complex. Similarly, it is common to see manioc referred to as a food to which Africans turn with reluctance, or only when they are obliged to do so, for example, because with reduced soil fertility yams are no longer sufficiently productive to satisfy the food requirements in a heavily populated district. As with all such general views concerning prefer-

TABLE 6-8.—INDICES OF STAPLE FOOD PRICES PER 1,000 CALORIES: NIGERIA, GHANA, AND BELGIAN CONGO*

(Maize = 100)

Area	Maize	Gari	Yams	Manioc	Cocoyams	Rice	Plantains	Sorghum (Guinea corn)	Millet
Nigeria:									
Western Region	100	62	216					118	117
Eastern Region	100	62	247	114		194		78	77
Northern Region	100	—	255			302			
Nigeria composite	100	75	243	76		213			
Nigerian cocoa farmers	100	112	198	76	137	118	126		
Ghana, wholesale:									
Accra	100	143	547	217	476	290		149	
Kumasi	100	120	295	—	228	306		130	
Sekondi	100	103	394	67	271	236		144	
Tamale	100	183	307	134	390	223		122	
Ghana composite	100	136	383	136	337	261		136	
Belgian Congo:									
Leopoldville	100		(327)a	121		356	598		65
L'Equateur	100		—	139		127	285		—
Orientale	100		(143)a	178		235	330		117
Kivu	100		—	408		258	346		117
Katanga	100		(333)a	296		313	800		159
Kasai	100		—	262		178	—		89
Belgian Congo composite	100		(317)a	225		256	517		106

* Calculated from Appendix Table II.
a Sweet potatoes.

ences, it is difficult to evaluate how significant this attitude may be. But data on relative prices examined in the following section reveal that consumers are willing to pay a substantial price differential for yams as compared with manioc and several other staples.

With maize, and probably certain other staples as well, the methods of preparation in vogue can have a pronounced influence on consumer attitudes. Barrett has argued that only in a few countries is maize properly prepared (2, pp. 346–47):

Very unfortunately most peoples have not yet learned how to cook maize. They fail to comprehend that the flinty particles of this seed require not twice but four times as long to cook as does rice. Eating partially cooked maize meal may cause intestinal disturbances, and this, not any lack of flavor or richness nor any question of cheapness, explains why maize is today unpopular in most countries as a human food.

Relative prices.[4]—Views concerning preferences are not only subjective but usually suggest a ranking of only a few crops and often refer to attitudes within a single, limited area. More objective information illuminating consumer preferences can be obtained by examining relative prices, and this has the further advantage of pointing up differences in the pattern as between territories and smaller units for which price data are available. It must be stressed at the outset, however, that the price data analyzed apply mainly to three areas—Nigeria, Ghana, and the Belgian Congo—and virtually no information is at hand concerning the nature of the markets to which these prices apply, the methods used in collecting the price information, or the degree of confidence which can be placed in them. More specific qualifications, particularly related to the extent to which annual average prices are meaningful in this context, are considered below. The present analysis of staple food price relationships is accordingly to be regarded as a preliminary and tentative venture.

Relative prices of the major staples are summarized in Table 6-8 for the three regions of Nigeria, for four markets in Ghana, and for the six provinces of the Belgian Congo. To facilitate analysis of the pattern of price relationships, average prices have been expressed as a price per 1,000 calories and indices computed on that basis for the different areas. Since maize is widely grown and is a relatively homogeneous product, its average price in each area has been used as the base for deriving the indices for that area. The more detailed

---

[4] I have been assisted considerably in the preparation of this section by the work of several graduate students at Stanford University: J. W. Madill, L. Norman McKown, Ben Uzoukwu Nzeribe, and Bill J. Pace.

data for selected markets on which Table 6-8 is based, together with the source, are shown in Appendix Table II. Some fragmentary information concerning staple food prices in Senegal, Dahomey, French Guinea, Ivory Coast, and Angola is presented in Appendix Table III, again in terms of prices per 1,000 calories. This table also presents supplementary data for the Belgian Congo based on selling prices of certain staple foods in each of its provincial capitals rather than the average official purchase prices on which Table 6-8 and Appendix Table II are based.

The price relationships revealed by Table 6-8 suggest a definite tendency toward a consistent hierarchy of staple food prices, and they also show some conspicuous departures from the general pattern. Chart 6-1 affords a summary picture of these relationships.

CHART 6-1.—INDICES OF STAPLE FOOD PRICES*
(*Base, maize price = 100*)

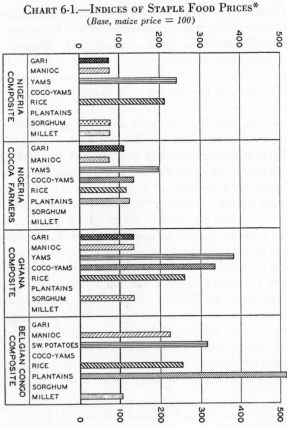

* Data in Table 6-8.

The most significant conclusion is that in terms of annual averages, at least, maize, manioc roots, gari, and millets and sorghums are consistently the cheapest staples, whereas yams and rice rank considerably above them in the price hierarchy. The position of plantains as shown in Chart 6-1 is anomalous, standing as it does as a relatively cheap staple according to the price data collected for Nigerian cocoa farmers and as the most costly of all staple foods in the Belgian Congo. This sharp contrast is to be explained in part by the fact that the composite figure for the Congo is heavily influenced by very high prices reported for plantains in Katanga and Leopoldville provinces where transportation and handling costs bulk large in the market price.[5] The prices for the Nigerian cocoa farmers were derived from data on the value and quantity sold and thus correspond, more or less, to producer prices. Although plantains do not appear in the wholesale price data for Ghana on which Table 6-8 is based, they are included in a published series of retail prices; and again considerable differences in the plantain index as between markets stand out, differences that seem to be related to the proximity or remoteness of the markets in relation to plantain-producing areas. The average index of 143 for plantains in Ghana (with a low of 113 at Kumasi and a high of 173 at Tamale)[6] is, however, considerably below even the lowest figures for the Congo. The limited information at hand for cocoyams seems to suggest that their relative price also varies substantially according to proximity to producing areas. And it would appear from the price data that cocoyams are esteemed more highly by consumers in Ghana than in Nigeria, a conclusion suggested by the greater importance of that staple in total production and consumption in the former country.

The staple food price relationships revealed by Table 6-8 are of considerable interest as an indication of consumer preferences and for other purposes as well. But, as noted briefly above, important qualifications are necessary. First of all, there is undoubtedly a substantial margin of error in the price data from which the indices have been computed. Collection of satisfactory price data is always difficult, but the difficulties are compounded under African conditions. Since bargaining over prices is common, the average price at which transactions occur may differ appreciably from the quoted

[5] This point has been stressed by V. Drachoussoff, Director of Agriculture in Leopoldville Province, who further observes that "prices on rural markets in the rainforest equatorial region are indeed very low" (personal communication, Nov. 4, 1957).

[6] Average of 1954 and 1955 prices from 41.

price. Moreover, if an official price exists, it will often be quoted whether or not it is used in actual transactions. Measurements used in quoting prices may be highly variable. Yams, for example, may be sold by the heap or pile. In Ghana the published yam prices are per 100 tubers, and it has been necessary to convert to a price per pound by the official but quite arbitrary factor of six pounds per tuber. Despite the formidable difficulties to be overcome in order to collect meaningful and comparable price data, it seems safe to assume that the personnel and other resources devoted to the collection of price data are very limited in these African areas where statistical services generally are poorly developed. Perhaps it is not too sanguine, however, to believe that to a considerable extent the errors are compensating and, in particular, that the picture of relative prices which emerges is not too far from reality.

Quite apart from the margin of error in the underlying data, relative prices are not necessarily valid indicators of the esteem in which consumers hold different staple foods. Relative prices of commodities can be taken as valid indicators of consumer preferences at the margin; but differences in marginal valuations of commodities are a function of the quantity consumed as well as differences in preference ratings. Although price data provide the only objective information concerning consumer preferences—and that in terms of an indication of marginal valuations—for the problem at hand there is a more interesting though unanswerable question: What is the relative strength of market demand for the various staples in a *schedule* sense—i.e., at various prices that might prevail according to the point of intersection between the demand schedule for a particular staple (reflecting consumer preferences and including the reservation demand of the farmer for his own produce) and a supply schedule determined by cost factors? Only if the costs of production for the crops being compared were about the same, resulting in closely similar supply schedules, would it be possible to interpret differences in relative prices unequivocally as a reflection of consumer preferences in a schedule sense. The authors of the Cocoa Marketing Board survey of western Nigeria express the opinion that, for the area which they studied, market prices of staple foods seem "to reflect less the relative abundance of the crops in the market than the consumers' preferences . . ." (17, p. 324). Although differences on the demand side may be of particular importance, it seems likely that the consistently high prices for yams and rice are a result both of relatively high costs of production and a strong position in the hierarchy of consumer preferences.

A more fundamental reservation concerning any attempt to generalize about African food price relationships is dictated by special features of the structure of prices in economies such as Nigeria, Ghana, or the Belgian Congo. Certain distinctive characteristics of underdeveloped economies, where transportation facilities are inadequate and costly, and long-distance trading and regional specialization are of limited importance, have suggested a useful distinction between "local-market" and "national-market" economies (*34*, p. 17). Oshima has argued that in contrast with developed economies (*34*, p. 21):

the tendencies toward the equalization of product-prices and real earnings in Asian economies are probably very weak and usually overpowered by local market forces. Prices of commodities may vary considerably from locality to locality, and the changes of these local prices over time may show very little concordance. Real earnings may also differ from locality to locality, varying generally with the degree of productivity of the locality. (Thus the frequent characterization of Asian villages within a province as rich or poor.)

Oshima is concerned with the problems these characteristics of a "local-product" economy pose in arriving at meaningful estimates of national income. "There is," he says, "an element of arbitrariness in the addition of such values into an aggregate to be designated as national income, since the forces generating the different prices and incomes do not belong to the same system or universe" (*34*, pp. 26–27). Great variation in prices, seasonally and annually, combined with weak links between different markets also impair the significance of a pattern of price relationships derived from average prices. Prest and Stewart have pointed out (*40*, p. 20):

there is a tremendous range of price variations in Nigeria from one month to another and from one town to another. It is not uncommon, for instance, to find identical commodities selling on the same day in two villages fifty miles apart with the price in one village double or three times that in the other even when errors in price-reporting are discounted.

Striking variations in the relative prices of plantains and cocoyams as revealed by the indices of Table 6-8 and Chart 6-1 have already been mentioned. For the other commodities there is some variation in their ranking in the price hierarchy, and the magnitude of the differentials differs substantially from area to area. For example, whereas yam prices per 1,000 calories averaged only some

75 per cent higher than maize for the sample of Nigerian cocoa farmers, yams appear to have been on the average five times as costly as maize in Accra.

Scrutiny of the level and seasonal movement of monthly staple food prices in selected markets in Nigeria and Ghana calls attention to additional limitations of the average indices. Particularly striking are the sharp seasonal fluctuations, especially pronounced in the case of yams and rice. There appears to be some similarity between markets in the seasonal patterns, heavily influenced as they are by the growth cycle and harvest periods for the various crops. In western Nigeria, for example, peak yam prices occur most commonly in May and June, and in the Eastern Region the seasonal highs commonly occur during June and July. These are the periods just prior to the main yam harvest, and in both areas as harvesting of the yam crop proceeds prices decline and continue at a lower level for several months—July or August through October in the Western Region and August through September in the markets of the Eastern Region. While these tendencies appear in the price data, there are considerable variations as between markets and from year to year. Seasonal variation of maize prices is less but still considerable. In the Western Region these typically decline in July and August coincident with the harvest season for early maize. Prices of gari seem to show considerably less seasonal variation than the other staples, presumably because of the fact that manioc can be harvested and gari manufactured throughout the year.

As a result of these sharp seasonal fluctuations, price relationships between the staple foods change considerably during the year. Yams and rice, for example, stand far above maize and gari in the months when their prices are seasonally high, but during trough periods their prices (per 1,000 calories) sometimes approach maize and gari quite closely.

With such large seasonal variations, the suspicion arises that perhaps only very small quantities are purchased at periods when prices are at their seasonal peaks so that the highest quotations may have little more economic significance than the January price of fresh strawberries in London. The Nigeria Cocoa Marketing Board's survey of Yoruba cocoa-farming families provides valuable information concerning seasonal variations in sales, purchases, and consumption of staple foods. The scarcity value of this type of concrete information is high; it is an open question whether these data throw valuable light on conditions in other areas, and indeed it may be questioned whether the sample was truly representative of the cocoa region of western Nigeria. The data for this particular group seem to indicate that appreciable quantities of major staples are purchased through the year and that the peak price quotations are not mere "token" prices. There is, however, considerable substitution between staple foods related to the seasonal availability of supplies, so that consumption of particular products displays a rough inverse relationship to the variations in price.

Galletti and his associates observe that cash expenditures for food by the sample of cocoa farmers studied remained very stable throughout the year (*17*, p. 595). Summary data showing the average calorie contribution of different foods by quarter for all areas surveyed show surprisingly little seasonal variation in quantities purchased; and the stability in food expenditure in the face of substantial seasonal fluctuation in staple food prices seems difficult to explain on the basis of these over-all figures. The major stabilizing factor suggested by these data is simply the important influence of the rather moderate fluctuations in the price of gari; gari and manioc flour occupy an overwhelmingly important position among the purchased foodstuffs, with daily purchases of these items ranging from 740 to 880 calories per "standardized person." Purchases of maize, next in importance as a purchased foodstuff, contributed a maximum of 321 calories per day in the December–February quarter and a minimum of 234 in the June–August period. Yams were the most important of the home-produced foods, with "own produce" of yams providing nearly 600 calories in the September–November quarter and a minimum of a little over 300 calories daily during the March–May quarter. But purchased yams contributed no more than 135 calories daily in any quarter and not less than 115. A seasonal peak in consumption of plantain flour and cocoyams in the March–May quarter, almost entirely home-produced, offset the relatively low intake of yams during that period and in combination with a high intake of manioc and its products accounted for a total average calorie intake (3,135 per "standardized person") for the March–May period, some 50–100 calories higher than for the other quarters (*17*, p. 717).

A somewhat different picture emerges from analysis of the seasonal variation in staple food consumption in four separate areas as indicated by food consumption surveys carried out during four two-week periods—in August and November 1951 and in February and June 1952. These data, which do not give a breakdown between home-produced and purchased food, show a more pronounced seasonal variation in the composition of the diet and in total calorie intake as well. In the Ondo area an indicated decline in consumption of yams from an average of 1,150 gms daily during a two-week period in November to about 665 gms during the February and June survey periods was partially offset by increased consumption of cocoyams but was reflected mainly in an apparent reduction in calorie intake from approximately 2,900 calories daily in November to 2,600 and 2,300 in February and June (per head rather than per "standardized person").

For the sample of 60 persons in the Ife-Ilesha area of western Nigeria, a sharp decline in yam intake from some 600 gms in the August and November survey periods to 350 and 300 in February and June, respectively, was offset to only a small extent by increased intake of other staples. Hence, the reported calorie intake declined from about 3,100 and 3,200 in the first two periods to roughly 2,800 and 2,600 in February and June. Cocoyam and plantain intake varied substantially, but not in such manner as to compensate for the fluctuations in yam consumption. Possibly more significant as a factor that might contribute to stability in the level of food expenditures is the fact that consumption of meat and fish declined from a combined intake of 126 and 80 gms daily in the first two periods to 56 and 30 gms, respectively, in the February and June periods, when prices of purchased food were presumably higher.

For the small sample surveyed in the Ibadan area (44 persons) a somewhat different pattern appears. Peak consumption of yams (600 gms per head per day) in the February survey period was associated with a marked reduction in intake of gari and manioc flour as compared with the August and November levels. But a reduction of yam intake in the June period to 400 gms was associated with a further reduction in consumption of manioc products and a decline in the indicated calorie intake to 2,025 calories compared to about 2,850 and 2,350 in November and February; but this was partly owing to the fact that the fast of Ramadan began during the June period and a fifth of the sample omitted their midday meal.

An even smaller sample (25 people) in the Abeokuta area showed the greatest variation in calorie intake, mainly resulting from a reduction in intake of gari and manioc flour from 470 and 450 gms per head daily in the August and November periods to about 350 and 250 gms in the February and June periods. The seasonal increase of cocoyam consumption from a level of some 30 or 40 gms in the earlier periods to 200 gms in June offset to only a small extent the reduced intake of gari and manioc flour, and of yams as well, with the result that the indicated calorie intake was only about 1,875 calories in the June survey period, compared with 2,950 calories in August (*17*, pp. 657–60). Such marked seasonal variation in consumption of manioc products seems surprising in light of the comparatively moderate seasonal fluctuations in the price of gari.

Seasonal variations are indicated in the quantities of various staples sold by the 187 families covered by this study of cocoa farmers of western Nigeria. Sales of manioc roots fell to 53,000 pounds for the September–November quarter, compared to a range of 70,000–90,000 pounds for the other quarters. Seasonal fluctuations in sales of gari and manioc flour were comparable in magnitude but did not vary in consonance with the seasonal pattern of sales of manioc roots. Sales of these manioc products, mostly manufactured from purchased roots, were roughly 35,000 pounds in the June–August and September–November quarters, but then declined to some 25,000 and 20,000 tons, respectively, in the December–February and March–May quarters. Of all the staple crops covered by the cocoa survey, sales of rice and maize were most heavily concentrated; 12,500 pounds of rice were sold in the June–August quarter out of a total of 14,000 pounds for the year, and maize sales in the June–August quarter were something over 20,000 pounds out of 31,000 pounds for the year. Yam sales also bulked largest during the June–August quarter—some 37,000 pounds compared to 15,000–20,000 pounds in each of the remaining quarters. Plantain sales were most evenly distributed of all the staple crops; peak sales of 31,000 pounds in the September–November quarter were only a little above the June–August and December–February quarters and not greatly in excess of the sales of close to 21,500 pounds in the March–May quarter. Since the bulk of the sales of cocoa takes place in the September–November and December–February quarters, the concentration of cash receipts during these months may have an appreciable influence on the intra-year variation in food prices; but it is a factor which is probably overshadowed by the impact on market prices of seasonal variations in the supplies of different staple foods (*17*, pp. 699–701).

The indices of Table 6-8 and Chart 6-1, based as they are on the average price of maize in each area, fail to illuminate differences in the level of prices as between markets and regions. Such variations in the price levels prevailing in different markets, which show up clearly in the data on price per 1,000 calories given in Appendix Table II, are one of the striking features of the price structure in these economies. Particularly large intermarket variations seem to be as characteristic of yams as of plantains and cocoyams. Thus within the Western Region of Nigeria we find that yams averaged nearly seven pence per 1,000 calories in Delta Province and at Ijebu-Ode and 8.5 pence at Agege in Colony Province, but in Oyo and Ibadan yam prices per 1,000 calories averaged only 3.2 and 3.9 pence, respectively. The dispersion of maize prices within Nigeria is nearly as great. The average price of maize in Kabba-Okene in the Northern Region, used as a base for the indices of relative prices in that region, was 1.3 pence per 1,000 calories compared with average prices of 2.5 and 2.3 pence in the Western and Eastern regions. And within the Western Region the range was from 1.8 to 3.3 pence per 1,000 calories. Although there is some similarity in the general seasonal patterns, many instances appear in which price movements of even neighboring markets diverge markedly. For example, a scarcity of maize at Ijebu in late 1953 (August through September) resulted in prices some 100 per cent above those prevailing in other Western Region markets. As harvest of the late maize crop at Ijebu got under way in December and January the price of maize fell to approximately the level of the other Western Region markets.

Intermarket price comparisons in Ghana for the most part seem to confirm reasonable expectations about the effects on the dispersion of prices resulting from location of markets and the nature of the various staple crops. Thus the bulky and comparatively perishable products—yams, cocoyams, manioc roots, and plantains—show much wider dispersion from market to market than do the cereal crops and manioc meal, which are better suited to transport and storage. Appendix Table II shows a moderate range in average prices of maize from 1.9 pence per 1,000 calories in Accra to 2.4 pence in Sekondi. The spreads for sorghum (from 2.4 pence in Kumasi to 3.4 pence in Sekondi) and rice (from 4.7 to 5.9 pence in Tamale and Kumasi respectively) are also moderate. Gari fits the pattern for three markets, with prices ranging from 2.3 to 2.7 pence per 1,000 calories; and the price at Tamale, which is some 65 per cent above the lowest market, is perhaps partly due to a relatively small consumption of gari in that northern market. According to retail price data, manioc roots showed a much higher spread between Tamale and Kumasi, the cheapest market, and the dispersion of prices as between Kumasi, Sekondi, and Accra was also much greater for manioc roots than for gari (*41*). For yams, the wholesale prices per 1,000 calories shown in Appendix Table II show a range from

5.7 pence in Kumasi to 10.2 pence in Accra and an even larger spread for cocoyams—4.4 pence in Kumasi compared to 8.9 pence in Accra. In the Tamale market, yams were only a little above the Kumasi price, whereas cocoyams were nearly as high there as in Accra; but those relationships were reversed in the prices at Sekondi.

A contrast in the degree of dispersion between cereal crops on the one hand and roots and plantains on the other is also evident in the Belgian Congo. The dispersion of the prices of both cereals and roots is considerably larger than in Ghana, but this is not surprising considering the vast distances which separate the Congo provinces; and relatively high money incomes in the Leopoldville and Katanga provinces no doubt contribute to the consistently higher food prices quoted for those areas.[7] Maize prices range from .23 franc per 1,000 calories in Orientale to .48 in Leopoldville. The low for rice is .52 franc in Equateur Province, the high, 1.71 francs—again the Leopoldville price. The Katanga quotation for manioc, 1.36 francs per 1,000 calories, is nearly four times as high as the lowest price—.41 franc in Orientale. But in this instance the Leopoldville price is only a little above the lowest quotation, which is not too surprising since there are important centers of manioc production close to Leopoldville. In the case of plantains, the Leopoldville and Katanga prices of 2.9 and 3.7 francs per 1,000 calories are respectively a little less and a little more than four times as high as the prices in Orientale and Kivu provinces.

A general ranking of the staple food crops according to their relative prices is obviously subject to great reservations. Beyond the qualifications to be stressed because of the uncertain reliability and incomplete coverage of the price data, there is a further difficulty in generalizing because of the way in which the pattern of price relationships varies from market to market. This no doubt reflects in part local differences in consumer preferences for the various staples; but the influence of a market's location, and of the characteristics of the production area it serves, on relative costs of production, of transportation, and of handling the various staples is probably of more general importance.

The intermarket variations considered above point strongly to a systematic tendency for bulky and semiperishable foods—notably

[7] The observations in the text which are related to Leopoldville Province are reinforced by examination of the breakdown by district given for 1952 (*3*, Table C ff. 155), which shows that staple food prices in Moyen Congo District (which includes the city of Leopoldville) are consistently the highest in the province.

plantains, yams, and cocoyams—to be relatively more costly in areas such as Accra, Leopoldville, or the Katanga, where transport and handling charges have added a good deal more to producer or rural market prices, than concentrated and storable products such as maize, rice, and gari. The strong influence of the location of the various markets on the price structure prevailing also complicates the task of defining a general hierarchy of staple food prices. Since millets and sorghums are so dominant in the drier regions, and relatively unimportant elsewhere, there are few meaningful price comparisons available between those crops and, say, forest-zone crops such as cocoyams or plantains. Even for a versatile crop such as manioc, the reason that manioc is more than twice as costly as millet (in terms of calories) in Dakar and close to four times as costly in Saint Louis is largely because growing conditions in those areas are not favorable to manioc, so that its cost of production is relatively high. Finally, there are certain difficulties in making intercommodity price comparisons. It is often necessary to compare, for example, the price per 1,000 calories of whole-grain maize, which must be ground into meal before it is ready to be cooked, with the price of gari, which is a processed product more nearly comparable to a breakfast cereal than to unmilled grain. Even as between different varieties of a single commodity such as "manioc roots" there may be important differences, for example, between so-called "sweet" varieties grown for use as a vegetable and the typically higher-yielding bitter varieties generally used for gari or manioc flour. Surmise suggests that this may explain, in part at least, the surprising situation reported for Accra where manioc roots appear to be 50 per cent more expensive per 1,000 calories than the processed product, gari.

Although any general ranking of staple food prices must be highly arbitrary and uncertain because of these difficulties and qualifications, it is nevertheless useful to suggest a hierarchy of staple food prices in western tropical Africa. A ranking is given below on the basis of price per pound as well as price per thousand calories. It would be unduly rash to attempt to rank the crops according to the return per acre, since the value of product per unit of land will naturally reflect the large variation from area to area in yields as well as in prices. The indices of "money value efficiency" shown in Table 6-4 above for a number of villages in the Western Region of Nigeria illustrate the considerable variability in the return per acre for various crops within a comparatively small area. In suggesting the ranking in terms of price per thousand calories, the staple foods have been divided into a relatively cheap and a somewhat more expensive group. The position of plantains is uncertain even as to categorizing them as a "lower-cost" or "higher-cost" source of calories, owing to the fact that they are such a cheap food in producing areas but apparently the most costly of all the staples, on a calorie basis, in urban markets of the Belgian Congo. Of the other staples the division into a "lower-cost" and "higher-cost" group in terms of price per thousand calories seems to apply quite widely; but the ordering within each category is much more doubtful.

Relative prices of the staple food crops (lowest to highest):

Per thousand calories	*Per pound*
Lower-cost sources:	Manioc roots
Maize	Cocoyams
Manioc roots	Plantains
Gari/Manioc flour	Yams
Sorghum	Maize
Millet	Gari/Manioc flour
Higher-cost sources:	Sorghum
Rice	Millet
Cocoyams	Rice
Yams	
Plantains (?)	

NUTRITIONAL CONSIDERATIONS

Discussion of the relative yield of the staple food crops indicated that some of the crops ranking high in yield of calories per hectare are rather poor sources of protein and other essential nutrients. It seems highly unlikely that the nutritive quality of different staples is a factor consciously considered by African cultivators in selecting crops, and its present influence on consumer demand for various staples must be virtually nil. Nutritional considerations do, however, carry some weight in fixing the direction of government programs for encouraging the expansion of particular crops. Furthermore, with the gradual spread of even rudimentary knowledge of nutrition, one could expect this factor in the future to exercise a perceptible influence on consumer demand for different staple foods. Clearly the tremendous increase in consumption of citrus fruit in the United States—from 18 pounds per capita in 1910 to 85 pounds in 1954— was encouraged by the wide recognition that oranges are an outstandingly good source of vitamin C. In Japan attitudes toward soy products, which play such a significant role as a source of high-quality protein in that country, suggest that awareness of their nutritional

TABLE 6-9.—NUTRIENT COMPOSITION OF SELECTED STAPLE FOODS PER 100 GRAMS*

(In terms of retail weight "As Purchased")

Commodity	Calories	Protein (%)	Protein per 1,000 calories (in grams)	Calcium (mg)	Iron (mg)	Vit. A I.U.	Thiamine (vit. B₁)	Riboflavin (vit. B₂)	Niacin	Ascorbic acid (vit. C)
								(milligrams)		
Rice:										
Husked or brown	357	7.5	21.0	15	1.4	(0)	.33	.05	4.6	(0)
Home-pounded, undermilled	359	7.1	19.8	14	1.0	(0)	.16	.04	2.5	(0)
Milled, white	360	6.7	18.6	10	.9	(0)	.08	.03	1.6	(0)
Maize:										
Meal, coarse, bolted	360	9.3	25.8	6	1.8	400ᵃ	.35	.09	(1.3)	(0)
Meal, fine, bolted, and degerminated	363	8.4	23.1	5	1.2	300ᵃ	.18	.08	(.6)	(0)
Sorghum (S. vulgare)	343	10.1	29.4	39	4.2	200	.41	.15	4.0	(0)
Millet:										
Pennisetum glaucum	348	11.7	33.6	28	(4.0)	(200)	.33	.15	2.1	(0)
Unspecified	340	9.7	28.5	(30)	(4.0)	(0)	(.3)	(.10)	(1.0)	(0)
Wheat:ᵇ										
Flour, medium extraction	350	11.7	33.4	24	2.4	(0)	.32	.07	1.7	(0)
Flour, white, low extraction	364	10.9	29.9	16	1.0	(0)	.13	.04	1.1	(0)
Sweet potatoes	97	1.1	11.3	28	.8	420ᶜ	.08	.04	.5	19
Manioc:										
Fresh	109	.9	8.3	25	.5	ᵈ	.04	.02	.4	27
Meal and flour	338	1.5	4.4	12	1.0	ᵈ	(0)	(0)	(1.0)	0
Cocoyams										
(Colocasia spp.)	86	1.5	17.4	19	.9	ᵈ	.12	.02	.7	4
Yams (Dioscorea spp.)	90	2.1	23.3	19	.7	ᵈ	.08	.03	.4	9
Plantains (Musa paradisiaca)	75	.8	10.7	5	.5	220ᵉ	.04	.03	.4	11
Bananas and plantains, unspecified	71	.8	11.3	6	.4	180ᵉ	.03	.03	.5	9

* Data from FAO, Food Composition Tables—Minerals and Vitamins—for International Use (Nutr. Studies 11, Rome, 1954), pp. 10–12 and 18. Figures in parentheses are imputed values.

ᵃ Yellow meal only.

ᵇ When enriched to minimum U.S. standards wheat flour contains not less than 2.9 mg iron; 0.44 mg thiamine; 0.26 mg riboflavin; and 3.5 mg niacin per 100 gms of flour. W. W. Leung, R. K. Pecot, and B. K. Watt, Composition of Foods Used in Far Eastern Countries (U.S. Dept. Agr., Handbook 34, March 1952), p. 11.   ᶜ For pale yellow varieties.   ᵈ Negligible.   ᵉ Varies from 0 to over 600 for plantains, and from 14 to 1,400 for bananas.

value has contributed to the strong consumer demand for those products (*25*, pp. 86–87).

In the opinion of many nutritionists, nutritional considerations should be advanced primarily to discourage the consumption—or at least increases in the consumption—of manioc and other roots and tubers. Professor Platt is most exceptional among nutritionists in asserting, "The first stage in the arithmetic is not in fact 'protein arithmetic' but 'calorie arithmetic.' A first step is to secure more food for the people so they can do more work . . . thus breaking the vicious chain of an inadequate supply of food, low energy intake, limitation of physical effort and so on" (*39*, p. 136). Much more characteristic is Dr. Brock's stress on deficiency of protein (*8*, pp. 523, 533):

> Throughout the African continent recent work, particularly arising out of interest in the disease kwashiorkor, suggests that protein malnutrition may be of equal importance with tropical parasitic disease and enervating climates in determining a high incidence of disease and backwardness in cultural and economic development. . . . It is steadily becoming clear that deficiency of protein foodstuffs may constitute the limiting factor in world nutrition and that attempts to satisfy the pangs of hunger by the development of crops such as cassava (manioc) with very high calorie yields per acre may merely shift the emphasis from starvation and undernutrition to protein malnutrition with its serious and disabling sequelae.

Statements stressing the problem of protein malnutrition could be multiplied indefinitely, but an observation by Dr. Nicol, adviser on nutrition to the Medical Department of Nigeria, deserves attention because of his wide experience and practical approach to the nutritional problems of tropical areas (*32*, p. 6):

> In the roots eating areas of Nigeria the total intake of protein is low, because its concentration in root vegetables and plantains never exceeds 2%. Here also the bulk of the protein is supplied either by one, or at most two, staples (yam and cassava), resulting in a deficiency of certain essential amino acids.

The most noteworthy differences among the staple foods in their nutrient composition, as summarized in Table 6-9, is the much higher protein content of the cereals as compared with the roots and tubers when protein is expressed as a percentage of the total weight of the product. Manioc has a protein content of only .9 per cent, and yams, ranking highest of the roots, have only 2.1 per cent protein, whereas milled rice, lowest ranking of the food grains, contains some 6.7 per cent protein and millet contains 11.7 per cent. Nutrient values given

in other food composition tables vary appreciably from the FAO estimates presented in Table 6-9, but the general conclusion is not altered.
If the comparison were in terms of protein per 1,000 calories, however, the contrast between the roots and cereals would not be nearly
so unfavorable. In fact, on such a basis yams would compare favorably with the cereals in protein content and actually would be rated
a little above the food grains in relation to their contribution of most
of the other nutrients. (Varietal differences are often associated with
appreciable differences in nutritive value, and it seems likely that for
certain species of yams the average nutrient content would differ considerably from the composition shown in Table 6-9.) Fresh manioc
roots do not rate so well in that type of comparison, and the position
of processed manioc is even more unfavorable. Manioc meal and flour
characteristically contain a mere 1.2–1.8 per cent protein although
they have nearly the same calorie value per 100 gms as the food
grains. Moreover, manioc protein is of poor quality, notably because
of a deficiency in the sulphur-containing amino acids (methionine and
cystine). The "protein score" of manioc roots, according to the provisional method of rating protein quality suggested by the FAO committee on protein requirements, is exceptionally low—22 compared
with a score of 72 for rice, 66 for sorghum, and 42 for corn meal (*14a*,
p. 28; see also *6, 5,* and *1*). Manioc roots and flour are also very low
in thiamine (B_1) and riboflavin (B_2) although the imputed zero
values given in Table 6-9 should be viewed skeptically. Knowledge
of the nutrient composition of tropical foods such as manioc is still
decidedly incomplete, and there is reason to believe that the content
of the B vitamins, which are water soluble, and of calcium in processed
manioc will depend largely on whether the roots have been soaked.
In preparing manioc flour they may or may not be soaked, whereas
they are never soaked in the preparation of gari. Fresh manioc ranks
as a fairly good source of vitamin C, although virtually all of this
nutrient is lost in the processing of manioc into meal or flour.

Of most of the root crops the leaves are frequently eaten, and
when this is so they make an appreciable contribution to the intake
of protein, minerals, and vitamins. Use of young manioc leaves as
"spinach" is especially important, and they are likely to be of appreciable importance as a source of both vitamins C and A as well as
other needed nutrients. Cocoyam and sweet potato leaves are also
used both as human food and for animal feed (see *35*, pp. 91–93).
No reference appears, however, of the use of yam leaves as food or
feed. Little quantitative information is available concerning the im-

portance of food use of root leaves. For Nigeria, Forde and Scott report (*16*, p. 40):

in addition to the cultivated plant production a considerable and, from the nutritional point of view, a crucial part of the food supply is obtained by the collection of wild vegetable products of the forest and bush . . . Outstanding among the collected products are palm-oil, palm wine, and a wide variety of edible leaves and shoots, all of which contribute essential mineral or vitamin elements to the diet.

According to F. R. Irvine, there are over 150 species of plants in West Africa of which the leaves are used as human food including some 30 plants that are cultivated and another 25 or more that are semicultivated (*23a*, p. 35). Dr. Pierre Bascoulergue, chief of the nutrition service in French Equatorial Africa, reports that daily per capita consumption of green leaves in Kibouendé village in the Moyen Congo averaged over 90 grams and that comparable quantities were being consumed in other Moyen Congo villages where he has carried out nutrition surveys. In his view the rather limited incidence of symptoms of nutritional deficiency in this area, where manioc and plantains are the chief staples, is probably largely owing to the considerable intake of manioc leaves (personal communication, May 14, 1958). Bundles of fresh manioc leaves are one of the most conspicuous items on sale at the Brazzaville market.

Appraisal of the nutrient composition of the staple food crops is, of course, inconclusive since the significance of any deficiencies characteristic of these items depends on the foods which complete the diet. In areas where palm oil is consumed, vitamin A requirements are abundantly supplied by the carotene contained in red palm oil. Yet the fact that the starchy staples provide a very high percentage of total calories means that the other ingredients of the diet may have a heavy nutritional load to carry. Hence a good deal of interest attaches to measures for preserving or enhancing the nutritional value of the staple foods. Brock reports, for example, that the South African Ministry of Nutrition and the National Institute for Nutrition Research are experimenting with the fortification of wheat and maize flour with vitamins and with protein from skimmed milk, soybeans, and fish meal (*8*, p. 524).

R. Masseyeff has set forth convincing arguments concerning the desirability and feasibility of using peanut flour to offset the deficiencies in protein and in the B vitamins likely to characterize a diet based heavily on starchy roots or cereals (*30*). He reports, on the basis of several investigations of consumer acceptance carried out in the Cameroons and in Senegal, that biscuits containing one-third peanut flour are well appreciated and that peanut flour is also used with satisfaction by housewives in preparing the sauces traditionally eaten with the starchy staple foods. Not only is the flavor of these products highly regarded, but women also appreciate the saving in time in using a manufactured product that does not have to be shelled, grilled, and pulverized. Masseyeff reports that Les Moulins de l'A.O.F. at Dakar are producing a peanut flour that is sold in a 10 per cent mixture with maize meal.

In Nigeria the possibilities of using peanut flour to increase the quantity and improve the quality of protein in the diet are being intensively studied. The Nigeria Oil Mills at Kano have produced low-fat peanut flour of excellent quality in terms of its palatability, storage qualities, and amino-acid content.[8] Nicol reports that a number of consumer acceptability trials have given favorable results. One interesting use of the flour is in combination with gari, and mixtures up to 50 per cent peanut flour have been found acceptable although somewhat lower levels are preferred. When the gari and flour are mixed dry the resulting product can be prepared simply by mixing with cold water in the manner in which gari is commonly prepared.

As a means of offsetting the shortage of protein in southern Nigeria, Nicol looks with favor upon enlarged consumption of rice. "If rice can replace the roots now used in such large quantities as a staple food, the protein deficiency in these southern diets would be greatly reduced, if not entirely overcome" (31, p. 12). Nicol's enthusiasm for increased consumption of rice is, however, qualified in two respects. In the first place, he points out that the nutritional advantage of a shift from roots to rice would be reduced if the rice is highly milled because of the large loss of B vitamins unless it is properly parboiled prior to milling (32, p. 5). It is not clear whether rice mills in Nigeria are following that practice to any degree, but a report of the Applied Nutrition Unit at the London School of Hygiene and Tropical Medicine expresses concern that the new rice mills being built in Nigeria apparently do not provide for parboiling (29). The second qualification made by Nicol is that substitution of rice for the millets and sorghums consumed in northern Nigeria would

---

[8] The flour, which is produced with special expellers and a microcyclomat mill, contains 50 per cent protein, has a fat content of 10 per cent or less, and a particulate size which does not exceed 20 microns (thus promoting digestibility which, for the protein fraction, is as high as 92 to 97 per cent) (31a).

mean a loss from the nutritional standpoint since rice has a lower content of the B vitamins than these grains (*32*, p. 5).

Table 6-9 shows that rice, especially white milled rice, contains appreciably less protein and considerably less of the B vitamins than millets or sorghums. As noted earlier, however, the quality of rice protein appears to be a little superior to that of millets and sorghums, although the available data concerning the amino acids contained in millets and sorghums is inadequate. The quality of rice protein is clearly superior to that of maize. Finger millet (*Eleusine coracana*), not shown in Table 6-9, is of nutritional interest because of its extraordinarily high content of calcium—some ten times higher than the highest of the calcium values shown in Table 6-9. In general, however, differences in the nutritional value of different cereals are probably not very significant and certainly less important than differences resulting from the processing which they receive. Particularly are the processing losses great for rice which, according to Kik and Williams, loses 76 per cent of the thiamine, 57 per cent of the riboflavin, 63 per cent of the niacin, and 15 per cent of the protein as a result of being highly polished. Moreover, the substantial loss of nutrients which may occur as a result of washing rice is much higher with polished than with undermilled rice (*28*, pp. 15, 19). Therefore, it is not surprising that much attention has been given to developing practical and economic ways to retain or restore nutrients in milled rice by undermilling, by parboiling or "conversion," or by enriching with a "pre-mix" of rice impregnated with a concentrated solution of certain vitamins and minerals (*15*, pp. 21–29). Inasmuch as these processes improve the nutritional value of rice and at very low cost, a particularly strong case can be made for utilizing whichever of these techniques seem most appropriate to the various African conditions. Consumer attitudes, so important to the acceptance of undermilling, parboiling, or enriching, seem to be largely a matter of preference for the rice product that is familiar. Hence early introduction of the process in areas where rice consumption is on the rise would minimize the problem of modifying consumer preferences. In Sierra Leone parboiling is practiced by the village women in their preparation of home-pounded rice; and the rice mills, which are operated by the Department of Commerce and Industry, parboil the paddy they receive prior to milling. It is reported, however, that with the increased consumption of imported rice in recent years there is evidence of a shift in preference in favor of polished rice. A pilot rice mill built in Liberia under FAO supervision "is designed to produce an unpolished rice retaining valuable nutrients" (*13*, p. 17).

Some points on the nutritional characteristics of maize need brief comment. It has been known for some time that a high incidence of pellagra is commonly found in areas which depend heavily on maize as a staple food. In 1937, Elvehjem and his co-workers identified niacin as the "pellagra-preventive" factor which Goldberger had postulated but had not identified. Among the cereals maize is particularly low in niacin, though this proved to be only part of the reason for the correlation between maize diets and pellagra (*14*, pp. 38–39). It is now known that maize also ranks low in content of the amino acid, tryptophan, which can be converted to niacin in the body.[9] This relationship explains the value of milk as an anti-pellagra factor, since milk is high in tryptophan but is not a good source of niacin.

The report of the Applied Nutrition Unit, mentioned above, expresses concern over the introduction of new, hard varieties of maize in Nigeria which, they believe, will lead to the substitution of commercial hammer mills for the present time-consuming but nutritionally superior methods, with the result that "Nigeria may develop a pellagra problem similar to that in parts of East and Central Africa" (*29*, p. 25). But with the small power-driven maize grinders so extensively used in Ghana, and which are likely to spread to other areas, there would appear to be virtually no loss of the germ. Moreover, since the niacin value is very low even in whole maize, attention has more commonly been directed toward ways of insuring adequate supplies of niacin, either by enriching the corn meal itself or by supplementing a maize diet with legumes, fish, animal products, or other foods richer in niacin and tryptophan. Pellagra, it is noteworthy, is not at all common among a number of the maize-eating groups in Mexico, Central and South America, and Java, probably in large part owing to the widespread use of beans and other pulses, which are good sources of the B vitamins. In 1947 the South African National Nutrition Council recommended compulsory fortification of maize with food yeast, exceptionally rich in niacin and also a very good source of protein, thiamine, riboflavin, and calcium. Fortification of maize meal with soybean meal, to the extent of 10 per cent rather than

---

[9] A further problem related to the nutritional characteristics of maize is the fact that zein, the protein in maize, is very rich in the amino acid, leucine; and some evidence has been obtained indicating that with high intake of leucine the body needs extra amounts of isoleucine to offset the growth-retarding effect of a high level of leucine (*12*, p. 84; *14a*, p. 24).

the 1–1½ per cent fortification recommended in the case of food yeast, was also endorsed. Although the contribution of soya meal to the availability of niacin would be small, it would provide a valuable supplement of protein and of the amino acid, tryptophan (*14*, pp. 48–49).

In the United States enrichment with synthetic niacin, thiamine, and riboflavin has been found to be a simple and inexpensive means of enhancing the nutritional value of maize meal as well as wheat flour. At the present time enrichment of maize meal is carried out on either a compulsory or voluntary basis in a number of southern states where maize is an important component of the diet. Enrichment programs in tropical Africa would, however, be limited in their impact since only a relatively small proportion of the indigenous cereals are commercially milled, and only the larger mills would be able to finance the needed enrichment equipment.

The technical problems of enriching rice are more difficult than for maize meal. For one of the nutrients commonly added to maize meal and wheat flour—riboflavin—no practical solution has been found, since impregnating rice with synthetic riboflavin causes a discoloration which, thus far, seems to render the product unacceptable to consumers. Moreover, fortification of maize meal with products rich in high-quality protein such as food yeast and soybean meal is simple, but such admixture is not feasible with rice, which is ordinarily eaten as whole grains. Enrichment or fortification of manioc meal or flour does not appear to pose any special technical problems apart from some possible difficulties with consumer acceptance and the problems of organizing the processing of manioc on a reasonably large scale—which in the case of gari, at least, seems to encounter obstacles because of consumer preferences for particular local techniques of preparation. If government policy in some of the areas considered in this study should turn to enrichment or fortification as a low-cost and quick method for enhancing the nutritional quality of urban diets, the relative ease with which these three staples can be enriched may have some slight influence on their competitive position.

The Ten-Year Plan for the Belgian Congo notes the nutritional shortcomings of manioc while recognizing that it must continue to play a dominant role as a food crop in the Congo. Some attention is being given to the possibility of enriching manioc flour, but more emphasis is apparently being placed on increased production of peanuts and other legume crops with high content of good-quality protein to provide a valuable supplement (*4*, p. 379). There appears to be a good deal of local variation in the extent to which legumes are grown and eaten; but in general it can probably be said that in tropical Africa they are more important as a source of good-quality protein—well supplied with suitable proportions of the 8 or 9 essential amino acids that the body cannot produce itself—than either livestock products or fish. However, development of ponds for production of fresh-water fish—mainly various species of *Tilapia* which thrive in warm, tropical regions—has received considerable attention in the Belgian Congo and elsewhere. And fish are, of course, of appreciable importance in coastal and riverine areas.

The much-debated question of whether satisfactory nutrition requires a sizable percentage of animal protein has a good deal of relevance to agricultural development in Africa. Insofar as expert opinion on this subject influences agricultural programs and consumer demand, views on the question will have some bearing on the extent to which the staple food crops continue to be used almost entirely for direct human consumption or come to be used in part as animal feed. Prospects for the use of certain of the staple food crops, notably manioc, as livestock feed will be considered briefly in Chapter 9, but it is pertinent at this point to note that divergent views prevail on the nutritional importance of increasing consumption of animal products. Léon Pales, the French authority who directed the "Mission Anthropologique" which carried out important investigations of food consumption in French West Africa, has recently expressed the view that for a proper diet ("une ration correcte") half of the protein should be of animal origin (*36*, p. 3014). In similar vein the ten-year plan for the economic development of Ruanda-Urundi states that of the proteins required to satisfy nutritional needs "at least a quarter should be of animal origin" (*4a*, p. 54). Many if not most nutritionists have now rejected this earlier view that from 25 to 50 per cent of the protein intake should be in the form of animal protein. H. C. Sherman has asserted that on the basis of chemical research and balance experiments, we should "rank the proteins of soybeans and peanuts with animal proteins in chemical nature and nutritional efficiency," and that the proteins of "ordinary beans and peas need but little supplementation in order to nourish us equally well" (*43*, p. 45). In a recent discussion of the problem of amino acid balance in nutrition, C. A. Elvehjem is somewhat less emphatic than Sherman's 1946 statement, but seems confident that many legume proteins are as valuable as animal proteins in overcoming inadequacies of cereal proteins. He goes on to emphasize that: "In many parts of the world we must rely on these proteins rather than increasing the level of animal proteins" (*11*, p. 308). A closely similar point of view has been expressed by Dr. Oomen, who has urged that measures be taken to encourage increased consumption of soybeans, peanuts, other legumes, and "vegetable" milks as the most practical approach to the problem of infant malnutrition in Indonesia (*33*, p. 35). Reference has already been made to the amino acid deficiencies which seem to be prevalent in southern Nigeria where manioc or yams bulk large in the diet. Dr. Nicol points out, however, that (*32*, pp. 6–7):

An exceptional area is the south east, where a very good state of physical development is achieved on a low protein intake, 98% of the protein being of vegetable origin. This can be attributed to the wide range of plant foods which are eaten to supplement the staple yam, including many varieties of leaves, legumes, nuts, and fruit.

The evaluation of protein quality by the FAO committee on protein requirements is focused entirely on the pattern of amino acids in foods in relation to a desirable pattern defined on the basis of available knowledge of requirements of human beings for the essential amino acids. While it is true that animal proteins have an amino acid composition that corresponds very well with what is believed to be the ideal pattern, various vegetable proteins and notably the legumes also rate rather high (*14a*, pp. 21–31). It may also be noted that since the various starchy roots and cereals tend to be defficient in different amino acids, a combination of staples provides a superior balance of the supply of the essential amino acids.

CITATIONS

1 E. L. Adriaens, "Recherches sur la composition en acides aminés des protéines d'aliments végétaux du Congo Belge et du Ruanda-Urundi," *Bull. agr. du Congo Belge* (Belg., Min. Col.), June 1956.

2 O. T. Barrett, *The Tropical Crops* (New York, 1928).

3 Belg., Min. Col., *L'Agriculture au Congo Belge et au Ruanda-Urundi de 1948 à 1952* (1954).

4 ———, *Plan décennal pour le développement économique et social du Congo Belge*, II (1949).

4a ———, *Plan decénnal . . . du Ruanda-Urundi* (1951).

5 E. J. Bigwood, "Sulphur Deficiency and Kwashiorkor," in *Malnutrition in African Mothers, Infants, and Young Children*, Rept. of Sec. Inter-Afr. (CCTA) Conf. on Nutr., Gambia, 1952 (London, 1954).

6 E. J. Bigwood and E. L. Adriaens, "Amino-acid Composition of Cassava Meal," in *5.*

7 C. Bonnefoy, "Tiagba—notes sur un village aizi," *Études Éburnéennes III* (Inst. Français d'Afr. Noire, Abidjan, 1954).

8 J. F. Brock, "Nutrition," *An. Rev. Biochemistry*, Vol. 24, 1955.

9 R. Cerighelli, *Cultures tropicales. I. Plantes vivrières* (Nouvelle Encycl. Agr., Paris, 1955).

10 E. S. Clayton, "Research Methodology and Peasant Agriculture," *Farm Economist* (Oxford), VIII, No. 6, 1956.

11 C. A. Elvehjem, "Amino Acid Balance in Nutrition," *J. Am. Diet. Assn.*, April 1956.

12 ———, "Corn in Human Nutrition," in *Proc. Fourth Ann. Meeting of the Agr. Res. Inst.*, *1955.*

13 Food and Agriculture Organization of the United Nations (FAO), *Activities of FAO under the Expanded Technical Assistance Program 1953/54* (Rome, 1954).

14 FAO, *Maize and Maize Diets* . . . (FAO Nutr. Studies 9, Rome, 1953).

14a FAO, *Protein Requirements* (Rept. of FAO Com. on Protein Requirements, FAO Nutr. Studies 16, Rome 1957).

15 FAO, *Rice and Rice Diets* . . . (FAO Nutr. Studies 1, Washington, D.C., 1948).

16 Daryll Forde and Richenda Scott, *The Native Economies of Nigeria*, Vol. I of *The Economics of a Tropical Dependency*, edited by Margery Perham (London, 1946).

17 R. Galletti, K. D. S. Baldwin, and I. O. Dina, *Nigerian Cocoa Farmers* . . . (Nigeria Cocoa Mkt. Bd., London, 1956).

18 G. Geortay, "Données de base pour la gestion de paysannats de cultures vivrières en région équatoriale forestière," *Bull. inf. de l'INÉAC* (Belg., Min. Col.), August 1956.

19 Ch. Godard, "Les Cultures vivrières du Tchad," in *Encycl. Col. et Mar: Afrique Équatoriale Française* (Paris, 1950).

20 Pierre Gourou, *The Tropical World* . . . (London, 1953).

21 Groupe d'Économie Rurale, "Évolution de l'agriculture indigène dans la zone de Léopoldville," *Bull. agr. du Congo Belge*, October 1954.

22 M. R. Haswell, *Economics of Agriculture in a Savannah Village* . . . (Gr. Brit., Col. Off., Col. Res. Studies 8, 1953).

23 T. Hunter and T. V. Danso, "Notes on Food Farming at Ejura," in Gold Coast, Dept. Agr., *Year-book, 1930* (Accra, n.d.).

23a F. R. Irvine, "The Edible Cultivated and Semi-Cultivated Leaves of West Africa," *Materiae Vegetabiles* (The Hague), II, No. 1, 1956.

24 N. Jasny, *Competition Among Grains* (Stanford, 1940).

25 B. F. Johnston, Mosaburo Hosoda, and Yoshio Kusumi, *Japanese Food Management in World War II* (Stanford, 1953).

26 Phyllis M. Kaberry, *Women of the Grassfields* . . . (Gr. Brit., Col. Off., Col. Res. Pub. 14, 1952).

27 Kellermann, "Les Cultures vivrières des régions forestières et guinèennes et la riziculture," in *Encycl. Col. et Mar: Afrique Équatoriale Française* (Paris, 1950).

28 M. C. Kik and R. R. Williams, *The Nutritional Improvement of White Rice* (Natl. Res. Coun. Bull. 112, Washington, 1945).

29 London Sch. of Hygiene and Trop. Med., Applied Nutr. Unit, *Nutrition in Nigeria* (London, 1954, mimeo.).

30 R. Masseyeff, *La Farine d'arachides: Intérêt—Acceptabilité—Possibilité de production au Cameroun* (Off. de la Rech. Sci. et Techn. Outre-mer, Inst. de Rech. du Cameroun, Yaoundé, 1955).

31 B. M. Nicol, *Feeding Nigeria* (Fed. Inf. Serv. Pub., Lagos, n.d.).

31a ———, *Memorandum on the Quality, Acceptability and Uses of the Groundnut Flour Produced by Nigerian Oil Mills, Kano* (no place, Aug. 22, 1955, mimeo.).

32 ———, *A Report of the Nutritional Work Which Has Been Carried Out in Nigeria Since 1920, with a Summary of What Is Known of the Present Nutritional State of the Nigerian Peasants* (Nigeria, Eastern Region, Min. Health [no place], 1954, mimeo.).

33 H. A. P. C. Oomen, "Infantile Malnutrition in Indonesia," *Nutr. Revs.*, February 1954.

34 H. T. Oshima, *Critique of National Income Statistics in Underdeveloped Countries* (U.S. Lib. Cong., January 1956, microfilmed).

35 V. A. Oyenuga, "The Composition and Nutritive Value of Certain Feedingstuffs in Nigeria . . . ," *Emp. J. Exp. Agr.* (London), April 1955.

36 Léon Pales, "Les Problèmes alimentaires africains," *Marchés trop. du monde* (Paris), Nov. 24, 1956.

37 Edgar Pauquet, "La Culture du riz en région Itimbiri," *Bull. agr. du Congo Belge* (Belg., Min. Col.), October 1955.

38 T. A. Phillips, *An Agricultural Note Book (with Special Reference to Nigeria)*, London, 1956.

39 B. S. Platt, "Food and Its Production—in Relation to the Development of Tropical and Sub-tropical Countries, Particularly Africa," in A. L. Banks, ed., *The Development of Tropical and Sub-tropical Countries* (London, 1954).

40 A. R. Prest and I. G. Stewart, *The National Income of Nigeria, 1950–51* (Gr. Brit., Col. Off., Col. Res. Studies 11, 1953).

41 *Quarterly News Letter* (Gold Coast, Dept. Agr.), March and December 1955 issues.

42 P. de Schlippe, "Sous-station d'essais de l'I.N.É.A.C. à Kurukwata (extraits du premier rapport annuel)," *Bull agr. du Congo Belge*, June 1948.

43 H. C. Sherman, *Foods: Their Values and Management* (New York, 1946).

44 Sierra Leone, Soil Conservation Com., *Soil Conservation and Land Use in Sierra Leone* (Sess. Paper 1, Freetown, 1951).

45 A. Van Parys, "La Culture continue des plantes vivrières à la Station de Nioka," *Bull. inf. de l'INÉAC* (Belg., Min. Col.), April 1956.

46 R. A. Young, *Cultivation of the True Yams in the Gulf Regions* (U.S. Dept. Agr., Dept. Bull. 1167, August 1923).

CHAPTER 7

SOCIAL, CULTURAL, AND HISTORICAL INFLUENCES

Owing to the widespread importance of subsistence production which tends to obscure the operation of price and cost relationships, various noneconomic factors appear to have exerted considerable influence on the pattern of crop distribution in tropical Africa. The first of these cultural and historical factors examined here is the "yam culture" in the coastal zone of West Africa lying east of the Bandama River and a "rice culture" among the peoples west of the Bandama. The existence of these zones has significantly affected the response of the local populations to the introduction of manioc and maize from the New World and to the introduction of Asiatic varieties of rice. Other factors influencing the introduction and spread of manioc and maize also receive attention because of their bearing on the position of those two crops and of certain crops which they have replaced. As an illustration of the influence of certain local mores and customs on cropping patterns in Africa (for example, the respective roles of men and women in agriculture), some of the findings of Miss Haswell's intensive study of a Gambia village are reviewed (14). And finally, an effort is made to discern relationships between population distribution and the pattern of production of the staple food crops.

Two other influences which might be described broadly as "social" are discussed elsewhere in the volume. In the description of the distribution of staple food crops in the Belgian Congo in Chapter 4 it was pointed out that the imposition by the administration of compulsory acreage quotas probably had a good deal to do with the early expansion of certain crops, notably rice and maize among the food crops. Governmental encouragement of a more general character appears to have had appreciable influence on the position of individual crops in a number of territories; the measures to encourage rice cultivation, which are reviewed in Chapter 9, have undoubtedly contributed to the increased importance of that crop and are likely to lead to further expansion.

172

INFLUENCE OF THE "RICE CULTURE" OF THE WESTERN AND "YAM CULTURE" OF THE EASTERN GUINEA COAST

It has been noted that the rice production zone which stretches south and east from the Gambia and the Casamance district of Senegal is characterized by a fairly definite eastern limit—the Bandama River that bisects the Ivory Coast. To the east of the Bandama, the region lying south of the millet-sorghum belt is a zone where roots and tubers are dominant. And throughout this zone of roots and tubers, yams are of great importance.

Studying the distribution of the staple food crops in the Ivory Coast, Jacques Miège concluded that this fairly sharp division between the rice region to the west and the yam region to the east of the Bandama can be fully explained by historical and cultural factors. The boundaries of the Ivory Coast, which are of course rather recent, encompass two distinct cultures. Miège suggests that the two ethnic regions referred to by Baumann and Westermann as "Atlantic east" and "Atlantic west" can be aptly described as "the civilization of the yam" and "the civilization of rice." The eastern half, territory of the yam, is as Miège points out inhabited mainly by the Baoulé and Agni tribal groups, which are matriarchal societies, whereas in the western half, the rice region, patrilineal succession is followed. He also notes that the Baoulé or Agni influence on other tribal groups in the east is marked; and that west of the Bandama the cultural homogeneity of the people suggested by adherence to patrilineal succession is reinforced by language affinities and religious and artistic similarities (*19*, p. 33). Furthermore, this dividing line between two distinct cultures within the Ivory Coast can be generalized, Miège believes, to all of West Africa (*19*, pp. 36–37):[1]

The western region of West Africa is a zone devoted to rice. There the role of the yam is strictly secondary, so much so that the most recent agricultural statistics for French Guinea and Senegal do not even mention its existence. . . .

To this immense rice zone, is opposed the domain of the yam (*Dioscorea*). Between the Baoulé and the Cameroons, the yam becomes the essential crop

---

[1] Daryll Forde speaks of a rice region of the western Guinea Coast as the "outstanding exception to the general pattern of indigenous cultivation in the forest belt" of West and Central Africa (*5*, p. 211). The "general pattern," according to Forde, was a food economy dominated by yams, cocoyams, and plantains which, following Burkhill and Sauer, he regards as having reached West Africa from the east, having been "first domesticated in an archaic planting area in southern Asia." Forde's notion of the ancient rice region of West Africa differs from Miège's, however, for he describes the area as extending from the Gambia only as far east as western Liberia.

about which agricultural activities revolve. If, as happens in portions of the region, it yields its dominant position to another crop, its social importance remains considerable. It manifests itself in a yam festival, object of rejoicing, which is one of the outstanding dates of the year in the life of these tribal groups. This is the case, for example, in the Agni District where yams as a crop have come to be of secondary importance.

Miège suggests that this east-west division of the crop zones was probably even more distinct in the past when the cultures and tribal groups were more stabilized. The expansion of manioc and maize as important crops within the "civilization of the yam" has obscured to a considerable extent the dominance of yams. But, as will be noted shortly, the ease with which manioc and maize penetrated West Africa east of the Bandama may have been related to certain affinities between the cultivation of those New World plants and the traditional yam crop. Although that is surmise, the fact seems established that the adoption and spread of the Oriental varieties of rice (*Oryza sativa*) was until recently confined almost entirely to the traditional domain of rice where the indigenous varieties of *Oryza glaberrima* had been cultivated for centuries (*25*, p. 491).[2] Portères estimates that rice cultivation dates back at least 3,500 years in the districts where it was first cultivated, and that by the sixteenth century cultivation of *Oryza glaberrima* had spread along coastal West Africa as far east as Axim near the western boundary of the present Ghana. And Portères suggests that cultivation of *Oryza sativa*, introduced by the Portuguese, was accepted only within this region where the indigenous rice had spread "because rice is the cereal which demands the greatest care, the most work, and the most extensive practical knowledge in order to obtain an adequate return" (*25*, pp. 491–92).

INTRODUCTION AND SPREAD OF MAIZE AND MANIOC

Since maize and manioc are both New World crops, their present position has necessarily been influenced by the timing and nature of their introduction and spread in Africa. Many details surround-

---

[2] S. D. Onabamiro states that: "Fifty years ago rice was practically unknown in Nigeria and the Gold Coast" (*24*, p. 24). Writing of Oubangui Territory in French Equatorial Africa, R. P. Ch. Tisserant states that rice was introduced at an early date by the Europeans but that as late as 1911 it was found only near European settlements where it was planted under orders of the Europeans or their Senegalese assistants (*27*, p. 224).

ing their introduction are obscure or controversial, but enough is known to throw some light on the present pattern of distribution of the staple food crops.

It appears highly probable, as was indicated in Chapter 2, that maize was brought to western tropical Africa across the Atlantic by the Portuguese and other Europeans; and that it also reached the interior of West Africa by the overland route from Egypt, where the New World plant had been received by way of the Mediterranean. Being well adapted to much of tropical Africa, maize seems not to have encountered formidable obstacles in securing an important position as a secondary and sometimes as a dominant crop throughout a major part of the region under study. The only exception to be signaled, and it is a difference of degree, is that maize has penetrated the "rice culture" of the western Guinea Coast to a much smaller extent than elsewhere in West and Central Africa. Portères, in noting that maize has tended to be confined to a compound or garden crop in the western half of West Africa, suggests that it did not become important there because rice was already well established as a cereal crop (25, pp. 492, 504).[3] On the other hand, he believes that maize was so readily adopted in the "yam culture" of the eastern Guinea Coast in part because it lends itself to planting in hills in a manner similar to the culture of yams.

Maize apparently has gained ground as a staple food mainly at the expense of yams and sorghums. Of the Bamenda District of the British Cameroons, Phyllis Kaberry reports that production of Guinea corn "has decreased and its place as a staple cereal has been taken by maize, particularly when this crop can be planted twice a year" (18, p. 61). Physical attributes of the plant, including a short growth period and this frequent possibility of planting two crops a year, as well as the fairly good yields obtained even with a low level of farm practice, are probably the principal factors accounting for the position it holds. A. Adandé has suggested that the exceptional importance of maize in Lower Dahomey, Lower Togo, and western Nigeria

---

[3] Miss Haswell's study of the Gambia village of Genieri explains the position of maize as a compound crop in terms of a soil deficiency of that district: "Maize is only cultivated inside the compound area where the women throw their refuse and domestic animals roam; phosphorus deficiency in the soil precludes its cultivation farther afield" (14, p. 42). I am unable to offer an opinion whether such a situation may occur more frequently in the western than in the eastern portions of West Africa. It is, however, probably more a characteristic of a savanna region as phosphorus deficiency has been stressed in discussions of the soils of northern Nigeria and parts of the Northern Territories of the Gold Coast (31, p. 4 and 23).

is the result of a tradition among the tribal groups of that region that millets and sorghums were "reserved exclusively to the kings and their descendants" (*1*, p. 279). And if that is true, one might further speculate that maize was particularly successful in replacing yams in this part of the Guinea Coast owing to the "semiarid" and "dry subhumid" climate.

One is also tempted to speculate on the reasons why maize is so enormously more important than sorghums or millets in the savanna region of the Belgian Congo. In recent decades, cultivation of maize has been expanded there as a result of governmental encouragement and coercion because it is a crop that is well suited for provisioning urban areas and mining centers. It was noted in Chapter 4 that in 1936 the compulsory quota for maize was raised to 135,000 hectares from the 85,000 hectares in effect the previous year (*13*, p. 893). The present position of maize in the Congo is probably also related in part to the circumstances under which it was introduced. But since those circumstances were basically the same as surrounded the adoption of manioc in the Congo, it is convenient to examine this aspect in terms of the account that W. O. Jones has given of the introduction and spread of manioc.[4]

Late in the fifteenth century the Portuguese established relations with the King of Congo at his capital some 200 miles inland from the mouth of the Congo, and for over a hundred years they maintained close relations with the Congolese. The rulers of the Kingdom of Congo apparently looked upon the Europeans as representatives of a superior culture and were highly receptive to the innovations which they brought—so much so that by "1506 the King of Congo was the Christian ruler of a more or less Christian realm and recognized as such by the King of Portugal and by the Pope" (*17*, p. 104). It would appear that at an early stage the Portuguese introduced manioc, the extremely useful food crop with which they had become familiar in Brazil. Details of the spread of manioc within the Kingdom of Congo are lacking, but Jones cites evidence showing that it was an important food in northern Angola by the 1660s. (The influence of the Kingdom of Congo extended inland as far as the present city of Leopoldville and perhaps beyond and south from the Congo to the site of the present city of Luanda.) The oral traditions of the Bushongo or Bakuba Kingdom located in the central portion of the

---

[4] The following is based mainly on Chapter 3, Introduction and Spread of Manioc, in Jones' forthcoming book, *Manioc in Africa* (*16*), as well as his article, "Manioc: An Example of Innovation in African Economies" (*17*).

southern savanna belt of the Belgian Congo indicate that manioc reached that area about 1650 or earlier.[5] It appears, however, that manioc did not become a staple of general importance among all the Bushongo until early in the present century.

Edmond Verhulpen states that the Bena Kalundwe, one of the important chiefdoms of the Baluba Empire which covered most of the present Katanga Province, adopted manioc in about 1885. Prior to that time maize alone was cultivated, but following the introduction of manioc by a famous chief it virtually replaced maize, which at present is important only for a matter of weeks after its harvest. Manioc was well received by the Bena Kalundwe because it could be harvested late in the dry season when the seasonal hunger was most acute; and the "name of the new crop was therefore on everyone's lips, and it was in this way that they came to be called the Manioc People"—the meaning of their name Bena Kalundwe (*17*, p. 107; *30*, pp. 232, 307).

A different factor is stressed by Jones in explaining the spread of manioc among the forest peoples of the Congo basin (*16*). He points out that until fairly recently, perhaps until the beginning of the seventeenth century, the Congo rain forest was inhabited chiefly by Pygmies and other hunting, fishing, and gathering peoples who practiced no agriculture. During the past three or four hundred years successive waves of Bantu Negroes were driven into the rain forests of Central Africa by more powerful peoples. The evidence suggests that these people came from savanna areas, initially from regions to the northeast and later from the northwest, where they had cultivated chiefly millets and sorghums.[6] They were not acquainted with forest agriculture and were therefore receptive to a crop such as manioc which was being introduced in the coastal areas by the Portuguese at about the same period as the early migrations of Bantu Negroes into the forest zone.

Manioc was so ideally suited as a crop for the rain-forest zone that it would not be surprising if its spread in the Congo basin was rapid and complete. In the savanna woodland of the southern Congo, however, there are indications that to the east of the Kingdom of

[5] Jones draws upon the studies by Torday and Joyce during the years 1907–09; because of the occurrence of an eclipse of the sun in 1680 it was possible for Torday and Joyce to attach dates with tolerable accuracy to the events of the oral tradition which they recorded (*17*, p. 106; *28*, pp. 28, 131–32, 249).

[6] Jones draws heavily here on A. Moeller (*20*) and an article by B. Tanghe (*26*).

Congo, maize may have spread more rapidly than manioc. Thus it has been noted that maize was the dominant staple of the Baluba group, now known as the Bena Kalundwe, prior to their adoption of manioc in the late nineteenth century. Similarly, Joyce and Torday recall the statement by Wolf, who visited the southern part of the Bushongo Empire in 1884, that manioc was not cultivated and that at that time maize alone was the important staple (*28*, p. 249; *17*, p. 106). Mary Douglas' description of the Lele of Kasai, a people who live in mixed savanna and forest on the extreme southern edge of the equatorial forest belt, suggests that manioc has been displacing maize rather recently. After noting that maize is the staple food of the Lele, she observes in a monograph published in 1954 that "in recent years manioc has become nearly as important as maize" (*4*, p. 2). Similarly, a recent report on the agriculture of the Mumosho-Mugabo groups of Kivu in the eastern Congo states that manioc "was not at all widespread five years ago, but has become increasingly important . . ." (*3*, p. 80). This expansion of manioc in Nord-Kivu seems to have been mainly at the expense of sweet potatoes, and seems to be related to the fact that manioc can be stored easily by being left unharvested and does not suffer from grasshopper attacks.

It is not surprising that the spread of maize would have proceeded more rapidly than manioc. And when we turn to the introduction of manioc in West Africa, it seems clear that it was fairly slow in being adopted, much slower than maize or sweet potatoes. To some extent the difference between the relative ease with which maize and manioc would be spread might simply be owing to the fact that seed for planting maize could be transplanted more readily than the cuttings required for the introduction of manioc. Jones believes, however, that the really important consideration is that the introduction of manioc required adopting a "manioc complex," including processing techniques to remove the prussic acid found in lethal amounts in many varieties of manioc (*16*). As Jones observes: "If the manioc root is handled in just the same way as the yam, which was the staple food for most of the region east of the middle Ivory Coast, it is very apt to contain dangerous amounts of prussic acid. A few unfortunate adventures with a new food plant would be sufficient to discourage its use for years to come" (*17*, p. 109). Moreover, with the well-established yam and rice cultures of the Guinea Coast there was no pressing need for a new food resource. Also the West Africans were not nearly so impressed with the culture of the Europeans as were the Congolese, so that the relationship was not particularly favorable to the transmission of the "manioc complex." Maize and sweet potatoes were more readily adopted because they were easy additions to the traditional food and agricultural pattern.

In a few areas—the islands of São Tomé, Principé, and Fernando Po, and at Owerri on the mainland—manioc was important by 1700. "But nowhere else on the mainland was it a crop of more than casual importance prior to the nineteenth century" (*17*, p. 109). The true importance of manioc in West Africa dates from its reintroduction by freed slaves migrating from Brazil to the Lagos-Dahomey coast beginning in about 1780. These "Brazilias," as they were called, brought not only the manioc root but also a knowledge of the preparation of manioc meal (and tapioca). The fact that manioc meal—gari—is such an important product of manioc in West Africa undoubtedly stems from the fact that it was part of the "manioc complex" as introduced by the Brazilias (*17*, p. 110).

It appears that cultivation of manioc in West Africa has been spreading steadily since about 1800, but much of the expansion has occurred only in the past few decades. Daryll Forde observes that manioc has been adopted only recently among the Yoruba, and while yams are still the dominant food crop in that part of Nigeria, manioc has become a major staple (*6*, p. 154). With respect to Lower Dahomey, A. Adandé observes: "The fame of manioc meal is very recent in Dahomey; until recently maize was the only staple food of the natives. Currently, it is facing serious competition from gari in the area extending from Agoué to Cotonou, including the regions of the Mono and the Ouidah" (*1*, p. 233). In 1900 manioc was still regarded as a food of the lowest class, according to Adandé. It was only during the period of food shortage during World War I that it became a part of the general diet, and as late as the 1920s the consumption of gari "was not widespread as it is today" (*1*, p. 233).

The great importance of manioc and gari in eastern Nigeria is also a fairly recent development. Older people in that region still regard manioc as an inferior food, lacking the prestige of yams, the traditional staple. But with the growth of population density, decline in soil fertility, and the loosening of older dietary preferences, manioc has come to be more important than yams throughout a large part of the Eastern Region. As noted in Chapter 5, the ability of manioc to produce a fair crop on very poor soils is an important element in its competitive position; and there are many districts throughout West Africa where it has expanded in recent decades because of this quality. Jones also points out that the "growth of cities and of a class of single men working in them also stimulated gari consumption, for it is one of the easiest foods to prepare, being edible when mixed with hot or cold water, or even when dry" (17, p. 110). And closely related to this influence of urbanization has been the way in which migrants have introduced manioc and gari into new areas.

Finally, a word about the recent expansion of manioc in the millet-sorghum belt. Jones states that in Nigeria, manioc probably entered the area north of the Niger and Benue rivers after World War I, but its spread has been fairly rapid owing to its ability to resist drought and to the influence of Ibos migrating from the Eastern Region. In the French territories, it has been official policy in recent years to promote the cultivation of manioc in savanna areas because of its resistance to grasshopper attacks and its value as a famine reserve crop. Reference has already been made to the vigorous campaign for distributing manioc cuttings in Niger territory and the remarkable increase in production during the past 10 or 15 years (2, p. 3075). Elsewhere in the interior territories of French West Africa and in the north of the French Cameroons, a similar policy of promoting the cultivation of manioc has been pursued.

The recent introduction of manioc in the savanna region of Ubangi-Shari in French Equatorial Africa has been described in some detail by R. Guillemin (12). As late as 1900 manioc was confined to the southern and western portions of the savannas of Ubangi; and sorghum, which had held undisputed sway a century ago, was still of substantial importance. But today manioc has become the dominant staple throughout this savanna region. In part this substitution of manioc for sorghum reflected the characteristics of manioc that often explain its strong competitive position—its drought resistance, the security provided from grasshopper attacks, and its ease of cultivation (12, p. 281). In this region, however, it seems that the rapid and almost total replacement of sorghum by manioc was also directly related to the compulsory cultivation of cotton enforced by the French to develop an export crop. The heavy labor requirements for cotton coincided exactly with the planting period for sorghum, which therefore suffered through being planted too early or too late (12, p. 299):

The result of this instability of the production of sorghum was not long in appearing and was the categorical abandonment, pure and simple, of the cereal. Thus, as a result of the introduction of an industrial plant, a traditional staple food disappeared and was replaced by manioc with all its drawbacks—nutritional, psychological, and agronomic.

Although sorghum has not altogether ceased to be cultivated, Guillemin asserts that it is cultivated only in a sporadic and limited way and exclusively for beer; and even that use is on the decline owing to increasing consumption of alcoholic beverages produced from manioc and plantains (12, p. 169).

In the drier climate of the Chad, northernmost territory of French Equatorial Africa, the introduction of manioc was still more recent and a good deal more limited in its impact on the traditional agriculture. M. Gaide has given the following account of the recent spread of manioc in that savanna region (7, p. 724):

In Chad, before 1930, manioc was a plant unknown to the local inhabitants . . .

In 1930, after a serious grasshopper attack which threatened the food economy of the territory which is based on the cultivation of millets and sorghums, manioc was introduced . . .

In 1940, the plant could be regarded as well established in the southern districts of the Territory among the Saras . . .

In subsequent years manioc continued to expand toward the north as a result of further administrative action to promote cultivation of the crop and because of the influence of Saras migrating to the north. At present, Gaide reports, manioc is no longer being encouraged by the French administration, but it continues to expand. He attributes this to its good price as a cash crop and to certain characteristics which have already been considered: its ability to return a fair crop in mediocre soils or soils exhausted by other crops; the light labor requirements; the good yields that may be obtained; and the fact that manioc is not vulnerable to the depredations of birds, often a major problem for grain crops.

AN EXAMPLE OF THE INFLUENCE OF "MICRO-FACTORS"— GENIERI VILLAGE, GAMBIA

Throughout this study it has been necessary to deal with influences of a general nature which bear on the distribution of the staple food crops. It seems certain, however, that under the conditions of small-scale, semisubsistence production prevailing in tropical Africa the choice of crops is often determined by strictly local considerations. The traditional attitudes within a locality as regards the appropriate crops to be grown, together with local food preferences, are, of course, extremely important as the proximate factors influencing the pattern of crops produced. In commenting on the uneven manner in which the cultivation of rice has been taken up in Chad

Territory in French Equatorial Africa, M. Gaide observes that an important factor seemed to be simply a matter of taste: "Certain of the millet eating people rapidly accepted a main dish made of rice whereas others would not accept it" (7, p. 728). It is probable, however, that over a long period these traditional attitudes have been heavily shaped by empirical knowledge of the suitability of various crops for the locality as determined primarily by the rainfall regime and soils.

In Miss Haswell's detailed description of the agricultural economy of Genieri village in the Gambia, based on a three-year field study (1947–49), we have an analysis of certain more specific local factors influencing the choice of crops grown (14). Owing to uncertain and poorly distributed rainfall of 30–50 inches a year, the staple food crops at Genieri are limited to early millet, fonio (*Digitaria exilis*), sorghum, maize (in the vicinity of the compounds), rice (on plots near the river), and late millet (planted in the same areas used for peanuts). The relative size of the areas planted to these crops varies a good deal from compound to compound. It appears that the sex composition of the labor force is one of the chief factors determining the relative areas planted to different crops—especially the extent to which swamp rice is grown as a chief food crop. Cultivation of peanuts and millet is a task performed by men, whereas the cultivation of food crops other than millet is almost entirely the work of women and girls. The influence of the number of able-bodied women in a compound and of the willingness of the men to lend a hand with the cultivation of rice is described by Miss Haswell in these terms (14, p. 9):

The choice of the women as a whole, and of individual compounds, seems to be determined mainly by size of the female labour force—in very small compounds where the work on rice production may be in the hands of one woman only, she will invariably concentrate more on upland rice and *Digitaria exilis* where she can obviate the long and tedious walk to the field; greater effort is made on the swamp in those cases where the men help out their womenfolk during the heavy transplanting period . . .—in one or two compounds they helped to carry headloads of seedlings to the swamp and with transplanting . . .

This appears to be a problem applying generally to the Gambia and perhaps to other areas as well. At a 1952 Conference of Protectorate Chiefs the Governor of Gambia, Sir Wyn Harris, urged the chiefs "to continually impress on your people that the belief that the production of rice is only a woman's crop is a thing of the past and that the men, particularly younger men, must realize that the production of essential foodstuffs of this territory is important—in fact is more important than planting of groundnuts" (8, p. 8).

The fundamental choice made by African farmers between food crops and industrial cash crops has been ignored in this study, which has focused on competition between the staple foods. In Genieri village, as in most areas, decisions vary a good deal between families and compounds regarding the relative areas planted to food crops and the cash crop—here peanuts. To some extent the planting of peanuts in Genieri is determined by the availability to a family of the "ochre-brown sandy soils" on which the peanut crop is mainly grown. But since the seasonal peak of labor requirements is the same for peanuts and late millet, also a "man's crop" and second only to swamp rice as a food crop in the village, an economic decision must be made in the priority to be given these crops. Owing to a scarcity of the "ochre-brown soils" best suited to peanuts, some of the crop is grown on the inferior "grey soils," and as a result the marginal return per hour of labor spent on peanuts is probably less than the average return. This complicates comparison of the relative returns from the two crops, but on the basis of an analysis of labor inputs and yields obtained, Miss Haswell is able to give a rough indication of the basis for allocating labor to peanuts and late millet respectively (14, p. 8):

No precise measurement is possible, but probably a fair conclusion is that, partly as a result of custom, and partly as a result of cash incentives to individuals, the men of Genieri, as a group, chose their crops and spent their time as if, in their minds about 550 lbs. of groundnuts [unshelled] were worth 100 lbs. of millet.

It is further pointed out, however, that the relative priority assigned to peanuts and to food crops by members of a particular compound seems to depend on their willingness to risk finding themselves in a position in which they must rely on relatives or cash purchases in order to have sufficient food to meet their needs for the year. As an illustration of this fact, Miss Haswell points out that one compound, made up of "descendants of founder-settlers with extensive kinship ties upon which to draw in times of extreme need, risked concentration on the commercial crop and neglected the food grain": eight times as large an area was planted to peanuts as to late millet (14, p. 8). In contrast, she notes that a small compound of newcomers to the village, which found it "imperative to be fairly self-reliant," did not push specialization in peanuts nearly so far.

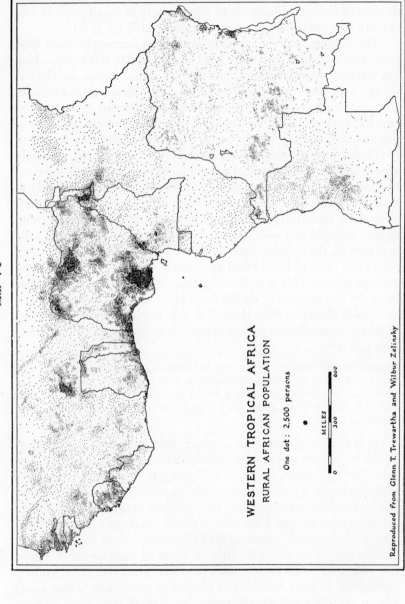

MAP 7-1

WESTERN TROPICAL AFRICA

RURAL AFRICAN POPULATION

One dot : 2,500 persons

MILES

0   300   600

Reproduced from Glenn T. Trewartha and Wilbur Zelinsky

RELATION TO POPULATION DISTRIBUTION

Factors influencing the distribution of population in tropical Africa are so numerous and so complex that it would be naïve to expect clear-cut correlations between relative density of population and the position of different staple food crops. The distribution of rural population in western tropical Africa is shown in Map 7-1, reproduced from a map prepared by Trewartha and Zelinsky (*29*, following p. 138). Various attempts to explain the distribution of population in tropical Africa are summarized in their study. After examining explanations which give primary emphasis to cultural, historical, or physical factors, they suggest that the most promising approach is to consider all of those factors "both as they react directly on population and as they affect one another, rather than any single-factor hypothesis" (*29*, p. 152).

Among the factors invoked to explain areas of particularly sparse population are slave raids and wars which may partially account for such relatively empty districts as Nigeria's "middle belt"; the presence in a particularly virulent form of tropical diseases, notably malaria or sleeping sickness; and water deficiencies in terms either of an annual deficiency or simply of a lack of usable surface or ground water during the dry season. Explanations of population concentrations are also diverse. Income from export crops, which permits purchase of supplementary foods, is mentioned as a key factor. Gourou, who has given particular attention to the distribution of population in the Belgian Congo, Ruanda-Urundi, and southern Nigeria, has stressed the primary importance of cultural differences among various tribal groups in their capacity to "organize space" (*10*, pp. 83–94; *9*, pp. 160–64). Most pertinent in this regard is, of course, superior skill in food production and in political organization. In a somewhat cryptic statement, Gourou suggests that the explanation of the high density of the Ibo population in parts of eastern Nigeria (in some areas as high as 700 per square mile, which is high indeed for tropical Africa) lies in "an elaborate use of the soil and long-standing peace, not with an advanced civilization" (*10*, p. 88). He believes that this density is recent and that it is unstable because it is leading to a shortening of the fallow period with consequent deterioration of the soil.

Several studies have been made of these areas of population concentration in southeastern Nigeria, and they throw light on what appears to be the most significant relationship between population density and the position of different staple food crops (21, 11). This relationship, which has already been referred to in stressing the ability of manioc to produce a tolerable crop on exhausted soils, is simply the tendency to rely increasingly on manioc as a major staple in areas where population density has led to shorter fallows and a loss of soil fertility. This relationship is evident in the 1951–52 report of the Department of Agriculture of the Western Region of Nigeria which noted that a "tendency toward declining acreage [for yams] is reported from some areas of relatively dense population, with a compensating expansion in the plantings of cassava" (22, p. 2). In a study of farming practice and population in southeastern Nigeria, Morgan points out that here also manioc production has expanded at the expense of yams, and one of the reasons cited is that manioc "is generally more productive on land with short fallows" (21, p. 331). But Morgan also stresses several other factors that have contributed to the expansion of manioc, and it is obviously difficult to assess the relative importance of different influences. As usual, the relatively low labor requirements for manioc are cited as favoring its competitive position: "Both men and women are on the whole devoting less time to farming and therefore tending to concentrate more on cassava since it is the easiest crop to plant and tend" (21, p. 331). The tendency for men to seek employment outside of agriculture has further contributed to the shift from yams to manioc because, in the areas studied by Morgan, yams are a "men's crop" and manioc is a "women's crop." Moreover, manioc is a "food of increasing popularity," the demand for which has been augmented by the trade in gari, which has undoubtedly increased considerably in recent decades.

W. O. Jones has also called attention to the way in which manioc has come to be of appreciable importance in certain parts of the Sudan region where population densities are relatively high. Thus in one production area near Saint Louis, manioc occupies some 12 per cent of the land in food crops. Manioc is also relatively important, for a Sudan region, in the southern part of Upper Volta where population density is relatively high (16). Striking examples of the sequence of population density, soil exhaustion, and a shift to manioc are provided by M. Gaide in his study of agriculture in the Chad Territory of French Equatorial Africa. In one of the areas he describes, the village of Mousgougou, the local people stated that they had been familiar with manioc for only 10 years, but half of the cultivated area was devoted to that crop. Gaide finds the extension of manioc under these conditions disturbing because of the manner in which it is grown without regard to any rotation and until the soil is completely exhausted. In concluding his discussion of the introduction of manioc in the Chad, he expresses this belief (7, p. 727):

its extension is now more of a danger than a blessing. The increase of population in the centers and the growing scarcity of good land for millets and sorghums will inevitably accelerate this extension. The systematic extension of manioc without regard to any rotation is certain to contribute to the disorganization of native agriculture.

Differences in population density are often associated with differences in the intensity of the farming practiced unrelated to the particular crops grown. Apart from the manioc relationship just noted, the only correlation of moment between population patterns and choice of staple crops concerns rice. The text accompanying the ethno-demographic maps of French West Africa prepared by Richard-Molard suggests the following relationship (15, pp. 2–3):

The valleys of the Gambia, of the Casamance, and of the "rivers to the south" are, it would seem, areas of population concentration only to the extent that their inhabitants are familiar with satisfactory techniques for utilizing the water, in particular the cultivation of irrigated rice.

It is pointed out that both in the Casamance district of Senegal and in Portuguese Guinea there are areas of relatively dense population, which are inhabited by rice cultivators; whereas nearby areas, with a similar physical environment but inhabited by tribal groups which do not cultivate rice, have a much lower concentration of population. A. T. Grove has suggested a different sort of relationship between rice and population density in his study of soil erosion and population problems in southeastern Nigeria. He expects that, as a result of mounting population pressure in the congested upland, people will be obliged to move to certain relatively sparsely populated riverine lowlands; and it is to be anticipated that rice will become more important as a consequence of this movement (11, p. 304).

Apart from these relationships for manioc and rice, the bearing of population density on the pattern of staple food crops does not appear to be highly significant. After exploring possible relationships of this nature in his monograph on population distribution in the Belgian Congo, Gourou concludes that there is no significant correlation between population density and the position of various staple food crops (9, pp. 160–64).

In calling attention to the area of population concentration on the Guinea Coast between Lagos and Accra and a lesser area in western Senegal, Trewartha and Zelinsky comment that "in areas of such low rainfall . . . it is difficult to understand how so many people can subsist on local resources" (29, p. 151). In the important concentration between Lagos and Accra, a large part of the explanation no doubt lies in the role of manioc and maize as the dominant staple crops throughout the drier portions of that area. Manioc's contribution under such conditions is readily apparent in the light of its high calorie yield per acre and its ability to resist drought. Presumably, maize is a productive crop in this area because early-maturing varieties can be grown during the "long" rainy season and quite often the "short" rains also suffice for maize with a short growth period, so that double-cropping is possible. It is also significant that despite the low annual rainfall, maize does not encounter the dry, hot air which is so unfavorable to its cultivation.

CITATIONS

1 A. Adandé, "Le Maïs et ses usages dans le Bas-Dahomey," Bull. Inst. Français Afr. Noire (Dakar), January 1953.

2 "Alimentation en Outre-mer. Niger," Marchés trop. du monde (Paris), Nov. 24, 1956.

3 Belg., Min. Col., Monographie des groupements Mumosho-Mugabo (par la Mission Anti-Erosive, 1952).

4 Mary Douglas, "The Lele of Kasai," in C. Daryll Forde, ed., African Worlds: Studies in the Cosmological Ideas and Social Values of African Peoples (Oxford, 1954).

5 C. Daryll Forde, "The Cultural Map of West Africa . . . ," Transactions of the N.Y. Acad. of Sciences, April 1955, Ser. II.

6 ———, Habitat, Economy, and Society (8th ed., London, 1950).

7 M. Gaide, "Au Tchad les transformations subies par l'agriculture traditionelle sous l'influence de la culture cotonnière," Agronomie trop. (France, Min. Outre-mer), Nov.–Dec. 1956 [Pts. I–IV in Sept.–Oct. 1956 issue].

8 Gambia, Summary of Proceedings of the Ninth Conference of Protectorate Chiefs Held at Georgetown, in the MacArthur Island Division, from the 19th to the 23rd February, 1952 (Sess. Paper 5/52, Bathhurst, 1952).

9 Pierre Gourou, La Densité de la population rurale au Congo Belge (Acad. Roy. des Sci. Col., Classe des Sci. Naturelles et Med., Mem. in 8°, Nouvelle sér. Tome I, fasc. 2, Brussels, 1955).

10 ———, The Tropical World . . . (London, 1953).

11 A. T. Grove, "Soil Erosion and Population Problems in South-East Nigeria," Geog. J., September 1951.

12 R. Guillemin, "Évolution de l'agriculture dans les savannes de l'Oubangui," Agronomie trop., Mar.–Apr. 1956 and May–June 1956.

13 Lord Hailey, An African Survey . . . (London, 1938).

14 M. R. Haswell, *Economics of Agriculture in a Savannah Village* (Gr. Brit., Col. Off., Col. Res. Studies 8, 1953).

15 Inst. Français d'Afrique Noire (IFAN), *Cartes ethno-démographiques de l'Afrique Occidentale, feuilles No. 1* (prepared by J. Richard-Molard, Dakar, 1952).

16 W. O. Jones, *Manioc in Africa* (to be published in 1959).

17 ———, "Manioc: An Example of Innovation in African Economies," *Econ. Devel. and Cultural Change* (Univ. Chicago), January 1957.

18 Phyllis M. Kaberry, *Women of the Grassfields* . . . (Gr. Brit., Col. Off., Col. Res. Pub. 14, 1952).

19 Jacques Miège, "Cultures vivrières en Afrique Occidentale . . . ," *Cahiers Outre-mer* (Bordeaux), Jan.–Mar. 1954.

20 A. Moeller, *Les Grandes lignes des migrations des Bantous de la Province Orientale du Congo Belge* (Inst. Roy. Col. Belg., Sec. des Sci. Morales et Politiques, Mem. Coll. in 8°, Tome VI, Brussels, 1936).

21 W. B. Morgan, "Farming Practice, Settlement Pattern and Population Density in South-Eastern Nigeria," *Geog. J.*, September 1955.

22 Nigeria, Dept. Agr., *Annual Report . . . Western Region, 1951–52* (Ibadan, 1954).

23 P. H. Nye, "Studies on the Fertility of Gold Coast Soils: Part III. The Phosphate Status of the Soils," *Emp. J. Exp. Agr.* (London), January 1952.

24 S. D. Onabamiro, *Food and Health* (London, 1953).

25 Roland Portères, "Vieilles agricultures de l'Afrique intertropicale," *Agronomie trop.*, Sept.–Oct. 1950.

26 B. R. P. Tanghe, "Histoire générale des migrations des peuples de l'Oubangui," *Congo: Rev. gen. de la Col. Belge* (Brussels), November 1938.

27 R. P. Ch. Tisserant, "Agriculture dans les savanes de l'Oubangui," *Bull. Inst. d'Études Centrafricaines* (Brazzaville/Paris), New Ser. 6, 1953.

28 E. Torday and T. A. Joyce, *Notes ethnographiques sur les peuples communément appelés Bakuba, ainsi que sur les peuplades apparentées.—Les Bushongo* (Belg., Min. Col., Ann. Musée du Congo Belge, Ethn., Anth.—Ser. III: Doc. ethn. concernant les populations du Congo Belge), Tome II, Fasc. 1, February 1911.

29 G. T. Trewartha and Wilbur Zelinsky, "Population Patterns in Tropical Africa," *Ann. Assn. Am. Geog.*, June 1954.

30 Edmond Verhulpen, *Baluba et Balubaïsés du Katanga* (Antwerp, 1936).

31 H. Vine, *Notes on the Main Types of Nigerian Soils* (Nigeria, Agr. Dept. Special Bull. 5, Lagos, 1953).

CHAPTER 8

THE PLACE OF THE STAPLE FOODS IN AFRICAN DIETS

The purpose of this Chapter is to indicate briefly how the staple foods figure in African diets—the typical ways in which they are prepared and how they are combined with other foods. Attention will also be drawn to the marked seasonal variations which characterize food consumption in tropical Africa.

TYPICAL METHODS OF PREPARATION

Techniques of preparation vary a good deal with different ethnic groups and localities.[1] Certain general features, however, are broadly similar throughout tropical Africa. The exaggeration is not great when a British resident of Kenya, visiting the Gambia, speaks of an African woman cooking "in the rounded black pot that caters to hunger from one side of Africa to the other; and in the pot simmered that stodgy, spiced, glutinous porridge that fills every belly from the Nile to the Zambezi" (17, p. 10).

Most commonly the staple foods, especially if the staple is a cereal, are pounded into a meal or flour by the housewife before cooking. With the cereals this is done either with pestle and mortar or with grinding stone. Plantains and yams are sliced and dried in the sun before being pounded into a meal. They are often soaked and sometimes boiled before drying. Manioc flour is prepared in the same way, while the preparation of manioc meal or gari, described in Chapter 2, differs mainly in that the manioc is grated and the drying process includes draining and drying in the sun followed by drying over a slow fire. Alternatively, the roots and tubers, and also maize,

---

[1] More detailed descriptions of common dishes and methods of preparation are given in: Léon Pales, *L'Alimentation en A.O.F.* . . . (ORANA, Dakar, 1954) ; W. R. Bascom, "Yoruba Food," *Africa* (Internatl. Afr. Inst., Oxford), January 1951, pp. 41–53 and Bascom, "Yoruba Cooking," *ibid.*, April 1951, pp. 125–37; Gold Coast Govt. (?), *Gold Coast Nutrition and Cookery* (Edinburgh, 1953) ; J. A. Mars and E. M. Tooley, *The Kudeti Book of Yoruba Cookery* (7th ed., Lagos, 1948) ; G. Plummer, *The Ibo Cookery Book* (Port Harcourt, n.d.) ; A. Adandé, "Le Maïs et ses usages dans le Bas-Dahomey," *Bull. Inst. Français Afr. Noire* (Dakar), January 1953, pp. 220–82; Faye W. Grant, "Nutrition and Health of Gold Coast Children. I. Food in Four Communities," *J. Am. Dietetic Assn.*, July 1955, pp. 685–93.

may be converted to starch before being used for cooking. This is most common with manioc, which is processed by soaking peeled roots for about four days, and grating or beating the roots into a pulp which is placed in a sack or basket and allowed to drain for several days under the pressure of heavy stones. The pulp is then put in water once again, and after the starch settles, the water is removed.

The flour, meal, or starch obtained by these methods may be used in a variety of ways. But the three most common are for the preparation of a thin gruel, a thick porridge, or a doughy paste which Bascom (2, p. 128) prefers to describe as a "loaf." A gruel of corn-starch or other staple is the common breakfast dish of the Yoruba in western Nigeria, but it may also be consumed at other meals as a beverage with such dishes as yam fritters or mashed beans. More universal, however, is the preparation of a porridge by adding flour, meal, or starch to boiling water and cooking until smooth. Manioc meal (gari) is mixed with boiling water but is not cooked. These porridges may be eaten hot or cold, commonly hot at the evening meal and the residue finished cold the following day. Finally, various types of doughy pastes are made from flour or starch. Important examples are the *couscous*, round balls made from finely ground millet or sorghum flour, which are prominent in French West Africa, and the dough balls made of corn meal known as *kenkey*, a staple dish in Ghana.

With few exceptions, the porridges and starchy pastes are eaten with a highly seasoned sauce or "stew," and bits of the porridge or paste are dipped into this sauce. Ingredients of the sauce vary greatly from area to area and seasonally, depending on the availability of vegetables, meat or fish, and condiments. Peppers, melon seeds, and leaves of various sorts are common ingredients; certain leaves may also be added directly to the porridge to increase its bulk (34, p. 163). Palm oil is a standard ingredient of sauces in the humid regions, while in the savanna areas it may be replaced by shea butter, shea oil, or by a paste made of peanuts.

Although the root crops and plantains are often processed into a flour or meal, other techniques of preparation are also common. Yams, cocoyams, plantains, and "sweet" manioc are often simply sliced and boiled and then eaten alone or with a sauce. Alternatively, they may be mashed after boiling, perhaps with added seasoning of palm oil, peppers, and onions (2, p. 130).

A prevalent technique for preparing root crops involves softening the root or tuber by boiling or soaking, and then pounding or grating until a thick, doughy mass is obtained. When it has reached the desired consistency it is molded "into a large doughy loaf somewhat resembling an unbaked loaf of bread" (*2*, p. 132), or into round balls. The term *fufu* (or *foofoo*) is applied to various versions of these thick pastes. In Ghana the product known as fufu can be made of manioc, yam, plantain, or cocoyam (*11*, p. 80).[2] The *Kudeti Book of Yoruba Cookery* (*24*, pp. 28–29) and the *Ibo Cookery Book* (*41*, pp. 43–44) limit the term fufu to manioc starch or a porridge made of manioc starch, which is the same usage Bascom reports for the Yoruba groups (*2*, p. 132n). A food of considerable importance in the Belgian Congo and parts of French Equatorial Africa is the chickwangue, which is a kindred product. Chickwangues are usually made of manioc, but sometimes of plantain, soaked and pounded directly into a starchy paste, or of manioc flour, mixed with water to obtain a thick paste. The resulting doughy substance is wrapped in leaves, typically of the plantain, and steamed. Although sometimes described as a bread, the cooked chickwangue is more like a soft dumpling. The balls of corn meal dough known as kenkey in Ghana are frequently wrapped in corn husks and steamed.

Frying is another technique of cooking the staple foods, especially common in the forest areas where yams and palm oil are important. Yams and plantains may simply be peeled, sliced, and deep fried in palm oil; or they may be pounded or grated and mixed with pepper, salt, onion, possibly eggs, and moulded into balls and fried as "fritters." The *Ibo Cookery Book's* recipe for "cassava cake" is similar except that the manioc is grated and allowed to drain in the sun for two days before being made into balls for frying. Millet flour or corn meal is commonly made into dough balls and fried. In rural areas, market stalls selling these fried balls—often known by the French terms, *beignet* or *galette*—perform the role of restaurants. A Ghana recipe for "corn dough cakes" calls for a mixture of maize and plantain; and the versatile gari may also be made into dough balls for frying (*11*, pp. 138–39).

Although maize is typically prepared according to the various techniques outlined above, roasted corn on the cob is also a popular dish. Rice is sometimes made into a flour or meal and cooked as a doughy paste to make a "loaf," in Bascom's terminology, or allowed to rise before cooking in order to make "rice kenkey" (*11*, p. 97). More common, however, is the conventional preparation of rice by

---

[2] With respect to cocoyams it appears that only the *Xanthosoma* variety is used for fufu (*46*, p. 201).

boiling or steaming rice kernels which have been hulled and skinned but not ground into flour or meal.

Considerable quantities of the starchy staple foods are made into beer, especially at times when grain is abundant. Certain varieties of millet are usually favored for this purpose. But maize and sorghum are also used for beer; and large quantities of certain varieties of plantain, referred to in the Belgian Congo as "plantains à bière," are made into a thick beer which is literally a staple food in certain districts. In a most interesting discussion of the role of beer and other alcoholic beverages in Africa, Professor B. S. Platt concludes that the loss of energy resulting from the conversion of grain to beer is probably fairly small. And he suggests that there is probably some nutritional benefit from the "biological ennoblement" associated with the brewing process as a result of the products of germination and the ascorbic acid, B-vitamins, and microbial proteins derived from fermentation (*40*, p. 121).

THE STARCHY STAPLES IN RELATION TO OTHER FOODS

It has been suggested earlier that in the savanna areas the starchy staples contribute something like 85 per cent of the calorie intake, while in the forest regions, where palm oil is also a cheap source of calories, the starchy staples still account for as much as 60–80 per cent of total food calories. Valuable evidence with regard to the relative importance of various foodstuffs is provided by B. M. Nicol's dietary surveys of selected population groups in Nigeria. In his first survey in Niger Province of northern Nigeria he selected at random three families in each of three hamlets. "All food eaten by the adult occupants of the nine compounds was weighed and measured in detail for four periods of 7 days each, between March 1947 and March 1948, the periods being distributed throughout the year in accordance with the expected seasonal variation in availability of the staple foodstuffs" (*29*, p. 26). Efforts were also made to take account of all food eaten outside the compounds. Nicol made a similar survey in 1949/50 in swamp and high forest areas of Warri Province in southern Nigeria (*30*). Table 8-1 shows the percentage of total food calories contributed by all items any of which accounted for as much as 0.5 per cent of the total in any district. Thus beef is shown because it provided 6.5 per cent of the average calorie intake of the relatively prosperous Warri traders of southern Nigeria although in Bida, the group with the next highest consumption of beef, it accounted for only about 0.1 per cent.

TABLE 8-1.—CALORIE CONTRIBUTION OF SELECTED FOODSTUFFS AS PER CENT OF TOTAL, BASED ON A SURVEY OF ADULTS IN SIX DISTRICTS OF NORTHERN AND SOUTHERN NIGERIA*

| | Northern farmers (Niger Province) | | | Southern farmers (Warri Province) | | |
Food item	Bida	Konta-gora	Zuru	Warri traders	Illu farmers	Soragbemi fishermen
Average daily calorie	*Per cent of total calorie intake*					
intake[a]	2,639	2,431	2,947	3,003	2,252	2,191
Cereals and products						
Guinea corn	56.5	74.4	90.4	—	—	—
Bulrush millet	17.0	11.3	2.7	—	—	—
Maize						
Grain (mature)	—	5.7	—	3.8	2.3	5.5
Starch	.7	—	—	—	—	—
Cob (immature)	.1	.2	.4	.3	.2	—
Rice						
Home pounded	[b]	[b]	—			
Milled	—	—	—	9.5	—	—
Wheat flour	—	—	—	8.8	—	—
Subtotal	(74.3)	(91.6)	(93.5)	(22.4)	(2.5)	(5.5)
Roots and tubers						
Manioc						
Meal	—	—	—	12.3	19.3	31.6
Starch	—	—	—	12.7	25.5	17.2
Fufu	—	—	—	—	3.5	—
Fresh	.7	.3	.2	—	—	5.5
Yams	.3	—	[b]	10.8	27.2	3.4
Cocoyams	—	[b]	[b]	—	—	.6
Sweet potatoes	7.2	.7	—	—	—	1.2
Subtotal	(8.2)	(1.0)	(0.2)	(35.8)	(75.5)	(59.5)
Cereals and roots subtotal .	(82.5)	(92.6)	(93.7)	(58.2)	(78.0)	(65.0)
Bananas	—	—	—	.8	—	—
Plantains	—	—	—	.6	.6	.7
Red palm oil	7.2	—	—	11.6	13.5	13.1
Shea-nut oil	—	.7	.3	—	—	—
Shea butter	—	.2	—	—	—	—
Cow peas	3.0	1.5	1.4	1.5	1.6	—
Groundnuts	.4	—	—	.8	.5	—
Bambara nuts	.3	.1	—	—	—	—
Peppers						
Red	[b]	[b]	[b]	.3	.6	.6
Green	—	—	—	.1	[b]	[b]
Avocado				1.9	—	—
Beef	.1	.1	—	6.5	—	—
Mutton	.1	—	—	.6	—	—
Pork, fat	—	—	—	3.4	—	—
Eggs	—	—	—	.6	—	—

TABLE 8-1 (*Continued*)

Food item	Northern farmers (Niger Province)			Southern farmers (Warri Province)		
	Bida	Konta-gora	Zuru	Warri traders	Illu farmers	Soragbemi fishermen
Milk						
Fresh	.1		.3	—	—	—
Condensed	—	—		.6	—	—
Evaporated	—	—		1.4	—	—
Butter	—	.6		—	—	—
Margarine				1.4	—	—
Sugar cane stem	—	—	.1	.5	.1	.1
Fish						
Fresh	—	—	—	2.1	.7	8.5
Dried	.8	.1	.1	2.7	2.1	11.5
Monkey, dried				—	.8	
Pumpkin seed	—	—	—	.6	.3	—
Jams, imported				.7	—	—
Baobab leaf	.4	.7	1.4			
Shea-nut husk	—	.6	.4			
Mango	4.0	1.8	.9	.4	.1	—
Kaffir potato	—	—	.5	—	—	—
Locust bean cake	.7	.3	.1	—	—	—

* Data from B. M. Nicol, "Nutrition of Nigerian Peasant Farmers . . ." and "The Nutrition of Nigerian Peasants . . . ," *Brit. J. Nutr.* (London), Vol. 3, No. 1, 1949, pp. 25–43 and Vol. 6, No. 1, 1952, pp. 34–55. On the basis of information provided by Dr. Nicol, the figure for bulrush millet in Kontagora has been changed to 75 grams and the figure of 29 grams of yellow maize for Illu farmers has been changed to 15 grams and the reverse change made for the Soragbemi fishermen.

a Totals as given by Nicol. The FRI calorie calculations on which this percentage breakdown is based give a total about 200 calories lower for the Warri trader group and nearly 350 calories lower for the Soragbemi fishermen. A report issued by the Applied Nutrition Unit gives calorie figures of 2,360 for the Illu farmers and 2,660 for the Soragbemi fishermen which are based on Nicol's data but which include alcohol (London Sch. of Hygiene and Trop. Med., Applied Nutr. Unit, *Nutrition in Nigeria*, London, 1954, mimeo., p. 16).

b Less than .05 per cent.

The striking features of the patterns of food consumption portrayed in Table 8-1 are the great importance of the starchy cereals and roots and tubers, and the contrast between the north, where cereals are all-important, and the south, where root crops are dominant and cereals are negligible except for the Warri traders who buy appreciable quantities of wheat flour and milled rice. The Warri traders are also exceptional for their consumption of condensed and evaporated milk, margarine, and pork, items which do not figure in the diets of any other group. While these features of the traders' diet are a consequence of their higher purchasing power, differences among the other groups are related chiefly to climate, custom, and the localized production of particular foodstuffs. Lying toward the southern limit of the millet-sorghum area, Bida at 9° N is in a Guinea savanna region where oil palms are cultivated along stream banks, whereas Kontagora and Zuru lie farther north (about 10° 20′ N and 11° 20′ N) beyond the limits of oil palm cultivation. Accordingly, palm oil is not consumed in the two northern areas but accounts for seven per cent of total calories in Bida. For the three southern groups, which lie at about 5° 30′ N, palm oil provided from 11½ to 13½ per cent of the calorie intake.

Also noteworthy is the low consumption of meat and fish by all groups other than the Soragbemi fishermen and the Warri traders, the former with an average intake of 68 grams of animal protein per person per day and the latter with 50 grams of animal protein out of a total protein intake of 84 grams. Owing mainly to relatively high consumption of fresh and dried fish (18 grams per day of each) and about the same amount of dried monkey, animal protein accounted for 17 grams of a total protein intake by the Illu farmers amounting to 43 grams. Beef, mutton, goat, rat and snake meat, and dried fish were all consumed by one or more of the northern groups but in quantities so minute that the average intake of animal protein for the Bida, Kontagora, and Zuru farmers was only 5, 1, and 2 grams respectively. Total protein for these groups was, however, fairly high—75, 73, and 89 grams respectively—because of the large quantities of sorghum and millet consumed (30, p. 40). Although rating low in comparison with high-protein foods such as meat or legumes, the 10 or 11 per cent protein content of Guinea corn and bulrush millet is considerably above the protein values of only 1 or 2 per cent for manioc and yams.

The groups studied by Nicol in the Northern and Eastern regions of Nigeria are of course not certainly representative of all similar climatic zones of West Africa. That wide geographical variation in the chief staple is common has already been suggested; and the seasonal variation in the staple foods of the diet is considered below. But it appears that these two groups well illustrate certain basic features of the role of staple foods throughout western tropical Africa. The overwhelming importance of starchy staples—cereals, roots, or plantains—and the small importance of animal products revealed in these surveys is stressed by many writers. Jean Adam, speaking of French West Africa, states that meat consumption is scarcely one kilogram per year per person in the lower Ivory Coast and lower Dahomey, ranges from 3 to 5 kgs per year in much of Senegal and French Sudan, from 5 to 8 kgs in French Guinea, but exceeds 20 kgs in Mauritania and the northern Sudan where nomadic cattle raising is prevalent (*1*, p. 28). Even the highest figure is not much more than one-fourth of the per capita meat consumption in the United States.

As would be expected, consumption of meat and dairy products is considerably higher among the pastoral peoples than for the people generally; and while the pastoralists are by no means numerous, they are widely scattered through the savanna regions of West Africa. Diets among cultivators living in areas where pastoralists are relatively numerous are also likely to contain above-average quantities of animal products; Nicol apparently attributes the rather good physical development and nutritional status of peasants of Bornu Province in a wide area around Lake Chad to this factor (*31*, p. 6). But the dependence of the pastoralists on animal products is not nearly as complete as some statements suggest. Léon Pales has noted that agriculture and stock raising are generally quite distinct, being carried on by groups of different ethnic origin, but he also stresses that these groups are generally "living in symbiosis" (*34*, p. 102). Consequently the exchange relationships existing between these groups provide the pastoral peoples with significant quantities of millets, sorghums, or other staples by barter of their milk products or as payment for the manure deposited by their herds. Furthermore, there is a tendency, according to Labouret, for the Fulani (Peul) pastoralists to evolve toward a more sedentary agriculture (*20*, pp. 25–26).

The extensive study of food in French West Africa by the "Mission Anthropologique"[3] offers much useful information about African diets and also underscores in a general way the key importance of the starchy staples. Unfortunately, however, the published summaries of the quantitative surveys do not give a breakdown by commodity. There is a breakdown into several categories according to the total calories consumed (e.g., the number in the sample consuming 1,000– 1,999 calories, 2,000–2,999 calories, and so on) and the per cent of total calories consumed as protein, fat, or carbohydrate. The ratios for calcium/phosphorus and vitamin B/carbohydrate are also given, but little quantitative information appears for individual foodstuffs. At the village of Dialokoro in the French Sudan, the observers saw no meat or fish in the meals eaten by the village farmers although some cattle, goats, and poultry were kept—evidently almost entirely for sale (*34*, p. 163).

Surveys carried out in recent years provide quantitative informa-

[3] The group has been renamed the Organisation de Recherches sur l'Alimentation et la Nutrition Africaines (ORANA).

tion on food consumption, by commodity as well as in terms of calories and nutrients, for three additional territories under French administration: a sample drawn from nine villages of the Bongouanou subdivision, Dimbokro *cercle*, in the forest zone of the Ivory Coast; at Attitogon village, which lies some 35 miles northeast of Lomé in French Togo; and at Evodoula village, located in the forest zone about 40 miles northwest of Yaoundé in the French Cameroons (*18, 36, 37, 38*, and *26*). The investigations in the Ivory Coast and French Togo reveal the usual preponderance of starchy staples as a source of calories, but the data for the French Cameroons show an appreciably lower percentage of calories derived from roots and cereals.

Diets in the Ivory Coast villages were dominated by root crops and plantains. The daily average per capita consumption in calories and as a percentage of total calorie intake were (*18*, p. 84):

Food	Calories	Per cent of total calories
Yams	1,065	49.5
Plantains	573	26.6
Cocoyams	117	5.4
Manioc	11	0.5
Total	1,766	82.0

Whereas the calorie intake from these crops represented over 80 per cent of the estimated intake of 2,153 calories per person per day, cereals, mainly maize and rice, accounted for only about 3 per cent of the total. At Attitogon village in French Togo, maize and manioc were dominant. Their relative importance changed considerably through the year because of the seasonal variation in maize supplies, but in none of the survey periods did their combined contribution represent less than 80 per cent of the estimated total intake of 2,087 calories (*38*, pp. 6 and 22):

Food	Per cent of total calories		
	May	September	January
Maize	21.0	35.5	45.5
Manioc	59.5	51.8	37.5
Total	80.5	87.3	83.0

Manioc, cocoyams, and plantains are the major staples in the Cameroon diets studied in the village of Evodoula. But the relative importance of starchy staples is not so great as in other areas studied. Nearly as many calories were obtained from palm oil as from manioc, the

leading staple, and the calorie contribution of peanuts was also high
(*27*, Table XXV):

Food	Per cent of total calories
Manioc	16.4
Cocoyams	14.0
Plantains	10.1
Subtotal	40.5
Palm oil	14.2
Peanuts	10.2

These five items thus accounted for some 65 per cent of the estimated
intake of 1,634 calories per person per day. The remaining calories
were widely distributed, with the small contribution of cereals being
less than the calories obtained from fruits, leaves, and green vegetables. Although the consumption of palm oil in this Cameroon village
was much higher than shown in the Ivory Coast and Togo surveys, it
is similar to the intake reported by Nicol for the forest region of
Nigeria. The intake of peanuts, seems very high by comparison with
the data for the Ivory Coast, French Togo, and Nigeria; but the reported consumption of approximately 35 grams per day is less than
the 50 grams estimated by Drachoussoff for the Bas-Congo and is not
greatly above the 20 grams per day estimated for the city of Douala
(*25*, p. 5).

A study carried out some 20 miles north of Accra in Ghana provides another example of the great importance of root crops, plantains, and palm oil in such a coastal area. The estimates of quantities
of these items consumed during 1952/53 correspond to the following
breakdown in calories per day (*12*, p. 10):

Manioc	645
Other roots (mostly cocoyams)	330
Maize	80
Plantains	312
Palm fruit	420
Other items listed	33
Total from starchy staples and palm fruit	1,820

The estimated annual consumption of other foods, which are lumped
together in a category of "miscellaneous crops," amounts to a little
over 2,000 tons against 25,000 tons for the crops tabulated above.
Hence, it seems unlikely that these other foods contributed more than
another 100–200 calories. On this assumption, it would appear that

the roots accounted for about half of the total calorie intake, plantains for another 15 per cent, and palm products for 20 per cent.

A similar pattern is suggested for Liberia. In reporting on observations in the Western, Central, and Eastern provinces of Liberia, an American nutritionist cites several meals said to be typical of many mission schools and also indicative of Liberian diets generally (19, pp. 13–14). These menus featured either manioc, cocoyams, or plantain as the noon meal and rice or some type of soup as staples for the evening meal. The noon meal was served with a sauce made of palm oil, chopped greens, and a little chopped meat or fish, and it seems that the boiled rice is commonly served with a little palm oil.

Valuable information concerning diets in another region of Nigeria is provided by the economic survey of the cocoa farmers of the Western Region. The detailed analysis of diets was carried out by Miss M. W. Grant of the Applied Nutrition Unit in the London School of Hygiene and Tropical Medicine on the basis of consumption data collected during two-week periods in August and November 1951 and February and June 1952. The dietary pattern summarized in Table 8-2 is based on records for 33 families in four areas; and in

TABLE 8-2.—CALORIE CONTRIBUTION, AS PER CENT OF TOTAL, OF MAJOR FOOD GROUPS, IN FOUR DISTRICTS OF WESTERN NIGERIA, 1951/52*

Food group	Abeokuta	Ibadan	Ife-Ilesha	Ondo
Starchy roots and fruits	64.9	59.3	64.0	78.2
Cereals	5.1	7.8	2.6	2.1
Pulses and oil-seeds	2.4	7.0	4.5	1.5
Fresh fruits and vegetables ..	2.1	0.8	1.7	1.0
Meat and fish	9.7	3.7	4.7	2.8
Oil	13.1	18.3	20.7	12.8
Palm-wine and beer	2.7	3.1	1.8	1.2
Sugar	...	...	...	0.4

* R. Galletti, K. D. S. Baldwin and I. O. Dina, *Nigerian Cocoa Farmers* . . . (Nigeria Cocoa Mkt. Bd., London, 1956), p. 241.

addition to the small size of the sample caution is indicated because of the limited training of the recorders and the difficulties involved in obtaining accurate estimates of quantities consumed and, for some dishes, of assigning appropriate calorie values (9, pp. 234–37). Nevertheless the composition of the diets and the calorie-intake levels seem reasonable and are well worth examining. The percentage of total calories contributed by various food groups shown in Table 8-2 summarizes appendix tables for each area which show a breakdown by commodity and the nutrient composition of the diets for each of the four periods covered.

Perhaps the most striking feature of Table 8-2 is the resemblance of the diet pattern in the four areas to Nicol's data for groups in the Eastern Region of Nigeria as well as the reports on diet composition in other coastal areas of West Africa. In no area is the contribution of starchy roots and tubers less than about 60 per cent of the total calorie intake, and there is the usual indication of the importance of palm oil in a forest region. The contribution of meat and fish, however, is particularly high in Abeokuta and is higher in all four areas than for other groups studied (with the exception of the Warri traders). This no doubt reflects the relatively prosperous position of the cocoa farmers and is perhaps somewhat higher than usual since incomes were high during the survey year. Although maize accounted for the greater part of the cereal calories, its importance was understated as the survey periods all occurred when maize supplies were at seasonally low levels. Rice is shown as a little more important than maize in Ondo and Abeokuta provinces, but its contribution is only some 35–55 calories per person per day. More important are the differences in the starchy roots or tubers which are dominant in the different areas. Thus consumption of yams averaged only about 150 grams in Abeokuta, but nearly 850 grams in Ondo. Consumption of root crops and plantains was exceptionally high in Ondo; it showed the highest consumption of cocoyams and plantains — nearly 200 grams of each — as well as of yams. In Abeokuta, on the other hand, the recorded intake of manioc meal and flour was close to 400 grams, almost twice as high as in Ondo which had the lowest consumption of these products (9, pp. 237, 657–60).

Finally, we may consider three daily rations presented by Drachoussoff as typical of three localities in the Bas-Congo District of the Belgian Congo. These localities are some 75–100 miles south and slightly west of Leopoldville at about 5° S. The area, a little to the south of the Congo tropical rain forest, is classed as wooded savanna with the higher elevations fairly well covered with forest (7). Table 8-3 shows the consumption of various foodstuffs which Drachoussoff believes to be typical of the daily "ration" in these three localities and of the Bas-Congo on the basis of his observations and interviews, and the estimates of people familiar with the area.

These consumption patterns provide still another indication of the overwhelming importance of the starchy staples and the minor role

TABLE 8-3.—ESTIMATES OF TYPICAL DAILY CONSUMPTION OF FOODSTUFFS BY
A NORMAL ADULT MALE IN SELECTED AREAS OF THE BAS-CONGO
DISTRICT, BELGIAN CONGO*

Foodstuff	Bangu (Lombo)		Bangu (Sanga)		Inkisi	
	Calories	% of total calories	Calories	% of total calories	Calories	% of total calories
Manioc:						
Flour	368	13.6	736	26.3	920	33.0
Chickwangues ..	820	30.2	984	35.1	984	35.4
Fresh	63	2.3	63	2.2	126	4.5
Subtotal	1,251	46.1	1,783	63.6	2,030	72.9
Bananas/plantains.	47	1.7	47	1.7	24	.9
Maize	74	2.7	74	2.6	74	2.7
Rice	—	—	69	2.5	—	—
Meat or fish	6	.2	6	.2	12	.4
Peanuts	274	10.1	274	9.8	274	9.8
Beans (dried)	684	25.2	171	6.1	34	1.2
Palm oil	180	6.6	180	6.4	135	4.9
Other^a	200	7.4	200	7.1	200	7.2
Total	2,716	100.0	2,804	100.0	2,783	100.0

* Data from V. Drachoussoff, *Essai sur l'agriculture indigène au Bas-Congo* (Brussels, 1947), pp. 80–81.

ᵃ An arbitrary amount has been added to cover other items such as fruit, vegetables, and melons. The figure of 200 calories was chosen because Drachoussoff's estimates are based on a normal male adult believed to require about 2,800 calories per day.

of meat and fish. The consumption of beans in the Lombo area of Bangu stands out, production for both local consumption and sale being highly developed and resulting in an exceptionally high level of consumption. Likewise the consumption of peanuts, placed by Drachoussoff at 50 grams per day in all three localities, is conspicuously high in comparison, for example, with Nicol's data for Nigeria. Conversely, the figure given for palm oil seems low in comparison with the estimates for districts of the French Cameroons, Nigeria, and Ghana where the oil palm is found.

All estimates of food consumption in rural areas in Africa are likely to understate the importance of various fruits, vegetables, minor root crops, and other items growing more or less wild and gathered rather than cultivated. Pales stresses this point in declaring that from the native's point of view ". . . *the products of collecting (la cuillette)—animals, vegetables and fruits—do not count* [italics his]. It is significant that fruits were not mentioned in any of our African investigations" (*34*, p. 163). With regard to fruit, however, ignorance or traditional taboos may significantly limit consumption in some areas. Speaking of this factor in relation to the food resources of West Africa, S. D. Onabamiro asserts (*33*, p. 31):

For this reason, even though these fruits grow profusely and are easily accessible to both the rich and poor, people have seldom taken them, except in the last decade or so when the fruit-eating habit has begun to gain ground in the larger towns. In the smaller towns and villages in the hinterland, where boys have to work with their parents on the farm from early years, and are expected to grow up tough and hard-working, the eating of an orange or a banana is still strongly frowned upon as unworthy of a *man* [italics his].

A final point is that the starchy staples are of dominant importance in the diets of infants and children as well as adults. After describing typical infant feeding practices in the Belgian Congo, Nigeria, the Gold Coast, and French West Africa, Brock and Autret state that "the general habit of most parts of tropical Africa is to give young children the portions of the food prepared for adults which seem to be the most digestible and which require least mastication" (*5*, pp. 41–43). Thus in the Kasai District of the Belgian Congo infants from three months "are literally stuffed with manioc flour, in the form of fermented paste of 'luku' " (*5*, p. 41). In Kwango infants receive manioc and plantain, supplemented occasionally by small quantities of beans, fish, or mango but never by meat or by milk, except that obtained at the breast. Children two years old, examined in Accra, had been fed on maize gruels, and in Nigeria infants typically received gruels made of manioc, yams, or plantain. According to Mme Comhaire, gruels made of manioc flour or a fine corn flour are the staple foods of infants in the large native ward of Leopoldville that she studied (*6*, p. 41).

SEASONAL CYCLES IN FOOD CONSUMPTION

A final factor requiring special mention in describing the place of staple foods in African diets is the strongly marked seasonal pattern of food consumption. The most striking feature of the seasonal cycle is the preharvest shortage period (*soudure*); it is especially pronounced in the savanna regions occupying such huge areas in the northern belt of French West and Equatorial Africa, and in the northern regions of Nigeria and Ghana. Here the combination of insufficient production and storage of grain, perhaps heavy consumption and considerable use of grain for beer in the period of abundance following the harvest, and a long dry season and irregular timing of

rainfall, commonly results in a period of acute shortage just before
the harvest of the new crop.

Preharvest hunger.—In their study of food in French West Africa,
Léon Pales and the "Mission Anthropologique" pay much attention
to seasonal changes in the composition of the diets studied and to the
prevalence of seasonal hunger.[4] Several of the villages they studied
were experiencing preharvest shortage at the time the consumption
surveys were made. In the village of Dialakoro, in French Sudan, the
shortage was acute when the survey was made in August 1946. The
storage bins for grain were empty, or nearly so, and the observed
calorie intake of the 64 families surveyed was only 802 calories per
person per day. With the depletion of stocks of the principal cereal,
millet, many families were relying on fonio and sweet potatoes, while
some with a little millet were stretching out their stock by winnowing
their grain so sparingly that at times they were eating pure bran.

Several villages located on the plateau of the Futa Jallon were
studied during the early phase of a preharvest shortage period. A
small sample in three villages (Labe, Pita, and Telimele) indicated
an average daily intake of 1,412 calories; a somewhat larger sample
in the village of Dalaba showed an average of 1,952 calories (*34*,
pp. 171–72). It is pointed out that in all these cases the meals, as
measured by the investigators, were supplemented by items gathered
from the brush, including certain poisonous roots which are not always rendered safe by the preliminary washing and maceration.

The situation is less grave [the report observes] than one would suppose relying only on an examination of the family meals. . . . The gathering of insects (termites, locusts, crickets), hunting of small rodents and the trapping
of all sizes of birds, will help to sustain both large and small in the work in
the fields or the tending of the herds. But it will come to pass also that certain
roots of the famine period (*Pouri dané, Pouri balé*) will poison and kill (*34*,
p. 173).

So general is this problem of seasonal shortage in the areas studied
by the "Mission Anthropologique" that their report suggests at one
point that a study of native diets might be oriented around three questions (*34*, p. 102):

1. What are the staple and secondary foodstuffs?
2. What are the foodstuffs of the preharvest period (*soudure*)?
3. What are the foodstuffs of a famine period (*disette*)?

---

[4] Henri Labouret also gives a brief but very interesting account of "the seasonal
rhythm of the food supply" (*21*, pp. 186–91).

The report also presents a schematic diagram, reproduced here as Chart 8-1, giving the Mission's impression of the wide swings that

CHART 8-1.—SCHEMATIC APPROXIMATION OF SEASONAL PATTERN OF FOOD INTAKE, RURAL AND URBAN WORKERS, FRENCH WEST AFRICA*
(*Calories per person per day*)

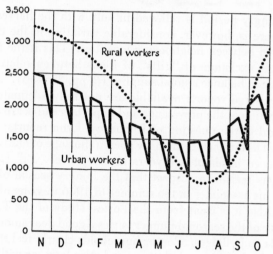

* Adapted from Léon Pales, *L'Alimentation en A.O.F.* . . . . (ORANA, Dakar, 1954), p.71.

characterize the calorie intake of farm villages and the smaller, but marked variations attributed to urban diets as well. The sawtooth effect in the curve for urban workers reflects the Mission's view that food consumption in the cities is relatively high early in the month shortly after wage payments have been made and then falls off appreciably toward the end of the month.

M. and S. L. Fortes and C. W. Lynn have given valuable descriptions of the food economy of Mamprusi District in the extreme northeastern corner of the Gold Coast (*8, 22*). A calendar of the hungry season as reported by the Fortes for 1934, described by the local people as "a fair year," provides a graphic and concise picture (*8*, pp. 252, 254–55).

May

Poorer households suffer two or three days' hunger a week, living on vegetable soup, groundnuts and wild fruits. Householders send their wives abroad to purchase grain for re-sale if they have money. Many selling livestock bit by bit to buy grain in market. Prices of all commodities rising.

June

Peak of "hunger" reached. Granaries empty among poorer households. Much live stock sold or bartered for grain very cheaply; grain scarce and dear. . . . Towards the end of the month many people are staunching their hunger by cutting the ripe or half ripe heads of early millet which they roast on the embers and nibble at.

The hungry period is relieved in July with the harvest of early millet. There is, however, considerable variation in the time of the harvest even between neighboring localities. This is the basis for a considerable exchange of "gifts" of foods between relatives, which helps a little to balance annual supplies (8, pp. 255–56).

The scattered reports available are not fully adequate to give a clear indication of the prevalence and importance of seasonal hunger. With regard to the question of frequency, Lynn reports: "Enquiry showed that as far back as memory goes, a shortage of cultivated foods is experienced in about two years in every five . . ." (22, p. 34). There seems reason to suspect that the hungry season observed by Pales and his associates in the summer of 1946 was one of particular severity. Also it is clear from the Fortes' study of the Tallensi that the severity of the seasonal hunger varies a good deal among different households and villages. Poorer households clearly feel the shortage more acutely than those with more or better land, or with money or cattle to exchange for supplementary food. Also it appears that there are areas "rich in grain," as the Fortes describe Nabte or Mampuru land, the areas two or three days' foot-journey away, where the Tallensi wives go to purchase grain. On the other hand, the Nakansa and Builsa peoples "come to Taleland to seek a few days work (for payment in food), since their settlements are in a worse plight than those of the Tale" (8, pp. 246, 255n).

The evidence seems to suggest pretty clearly that the phenomenon of seasonal hunger occurs widely in the Sudan region of West Africa; and that its occurrence in an acute way is more commonly a matter of, say, two years out of five, as reported for North Mamprusi, rather than an annual event.

M. K. Bennett has expressed the view that perhaps seasonal hunger is simply a characteristic feature of diets among "peasant population groups who are accustomed to more or less seasonal irregularity of food intake—who, in short, eat heavily and gain weight after harvest, and as stored stocks dwindle, eat progressively less and become thin" (4, p. 203). Mme Comhaire's description of the experience of a Congolese youth newly arrived in Leopoldville seems to indicate that a condition of alternating periods of abundance and extreme shortage is preferred to a situation in which food intake is continuously at a restricted level owing to a limited income and the competing requirements for rent and clothing.

After three months [Mme Comhaire reports] he had learned how to manage to eat just enough to be able to go on, not enough to get rid of that hungry feeling that never left him. He was quite unhappy about his food situation till he found another boy who got him into an association. They were four in all who agreed to pool their resources; each week one of them got the four wages and rations and had a good time. From then on, my boy was adapted to life in town: in "his" week he had fresh fish, meat and spinach for which he was craving and though he might starve for the next three weeks, he had something to remember and something to expect (*6*, p. 56).

Bennett suggests that if, indeed, the seasonal variations in consumption are simply an accepted pattern, a mode of life that does not accord with western ideas, the preharvest shortage is scarcely to be regarded as a "food problem."

Most writers who have dealt with seasonal hunger in Africa take a more serious view. In particular, it is frequently stressed, as by Platt, that the shortage "occurs when extra physical effort is expended on getting the new season's crop in the ground" (*39*, p. 101). In similar vein, Lynn asserts that although the preharvest shortage "does not necessarily mean starvation," since some food is to be had by collecting and gathering, "it lowers resistance to disease and saps the energy of the people at the end of the dry season when they need strength to prepare their farms; thus setting up a 'vicious circle' " (*22*, p. 11). The Fortes also note that June, the month of greatest shortage, is the peak of farming activity (*8*, p. 254); and Guilloteau, after noting this same unfortunate timing of the hungry season in Senegal, observes that "an inadequately fed cultivator works little and badly" (*16*, p. 219). Furthermore, Guilloteau asserts, concern with the preharvest shortage prompts farmers to plant crops with a short growing season but poor yield, and offers as an example the planting of early Souna millet, with a yield of only 300–400 kilograms per hectare, whereas a later-maturing crop of Sanio millet would yield 600–800 kilograms per hectare.

If preharvest shortage is not merely a way of life but a condition that gives rise to acute discomfort and significant adverse effects, one is led to seek an explanation for this widespread and recurring phenomenon. After commenting on the serious consequences among the farmers of North Mamprusi, Lynn goes on to say: "It is not the shortage of food in itself which is so arresting, however, as the apathy of the people to the shortage" (*22*, p. 11). In the case of this Tallensi group of North Mamprusi, Lynn believes that the explanation for the apathy and lack of concern for the future stems from the unsettled conditions of life which prevailed in this area until recently, especially as a result of being harassed by frequent slave raids. The religious views of the people are also implicated, though Lynn regards these as an aspect of the insecure existence: "Ancestor worship causes them to dwell in the past and to think insufficiently of the present and future. This, too, is probably symptomatic of the unsettled conditions when only the past was certain" (*22*, p. 11). For these reasons, Lynn suggests, "A surplus in a good season is not stored against the possibility of a bad one, but is used lavishly in the performance of religious customs, or is sold or bartered for livestock" (*22*, p. 34). Purchase of stock does not really appear as a lack of foresight, however, for as Lynn himself points out: "Livestock may be regarded as a kind of bank . . . In years of food shortage, livestock are sold in order to buy grain . . ." (*22*, p. 34).

Unstable conditions of life are also cited by Thompson and Adloff as an explanation for the failure of native groups in French West Africa to fend off food-shortage periods by establishing grain reserves: "Only the strong states with a stable economy, such as that of the Mossi, regularly constituted grain reserves and, more occasionally, stocks of fodder. Periodic raids by nomadic warriors and the requisitions of conquerors furnish a historical explanation for the Sudanese Negroes' improvidence" (*45*, p. 355).

After citing "custom, habit, and taste" as factors which account for the fact that production of food is insufficient to last until the next harvest, Pierre Gourou lays special stress on the availability of food from wild sources: "the ancient tradition that, whatever happens, men do not die of hunger because they can always live by collecting until the next harvest" (*13*, p. 70).

Whatever may be the underlying factors responsible for the insufficient production and storage of food—and the efforts at explanation that have been cited are by no means conclusive—it seems clear that the immediate cause of truly acute preharvest hunger is a poor crop, most frequently as a result of inadequate or poorly timed rainfall or locust attacks (*22*, p. 34). Year-to-year variations in the amount and timing of rainfall are especially marked in the Sudan areas of West Africa where preharvest hunger is so widespread. A study of rainfall records of 31 stations of the African Sudan for the years 1900–1920 led G. T. Renner to conclude that: "rains begin and end with great uncertainty . . . [and] are liable to sudden interruptions or cessations, of from a fortnight to 2 months, after which they are resumed" (*42*, p. 591). Rainfall variations are, of course, of greater significance where crops are being grown under marginal conditions than in areas with more or less optimum moisture conditions. Thus, Renner asserts that "obviously a very small departure from normal precipitation is disastrous in a region like the Sudan where the average precipitation is little above the needs of agriculture" (*42*, p. 584).

Although climate is scarcely the full explanation, it seems clear that the phenomenon of seasonal hunger is much less significant in the more humid coastal regions, and especially where roots are the dominant staple. With respect to the yam areas of the Ivory Coast, Miège states that owing to the range of varieties utilized, the harvest of yams is spread over the period late-August to January. Yams can be stored moderately well, which permits a further extension of supplies with the result that the preharvest shortage is limited to a relatively few weeks, and in years of abundant harvest may not occur at all (*28*, p. 146). Beckett's account of Akokoaso suggests strongly that in this forest-zone village, preharvest shortage is not a problem. Plantains and cocoyams, the chief staples, are produced throughout the year (*3*, p. 20).

Finally, the frequency and severity of preharvest hunger has probably been changing to some extent in recent decades. It is reported that in Sierra Leone "the 'hungry season' which was so severe in the old days has been very much reduced, and compared with many other territories in Africa the people are well-nourished" (*44*, p. 10). British, French, and Belgian authorities all have given attention to measures to prevent famine and to eliminate the preharvest shortage periods. Most common has been encouragement of the planting of manioc as a famine reserve crop. Although manioc plays its most conspicuous role in moister areas, it has come to be widely cultivated in small plots in French Sudan, Niger, Senegal, and other territories of the Sudan zone. Jean Adam reports that "in order to give a greater security of food supply to the population, great efforts have been made in Senegal in recent years to develop the cultivation of manioc, with its underground roots which are protected from locust attacks" (*1*, p. 29). Moreover, as was noted in Chapter 5, manioc has the signal advantage that the roots can be left in the ground for a considerable time and harvested only as needed. Although outside the area considered in this study, the outstanding success achieved in controlling famine in densely populated Ruanda-Urundi by establishing manioc as a reserve crop deserves mention.

An interesting example of official attitudes toward the problem of preharvest hunger is found in the report on a conference of African chiefs held in Gambia. The Director of Development and Agriculture opened his address to the conference by urging increased food production "with a view to eliminating the hungry season," and then asked the chiefs to consider whether "a garden of reserve food such as cassava or sweet potato" should be made compulsory (10, p. 13). According to a recent statement on the development program in northern Nigeria, a project for storage of maize "to stabilize prices and form a famine reserve is . . . considered essential to the economy of the Region . . ." (32, p. 7). Provision is made in the development budget for the expenditure of £250,000 over a three-year period for further study of pit storage of maize and for payment of storage subsidies during the early years of the program. Severe famines in French West Africa in 1914, 1927, and 1931 prompted the administration to institute a program of compulsory grain reserves. By a decree of January 17, 1935 every family was required to deliver a quantity of grain, usually between 100 and 150 kilos per person over 2 years of age, to an official granary. After World War II the West Africans began to use their new political powers to agitate for the abolition of these reserves. Storage losses were a problem in maintaining them, and also there were accusations of favoritism and malpractice in distributing the supplies: 28 persons were killed in riots in Niger in 1946 following a local chief's refusal to distribute reserves under his control. Finally, in the spring of 1955 the French administration yielded to the demands for abolition of compulsory reserves, though it was hoped that the practice would be continued under voluntary arrangements (45, pp. 355–56; 23, p. 2725; 15; 43, p. 64).

In addition to the variations in total calories consumed, there is commonly considerable seasonal change in the composition of the diet affecting the starchy staples as well as more typically seasonal produce such as fruits and vegetables. For example, in the forest region of the Ivory Coast near Man, some 200 miles from the coast and about 60 miles from the Liberian border, the following seasonal pattern is indicated: overwhelming reliance on rice in November and December, the period of post-harvest abundance; in January and February the consumption of rice is curtailed and is supplemented by manioc, cocoyams, and plantains. The period March through June is marked by increasing difficulties, with the curtailed consumption of rice only partially made good by the supply of plantains and manioc. July is the month of greatest preharvest shortage when manioc and the sundry products of gathering activities are the main food resource. By August the maize and early rice are ready to be harvested; in September and October rice returns as the dominant staple (*34*, pp. 31–32).

The cycle of wet and dry season, planting and harvesting, and availability of various staple and other foods is presented by Pales for a number of other areas—the French Sudan, the Casamance region of Senegal, Upper Guinea, Sudan and Sahel regions of Senegal, and for a group of Moors along the Senegal River, and another farther to the north. In all instances a marked seasonal pattern in the consumption of staple foods is suggested. Although millets and sorghums are the dominant staple in the Sudan area through most of the year, sweet potatoes enter the diet as a supplementary food in December and January, manioc does so in May and June and probably on through the shortage period, and finally there is heavy reliance on collecting from wild sources until mid-August, when the situation is relieved by the harvest of maize. In August and September, maize and fonio are the principal staples, being superseded in October by millets and sorghum and rice (*34*, pp. 32–34).

Still another pattern is represented by the Kissi region of Upper French Guinea. The Kissi, known as the "gens du riz," look upon other staples as merely supplementary or substitute foods. By planting early-, medium-, and late-maturing varieties, the rice harvest is spread over a four-month period (September–December). In January cocoyams and sweet potatoes appear as supplementary staples, and by June, July, and August manioc, yams, and early-maturing varieties of fonio have become important, perhaps predominant (*34*, p. 37). Impressed with the fairly rich and varied agricultural possibilities of the Kissi, Denise Paulme found it somewhat surprising to hear the natives speak of their hungry season. She was not in the area during July and August, the shortage period; but she suspects that it is mainly a problem of their having to rely on fonio (referring to an observation by Richard-Molard that fonio is "perhaps the most miserable of all cereals") and root crops, which the Kissi regard as poor substitutes for rice (*35*, p. 38). A somewhat similar observation is made by Gourou relative to the Kwankos and Tures of the Ivory Coast, who eat cocoyams, sweet potatoes, and manioc from about May 1 to

August 15 after exhausting their supply of rice—and are very conscious of a deterioration in the quality of their diet during this period (*13*, p. 69n).

CITATIONS

1 Jean Adam, "Cultures vivrières," in *L'Encycl. Col. et Mar: Afrique Occidentale Française*, II (2 vols., Paris, 1950).

2 W. R. Bascom, "Yoruba Cooking," *Africa* (Internatl. Afr. Inst., Oxford), April 1951.

3 W. H. Beckett, *Akokoaso: A Survey of a Gold Coast Village* (London Sch. of Econ. and Pol. Sci., Monograph Soc. Anthropology 10, London, 1944).

4 M. K. Bennett, *The World's Food* . . . (New York, 1954).

5 J. F. Brock and M. Autret, *Kwashiorkor in Africa* (FAO Nutr. Studies 8, Rome, 1952).

6 Suzanne Comhaire-Sylvain, *Food and Leisure among the African Youth of Leopoldville (Belgian Congo)* (Communications from the Sch. Afr. Studies, New Ser. 25, Univ. of Cape Town, 1950).

7 V. Drachoussoff, *Essai sur l'agriculture indigène au Bas-Congo* (Belg. Min. Col., 1947) [Extract from *Bull. agr. du Congo Belge*, September 1947, pp. 783–880 and December 1947, pp. 471–582].

8 M. and S. L. Fortes, "Food in the Domestic Economy of the Tallensi," *Africa*, April 1936.

9 R. Galletti, K. D. S. Baldwin and I. O. Dina, *Nigerian Cocoa Farmers* . . . (Nigeria Cocoa Mkt. Bd., London, 1956).

10 Gambia, *Summary of the Proceedings of the Ninth Conference of Protectorate Chiefs Held at Georgetown, in the MacCarthy Island Division from the 19th to the 23rd of February 1952* (Bathurst, 1952).

11 Gold Coast Govt. (?), *Gold Coast Nutrition and Cookery* (Edinburgh, 1953).

12 Gold Coast, Off. Govt. Stat., *Agricultural Statistical Survey of South-East Akim Abuakwa, 1952/53* (Stat. and Econ. Papers 1, Accra, September 1953).

13 Pierre Gourou, *The Tropical World* . . . (London, 1953).

14 Faye W. Grant, "Nutrition and Health of Gold Coast Children. I. Food in Four Communities," *J. Am. Dietetic Assn.*, July 1955.

15 "Les Greniers de réserve dans le territoire du Niger," *Agronomie trop.* (France, Min. Outre-mer), May–June 1949.

16 J. Guilloteau, "Scheme for the Improvement of the Agricultural Economy of Senegal," *Afr. Soils* (Inter-Afr. Bur. Soils and Rural Econ., CCTA [London]), III, No. 2 [1955].

17 Elspeth Huxley, *Four Guineas: A Journey through West Africa* (London, 1954).

18 Ivory Coast, Conseil Supérieur des Recherches Sociologiques Outre-mer, *Enquête nutrition—Niveau de vie (Subdivision de Bongouanou 1955–1956)* [Paris, 1958].

19 Flemmie P. Kittrell, *A Preliminary Food and Nutrition Survey of Liberia, West Africa, Dec. 1946–June 1947* (Washington, D.C., mimeo.).

20 H. Labouret, *La Langue des Peuls ou Foulbé: Lexique Français-Peul* (Mémoires Inst. Français de l'Afrique Noire 41, Dakar, 1955).

21 H. Labouret, *Paysans d'Afrique noire* (Paris ?, Gallimard, 1951).

22 C. W. Lynn, *Agriculture in North Mamprusi* (Gold Coast Dept. Agr., Accra, 1937).

23 *Marchés col. du monde* (Paris), Oct. 8, 1956.

24 J. A. Mars and E. M. Tooley, *The Kudeti Book of Yoruba Cookery* (7th ed., Lagos, 1948).

25 R. Masseyeff, *La Farine d'arachides: Intérêt—Acceptabilité—Possibilité de production au Cameroun* (Off. de la Recherche Sci. et Tech. Outre-mer, Inst. de Recherches du Cameroun, Yaoundé, 1955, mimeo.).

26 R. Masseyeff and A. Cambon, *Une enquête sur la consommation alimentaire dans le Sud-Cameroun* (Off. Recherche Sci. et Tech. Outre-mer, Inst. Recherches du Cameroun, Yaoundé, 1956, mimeo.).

27 ———, *Enquêtes sur l'alimentation au Cameroun. I. Evodoula, Annexe* (Off. Recherche Sci. et Tech. Outre-mer, Inst. Recherches du Cameroun, Yaoundé, 1956, mimeo.).

28 J. Miège, "L'importance économique des ignames en Côte d'Ivoire. Repartition des cultures et principales variétés," *Rev. internatl. de bot. appliqué et d'agr. trop.* (Paris), March–April 1952.

29 B. M. Nicol, "Nutrition of Nigerian Peasant Farmers, with Special Reference to the Effects of Vitamin A and Riboflavin Deficiency," *Brit. J. Nutr.* (London), Vol. 3, No. 1, 1949.

30 ———, "The Nutrition of Nigerian Peasants, with Special Reference to the Effects of Deficiencies of the Vitamin B Complex, Vitamin A and Animal Protein," *Brit. J. Nutr.* Vol. 6, No. 1, 1952.

31 ———, *A Report of the Nutritional Work Which Has Been Carried Out in Nigeria since 1920* . . . (Kaduna?, 1956?, mimeo.).

32 Nigeria, Northern Region, *A Statement of Policy on the Development Finance Programme 1955–60* (Kaduna, 1955).

33 S. D. Onabamiro, *Food and Health* (London, 1953).

34 Léon Pales, *L'Alimentation en A.O.F.* . . . (ORANA, Dakar, 1954).

35 Denise Paulme, *Les Gens du riz* . . . (Paris, 1954).

36 J. Perisse, *Rapport concernant la première enquête d'Attitogon* (Off. Recherche Sci. et Tech. Outre-mer, Inst. Recherches du Togo, No. 1479, Paris, 1953, mimeo.).

37 ———, *Rapport concernant la deuxième enquête d'Attitogon* (Off. Recherche Sci. et Tech. Outre-mer, Inst. Recherches du Togo, No. 1480, Paris, 1954?, mimeo.).

38 ———, *Rapport concernant la troisième enquête d'Attitogon* (Off. Recherche Sci. et Tech. Outre-mer, Inst. Recherches du Togo, No. 1941, Paris, 1954, mimeo.).

39 B. S. Platt, "Food and Its Production—in Relation to the Development of Tropical and Sub-tropical Countries, Particularly Africa," in A. Leslie Banks, ed., *The Development of Tropical and Sub-Tropical Countries* (London, 1954).

40 ———, "Some Traditional Alcoholic Beverages and Their Importance in Indigenous African Communities," *Proc. of the Nutr. Soc.*, Vol. 14, No. 2 (1955), pp. 115–29.

41 G. Plummer, *The Ibo Cookery Book* (Port Harcourt [Nigeria], n.d.).

42 G. T. Renner, "A Famine Zone in Africa: The Sudan," *Geog. Rev.,* October 1926.

43 Edmond Séré de Rivières, *Le Niger* (Paris, 1952).

44 Sierra Leone, Soil Conservation Com., *Soil Conservation and Land Use in Sierra Leone* (Sess. Paper 1, Freetown, 1951).

45 Virginia Thompson and Richard Adloff, *French West Africa* (Stanford, 1958).

46 J. Wright, "Coco-yam Varieties in the Gold Coast," in Gold Coast Dept. Agr., *Year-Book, 1930* (Accra, n.d.).

CHAPTER 9

PROSPECTIVE CHANGES IN THE POSITION OF THE STAPLE FOOD CROPS

Numerous considerations suggest that during the next few decades marked changes will occur in the composition of African diets. If economic growth and rising incomes are general, it may confidently be expected that there will be the characteristic reduction in the "starchy staple ratio" as meat, dairy products, sugar, vegetables, and fruits tend to be substituted for the starchy staples that now supply some 60–85 per cent of total calories. But it can also be taken for granted that the starchy staples will continue to be the backbone of African diets for many years, despite impressive percentage increases in other items.

An effort is made in this chapter to examine some of the probable changes in the position of the different staple food crops. Even apart from the paucity and uncertain reliability of data on past trends of consumption in tropical Africa, the outlook must be obscure because the factors that will act upon the competitive position of the staple crops are numerous, complex, and far from stable. Among these factors, the most influential are likely to be:

1. Changes in relative prices resulting from (*a*) modifications in farming techniques or processing methods which have a differential impact on costs of producing various staple foods; or (*b*) differences among the crops with respect to costs of transport, storage, and handling which will have an increasingly important influence on retail prices with the extension of regional specialization and the growth of commerical production.

2. Government encouragement of particular crops through subsidies, investment, development schemes, and so on.

3. Growth of per capita incomes allowing more latitude for consumer choice and the possibility of enlarged consumption of relatively expensive but highly esteemed foods.

4. Changes in consumer preferences which are likely to occur (*a*) as a result of greater familiarity with staple foods other than those consumed in traditional local diets, or (*b*) because of the higher

215

premium urban consumers may place on such factors as ease of preparation or the prestige value of particular staples.

5. Expansion of animal feeding which may give rise to substantial demands for particular staples for feed use.

Important technical changes affecting African food production and processing are certain to occur in the years ahead, and it is probable that these advances will benefit certain crops more than others. It appears, for example, that a particularly large potential exists for raising rice yields through plant breeding, use of commercial fertilizers, improvement of farm practices, and in some instances through mechanization. It is conceivable that comparable advances might be achieved for, say, millets and sorghums if equal resources were devoted to research and experimentation in those crops, but this is not likely to be done. Judging by experience to date, one may hazard an opinion that technological advance will do more to lower production costs of rice, maize, and manioc than of the other major staples— millets and sorghums, yams, cocoyams, and plantains. Experience also suggests that introduction of mechanization can be expected to lower production costs of the grains earlier and to a greater extent than those of root crops. Mechanization of postcultural operations is likely to have an earlier impact on African agriculture than mechanization of field operations; but it is difficult to foresee the relative importance of this impact on individual crops. Reports from a number of areas—Ghana, the British Cameroons, Nigeria, and Dahomey—suggest that increasing use of small mills for shelling and grinding maize may be especially significant (*37*, p. 20; *47*, p. 46). Phyllis Kaberry found that in Bamenda in the British Cameroons, approximately one hour was required to grind three pounds of maize with the traditional stone pestle and mortar; the saving in time with even a simple handmill is considerable (*54*, p. 82). Stanton has suggested that the spread of mechanical milling of maize may have a further advantage in permitting "the use of grain of optimum yielding capacity irrespective of type (i.e., hardness)" (*94*, p. 34).

Considerably more can be said about the probable influence of the growing importance of commercial production to supply urban markets. The final section of this chapter examines the competitive advantage which cereals, and also storable root products, such as gari and manioc cosettes, are likely to enjoy in comparison with the bulky, semiperishable roots and tubers.

Among staple food crops, government programs have been concentrated to a surprising extent on rice; and that is one of the reasons the recent expansion of rice production is singled out for special consideration in this chapter.

Although it is to be expected that rising incomes will alter the relative position of the staple foods, the only evidence at hand which bears directly on this question is surprisingly inconclusive. Reports on budget surveys in three urban areas in Ghana—Accra, Kumasi, and Sekondi-Takoradi—reveal very little in the way of clear-cut correlations between per capita consumption of different staples and income levels (the grouping is actually by expenditure classes; see *39*, p. 4; *40*, p. 39, and *38*, p. 14). The Kumasi data display a clear tendency for consumption of yams and the corn product, kenkey, to increase with income, and there is also a tendency for per capita purchases of rice and bread to rise with income—although consumption in the highest income bracket shows a decline in each case to the level of the lowest category. In Sekondi-Takoradi, expenditures for bread rose sharply in the first three expenditure classes but then tapered off; aside from kenkey, which also showed a rising tendency, no other clear trends are to be discerned. Stronger correlations might emerge from a more thorough analysis of the original data. It is possible, for example, that a closer correlation between consumption and income would appear if consumption "per standardized person" had been computed rather than the simple per capita figures used in this analysis. The Accra report shows only the percentage of total expenditure allotted to each food item or category, so that per capita figures cannot be computed. The Accra data as presented do show a clear tendency for consumption of yams and bread to rise and for gari and *yekeyeke* (another inexpensive manioc product) to decline as income rises. Conceivably in one or more of these areas there is a correlation between various tribal groups and income classes which, because of persistence of traditional food habits, obscures the specific effect of increased income on consumption of various foodstuffs within groups with more homogeneous preference patterns.

It may confidently be expected that wider knowledge of various staple foods and changes in consumer preferences related to urbanization will alter patterns of food consumption, but at present it is impossible to specify how these changes are likely to affect the individual staple foods. Probably the widespread tendency for more consumers, notably in towns, to include some wheat flour in their diets is the clearest manifestation of a modification of preference patterns. And this, together with the very large percentage increases that have oc-

Wheat Reason

curred, is the justification for including a section on consumption of wheat products, notwithstanding the fact that per capita consumption is still slight and almost no wheat is grown in western tropical Africa. The possible influence of consumer attitudes on changes in consumption of rice and several other staples are touched upon below.

With growth in the importance of livestock products, large quantities of certain staple food crops will in time be used as livestock feed. Between 1933 and 1953, annual consumption of meat in the Katanga increased from 1.35 million to 8.5 million kgs, a striking indication of an upsurge in demand for meat resulting from mining and industrial development, urbanization, and rising incomes (*104*, pp. 62–63).

Manioc, with its high yields and low cost of production, offers excellent promise as a carbohydrate feed, and is already being used to a limited extent as feed for hogs in the Belgian Congo, Ghana, and no doubt other areas as well.[1] Maize, so enormously important as a feed grain in the United States, can also be expected to be in strong demand as livestock feeding becomes more important. In drier areas, sorghums will probably acquire appreciable importance as a forage and silage crop. It is reported that trials at Lyamungu Station in Tanganyika Territory have demonstrated the value of chopped banana stems as feed for cattle, so the competitive position of bananas and plantains may also be influenced by growth in livestock production and feeding (*51*, p. 1742). But information is not at hand to give precision to these possibilities or to go much beyond the surmise that manioc and maize will be the two staple crops that will figure most prominently as livestock feed.

[1] G. B. Masefield believes that increased production of pig meat is likely to be especially significant in supplying the rising demand for animal products: "There is already a chronic shortage of meat over most of Africa, and the easiest way of relieving this is by pig breeding, which produces more meat per pound of feeding-stuffs than any other animal, and also gives a rapid turnover in numbers" (*63*, p. 108). Thompson reports that experience at the Achimota College Farm has shown that "entirely satisfactory pork carcasses can be produced using cassava as the chief source of carbohydrate in the ration after the pigs are about 18 weeks old" (*95*, p. 86). He cautions that manioc should not constitute more than 40 per cent dry weight of the ration. Morrison reports that tests in Hawaii indicated that when manioc supplied more than one-third the dry matter in rations for pigs or dairy cows, scours resulted, and he also points out that varieties containing much prussic acid must be heated or dried before feeding (*67*, p. 454). The manioc fed at Achimota was cooked. V. A. Oyenuga has found in preliminary investigations at Ibadan that feeding raw manioc in a balanced ration leads to a higher rate of weight gain and at lower cost per pound of pork, up to the porker stage, than either cooked manioc or sorghum; and there are no adverse effects on the quality of the carcass.

Although the factors which will probably have greatest influence in altering the pattern of staple food consumption are easily identified in general terms, it is difficult to assess their relative importance or the net changes likely to occur. Indeed, some might argue that the conservatism of African consumers is so great that no substantial changes are likely to occur even over a period of two or three decades. The two sections which follow—reviewing trends in staple food consumption in other areas and evidence concerning the flexibility of African food habits—suggest that the change will probably be substantial. But as to alterations in the position of individual crops, only in the case of rice and wheat products does the evidence appear to point unequivocally toward increasing consumption. Considerations examined in the final section of this chapter suggest that maize and manioc may also increase in relative importance, whereas the other staples are likely to register some decline. But this is no more than a carefully considered opinion, and no basis exists for trying to estimate the magnitude of the changes in prospect.

CONSUMPTION TRENDS IN OTHER AREAS

Developments in other regions of the world afford a strong basis for expecting that substantial changes in food consumption will occur as economic development proceeds; but experience in other regions sheds relatively little light on the specific changes to be expected in the area considered here.

In Europe and the United States several general trends have characterized the long-term changes in consumption of cereal foods. In these temperate regions there has been:

1. a tendency to substitute flat breads for boiled cereals eaten as porridge;
2. substitution of raised breads for flat breads;
3. a shift from darker to whiter breads; and
4. substitution of wheat for barley, millet, corn, and rye.

Some of these changes took place simultaneously and were interdependent; the growth of wheat consumption has been fostered by the pervasive preference for white bread since only wheat and rye contain the gluten needed to make a raised bread; and wheat has superior leavening properties and yields a white flour at a higher extraction rate than does rye. In England the shift from rye, barley, and oats to wheat was largely completed by the end of the eighteenth century (6, p. 3). But the change—not yet so general—seems to have occurred considerably later elsewhere in Europe. Displacement of rye by wheat in Germany and the Scandinavian countries has largely occurred in the present century; and human consumption of rye in those countries is still something like a third as large as the consumption of wheat. In large regions of southern Europe, porridge made of maize is widely consumed, and spaghetti and other alimentary pastes rival or outdistance wheat bread as the major cereal product for sizable population groups. Although custom and local preferences are no doubt important contributing factors, low levels of income appear to be a major explanation of the important place these products retain in competition with bread in southern Europe. Consumption trends for the temperate zone grains, and the milling and baking qualities of wheat which give it such an advantage whenever bread becomes an important item in the diet, have been well summarized by Jasny and need not be pursued here (52, pp. 35–48).

Experience in Monsoon Asia, with climatic conditions somewhat more like those of tropical Africa, has been quite different. Throughout most of Asia rice has been the preferred cereal. With urbanization and rising incomes bread has gained a place in Asian diets, but it has not challenged rice as the staple food *par excellence*. In Japan, where statistics permit a review of long-term trends, the decades following 1880 were characterized by substantial increases in per capita utilization of rice and declining consumption of naked barley and barley, grains which were cheaper but not so highly esteemed by consumers. Between the First and Second World Wars, per capita utilization of rice changed little, though imports accounted for an increasing percentage of total supplies, while the declining trends for naked barley and barley continued. From a very low initial level, wheat production and consumption increased quite rapidly until the end of World War I. During the interwar period per capita utilization of wheat declined slightly, but government wheat policy was the prime mover: a large increase in domestic production in pursuit of self-sufficiency did not entirely offset a sharp curtailment in imports resulting from restrictions on foreign purchases of wheat (32; 53, pp. 73–82). Since World War II, as a result of persistent shortage and relatively high prices for rice in world markets, there has been some increase in the consumption of wheat flour and a marked increase in the share of wheat in Japan's total food imports.

Owing to inadequate data and contradictory evidence it is difficult to generalize about long-term trends in consumption of root crops —either in absolute terms or relative to cereals. In Europe, white potatoes are the only root crop that has competed with cereals as a staple starchy food. In Ireland, this New World crop established itself as the dominant staple within some 50 years following its introduction at the end of the sixteenth century. This resulted from a unique combination of circumstances—an unusually favorable natural environment, very great dependence on small-scale subsistence farming, and exceedingly difficult living conditions as a result of burdensome rents and efforts of English troops to subdue the island, including a scorched earth policy to which potatoes were less vulnerable than grain crops (89, p. 157). In the period prior to the Irish Famine (1845–46) dependence on potatoes was probably comparable to the present dependence on roots or tubers in African zones of root crop dominance.[2] In the decades since the famine, the establishment of a more diversified agriculture and more satisfactory economic conditions has greatly reduced this dependence, so that currently wheat contributes more calories than potatoes.

Elsewhere in Europe, potatoes became important at a much later date and never assumed the position of dominant staple as in Ireland. Salaman believes that in England between 1775 and 1850 potatoes increased considerably in importance during a period in which per capita supplies of wheat were declining. During that period, local wheat production failed to keep pace with the rapid population growth, and there was increased production and consumption of potatoes to supply cheap calories at a time when bread was relatively scarce and dear. With the availability of more abundant and cheaper supplies of wheat following the repeal of the Corn Laws in 1846 and the great increase in wheat shipments from the New World, the rise in potato consumption came to a halt and a decline set in after 1870 (89, pp. 537–42).

In the United States, annual estimates of food consumption dating back to 1909 show a very marked decline in per capita utilization of white potatoes (from 184 to approximately 100 pounds per year) and also of sweet potatoes (26 pounds to about 7 pounds). But this has been part of a general reduction in the consumption of starchy staples and, in lesser degree, of total calorie intake. Thus over the same

---

[2] Salaman speaks of current consumption of potatoes in Ireland as being "about 3 lb. per head, trifling no doubt compared with the 14 lb. per diem eaten in the pre-famine days . . ." (89, p. 331). His figures must include quantities eaten by pigs as well as by humans. The FAO *Food Balance Sheets* (30) estimate per capita food use at little more than a pound a day in 1947/48, but well over twice as large a quantity was used for animal feed than for food use. An average daily per capita intake of 14 pounds (some 4,550 calories) of potatoes is inconceivable.

period per capita consumption of wheat flour declined from some 215 to 125 pounds and consumption of corn meal and flour fell off most sharply of all—from 52 to 12 pounds (*101*, pp. 27–28).

In Japan sweet potatoes rank next to rice and wheat as a staple food though they supply only about a tenth as many calories as the all-important rice crop. It seems clear that at least since 1900 sweet potatoes have been declining in relative importance. This trend was sharply reversed, however, during World War II and in the postwar period as production of sweet potatoes was increased greatly to offset in part the shortage of other staples.

Other areas can be cited, however, where root crops have undoubtedly increased at the expense of grain crops. Enlarged consumption of manioc in substitution for rice in Travancore in India and in parts of Java come to mind as conspicuous examples. But it is questionable whether those changes were associated with rising per capita incomes.

FLEXIBILITY OF AFRICAN FOOD HABITS

Since "foreign" food crops—manioc, maize, sweet potatoes, and others—have found such an important place in African diets, it may seem superfluous even to raise the question whether food habits are likely to be modified substantially as a result of such influences as urbanization and economic progress. But it is not uncommon for writers to stress that African peoples are resistant to change. Particularly with respect to food, resistance to change is held to be a general characteristic of human nature: "In nothing is man more conservative than in his food" (*89*, p. 307). Numerous examples could be offered of authors who have stressed the conservatism of African consumers in their food habits. Suffice it to recall F. J. Pedler's reference to the "unwillingness—indeed the refusal—of consumers to accept near alternatives to these staple products . . ." (*80*, p. 147). As examples of consumer loyalty to particular staple items he cites the insistence of Nigerians on stockfish from Norway or Iceland as the only acceptable dried fish, while in Sierra Leone consumers were similarly insistent on the local bonga and refused to accept salted herring as a substitute even though it was offered at half the price. As usual, any generalization for a region as enormous and diverse as western tropical Africa is difficult to defend. But still more important is the question: flexible over what period of time? It seems to be almost universally true that consumers resist change in their food habits within a short period of time, but over years and decades there is much greater flexibility in modifying a traditional diet. Change comes, but it seems to come slowly.

Although no clear-cut answer to the question of the flexibility of African food habits can be expected, certain fragments of evidence afford some insight into the extent and nature of some of the probable changes. For the most part, statistical series of food production and consumption, which would reveal recent consumption trends, are unavailable. Even where estimates are available for two or more points of time, differences seem more likely to reveal a statistical discrepancy than an actual change in the level of consumption. Since these reservations probably apply with somwhat less force to estimates for the Belgian Congo than elsewhere in western tropical Africa, it is worthwhile to note the more conspicuous changes in consumption of staple foods in the Congo during the past two decades. Official estimates of production of the major staples are as follows, in thousand metric tons, for three selected years (8, p. 399 and 13, p. 786 ff.):

Staple food	1934	1947	1955
Manioc (flour equivalent) ...	1,042	1,175	1,875[a]
Rice (paddy)	57	148	198
Maize	295	370	321
Plantains	2,200	1,590	1,961
Sweet potatoes and other roots	590	530	371

[a] Converted from product weight on the basis of 1 ton = 250 kilograms of flour.

Particularly striking is the increase of rice production, nearly fourfold between 1934 and 1955, but the indicated expansion of manioc since 1947 is also substantial. Whether any trend can be inferred from the production data for maize and plantains is doubtful, but the decline in production of sweet potatoes and other roots since 1947 seems too large to be a mere statistical illusion.

More direct though limited evidence on the question of flexibility of food habits is provided by Dr. Masseyeff and his associates in their report on a sample study of consumer reactions to a new foodstuff in the French Cameroons. A type of fish paste of high nutritional value was offered to various groups of Cameroon natives, including a sample at a workers' restaurant in Douala and groups in several rural villages. Reaction to this new food was favorable among a high percentage of the individuals to whom it was offered. In the Fulani town of Mindif, however, the experiment failed owing to suspicion that the paste might include pork and the resistance of this Islamic group to outside influences: "They remain faithful to their traditions, showing only slight interest in the innovations of Europeans" (64, p. 169). These investigators concluded that their survey results refute or at least cast a great deal of doubt on the view that it is impossible to change the traditional food habits of African consumers (*64*, p. 170);

If it is true, that the introduction of certain new foods has encountered a passive reaction and complete lack of interest (soybeans being a case in point), it is no less true that these failures can be explained by a series of unfavorable circumstances and that on the other hand when the conditions are favorable the African is perfectly capable of modifying his diet.

Although the Union of South Africa is outside the area considered in this study, the dietary changes and attitudes of native consumers in the Union shed light on our question of the flexibility of African food habits. Ellen Hellman's description of urban diets in Johannesburg stresses the substantial dietary changes that have taken place. Most marked is the increased consumption of meat, but the rising consumption of rice is also noted. More generally, Miss Hellman observes that the African consumers attach a good deal of importance to the greater variety of their new food pattern and that they "assert their preference for their urban diet in no uncertain terms" (*50*, p. 282). J. F. Brock has also stressed the extent to which Bantu laborers moving to cities in the Union of South Africa modify their traditional dietary patterns. He notes in particular that "home pounded maize is often replaced by degerminated and purified mazie meal and later tends to be replaced by white bread" (*12*, p. 524).

Léon Pales has also called attention to the readiness of African consumers in urban areas to modify their eating habits. He asserts that any foodstuff requiring only limited work for its production or preparation will find a ready reception, especially if it is regarded as an element of western civilization. In particular, he notes the way in which bread enters into the diets of the educated Africans (*évolués*), of the relatively rich, and of single workers, and the way in which rice "tends to become the preferred food of city-dwellers of all types" (*78*, p. 207). These trends are particularly evident, he declares, in areas where industrial crops (peanuts or cotton) or industry have become important. By way of example, he mentions the Lébou living in Dakar who consume rice as their staple food, whereas in their native villages only a few miles away sorghums and millets are the dominant staples. And similarly: "The Sudanese transplanted to Dakar use rice and peanut oil in place of sorghum, millet, and shea butter (*karité*); the people from Guinea adopt maize and peanut oil whereas they had eaten yams and palm oil in their original habitat" (*78*, p. 209).

✓ The expanding role of rice and of wheat flour in African di..... are the two trends that appear to be in evidence in virtually all of the territories of western tropical Africa. After citing the early introduction of manioc, maize, and cocoyams as "the most notable instances" of changes in Yoruba diets, Galletti and his associates go on to report (*31*, p. 243):

More recently rice has begun to be relished while bread, baked to the Yoruba taste in light and almost excessively airy loaves from imported flour, is on sale not only in the big cities but in every large town and in smaller places, especially if passenger lorries regularly stop there. . . .

While it seems likely that urbanization will have a particularly strong influence in contributing to increased consumption of rice and wheat products, it will no doubt accelerate other changes in dietary patterns as well. Its probable effect on competition between root crops and cereals is examined in the final section of this chapter. But urbanization is significant in its influence on the modification of food habits not only because change may be expected to come earliest in the urban environment, but modifications once adopted by city-dwellers are likely to spread, at least in some degree, to the countryside.

EXPANSION OF RICE PRODUCTION AND CONSUMPTION

The limited importance of rice, at least by comparison with Monsoon Asia, was signaled in Chapter 2 as one of the distinctive features of the food economies of western tropical Africa. Later it was noted that until some 50 or 60 years ago rice was little cultivated and was an unimportant "luxury food" outside the rice zone extending south from the Gambia and Casamance rivers to the Bandama River in the Ivory Coast. But evidence is abundant that in the past decade or two widespread and significant increase in the importance of rice has occurred.

Production statistics for the Belgian Congo, which suggest nearly a fourfold increase in rice production between 1934 and 1955, have already been cited. Estimates of rice production in Sierra Leone, which point to an increase of close to 50 per cent between 1934–39 and 1951, should probably be given some credence since considerable official attention has been given to rice throughout that period. An estimated increase of rice production in French West Africa of some 30 per cent over the same period—1934–39 to 1951—is undoubtedly subject to a wide margin of error, but at the very least it represents a definite opinion on the part of the local officials that a sizable increase had taken place (*46*, p. 265).

Unquestionably a considerable expansion of rice production in Nigeria has occurred although the statistical evidence is meager. The Department of Agriculture's annual report for 1952/53 declares (*72*, p. 5):

Rice as a local crop continues to expand in all regions; this is particularly evident in the Eastern Region which has in part been stimulated by the introduction of rice mills. In the East attention is also being attracted to the utilization of the tidal mangrove swamps around Calabar and Rivers Province, where the potentialities for growing rice are vast.

A 1953 report of the government of the Eastern Region observes that the "cultivation of rice . . . increased from an acreage of 4,000 in 1942, to an acreage of 48,000 in 1952 . . ." (*74*, p. 4; see also *71*, p. 5). According to a document issued early in 1956 the rice area in the Eastern Region had reached approximately 100,000 acres (*75*, p. 20). A few references to the expansion of rice acreage in the Northern Region are noted below in reviewing some of the government-sponsored projects for promoting rice cultivation. For the Western Region, the only evidence at hand is the 1951/52 annual report of the regional Department of Agriculture, which observes that "the growing of rice is steadily growing in favour" and that acreage of both swamp and upland rice had increased considerably during the previous season (*73*, p. 2).

Since World War II, governmental programs for agricultural development and research have emphasized rice to a striking degree. So conspicuous has been this emphasis that one is tempted to speak of rice as "the glamour crop of West Africa." It is characteristic of this emphasis that in an account of the agricultural research stations in French West Africa by Arsène Renard, rice is the only cereal or root crop mentioned in the summary of "principal activities" (*84*, p. 336). And at least until recently rice was the only product given a price guarantee in most of the French territories (*99*, p. 79). Similarly, in the British territories of West Africa out of 15 agricultural development schemes described in a recent Colonial Office report, seven are concentrated on rice and one or two others include rice as an important crop in the rotation (*44*).

The introduction of wet rice production in tidal mangrove swamps in Sierra Leone in the late nineteenth century was noted in Chapter 4. In the 1930s a program of subsidies for swamp clearance for rice cultivation was launched, and in 1934 a rice experiment station was established at Rokupr, about 20 miles from the mouth of the Great Scarcies River. It has now been enlarged to become the West African Rice Research Station.

Since World War II Sierra Leone's major development effort for rice has been carried out in the south near the coast. Some 60,000 acres of comparatively level grassland exist in the Bonthe-Pujehun districts, with rich alluvial soil replenished by annual flooding. Although the flooding reaches a depth of as much as 12–15 feet during the rainy season, the land is dry enough to support crawler tractors during the dry season—mid-January to mid-April—and a promising start has been made in developing cultivation of floating rice. The problems of clearing this type of grassland for rice have been solved by the use of heavy, full-track crawler tractors, disc plows, and disc harrows for clearing the heavy grass cover. The mechanical cultivation is done on a contract basis with payment in kind at harvest time. It is reported that in this way a farmer can cultivate approximately 8 ½ acres and obtain a yield of about 1,800 pounds per acre, compared to 1–2 acres and a yield of some 1,300 pounds per acre with hand cultivation. The present experimental charge for plowing is only 3 bushels (180 pounds) per acre, a subsidized rate insufficient' to cover the full cost; but even with a doubling of the charge for contract plowing the profitability of this type of operation would be considerably greater than the traditional hand cultivation (*43*, pp. 80–83). The underlying philosophy of this Southern Grasslands Mechanical Rice Production Scheme has been stated succinctly in these terms (*44*, p. 47):

The whole essence of the scheme is a cautious gradual approach in the early years, gaining the confidence of local farmers and weaning them to the idea of paying for mechanized work, increasing their holdings and becoming small capitalist farmers instead of mere subsistence farmers.

The steady extension of the area under cultivation is impressive evidence of the results being attained: 70 acres in 1950; 312 in 1951; 868 in 1952; 1,777 in 1953; and 3,342 in 1954. Plans for expansion called for 6,500 acres in 1955 and a doubling of the area each year thereafter with the goal of having all plowable land in production by 1958–60. This seems to be one of the few schemes for mechanized cultivation in British West Africa that shows real promise of success. "Settlers and small traders from other areas are beginning to arrive," a recent official report observes, "and all the signs are that this backward area is well on the way to prosperity and to becoming one of the main rice producing centres of Sierra Leone" (*44*, p. 49). Major Taylor, Director of the Department of Commerce and Industry, reported early in 1958 that a farmers' cooperative had assumed responsibility for mechanical cultivation of approximately 3,000 acres.

Efforts are also being made in Sierra Leone to develop rice production in certain inland swamp areas (the Bobali-Tonkolili districts of Makeni). The soil in these areas is not so fertile as in the southern grasslands, the annual deposit of silt being less. But with the application of superphosphate good yields are obtained, and by 1954 this Northern Boli Land Mechanized Rice Production Scheme encompassed nearly 2,500 acres. The rice farms average 10 acres per cultivator, although some individuals have expanded their holdings to 40 or 50 acres (*44*, pp. 50–54). In some of the inland swamp areas of the north, rice cultivation is being developed with animal draft power; 89 plow teams of oxen had been established by 1953 (*45*, p. 35).

Another indication of the importance attached to rice cultivation and the prospects of its expansion in Sierra Leone is the emphasis accorded it in the *Plan of Economic Development* issued in 1949. The author, H. Childs, identified "the hope of developing large-scale swamp cultivation of rice for export" as one of the three principal factors upon which the "future economic progress of Sierra Leone" will depend (*91*, p. 1). He recognized, however, that such a goal hinged upon further research and experimental work. As late as 1954 Sierra Leone's rice exports were negligible; and in that year imports exceeded exports by 4,500 tons (*92*, pp. 9, 114). Largely as a result of the movement of population to the diamond areas, and the decline in food production and increase in incomes associated with the search for diamonds, rice imports increased sharply during the years 1955–57 and exceeded 30,000 tons in each of the last two years.

Recent expansion of rice cultivation in Nigeria has received official encouragement in the form of propaganda and distribution of improved seed by officers of the agricultural departments. In addition, rice cultivation has figured prominently in several governmental schemes for agricultural development and mechanization. The most ambitious of these was the Sokoto Mechanized Rice Scheme for bringing into cultivation substantial areas in the valleys of the Sokoto and Rima rivers, land previously "left untouched by reason of the heavy labor involved in breaking in by hand" (*70*, p. 23; *43*, pp. 20–24; *44*, pp. 175–79). This project was initiated in 1949 on a "quasi-commercial basis" with a grant of £136,000 from the Northern Regional Production Development Board. The mechanical operations are confined to plowing, since the initial cultivation was the main limiting factor in extending the rice area. In this scheme, land was held under "rights of user" by the peasants, but re-allocated in one-acre plots to facilitate the mechanized plowing. A recent report states that by 1953/54 it was apparent that the scheme would never be a commercial success. One of the native authorities that had never liked the pooling of land for mechanical cultivation, withdrew from the project, leaving only the Gwandu Native Authority. The project, now reorganized as the Gwandu Mechanized Rice Scheme, is operating at a loss and will no doubt come to an end when the heavy tractors and disc plows being used are worn out—perhaps in another five years. Rice yields have averaged only about 750 pounds per acre, so that returns have been insufficient to cover the costs of mechanized cultivation.[3] Flood damage, which has been ameliorated to some extent by small earth bunds, and destruction of rice plants by fish have been the chief adverse factors responsible for the poor yields in the Sokoto/Gwandu scheme. After reaching 25,000 and 23,000 acres in the 1951/52 and 1952/53 seasons, the area plowed fell off sharply to 6,000 acres in 1953/54 (*44*, pp. 175–79).

In the Kaduna River flood plain, the Edozhigi Irrigation Scheme was set up to provide controlled irrigation for some 2,500 acres of rice. Mechanical cultivation was contemplated although the participating farmers were reported to be cool to that feature, and difficulties were anticipated in re-allocating the land (*44*, pp. 36–38). The Shemankar Mechanized Rice Scheme in Plateau Province near the Jos tin-mining area is another Nigerian scheme concentrated on rice. No doubt more important in their impact on total output of rice in Nigeria are the many small-scale projects for extending the area under rice by construction of small earth dams and other measures to improve control of irrigation water.

A minor effort to develop rice production was initiated in Ghana as long ago as 1926. A power-driven mill was erected in E. Nzima in the southwest with the object of stimulating rice cultivation, and by 1930/31 production approached 300 tons (*85*, p. 175). As late as 1948/49, the Department of Agriculture observed that throughout

---

[3] The plowing charge of £2.10 per acre is the same as under the Northern Boli Land Mechanized Rice Production scheme of Sierra Leone where yields of 2,000 pounds or more are obtained on land receiving superphosphate. In Sierra Leone's southern grassland scheme, the plowing charge is £3 per acre against an estimated cost (including depreciation and supervision) of £5.8. Average yields there exceed 2,000 pounds to the acre without fertilizer.

"most of the Gold Coast rice is a luxury rather than a staple food," at the same time noting that interest in growing rice was increasing under the stimulus of high prices (*34*, p. 4).

The most significant recent extensions of rice production in Ghana have taken place in the Northern Region, particularly in Mamprusi District, and in Ashanti (*11*, p. 129). A 1937 report of the Department of Agriculture indicated that the value of rice had been proved by trials in North Mamprusi: "It yields a bigger weight of food for man and for beast from a given area, than any crop we have tried so far" (*59*, p. 49). At that time the local population resisted its introduction, asserting that they did not care for rice. It was the view of C. W. Lynn, the author of this report, that the true explanation for the reluctance to undertake rice cultivation was "the difficulty of hoeing suitable rice land with the implements available" (*59*, p. 39). In recent years considerable progress has been made in introducing draft animals, and the number of "plow farmers" in Mamprusi approached 1,200 in 1952, nearly double the number so equipped in 1950 (*35*, p. 13). As a result of the various measures of encouragement, rice shipments from Mamprusi have increased sharply in recent years, exceeding 1,500 tons in 1952.

Although particular attention has been given to efforts to improve and encourage rice production in the Northern Region and in northern Ashanti, the Department of Agriculture has had a general policy "aimed at increasing the acreage under swamp rice in areas where topography, soils and climate are suitable" (*11*, p. 131). This policy is being implemented by developing and distributing improved varieties, introducing better methods of cultivation, and by measures to improve water control and to provide better facilities for threshing, hulling, and milling. In some areas departmental extension teams have marked out contour bunds and carried out mechanical cultivation, and in Ashanti mobile threshing and hulling units "have operated successfully" (*11*, p. 131).

Emphasis on developing the production of rice has been an equally conspicuous feature of the agricultural programs in French West Africa. The Office du Niger Project in French Sudan is the largest irrigation scheme in West Africa and, contrary to original expectations, rice is the major crop being produced. Studies of a large-scale irrigation scheme in the central delta of the Niger were initiated in 1919–20 as a result of preoccupation with establishing a dependable source of supply of cotton following the difficulties experienced by France during World War I. In 1932 the Office du Niger was created as a public corporation to administer the proposed irrigation scheme. Work on the principal dam of the system, Sansanding, was begun in 1934 but not completed until 1947. In the period since World War II there has been renewed interest in the Office du Niger project because of a desire to obtain rice supplies for Senegal to replace imports from Indochina and to reduce French dependence upon cotton imports from the dollar area (*103*, pp. 341, 352). Rice, which accounted for $4.7 million of the $6.8 million total value of crops produced in 1952/53 by the Office du Niger, has proved to be more important than cotton for a variety of reasons (*100*, p. 95). In the succinct observation of Yves Coyaud, the Technical Director of the project, "rice has found better soil, economic, and human conditions" (*25*, pp. 275–76). A large part of the area developed to date has had soils characterized by slow drainage, a high content of clay or silt, and lack of humus—conditions that rice tolerates better than cotton. Rice has also had an advantage in that the labor requirements for its cultivation are typically about half of the 150 to 200 man-days per hectare required for cotton.

Starting with an output of rice of only 1,550 tons in 1934, production increased to a level of nearly 45,000 tons in 1954/55. Increase of yield accounted for some of this expansion, but most of it was due to the extension of the cultivated area from less than 5,000 hectares in 1937/38 to 23,000 hectares in 1954/55 and 26,000 in 1955/56 (*25*, p. 278). Despite the progress achieved, the area brought under cultivation in the Office du Niger project is but a small fraction of the original highly ambitious goal of developing a million hectares of irrigated land. Georges Spitz has recently affirmed the possibility of eventually developing rice and cotton cultivation on some 950,000 hectares, and he notes that the heavy investment in Sansanding and other facilities is excessive in relation to the area presently under cultivation (*93*, p. 90). Yves Coyaud, writing in 1956, asserted that "the extension of rice fields has in fact been limited only by the restricted availability of funds" (*25*, p. 276). And he reports that a four-year plan recently prepared by the Office du Niger envisages increasing the rice area to 47,500 hectares; this would permit an increase in the tonnage of rice commercialized to 50,000 tons of paddy, compared with 28,000 tons commercialized in 1954/55 (*25*, p. 283). It is the current view of officials of the Office du Niger that expansion of the total area under rice and cotton to some 200,000 hectares, which could be done with little increase in present overhead costs, would allow the project to become economically viable. Up to the present its continued operation has depended upon an annual subsidy from the French government.

Most of the cultivation of rice and cotton in the Office du Niger project is carried out by Africans brought in as colonists, numbering some 26,000 at present, including salaried employees and laborers. Cultivation by the colonists is organized mainly according to two systems. By one arrangement a settler is assigned a hectare of land and is equipped with a team of oxen. Every third year deep plowing is carried out on his field mechanically for a fee, and each year his crop is harvested by combines of the Office du Niger. In the other arrangement, in which a settler may have one or two hectares, depending on the availability of seasonal labor for harvesting, mechanical plowing, planting, and turning under of a green fertilizer crop are carried out each year on a contract basis. In addition, a rice farm of some 6,000 hectares is being operated directly by the Office du Niger with mechanical equipment and hired labor (25, pp. 279–80; 93, pp. 85–86). Owing to the influx of population and marked increase in local consumption, the supplies available for export have been less than anticipated. Sales of rice and broken rice by the Office du Niger for shipment to Senegal, other territories, and to other districts of French Sudan have been as follows (in metric tons; 25, p. 284):

Destination	1951/52	1952/53	1953/54	1954/55[a]
Senegal	4,218	1,707	6,230	8,889
Sudan and other territories ..	4,653	8,027	10,973	9,172
Total	8,871	9,734	17,203	17,061

[a] Figures as given in the source: items do not add to total given.

The increase in recent years has been marked and, as noted earlier, expectation of a further substantial increase in the next few years seems to be firmly based. The high cost of rail transport poses a problem, however, in exporting rice to Dakar and other Senegalese cities. In addition to the original emphasis on the Office du Niger project as a source of exportable supplies of rice and cotton, however, there seems now to be a good deal of stress on the improvement in levels of living enjoyed by the settlers taking part in the project; one recent report, in speaking of the goal of ultimately irrigating 910,000 hectares, observes that it is hoped that the project would then support a million indigenous settlers (100, p. 95).

For some years the Agricultural Service of the French Sudan has been seeking to promote rice production in other districts of the central delta and in the upper valley of the Niger through extending the area under cultivation and improving yields. The principal effort to date has been directed at construction of many small-scale irrigation facilities to regulate the floodwaters and reduce the uncertainty of production. These small dams together with the increase in height of the river banks help to prevent flooding of the fields before planting has been completed and to hold the water in the fields until the rice plants have reached maturity. The use of plows drawn by oxen has increased to such an extent during the past 20 years that most of the rice area is now cultivated with animal draft power. This has been encouraged by instruction in the use of draft animals and distribution of plows; some 20,000 plows are currently in use (*83* and *88*, pp. 34–36).

Interesting as an example of mechanized agricultural development is the Richard Toll Rice Scheme on the Senegal River some 60 miles northeast of Saint Louis. This project has involved the construction of a dam to control the waters of Lake Guiers so as to assure a supply of fresh water, for the Senegal River is often salty as much as 300 miles upstream during the dry season (*79*, p. 41; *87*, p. 35). Cultivation is fully mechanized, Richard Toll being an outstanding example of a type of scheme particularly favored in the first development plan for the French overseas territories launched by the law of April 30, 1946. Particular attention was to be given to achieving substantial increases in production by means of "concentrated and powerful enterprises" located in sparsely inhabited areas and compensating for the shortage of labor by use of modern mechanical equipment (see *5*, p. 12). This emphasis was influenced by the postwar shortage of primary products, which was believed to be a long-run problem, and by a conviction that this approach offered the only hope of obtaining substantial results speedily, since development of the native agricultural economy would be slow and fraught with difficulties. An experimental rice farm of 120 hectares was established in 1946 and by 1953 the planted area had increased to 1,100 hectares. Early plans called for rapid expansion to 6,000 hectares (4,500 in rice and 1,500 planted to a green manure crop), with further extension over a 10-year period to raise the total area to 50,000 hectares (*79*, pp. 41, 44). Following serious attacks on the rice crop by "millet-eater" birds (various species of *Quelea*) in 1952, the completion of the investment program was postponed to allow a trial on 1,500 hectares (*68*, pp. 4, 6). Ardent efforts have been made to control the birds, also a problem at the Office du Niger, by means of such measures as destroying nesting areas with dynamite or burning with flame throwers, use of poison bait, and noise devices (*60*, pp. 801–02). Considerable success is apparently being attained in these efforts, mainly through the dynamiting of nesting areas, and by 1956 the planted area at Richard Toll exceeded 4,000 hectares. A small part of that area was sown by airplane, a Piper Super-Cub, which was used more extensively and with better success for spreading fertilizer and spraying (*22*). In 1955 the management of Richard Toll was turned over to a private company, the Entreprise-africaine Ortal. This arrangement is for a 15-year period, and the company is to share any profits with the territorial government (*96*).

Another pilot project for mechanized rice cultivation is proceeding in the Casamance District of southern Senegal under the Compagnie Générale des Oléagineux Tropicaux (CGOT). The area involved, 305 hectares planted to rice in 1955, is still small, but the project is of interest because it differs in important respects from the Office du Niger and Richard Toll schemes. Whereas these two are directed at the development of irrigation for the production of wet rice, the CGOT experiment concerns cultivation of upland rice in a rotation, viz., green manure crop–peanuts–rice–peanuts. The field operations are completely mechanized except for some weeding by hand after tillering has proceeded to a point where mechanical weeding would be destructive. By application of chemical fertilizer —mainly nitrogen and phosphoric acid, but some potash—yields on the order of 1,800 to 2,000 kgs have been obtained, comparing rather favorably with yields in the irrigated culture at Richard Toll and the Office du Niger (*49* and *56*).

Roland Pré in 1951 devoted several chapters of his book on French Guinea to a description of measures being taken to extend the cultivation of wet rice (*82*, pp. 45–71). The first chapter of his enthusiastic report on these efforts and the possibilities for future development carries the optimistic title "La Guinée—Futur Grenier à Riz." Primary emphasis has been placed on encouraging production of wet rice as a substitute for the cultivation of upland rice, which is considered highly destructive of the soils. Some experimental work has also been done on "semimechanized" rice cultivation. Over 1,350 hectares were plowed and disked with mechanical equipment in 1952, and yields averaged about 1,200 kgs of paddy to the hectare (*4*, pp. 154–55). If we can trust the crop estimates, rice production in French Guinea, the highest of any territory in French West Africa, increased by some 50,000 tons between 1950 and 1954; the increase in area appears to have been on the order of 50,000 hectares. Despite the appreciable rise in production to a little over 250,000 tons in 1954, rice imports into French Guinea have been increasing steadily in recent years and were at a level of about 10,000 tons in 1956 and 1957.

Liberia is another West African territory where rice has been singled out for special attention. As Liberia's dominant staple food, it has in the past been grown entirely as an upland crop under a system of shifting cultivation. In recent years officials of the Department of Agriculture and Commerce and United States agricultural advisers have condemned this "wasteful use of high forest," which is said to be "fast depleting the country of its most valuable timber" (*102*, Preface; and *65*, Intro.). A "swamp rice production program" was initiated by the Department of Agriculture and Commerce in 1953, and American rice specialists have been assisting. Steps taken to date are directed at introducing the cultivation of irrigated rice in inland swamps. Techniques in use in Sierra Leone were studied prior to launching this program, but the transplanting of seedlings as practiced in the Scarcies tidal swamps is not being used. Very satisfactory yields of from 1,750 to 2,950 pounds per acre have been reported. Not only are these yields several times as high as those obtained in the usual upland culture, but in addition the same land can be planted to rice for several years before being rested, instead of for only a year or two as with the usual shifting cultivation. In 1954 the government planted 125 acres of swamp rice under its demonstration program, and a little over 500 acres were planted by tribal groups or individuals (*57*, p. 37). It is said that there are many of these swampy areas at the base of hills, with fertile soils that can be easily drained and therefore lending themselves to the growing of wet rice.

Little can be added to the earlier discussion (Chapter 4) of measures to extend rice cultivation in French Equatorial Africa, except to call attention to the emphasis accorded "the rice plan" in economic development plans for the Federation. Close to 10 per cent of France's contribution to the Investment Fund for Economic and Social Development (FIDES) in French Equatorial Africa was allotted to rice cultivation, more than for any other crop (*99*, pp. 18, 84). Despite a general attitude highly favorable to rice cultivation, the price policy pursued by the administration in recent years has, in the opinion of Jean Cabot, tended to discourage further expansion of rice (*21*, pp. 169–70).

A price policy much more favorable to rice producers has been pursued by the French administration in the Cameroons, which has promoted rice cultivation by means of an "Experimental Sector for the Modernization of the Cultivation of Rice in Yagona," a subdivision lying to the west of the Logone. A purchase price of 14 francs C.F.A. per kilogram for paddy rice was paid these producers in the northern Cameroons in 1955 compared with 8.50 francs C.F.A. being paid in the Chad. Other measures to encourage development of rice production in the Cameroons include an experimental station charged with the development and multiplication of improved seed; distribution of seed to farmers; construction of facilities for water control and irrigation; mechanical plowing and subsoiling on a fee basis; and construction of a modern rice mill with Italian equipment and under the direction of an Italian specialist. At the present time subsidization is required to enable the rice produced in Yagona—some 2,300 tons of paddy in 1955—to compete with imported rice in the urban market in the south. Rice is shipped to Douala by air at a cost of 15.50 francs per kilo and by truck to Yaoundé at a cost of nearly 12 francs per kilo. These high transport charges represent a considerable handicap; but with increased rice yields and a lowering of milling costs, mainly through reducing the percentage of brokens, the rice from this new center of production may become fully competitive (21, pp. 170–72).

Expansion of rice culture in the Belgian Congo was described earlier in this chapter and in Chapter 4. In contrast to most of the West African schemes, the rice grown in the Congo is almost exclusively upland. Abeele and Vandenput have summed up the position thus (1, p. 158):

> Some trials of irrigated rice have been carried out in the Bas-Congo by the government service, but the cost of the installations for irrigation was too high to be able to recommend this type of culture.

The reasons for this difference in emphasis are not at all clear. Part of the explanation is probably the more satisfactory rainfall regime in much of the Congo and perhaps greater availability of relatively level areas of sufficient fertility for rice, so that soil erosion induced by cultivation of upland rice is not considered a problem. The development of improved varieties in the Congo has also made it possible to obtain quite satisfactory yields with the upland culture. One may also conjecture that the additional cost of providing irrigation facilities has been given more weight in the Congo than in some of the territories of West Africa. Experimental cultivation of irrigated rice is being conducted, however, by L'Institut National pour l'Étude Agronomique du Congo Belge (INÉAC) on marshy or inundated land adjacent to the Congo. O. Tulippe has argued that irrigation would be of considerable value in parts of the Kasai Province because of the long dry season and sandy soils, but he indicates that the local authorities are not enthusiastic (97, pp. 64–65). Roger Jaspar, who carried out a study mission of the possibilities of extending the cultivation of irrigated rice in the Belgian Congo, has reported that huge possibilities for expansion exist; and he asserts that rice production in the Congo should be increased tenfold by the mechanized development of the culture of irrigated rice (51a, p. 93).

The reasons cited for giving such special emphasis to extending the cultivation of rice in tropical Africa are legion. But it is difficult to evaluate the importance of the various types of supporting arguments. To a considerable extent the stress on rice in British and French territories may be related to the fact that many administrators and technicians in those areas are familiar with rice, having had experience with it in India, Burma, Indochina, and other parts of Asia where rice is of such great importance. This type of influence seems particularly evident in the report of the British West African Rice Mission prepared in 1948 by W. M. Clark and F. H. Hutchinson, retired officials of the Indian Civil Service. Following a survey of the British territories of West Africa and brief visits to Liberia and parts of French West Africa, they argued for a large and energetic program to develop production of irrigated rice (23, p. 2):

We have found areas, totalling approximately 2,000,000 acres, where we believe satisfactory yields of paddy can be obtained. Many of these areas will, however, require major Civil Engineering Works. We are, therefore, proposing the immediate formation of 17 Engineering Survey Unit Sub-Divisions to carry out investigations with a view to preparing detailed Project estimates, so that the whole of the 2,000,000 acres can be brought into production in a period of 10 years.

This ambitious if not grandiose scheme was justified in the first instance by comparing their estimate of the cost of cultivating rice (on an initial 28,000 acres to be cultivated by state farms and 137,000 acres by "Hiring Units") with prevailing rice prices. More generally they observe: "The demand for rice is rising rapidly; we therefore believe that most of whatever is produced will be consumed in Africa" (23, p. 3). They further assert: "Before any large scale Agricultural or Industrial Developments take place, it is essential that food supplies (particularly paddy) should be augmented, as the diversion of a large number of people will inevitably result in a general shortage of food" (23, p. 4). As evidence to support their point of view, they cite the fact that in Liberia "one firm alone" (presumably Firestone) was subsidizing rice imports to the extent of £350 a day.

The Mission's report is highly critical of the local administrators in the four territories of British West Africa for failing to assign responsibility for development of inland waterways and for neglecting to obtain essential hydraulic information. Considering the background of Clark and Hutchinson, it is not at all surprising that they should also be critical of the "lack of attention to and competence in building of irrigation and drainage facilities" (23, p. 5).

Enthusiasm concerning possibilities for a large expansion of rice production in tropical Africa seems to be rather general. A notable example is the view of D. H. Grist in his book, *Rice*, published in 1953 (46, p. 262):

The possibilities here [Africa] are, in fact, enormous, there being literally millions of acres of swamp jungle suited to the crop provided that irrigation and drainage are feasible. In Sierra Leone alone the available area is probably a million acres, and taking into account possibilities in Nigeria, the Gold Coast, and Gambia, the potentialities in British territories alone are almost incredible.

Grist goes on to mention French Equatorial Africa and the Belgian Congo as territories with "vast areas of potential paddy-land"; and the assertion is made that the rice area in French West Africa "has practically doubled in the last decade" (46, p. 262). The preoccupation with rice in the British territories is also reflected in an official memorandum circulated in 1952 whereby "colonial governments were asked to examine as a question of particular importance the possibilities of increasing the production of rice . . ." (42, p. 42).

Of more fundamental importance in contributing to the emphasis on rice cultivation are certain characteristics of the rice plant which make it well suited to tropical agriculture. The attitude of Pierre Gourou, an able advocate of rice as the food crop *par excellence* in tropical regions, has already been noted briefly (Chapter 2). The essential point is that wet rice, alone among the important food crops, can return a satisfactory yield year after year in tropical areas of high rainfall and high soil temperatures where soils lose their fertility within a few years when planted to other food crops. Moreover, production of irrigated rice normally does not induce soil erosion and, particularly since rice is capable of giving high yields, this makes possible a reduction in the cultivation of various upland crops regarded as destructive of the soil. These considerations are not only pertinent to the high rainfall forest regions, but are also advanced

by agricultural officials in the French Sudan as the principal reason
for the heavy emphasis they have placed on the production of wet
rice in that savanna region wherever the waters of the Niger or its
tributaries make that possible. Robert Pendleton explains his view
that rice will become increasingly important in the humid tropics
by stressing that (*81*, p. 220):

lowland rice is a unique crop. Most of the principles of agronomy which apply
to the usual grain crops do not seem to apply to padi. Just why this is so cannot yet be satisfactorily explained. The fact remains that rice, if it is grown
on a soil that is well puddled, and can have a few inches of water standing on
it throughout the growing season, will produce some rice to eat when this soil
is too infertile to produce any other grain crop.

The British authority G. B. Masefield expresses the same point of view
in declaring (*63*, p. 108):

Of all the tropical cereals, swamp rice gives the most reliable (and with the
possible exception of hybrid maize) the highest yield. It has the further
unique advantage that it can apparently be grown continuously for centuries
on the same land without depletion of soil fertility or obvious decline in
yield. . . .

But even Clark and Hutchinson acknowledge that there are some
unfavorable factors to be reckoned with in Africa. As they point out
(*23*, p. 6), "The main watersheds in West Africa have, as a rule, very
steep slopes; they are also undulating and frequently have rock out-
crops; there are practically no broad flat plains as in India." This
means that a system of canals running between more or less parallel
rivers, as in parts of India, Burma, and Thailand, is not feasible. Thus
"irrigation in West Africa will be mainly from storage on tributaries
rather than perennial irrigation from the big rivers" (*23*, p. 6). In
addition, it seems clear that the rivers of West Africa do not carry
as heavy a load of nutrient-bearing silt to replenish fertility as do
the great rivers of Asia. Louis Papy has pointed out, for example,
that the Senegal River carries a very weak concentration of alluvial
matter owing to the rocky and sandy surfaces which it traverses.
Whereas the Nile carries approximately 1.5 kilograms of silt per
cubic meter of water, the Senegal carries only 100 to 150 grams.
Consequently, the addition to soil fertility brought by the annual
flooding is relatively small, and to obtain satisfactory yields it is often
necessary to plow under periodically a green manure crop or allow
rice land to lie fallow from time to time (*79*, p. 28; see also *41*, p.
105n).

In addition to the strictly agricultural considerations, rice is sometimes viewed favorably because, at least with irrigated culture, the growing of rice contributes to the establishment of more stable communities. This point was stressed by Aimé Drogué in relation to "The Rice Plan" in French Equatorial Africa in a statement interesting also for its general tenor (27, p. 292):

In all areas, even in the great forest, by development of the valleys, rice culture will be a powerful means of fixing the villages, of conserving the soil, of combatting undernourishment. To this end, it is necessary, by means of a far-seeing extension program, in the school and in the field, to acquaint people with rice, its cultivation, its properties as a food, its preparation. Rice should become everywhere a food plant that is generally cultivated.

Although his enthusiasm may seem a little extreme, it is certainly to be conceded that the stabilization of rural groups has a very definite value for social and economic development beyond the convenience to colonial administrators.

The nutritional advantages of rice, alluded to by Drogué, are emphasized by B. M. Nicol, the adviser on nutrition to the Medical Department of Nigeria. As already noted in the discussion of "nutritional considerations" in Chapter 6, Dr. Nicol believes that enlarged consumption of rice in the root-crop zones of southern Nigeria could do much to augment supplies of protein in such areas. The higher protein content of rice as compared to manioc is one of the chief factors stressed by Roger Jaspar in his eloquent advocacy of a great expansion of rice production in the Belgian Congo (51a, pp. 88–91).

A consideration in favor of rice which has been stressed in French West Africa is the fact that whenever mechanical milling is possible, and this is usual, the native women can be relieved of the time-consuming task of pounding millets or sorghums by hand. Thus Léon Pales comments: "In delivering the African woman from servitude to pounding, milled rice thus sees its success doubly assured" (78, p. 207).

A related consideration is that rice is a crop particularly well suited to commercial distribution. Mills, large or small, for mechanical milling are relatively easy to establish. Rice can be stored under tropical conditions as well as virtually any food crop; and not only is it rather easy to transport, either bagged or in bulk, but its monetary and food values are high enough to warrant long-distance shipment from producing to consuming centers. The survey data collected by Galletti and his associates bring out very clearly the commercial character of rice production in the cocoa region of western Nigeria. Thus, rice was being produced by only 14 of the 187 families surveyed, and these were all located at Ibesse in Abeokuta Province. Of their total output, which averaged just over 1,000 pounds per family, 97 per cent was sold. And viewing rice as an item of consumption, we find that the survey families consumed an average of 27 pounds of purchased rice per year (*31,* pp. 421, 717).

A fundamental factor certain to influence the competitive position of rice will be the attitude of African consumers. The scant evidence at hand suggests that, especially in urban areas, African consumers readily shift to rice. Particularly striking as evidence of the consumer preference for rice, at least in competition with millets and sorghums, is the way in which residents of Sudanese cities like Bamako and Segou seem to have adopted rice as their principal staple in preference to millets and sorghums despite the fact that the price of rice in those cities is some two or three times as high as the price of the competing staple foods. Moreover, the examination of the relative prices of the staple foods in Chapter 6 indicates clearly that consumers are willing to pay a premium for rice over most other staple foods.

The comparatively favorable prices obtainable for rice seem to be significant in determining the profitability of mechanized cultivation of rice in comparison with other staple food crops. In a study of 29 projects for mechanized cultivation in Nigeria, W. T. Newlyn found that the "contract schemes" (i.e., where mechanized services are provided at a prearranged cost) are in a much sounder economic position than "official schemes" or "partnership schemes." He concludes that the principal reason for this is simply that all but one of the "contract schemes" are based on cultivation of swamp rice—"a comparatively high revenue yielding crop." The gross return of £15 to £20 per acre obtainable from rice under favorable conditions is considered sufficient to meet "the full cost of mechanical cultivation and allow a reasonable return to the cultivator. This is true, however, of very few crops in Nigeria" (*69,* p. 35).

One of the significant factors likely to lead to expansion of rice was noted briefly in Chapter 6. In examining the problem of population concentration in the Eastern Region of Nigeria, A. T. Grove reached the conclusion that population and farming will tend to move increasingly into riverine valleys, with rice emerging as a major staple crop (*48,* p. 304). P. H. Nye anticipates that a similar trend will be evident throughout much of West Africa. In the savanna regions of West Africa, he suggests (*77,* p. 94),

the future lies not on the uplands, with their impoverished eroded sandy and shallow soils, but in the deeper, heavier, alluvial soils of the valleys. These are unexploited lands alternately bone dry and inundated by uncontrolled floods.

On the edges of the seasonal swamps and in the upper reaches of the streams, the numbers of small rice schemes are increasing rapidly, but they all face the difficulty that the flood cannot be relied upon to provide a reasonable depth of water for the right period, so flood control is essential.

Nye describes promising work to develop such lands in northern Ghana by constructing small, inexpensive earth dams in the smaller tributaries. In five land-planning areas where this development is under way, rice and some dry season vegetables are grown as irrigated crops in the valleys, the better soils of the valley sides are devoted to upland crops, while eroded or rocky areas are given over to fuel wood or controlled grazing. He regards this as "an example of a highly productive rational agriculture that could ultimately be repeated over thousands of square miles of the Savannah" (77, p. 95).

CONSUMPTION OF WHEAT PRODUCTS

The rate of increase of consumption of wheat products has been more rapid than for any of the indigenous staple foods examined in this book. Some attention to recent and prospective trends in flour consumption is, therefore, of considerable interest despite the fact that the quantity of wheat products currently consumed is very low and local production of wheat is negligible.

Wheat is not produced in the high-rainfall regions of tropical Africa because the combination of high temperatures and high humidity, and the plant diseases which they favor, are "fatal to wheat" (55, pp. 148, 345). In the Sudan and Sahel belts, cultivation of wheat appears to be precluded largely by lack of moisture even though large areas receive a larger annual rainfall than do some major wheat regions of the world. A number of factors combine, however, to greatly reduce the efficiency of precipitation in the huge Sudan Zone of West Africa: (1) the high temperatures and solar radiation throughout much of the year, the extremely low humidity, and the Harmattan winds which blow southwest from the Sahara in the winter cause very high rates of evaporation and transpiration; (2) the concentration of the rainfall in heavy deluges leads to rapid runoff; and (3) the short duration of the rainy season and its erratic timing reduce the agricultural value of the precipitation received. It is the last factor that probably gives the great advantage to millets and sorghums. They are drought-resistant in the specific sense of being able to go into a dormant period when soil moisture is depleted and then recover if rains arrive, whereas wheat and other small grains ripen prematurely and the crop is lost under such conditions (52,

p. 288). Wheat is also at a disadvantage because the soils in the savanna areas are characteristically too light for a plant as exacting as wheat. I find no reports of attempts to grow wheat in the African Sudan zone with modern dry-farming methods and adapted varieties.[4] But even were wheat production feasible it is unlikely that it would receive a price differential sufficient to offset its yield disadvantage. Although wheat is of great importance in certain other regions of the world inadequately supplied with moisture, wheat prices in those areas typically exceed the prices of competing grains by 30 per cent or more, a greater differential than is likely to exist when wheat is being grown for local consumption (52, pp. 13, 427–29).

Although wheat production with dry-farming methods is apparently not practiced in the African Sudan, there are areas where small quantities are grown under irrigation. In the Kanem District of the Chad Territory of French Equatorial Africa, a little wheat is grown in natural depressions called *ouaddi*. Sometimes the cultivation is in basins with natural connection with the lake, and elsewhere there is controlled irrigation with water drawn from wells by the Egyptian balance or *shadoof*. The rise in the level of Lake Chad (nearly 3 meters between 1950 and 1957) and exceptionally heavy rainfall for this area received in 1954 and 1956 made it necessary to replace a number of the dikes which had been constructed to make dry land available for cultivation; but there seems to be reason to hope that the level of the lake has been stabilized (2, p. 34). Total production of wheat in French Equatorial Africa is placed at only 720 tons (3, p. 100). Ch. Godard believes that wheat production can be expanded appreciably in the areas bordering on Lake Chad, a number of ouaddi suited to this culture not yet being utilized. Satisfactory development, however, would require installation of power pumps, and apparently all that is feasible in this remote area is to satisfy a local demand (33, pp. 306–07).[5]

In Kano Province of northern Nigeria, wheat is sometimes grown as a dry season (winter) crop on small irrigated plots of one-fourth

----

[4] It is of some interest to note that in the southern great plains in the United States wheat has been about four times as important as sorghum (1914–48). Rainfall in this area has averaged 24 inches, with July and August averaging 1.95 inches and 2.41 inches respectively, and the annual evaporation is given as 51 inches (58). The much cooler mean temperatures in winter in the southern great plains are, however, an important climatic difference.

[5] It was reported in late 1955 that the Director General of the Grands Moulins de Paris and a group of specialists were to study the possibilities of developing wheat production in the Chad area (28, p. 331).

to one-half an acre. The quantity must be almost insignificant, for the wheat is grown on these farms essentially as a garden crop along with onions and other vegetables (*76*, p. 521). Minute quantities of wheat are also grown in the Niger and Sudan territories of French West Africa. A figure of 371 tons is given for Niger, where wheat seems to be grown mainly as a garden crop in Aïr, a mountainous district (*90*, p. 65). It is reported that about a thousand hectares are planted to wheat in the Goundam-Tombouctoo region of Sudan (*93*, p. 68). This and the Chad wheat are identified as soft wheat, but in northern Nigeria some macaroni wheat (*Triticum durum* var. *leucurum*) is grown as well as an awnless soft wheat.

The Agricultural Service in the Belgian Congo has been experimenting with the cultivation of wheat on high plateaus since 1923. Great difficulty has been encountered with rust damage, but cultivation has been successful at elevations above 1,800 meters where the climate is sufficiently temperate to avoid serious rust damage. At Kisozi in Urundi, where wheat is grown successfully, the annual rainfall is about 60 inches. Yields ordinarily range between 500 and 1,000 kgs per hectare or sometimes more (*1*, pp. 186–90). The largest production of wheat in western tropical Africa is in Angola. Production, estimated at about 14,000 tons, is concentrated in the central plateau.

Local production of wheat is so slight in these territories of tropical Africa that consumption of wheat products can be taken as identical with net imports. By relying on import data, it is possible to review the trend of consumption of wheat flour over a considerable span of years. In a study of wheat consumption in tropical regions published in 1930, M. K. Bennett reported that for a group of African countries there appeared to be an increase from an annual average consumption of only 0.6 kg of wheat flour per capita for the years 1909–13 to 0.8 kg in 1923–27 (*9*, p. 348).[6] For the years 1951–54, average per capita consumption of wheat flour for the territories of western tropical Africa, shown in Table 9-1, was 2.0 kgs. This resulted from average annual net imports of 151,000 metric tons, a fourfold increase as compared with average imports during 1934–38 and nearly a twofold increase over the 1948–50 level. (For the coun-

---

[6] The tropical regions considered in this study were: Asia, Africa, Central and South America, the West Indies, Oceania, and Brazil. "Africa" was represented by data for Nigeria, Gold Coast, Gambia, Sierra Leone, Senegal, Ivory Coast, French Guinea, Dahomey, Gabon, Middle Congo, Belgian Congo, Mozambique, Mauritius, Réunion, Seychelles, Madagascar, Northern and Southern Rhodesia, British, French, and Italian Somaliland.

tries included in Bennett's study, per capita consumption in 1951–54 was 2.7 kgs.)

TABLE 9-1.—WHEAT FLOUR NET IMPORTS AND PER CAPITA CONSUMPTION, WESTERN TROPICAL AFRICA, 1951–54 AVERAGE WITH COMPARISONS*

(Thousand metric tons, and kilograms per capita)

Territory	Net imports			Per capita consumption[a] 1951–54
	1934–38	1948–50	1951–54	
Belgian Congo[b]	2.4	8.5	19.4	1.6
French Cameroons	1.0	4.3	11.7	3.8
Fr. Equat. Africa	1.0	4.3	7.5	1.6
Fr. Togo	.3	1.0	1.4	1.3
Fr. West Africa[b]	16.9	33.2	56.6	3.1
Gambia	.7	.7	1.4	5.0
Ghana (Gold Coast)	7.2	16.4	28.5	7.0
Liberia	...	.6[c]	.7	.6
Nigeria	2.7	8.6	19.8	.7
Sierra Leone	1.4	2.5	4.0	2.0
Total	33.6	80.1	151.0	2.0[d]

* Net imports from FAO, *Yearbook of Food and Agricultural Statistics, Part 2, Trade, 1954*, pp. 55, 59; and *ibid., 1955*, pp. 48, 52. The Belgian Congo and French West Africa are the only countries in the area that report imports of any wheat grain. Population as of mid-1953 from UN, *Demographic Yearbook, 1956*, pp. 135–39.

[a] Net imports (identical or nearly identical with consumption) divided by population as of mid-1953.

[b] Including flour equivalent of small net imports of wheat grain.

[c] Unofficial.

[d] Average.

Numerous descriptive accounts comment on the rapid increase in the consumption of wheat flour and provide additional information concerning the nature of the expansion. A report on the market for food products in French West Africa observes (*61*, p. 1687):

It is first of all bread which has benefited from the favor of consumers. In 1939, it was only consumed in the cities and in small quantities by the Europeans and the well-to-do African bourgeoisie. Today, it is to be found in all the centers, in the grocery shop, in the market stands in the same fashion as cola nuts and peanuts.

Data on flour imports and consumption in the French Cameroons show consumption by Africans and Europeans separately, and also indicate the great variation in per capita consumption between districts. It is estimated that between 1946 and 1952, while consumption of wheat flour by Europeans was increasing from 480 to 1,250 tons, there was nearly a tenfold increase in African consumption, from 960 to 8,961 tons. In the subdivision of Wouri, which includes the rapidly expanding port city of Douala, it is estimated that the per capita consumption of wheat flour had reached 41 kgs. Two other subdivisions with urban or port centers registered flour consumption of about 10 and 13 kgs, but in the other more remote and less developed districts flour consumption was very low indeed (62, pp. 1690–91). Marked variation is also apparent in estimates of flour consumption in the three regions of Nigeria. In the Western Region, the center of cocoa production and an area with higher incomes than the other regions, per capita consumption is estimated at 2.7 kgs per year compared with 0.6 and 0.4 kg in the Eastern and Northern Regions (31, p. 12).

Estimates of native consumption of wheat flour in the Belgian Congo also point to a striking increase. It is reported that consumption of wheat flour by the Congolese population rose from 3,000 tons in 1948 to 16,600 in 1955, well over a fivefold increase in seven years (29, p. 465). Consumption by Europeans apparently accounts for a considerable part of the wheat and flour imported into the Congo. Thus the increase in total imports of wheat and flour from 1948 to 1955 was from 9,000 to 36,000 tons in wheat equivalent (or from roughly 6,500 to 26,000 tons in terms of wheat flour), appreciably less than the estimated rate of increase in native consumption.

The increase in consumption of wheat flour is attributed primarily to a widespread tendency for urban residents to add wheat products to their diet as income permits. Explanations of this trend of consumption in urban areas stress particularly the convenience of bread and rolls as food staples, and the fuel economy of bread compared to indigenous staple foods is also mentioned. Some observers further stress the fact that many Africans acquired a taste for bread during military service in World War II.

Nearly all of the wheat is imported in the form of wheat flour. Only in the French West African territory of Senegal has a sizable milling industry been created. Largest of the mills is the Grands Moulins de Dakar, which, following substantial expansion during 1955, was estimated to have a capacity of about 100,000 tons a year. The Moulins de l'A.O.F., also located in Dakar, has a much smaller though nonetheless considerable capacity; production in 1955 reached 15,000 tons (26, pp. 3056–57). Imports of wheat by the Grands Moulins de Dakar during 1955 amounted to nearly 30,000 tons, all of it from Morocco. Total shipments into Dakar in 1955 were 45,000 tons; wheat imports reached nearly 63,000 tons in 1956 and exceeded 50,000 tons during the first six months of 1957. Recent shipments have come almost entirely from France. The Dakar mills are now capable of supplying all of French West Africa, and since January 1957 the French government has required the territories of French West Africa to purchase 75 per cent of their flour requirements from the Dakar mills. And as a further guarantee to the Dakar mills, the French Cameroons and French Equatorial Africa are obliged to obtain 65 per cent of their flour imports from Dakar.

In addition to the numerous small bakeries that have sprung up in African cities and outlying areas as well, several large-scale baking establishments have been built. Outstanding among the larger ones is La Panification Industrielle Christian in the Ivory Coast, which produced 14.5 million loaves or 9,400 tons of bread in 1955. Besides serving the capital city of Abidjan, deliveries are made by truck to areas as far as 90 miles in the interior and account for approximately half of the firm's sales (*26*, p. 3066).

Rising incomes, urbanization, and increasing familiarity with wheat products can all be expected to lead to further growth of wheat consumption. There seems every reason to expect that the rising trend of recent decades will continue, and statements to that effect are common. Abeele and Vandenput remark, for example: "It is to be expected that the consumption of bread will increase very rapidly" (*1*, p. 201). One European writer is so carried away by his expectation of rising consumption of wheat flour that he suggests, with far more enthusiasm than accuracy, that this development could "lead progressively to the abandonment of the traditional food crops which, for a small yield, exhaust the soil and furnish only poor food products" (*24*, p. 1611). In a final burst of zeal this same author declares, "We have the responsibility to lead the peoples of the overseas territories to political and social maturity, to integrate them, to imbue them with our civilization. And is not bread the typical food of civilized peoples?" (*24*, p. 1612).

Comparison of present levels of flour consumption with trends and levels of consumption in other tropical areas, Asia and the West Indies, is perhaps the strongest basis for anticipating a substantial increase in tropical Africa.[7] Current per capita consumption in a group of tropical countries in Asia is a little over five kgs per year

[7] The Asian countries considered are Ceylon, Indonesia, Malaya-Singapore; the Associated States of Laos, Cambodia, and Vietnam; the Philippines; and Taiwan. The West Indies group comprises Jamaica, Trinidad, and other islands of the British West Indies; Cuba, Puerto Rico; Haiti; Dominican Republic; Martinique; and Guadaloupe.

but with wide variations from country to country. In Indonesia and the Associated States of Cambodia, Laos, and Vietnam, consumption is about 1.6 kgs, but in the other areas it ranges from 9 kgs in the Philippines to 28 kgs in Ceylon. In the West Indies there is also a wide range—from 8 kgs in the Dominican Republic to close to 70 kgs per capita in Martinique. But average per capita consumption in the West Indies—some 25 kgs per year—is much higher than in Asia and is more than ten times as high as the present level in western tropical Africa. In these calculations, tropical Asia and the West Indies have been defined in essentially the same way as in Bennett's study of the growth of wheat consumption in tropical countries; an indication of the trend of flour consumption over the past half century can thus be obtained by combining Bennett's data (9, p. 348) with the present calculations (kgs per capita per year):

Region[a]	1909–13	1923–27	1951–54
Tropical Africa	.6	.8	2.7
Asia	1.6	2.3	5.2
West Indies	24.2	26.2	24.7

[a] The composition of the African region as used here and in Bennett's calculations differs appreciably from the territories included in Table 9-1. Omission of North Vietnam and French India from the 1951–54 figures is the only change from Bennett's Asia grouping.

There is no reason to expect closely similar levels of flour consumption in all tropical areas. Quite apart from the variations which may be related to differences in consumer preferences or income levels, it appears that the degree of dependence on imported food often has a very strong influence on the level of flour consumption. This is, of course, to be expected; food imports to cover a considerable portion of a country's food needs almost always consist mainly of wheat, rice, or some combination of the two.

In spite of the qualifications that must be made, the indication is strong that there will be further substantial growth in the consumption of wheat flour in western tropical Africa unless imports are curbed by government action. It is possible, for example, that quantitative restrictions may be imposed on imports of wheat and flour because of a policy of limiting foreign exchange allocations for the purchase of consumer goods. Likewise import duties imposed for revenue purposes may cause flour and bread to be expensive relative to indigenous staples. On the other hand, concessional sales of wheat or flour by exporting countries holding burdensome surplus stocks may induce certain countries to import and consume larger quantities of wheat than would otherwise be purchased.

The extent to which wheat will secure an increasingly important place in African diets will naturally depend a good deal on the relationship between the price of wheat flour or bread and the prices of local staple foods. Two recent observations concerning experience in French West Africa stress the sensitiveness of consumers to the level of flour prices. J. A. Colombani attributed a considerable decline in wheat and flour imports in French West Africa between 1951 and 1952 to curtailed demand for bread resulting from an increase in its price (*24*, p. 1611). And Jean Denis, writing in 1956, anticipated a marked increase in consumption following a reduction in flour and bread prices as a result of export subsidies made available by the French government (*26*, p. 3057). According to preliminary trade returns for 1957, his expectation was borne out. On the basis of very fragmentary price data for wheat flour and for local staples, it would appear that flour is a little more expensive than rice and perhaps twice as costly as maize meal. The price relationship between wheat flour and bread, expressing both as a price per 1,000 calories, seems to vary a great deal in the quotations for different cities. In the coastal city of Conakry in French Guinea the price of bread is only some 10 per cent higher than the price of flour, whereas at Fort Lamy bread appears to be some 80 per cent more costly than wheat flour on a calorie basis. At Bangui, another city of French Equatorial Africa lying about half as far from the coast as Fort Lamy, the price quoted for bread is about 45 per cent more expensive, in terms of calories, than wheat flour.[8]

COMPETITION BETWEEN ROOT CROPS AND CEREALS

Since the time of Adam Smith, economists have regarded it as axiomatic that growth of regional specialization and production for commercial markets represents an important element in increasing productivity. This view is, however, sometimes challenged in its application to food production in tropical Africa. A report of the Agricultural Productivity Committee in Uganda published in 1954 has argued that government policy should aim at ensuring self-sufficiency with respect to staple food supplies (*98*, pp. 42–43). The Committee

---

[8] Based on an analysis by Mr. Bill J. Pace of price data published in the statistical bulletins of Guinea, the Ivory Coast, Dahomey, Senegal and Mauritania, Ubangi-Shari and Chad in French Africa, and of Angola (*10, 14, 15, 16, 17, 18, 19, 20*). In Conakry, and perhaps in the other areas as well, the actual weight of the bread was probably some 10 per cent less than the nominal weights used in the above computation owing to the leeway which bakers are permitted under the official price regulations.

recognizes the advantages of specialization in the production of certain cash crops, but for food crops they believe that any gains in production efficiency would not offset disadvantages such as the danger of famine and the cost and difficulty of transporting food to deficit areas.

A somewhat similar view is put forward at one point in the *Ten-Year Plan for Economic and Social Development of the Belgian Congo* (*7*, p. 22): "Every effort will be made to diversify local production in order to give the population the possibility of varying its diet while avoiding inter-regional shipments as much as possible." But the general view expressed in the development plan for the Congo is that interregional trade will become increasingly important (*7*, p. 23): "These facts will determine the future orientation of agriculture: exchanges of greater and greater importance, at greater and greater distances will be established between specialized but complementary regions."

Although it would be foolhardy to forecast the extent to which specialization and interregional trade will be developed in tropical Africa, the presumption is strong that improvement of transport facilities, the growth of urban demand for farm products, and technical advance and capital accumulation in agriculture will bring significant changes in that direction. In reporting on the needs for economic research in East Africa, E. A. G. Robinson bowed to local views to the extent of acknowledging that there may be "good technical as well as precautionary reasons" for a policy of self-sufficiency; but he then stressed the common view that "in more advanced countries the specialisation of agriculture and the development of large-scale production of foodstuffs has been one of the important sources of economic progress, and with improved transport facilities it is becoming easier to move grain to areas of shortage" (*86*, p. 19).

Owing to the comparative ease with which grain crops can be commercialized, their importance relative to the roots and tubers will tend to increase with the growth of interregional trade. This rather obvious but important proposition is summed up well in an observation pointed at Uganda (*66*, p. 65):

The country people therefore have little need to store food but subsist mainly on green bananas and sweet potatoes [and other foods which can be harvested more or less continuously through the year]. On the other hand the cost of transporting this bulky fresh food makes it expensive for town dwellers and for feeding large numbers of labourers. In consequence, there is a growing demand for dry foods which can be stored, particularly maize.

The crucial elements here are obviously the storage qualities of the different staples and the extent to which their price at the point of production is increased by transport and handling charges. The roots and tubers show considerable variation in their keeping qualities (see Chapter 5), but all of them in their fresh state are costly and difficult to store or ship as compared with grain. Dried manioc products such as gari, cosettes, and manioc flour approach the cereals in their storage and transport characteristics; but cosettes, the dried, sliced roots, are a good deal bulkier than a compact product like rice or flour even though moisture content and calorie value are similar. Although the safe storage period of gari and manioc flour is apparently shorter than for grain or wheat flour, the practical importance of this difference is reduced because of the fairly uniform flow of manioc production through the year. In the Congo, storage problems with manioc flour are also minimized by shipping and storing cosettes which are ground into flour only a short time before being sold for consumption.[9]

It was noted in Chapter 6 that the intermarket dispersion of prices of roots and tubers seems to reflect proximity or distance from the producing area much more sharply than do the grain crops. Experience in Jamaica throws light on price and consumption relationships between roots and cereals products because it is one of the few areas where root crops are of major importance and for which statistical data exist covering four or five decades. While production statistics are too meager to judge the trend directly, it appears that per capita consumption of starchy roots and plantains declined during the half century 1900–1950. Arthur Wood infers such a decline from the fact that imports of wheat flour, rice, and corn meal, which supplied some 325 calories per person per day in the years 1905–07, increased steadily and by 1951–52 their contribution measured in calories per capita had doubled. Wood believes that the increased consumption of these items was at least partly offset by reduced intake of roots and plantains, and as one causal factor he stresses that with increasing urbanization "more of the total food supply must be purchased at

---

[9] Roger Van der Aa estimates that manioc flour can be stored for five or six months at most (personal communication to W. O. Jones, Food Research Institute, Jan. 20, 1956). Cossettes can be stored longer, perhaps a year, but in fact mills manufacturing manioc flour receive a fairly steady flow, so that cosettes would normally not be stored more than two or three months. A year also appears to be a passably good estimate of the storage life of the specially processed wheat flour which is imported into the Congo, but the trade endeavors to avoid holding flour for more than three or four months.

retail prices where the cereal group appears to have the advantage of lower calorie costs" (*105*, p. 223). Another factor contributing to the rising importance of cereal products in Jamaica was simply the increasing reliance on imported food as a result of the doubling of population between 1900 and 1950, the limited availability of crop-land, and the fact that sugar, an export crop, occupied much of the better land. But it seems safe to assume that the increase in prices of roots and tubers relative to the price of wheat flour and rice con-tributed to the increased importance of the latter items. To indicate the relative importance of the staple foods in Jamaica, daily per capita consumption during a recent period is shown in addition to the price relatives for selected years (*105*, pp. 129, 220):

Commodity	Relative price per 1,000 calories *Flour = 100*			Estimated per capita supplies, 1946–50 (*calories per day*)
	1913–14	1938	1948	
Wheat flour	100	100	100	380
Corn meal	46	50	87	38
Bread	140	175	224	a
Rice	84	67	179	79
Yams	139	278	255	95
Sweet potatoes	57	171	...	52
Cocoyams	111	185	...	25
Bananas/plantains	121	162	89	45

a Included in wheat flour total.

The price relatives for bananas and plantains and for rice in 1948 seem to be contrary to the general relationship asserted above. I am unable to offer any explanation for the fact that bananas appear to have become cheaper than flour in 1948, but the higher price-relative of rice in that year can be attributed to the acute postwar shortage which caused rice to become dear relative to wheat and wheat flour.

To a considerable extent the advantages which grain crops enjoy in their suitability for long distance transport and storage merely re-inforce other considerations pointing to a growth in consumption of rice and wheat flour. A similar presumption applies to maize, already one of the cheapest staples, but the variable and uncertain nature of consumer preferences makes it especially difficult to anticipate the extent to which maize consumption may benefit from a shift away from roots and tubers. Not only are there striking contrasts between countries (for example, the strong position maize holds in Mexican diets), but within individual African territories its position varies markedly. In the urban centers of Katanga its position is preeminent, whereas in Leopoldville rice is the important cereal. Although the location of centers of production and lines of supply suggest part of the explanation for this contrast, much of it must be attributed to differences in the preferences of the Congolese populations in the two areas. Of millets and sorghums, it can only be said that in other areas of the world those crops have not held esteem as human food in areas where they have faced competition from other cereals—rice, wheat, or maize. They will undoubtedly remain highly important as the local staple food crops in those drier areas where they now predominate, but it is unlikely that they will be of much importance in supplying the food needs of urban and industrial centers, where they would enjoy a relatively small price advantage even in comparison with rice.

Among the root crops, several considerations suggest that manioc is likely to increase in importance. Clearly, it has expanded considerably during the past half-century; the advantages which it enjoys because of its low cost, ease of cultivation, ability to tolerate mediocre soils, resistance to drought and locusts, and the fairly satisfactory transport and storage characteristics of manioc products such as gari and cosettes, point to a continuation of that trend. On the other hand, rising incomes, widening familiarity with rice and wheat, and enlarged local production of the former could well mean that those staples, so generally esteemed by consumers the world over, may to some extent displace manioc in African diets. Yams, owing to the strong position they enjoy in the hierarchy of consumer preferences, presumably will be favored by increased per capita incomes. But a number of factors, including the transportation and storage problem just considered, indicate that yams are likely to become increasingly costly relative to other staples. In addition, the strong position of yams in consumer preferences appears to be, in part, a matter of tradition and prestige, and in an urban environment it is perhaps a less persistent preference than that for rice and bread. Scant basis exists for any observation concerning cocoyams, sweet potatoes, and plantains, but it seems probable that for them the general tendency will be toward a lower level of per capita consumption.

CITATIONS

1 Marcel van den Abeele and René Vandenput, *Les Principales cultures du Congo Belge* (Belg., Min. Col., 3d ed., 1956).

2 "Afrique Équatoriale Française," in *Chroniques Outre-mer* (France, Min. Outre-mer), June 1957.

3 Afrique Équatoriale Française, Haut Commissariat, *Annuaire statistique* . . . , *1936–1950,* I (Brazzaville, n.d.).

4 Afrique Occidentale Française, Govt. Gen., Dir. Gen. des Serv. Écon., Inspection Gen. Agr., *Rapport annuel, 1952* (no place, n.d., mimeo.).

5 M. G. Ancien, *La Modernisation du paysannat dans les territoires d'Outre-mer* (France, La Documentation Française, Notes et Études Documentaries, No. 2.129, Jan. 21, 1946).

6 Sir William Ashley, *The Bread of Our Forefathers* (Oxford, 1928).

7 Belg., Min. Col., *Plan décennal pour le développement économique et social du Congo Belge,* Tome I (1949).

8 ——, *Plan décennal* . . . , Tome II (1949).

9 M. K. Bennett, "Growth of Wheat Consumption in Tropical Countries," *Wheat Studies of the Food Research Institute* (Stanford), June 1930, VI.

10 Boletim Mensal de Estatística (Angola, Repartição Técnica de Estatística Geral), June 1957.

11 J. Bowden and J. T. W. Gray, "Rice Cultivation in Ghana," *The Ghana Farmer* (Ghana, Dept. Agr.), May 1957.

12 J. F. Brock, "Nutrition," *An. Rev. of Biochemistry,* Vol. 24, 1955.

13 Bull. agr. du Congo Belge (Belg., Min. Col.), June 1956.

14 Bull. inf. stat. de l'Oubangui-Chari (Afr. Équatoriale Française), various issues January to December 1956.

15 Bull. mensuel stat. (Territoire de l'Oubangui-Chari), May 1957.

16 Bull. stat. bimestriel (Territoires du Sénégal et de la Mauritanie, Serv. Stat.), June 1957.

17 Bull. stat. du Dahomey (Afr. Occidentale Française, Govt. du Dahomey), Année 1956.

18 Bull. stat. de la Guinée (Afr. Occidentale Française, Territoire de la Guinée), September 1957.

19 Bull. stat. mensuel (Govt. de Côte d'Ivoire), March 1957.

20 Bull. stat. du Tchad (Afr. Équatoriale Française), July 1957.

21 Jean Cabot, "Un domaine nouveau de riziculture inondée: Les Plaines du Moyen Logone," *Cahiers Outre-mer* (Bordeaux), April–June 1957.

22 R. Chateau, "Utilisation de l'avion en riziculture à Richard-Toll," *Riz et riziculture* (Paris), 3° année, 1ᵉʳ trimestre, 1957.

23 W. M. Clark and F. H. Hutchinson, *British West African Rice Mission's Report on the Possibilities of Expanding the Production of Rice in the British West African Colonies* (London?, 1948, mimeo.).

24 J. A. Colombani, "Les Importations de sucre et de farines panifiables en Afrique Noire française," *Marchés col. du monde* (Paris), June 6, 1953.

25 Yves Coyaud, "La Culture du riz à l'Office du Niger," *Riz et riziculture,* 2° année, 4° trimestre, 1956.

26 Jean Denis, "L'Alimentation Outre-mer: Sénégal Mauritanie," *Marchés trop. du monde* (Paris), Nov. 24, 1956.

27 Aimé Drogué, "Le Développement agricole de l'A.E.F. dans le cadre du plan décennal," in *Encycl. Col. et Mar: Afrique Équatoriale Française* (Paris, 1950).

27a Encycl. Col. et Mar: Afrique Occidentale Française (2 vols., Paris, 1949).

28 "Les Essais de culture de blé au Tchad," *Études Outre-mer* (Marseille), October 1955.

29 "L'Évolution de la consommation indigène au Congo Belge," *Bull. Banque Cent. du Congo Belge et du Ruanda-Urundi* (Brussels and Leopoldville), December 1956.

30 Food and Agriculture Organization of the United Nations (FAO), *Food Balance Sheets* (Washington, 1949).

31 R. Galletti, K. D. S. Baldwin, and I. O. Dina, *Nigerian Cocoa Farmers* . . . (Nigeria Cocoa Mkt. Bd., London, 1956).

32 Gen. Hqs., Supreme Commander for the Allied Powers, Natural Resources Sec., *Japanese Crop and Livestock Statistics, 1878–1950* (Rept. 143, Tokyo, 1951).

33 Ch. Godard, "Les Cultures vivrières au Tchad," in *Encycl. Col. et Mar: Afrique Équatoriale Française* (Paris, 1950).

34 Gold Coast Colony, Dept. Agr., *Annual Report* . . . *1948–49* (Accra, 1951).

35 Gold Coast, Dept. Agr., *Annual Report* . . . *1st April, 1952 to 31st March, 1953* (Accra, 1954).

36 ———, Min. Fin., *Economic Survey, 1953* (Accra, 1954).

37 ———, *Economic Survey, 1955* (1956).

38 ———, Off. Govt. Stat., *1953 Accra Survey of Household Budgets* (Stat. and Econ. Papers 2, Accra, December 1953).

39 ———, *Kumasi Survey of Population and Household Budgets, 1955* (Stat. and Econ. Papers 5, Accra, March 1956).

40 ———, *Sekondi Takoradi Survey of Population and Households Budgets, 1955* (Stat. and Econ. Papers 4, Accra, March 1956).

41 Pierre Gourou, *The Tropical World* . . . (London, 1953).

42 Gr. Brit., Col. Off., *The Colonial Territories, 1952–53* [Cmd. 8856].

43 ———, *Notes on Some Agricultural Development Schemes in Africa and Aden* (April 1953, mimeo.).

44 ———, *Notes on Some Agricultural Development Schemes in the British Colonial Territories* (2d rev., October 1955).

45 ———, Col. Repts., *Sierra Leone, 1953* (1954).

46 D. H. Grist, *Rice* (London, 1953).

47 R. Grivot, *Réactions Dahoméenes* (Paris, 1954).

48 A. T. Grove, "Soil Erosion and Population Problems in South-East Nigeria," *Geog. J.*, September 1951.

49 Maurice Guernier, "La Culture du riz en sec en Casamance (Sud-Senegal)," *Riz et riziculture*, 1ʳᵉ année, 4ᵉ trimestre, 1955.

50 Ellen Hellman, "Urban Food in Johannesburg," *Africa* (Internatl. Afr. Inst.), April 1936.

51 F.-L. Hendrickx and J. Henderickx, "La Jachère à bananiers," in *Comptes rendus de la Conférence Africaine des Sols, Goma* . . . *1948, II* (pub. as the June 1949 issue of *Bull. agr. du Congo Belge*, pp. 1725–44).

51a Roger Jaspar, "Du rôle de la nutrition dans l'économie indigène: Le riz," in *Vers la promotion de l'économie indigène* (Compte rendu du Colloque Col. sur Econ. Indigène, January 1956, Inst. Soc. Solvay, Brussels, 1956).

52 N. Jasny, *Competition Among Grains* (Stanford, 1940).

53 B. F. Johnston, Mosaburo Hosoda, and Yoshio Kusumi, *Japanese Food Management in World War II* (Stanford, 1953).

54 Phyllis M. Kaberry, *Women of the Grassfields* . . . (Gr. Brit., Col. Off., Col. Res. Pub. 14, 1952).

55 K. H. W. Klages, *Ecological Crop Geography* (New York, 1942).

56 Philippe Leblond, "La Culture du riz en Casamance (Sud-Senegal). Campagne 1955," *Riz et riziculture*, 2e année, 2e trimestre, 1956.

57 Liberia, Dept. Agr. and Comm., *Third Annual Progress Report of the Cooperative Program in Agriculture, Forestry, and Fisheries under the Joint Liberian-United States Commission for Economic Development* (1954).

58 F. Locke and O. R. Mathews, *Cultural Practices for Sorghums and Miscellaneous Field Crops* . . . *Woodward, Oklahoma* (U.S. Dept. Agr., Circ. 959, 1955).

59 C. W. Lynn, *Agriculture in North Mamprusi* (Gold Coast, Dept. Agr., Bull. 34, Accra, 1937).

60 A. Mallamaire, "Réunion internationale pour l'étude de Quelea (Mange-Mil)," *Agronomie trop.* (France, Min. Outre-mer), Nov–Dec. 1955.

61 "Le Marché de l'alimentation dans les principaux territoires: Afrique Occidentale Française," *Marchés col. du monde*, June 6, 1953.

62 "Le Marché de l'alimentation dans les principaux territoires: Cameroun," *Marchés col. du monde*, June 6, 1953.

63 G. B. Masefield, "African Agriculture," *Col. Rev.* (London), December 1953.

64 R. Masseyeff, A. Cambon, and B. Bergeret, "Les Camerounais devant un aliment nouveau," *Encycl. mens. Outre-mer* (Paris), April 1955.

65 G. C. Meaux, *Report on 6 Months Assignment in Liberia, West Africa as Rice Production Specialist Under Point IV Program, Nov. 30, 1952 to May 31, 1953* (U.S. Dept. Agr., For. Agr. Serv., in co-op. with Tech. Co-op. Admin., 1953, mimeo.).

66 A. P. G. Michelmore, "Food Storage Problems in Uganda in Relation to Insect Pests," *E. Afr. Agr. J.* (E. Afr. High Commis.), October 1955.

67 F. B. Morrison, *Feeds and Feeding* (21st ed., Ithaca, 1951) .

68 G. Nesterenko, *Richard-Toll au 1er juillet 1953* (Mission d'Amenagement du Sénégal, Saint Louis, Aug. 27, 1953, processed).

69 W. T. Newlyn, *Report on a Study of Mechanized Agriculture in Nigeria* (West Afr. Inst. of Soc. Econ. Res., Ibadan, 1955[?], mimeo.).

70 Nigeria, Dept. Agr., *Annual Report* . . . *1949–50* (Kaduna, 1951).

71 ———, *Annual Report* . . . *1951–52* (Insp. Gen. Agr., no place, 1954).

72 ———, *Annual Report* . . . *(Central), 1952–53, Part I* (Lagos, 1955).

73 ———, *Annual Report* . . . *Western Region, 1951–52* (Ibadan, 1954).

74 Nigeria, Eastern Region, *Agricultural Policy for Natural Resources* . . . (Sess. Paper 3, Lagos, 1953).

75 ———, Inf. Serv., *Eastern Nigeria* (Enugu, January 1956).

76 Nigeria, Northern, Dept. Agr., "Farming Systems in Kano Province,"

Afr. Soils (Inter-Afr. Bur. Soils and Rural Econ., CCTA [London]), Oct.–Dec. 1955.

77 P. H. Nye, "Some Prospects for Subsistence Agriculture in West Africa," *J. W. Afr. Sci. Assn.* (Achimota), February 1957.

78 Léon Pales, *L'Alimentation en A.O.F.* . . . (Orgn. de Recherches sur l'Aliment. et Nutr. Afr.—ORANA—Dakar, 1954).

79 Louis Papy, "La Vallée du Sénégal: Agriculture traditionelle et riziculture mécanisée," art. from *Cahiers Outre-mer*, Oct.–Dec. 1951, reprinted in *Problèmes agricoles au Sénégal* (Inst. Fr. Afr. Noire—IFAN—Études Sénégalaises 21, Saint Louis, 1952).

80 F. J. Pedler, *Economic Geography of West Africa* (London, 1955).

81 R. L. Pendleton, "The Place of Tropical Soils in Feeding the World," *CEIBA* (issued by the Escuela Agricola Panamericana), Nov. 15, 1954.

82 Roland Pré, *L'Avenir de la Guinée Française* (Conakry, 1951).

83 Arsène Renard, "Hydraulique agricole au Soudan," in 27a, II.

84 ———, "Les Stations agricoles," in 27a, I.

85 F. A. Robb, "Results at Esiama Rice Mill," in Gold Coast, Dept. Agr., *Year-book 1930* (Accra, n.d.).

86 E. A. G. Robinson, *Report on the Needs for Economic Research and Investigations in East Africa* (Uganda Protectorate, Entebbe, 1955).

87 Maurice Royal, "Economic Development in Senegal," *Col. Devel.* (London), Autumn 1954, No. 19.

88 G. Sagot, "Le Riz," in 27a, I.

89 R. N. Salaman, *The History and Social Influence of the Potato* (Cambridge [England], 1949).

90 Edmond Séré de Rivières, *Le Niger* (Paris, 1952).

91 Sierra Leone, *A Plan of Economic Development* by H. Childs (Freetown, 1949).

92 ———, *Trade Report for the Year 1955* (Freetown, n.d.).

93 Georges Spitz, *Le Soudan Français* (Paris, 1955).

94 W. R. Stanton, "Factors Affecting the Yield of Maize in West Africa," in W. Afr. Maize Rust Res. Unit, *First Annual Report, 1953* (London, 1954).

95 F. W. Thompson, "The Use of Cassava in the Feeding of Pigs on Achimota College Farm," *Farm and Forest* (Nigerian Govt., Forest Dept.), VII, No. 2, 1946.

96 Virginia Thompson and Richard Adloff, *French West Africa* (Stanford, 1958).

97 O. Tulippe, "Les Paysannats indigènes au Kasai," *Bull. soc. belg. d'études géog.* (Louvain), 1955, XXIV.

98 Uganda, *Report of the Agricultural Productivity Committee* (Entebbe, 1954).

99 United Nations (UN), *Special Study on Economic Conditions in Non-self-governing Territories* (New York, 1955).

100 UN, Econ. and Soc. Counc., *Aspects of Water Development in Africa*, companion vol. to *Economic Developments in Africa, 1954–1955* (New York, 1956).

101 U.S. Dept. Agr., *Supplement for 1954 to Consumption of Food in the United States, 1909–52* (Agr. Handbk. 62, October 1955).

102 U.S. For. Operations Admin., *Liberian Swamp Rice Production: A Success* (1955).

103 P. Viguier, "La Mise en valeur du delta central du Niger par l'irrigation," in *27a*, I.

104 R. Wauthion, "L'avenir agricole de la Province du Katanga," extr. from the *Sociéte belge d'études et expansion*, Aug.-Sept.-Oct. 1954, No. 162 in *Bull. de doc. et technique agr.* (Belg. Congo, Comité Natl. du Kivu et Off. des Produits Agr. de Costermansville, Bukavu), 1ᵉʳ trimestre 1955.

105 A. W. Wood, *Food in the Jamaican Economy, 1900–1950* (doctoral diss., Stanford Univ., May 1956).

CHAPTER 10

PROSPECTS FOR INCREASING PRODUCTIVITY AND ENLARGING STAPLE FOOD SUPPLIES

It is frequently asserted that food supplies in tropical Africa are particularly inelastic. Presumably these allegations refer to supply elasticity in the usual short-run sense of a supply schedule related to a given technology which indicates the supplies forthcoming at various prices; and they seem to have been influenced by the sharp increases in food prices that occurred in Nigeria and the Gold Coast in 1948/49 and 1950/51.

The common view is that aggregate farm output is "very" or "quite" inelastic in all countries, not merely in tropical Africa, since two of the major inputs—land and labor—are not likely to be altered significantly in the short run. With respect to economically advanced countries, there would probably be general agreement with the proposition expressed by B. D. Giles: "The supply schedule for farm output as a whole is probably very inelastic, and it shows a marked tendency to shift bodily to the right as a result of technical progress and capital accumulation" (*19*, p. 184). The really interesting question, in the writer's opinion, is the extent to which, in the years ahead, the supply function for food in tropical Africa can be expected "to shift bodily to the right as a result of technical progress and capital accumulation." But before considering the long-run potential for expanding food supplies in response to the secular growth of demand, allowing for possible increases in inputs of fixed factors and advances in productivity resulting from the discovery and application of improved farming techniques, it is well to examine the question of (short-run) elasticity in relation to staple food production in tropical Africa.

ELASTICITY OF AFRICAN FOOD SUPPLIES

Assertions concerning the inelasticity of African food supplies may be related to several rather different attitudes, including: (*a*) a view concerning the shape of the production functions of African food farmers as determined by present technology; (*b*) a view as to the psychology of African producers and the nature of their response to price changes; and (*c*) views concerning the difficulty of augmenting food supplies for urban centers because of dependence upon a restricted hinterland, owing to the poor development of transportation and distribution links with more distant producing areas. The conclusion is reached that the fears which have been expressed concerning food problems likely to arise in tropical Africa owing to the alleged inelasticity of supply have been much exaggerated. Problems related to dependence on a limited hinterland and poor transport links appear, however, to have been of considerable importance.

It seems clear that John Dalton's assertion that "domestic food prices would skyrocket" if producer incomes were allowed to rise is related to a characteristic of African food production: "But domestic food supply is quite inelastic. It will remain so until fundamental agricultural research can prescribe a secure substitute for the system of shifting cultivation" (*10*, pp. 415–16). No suggestion is offered to explain why dependence upon shifting cultivation implies a particularly inelastic supply function. Actually so little is known about the nature of the production functions of African food producers that it seems impossible to confirm or refute Dalton's assertion. In the same vein of general speculation, it might be argued that the elasticity of agricultural output will be especially low in an area such as tropical Africa, since purchased inputs of fertilizers and other requisites are so much less important than in an advanced country. This is presumably one of the factors Gunnar Myrdal had in mind when he spoke generally of the "relatively low elasticity of domestic supplies, which is a characteristic of underdeveloped countries . . ." (*38*, p. 241). It could also be argued that underdeveloped economies are likely to be characterized by a certain lack of mobility of labor and other productive factors, and a degree of rigidity in production patterns insofar as these are dictated by custom or traditional authority. On the other hand, there seems to be considerable scope in Africa for varying the area under cultivation and for intensifying the farming effort by increasing the number of hours worked per day or days per year.

It is to be emphasized that the elasticity of supply for food products is necessarily greater than for total agricultural output because of the possibility of shifting land and labor resources between production of export crops and food crops. Indeed, an important factor in the rise in food prices in the Gold Coast and Nigeria referred to above was the strong demand for labor for cocoa farming, as a result of the attractive prices prevailing, which led to a general increase in wage rates for farm laborers. Use of land for production of export rather than for local food crops is quite often cited as a major reason for concern about food supplies. Robert Buron has argued, for example, that food supply problems are likely to hamper economic development in French West Africa because concentration on cash export crops has led to neglect of food crops (5, p. 1054).

The elasticity of food supplies in different regions of tropical Africa probably varies to some extent according to the staple foods that bulk largest in local diets. The production characteristics of the root crops and plantains suggest a more elastic supply situation, as governed by conditions of production, than those of millets and sorghums. W. H. Beckett's description of the production of cocoyams and plantains in a cocoa district of Ghana, which is summarized below, points in that direction. And the production conditions for manioc seem to suggest a distinctly elastic supply because of the common practice of leaving the roots in the ground unharvested if the price, or the food needs of the producer, do not seem to justify the expense or labor of harvesting.[1]

One additional problem on the production side needs to be mentioned. Maize rust was introduced into West Africa from the Americas in 1949, and a severe epiphytotic developed rapidly between 1950 and 1953. The local maize was highly susceptible to the American rust (*Puccinia polysora*), and conditions for spore germination and infection were nearly optimum in the humid coastal areas of West Africa. Cammack estimates that in 1950 there was an over-all loss of maize yields of 20–40 per cent in the rain forest regions of West Africa (6). Speaking of rust damage in Dahomey which reached its peak between May and September 1950, Cammack asserts that the resulting decline of production in this maize-dominant area "resulted in a local food shortage which caused the price of maize to rise 500%" (7, p. 20). It may be doubted whether the sharp reduction in maize supplies as a result of rust damage was entirely responsible for such an increase; but it cannot be doubted that rust damage was a significant factor contributing to the 1950/51 price increases in the Gold Coast and Nigeria as well as Dahomey, and of food prices generally, and not merely maize. The elasticity of substitution among the starchy staples is so high that a reduction in the supply of maize would

[1] The proposition in the text is to be distinguished from the obvious fact that the supply elasticity for any individual crop will be greater than the elasticity of supply for all food crops since its output can be expanded by shifting resources from the production of other crops. The point stressed here is that the total food supply function is likely to vary considerably from area to area depending on the production characteristics of the staples which are dominant.

have a very strong influence on the prices of all staple foods. To the extent that the inflationary rise in food prices at this time was a result of the outbreak of American rust (*Puccinia polysora*), which began in 1950, it is hardly to be regarded as a general feature of the supply conditions for staple foods in West Africa. Between 1953 and 1956 the disease declined in severity for a variety of reasons. Considerable natural selection must have occurred as the most susceptible local varieties were attacked so severely that they produced virtually no grain (*6*, pp. 19–20). Moreover, it was soon found that rust damage could be minimized by early planting, and considerable success was achieved in breeding rust resistant varieties by utilizing varieties of Central and South American origin.

The statement by Seers and Ross quoted in Chapter 1 seems to suggest that the alleged inelasticity is due to a certain sluggishness in the response of producers to a price increase (*51*, p. 23). Data required for testing such a view of the psychology of African farmers do not exist; but there are fragments of information that certainly cast doubt on it, particularly as a proposition applicable to producer responses to changes in the relative prices of individual crops. A recent experience in Uganda suggests that in that East African territory there is little sluggishness in the response of producers to a price increase. Between 1952 and 1953 the area planted to maize increased from 201,000 to 662,000 acres and, we are told, "It is highly probable that this record crop was due primarily to the high prices for maize which prevailed during the previous season under a system of unrestricted marketing and disposal in a poor year" (*52*, pp. 4, 93). More generally, the impressive expansion of native production of cocoa in West Africa over the past half-century would also seem to refute any notion of a "backward-sloping supply curve" of farming effort. The whole question of whether African producers respond to economic incentives in a "normal" manner is complex, but the writer subscribes to Neumark's view that many of the alleged instances of a failure to respond have been based upon incomplete understanding of the relevant economic influences (*39*).

A review of developments in Nigeria and the Gold Coast in 1948/49 and 1950/51, when food prices rose sharply, throws light on several aspects of the problem of elasticity of African food supplies. The Nigerian Department of Agriculture summed up the situation in 1950/51 in these terms (*41*, p. 47):

Prices of staple foods rose steeply during the year due to a combination of factors, maize shortage caused by rust being one of the most important. Other factors were higher produce prices, and wage levels and the rapid development of the timber export trade all of which increased purchasing power and food consumption while diminishing labour available for farm work to some extent. Future food prospects are however quite encouraging as the high prices stimulated annual crop farming, and in most areas the acreages under cassava increased considerably.

Of particular interest at this point is the view that Nigerian food producers were showing a marked response to the increase in food prices.

Maize rust and increased cocoa incomes were both important factors in the rise in food prices in the Gold Coast as well. The producer price of cocoa rose sharply to 27 shillings 6 pence in 1946/47, compared with 14/6 the previous year, and rose in the next two years to 40 and 65 shillings respectively. Poor crop yields during 1945–47, because of a series of years with late rainfall, and curtailed planting of cocoyams and plantains appear to have been other factors which aggravated the 1948/49 food shortage. According to J. O. Torto, Deputy Director of Agriculture in Ghana, the slow rate of planting of cocoa during the war and until 1946/47 because of low prices also meant a significant curtailment in the planting of cocoyams and plantains which are used as nurse crops for young cocoa. Whatever the underlying causes of the situation may have been, fears were expressed that "the country would be faced with a chronic food shortage and greatly inflated prices" (*20*, p. 3). This greater concern in the Gold Coast was translated into several measures to do something about the food situation. In response to recommendations of a subcommittee of the Central Planning Committee set up in September 1949, the Gold Coast government appointed a Commissioner of Food Production, launched a "Grow More Food" campaign, and established a Bulk Purchase and Storage Organization to implement a system of guaranteed prices (*20*, p. 3). In November 1952, a National Food Board was created to examine "all problems connected with production, distribution and marketing of foodstuffs and to advise on means of ensuring an increase in the production of foodstuffs to meet the needs of the present and future population of the country" (*22*, p. 12).

By 1953 the supply-demand situation for food had changed appreciably and the weighted price index for seven Gold Coast cities showed a small decline from 197 to 186; important staples such as manioc, plantains, and maize registered declines of 20 per cent or more. The Department of Agriculture reported a "considerable increase in cassava production" as early as 1951/52 (*21*, p. 11); and by 1953 the maize crop had made a considerable recovery which was attributed to the adoption of early planting as a means of reducing rust damage (*23*, pp. 19–20). In addition, at least one significant component of demand was at a lower level in 1953; payments to cocoa farmers were reduced by some £7 million as a result of a decline in production (*23*, pp. 13–14).

The most interesting feature of the Gold Coast experience is the way emphasis seems to have shifted away from special measures to stimulate food production and toward measures to enlarge the hinterland supplying urban areas by developing the transport network. In fact, the effort to stimulate increased output of food crops by means of a propaganda drive making use of local Food Production Advisers seems not to have been very successful (*21*, p. 11). And in May 1954 the Guaranteed Prices Scheme was discontinued, although small quantities of maize were bought by the government in August of that year when the price was considered unduly low (*24*, p. 23). More and more attention has been given to the development of "feeder roads . . . required to open up places where foodstuffs were already available but from which lorry transport was not at present possible" (*21*, p. 11). By 1954 this appears to have become the principal concern of the Food Board which was giving "special attention to the construction or improvement and maintenance of 'feeder' roads," and by the end of that year grants of some £280,000 had been made for this purpose (*24*, p. 23).

A recent article by H. P. White suggests that road building to increase the movement of food supplies to markets is the crucial factor in satisfying urban food needs (*54*, p. 125). The view that inelasticity of food supplies for urban areas was related chiefly to inadequate and costly transportation and poorly developed trade channels had been suggested earlier by W. H. Beckett. On the basis of his studies in the Gold Coast during the 1930s, he concluded that "food problems in the Gold Coast have not been those of production, but of distribution. Centres of increasing population have sometimes outstripped the increase in cultivation of foodstuffs within the economic radius" (*3*, p. 76). His observations in Akokoaso, which he regards as sort of a "modal" village of the cocoa belt, suggest a high elasticity of supply at the point of production where "the bulk foods, plantain, cocoyams, etc., are over-produced and much is left to rot in the farms . . ." Owing to costly and inadequate transportation and the bulky nature of the starchy staples produced in this forest region, the elasticity of supplies available to urban areas was very much less. It seems most unlikely that this sort of "overproduction" would be duplicated in a millet-sorghum region where the staple crops are more easily stored and transported. Even in the forest zone of Ghana, significant changes have occured since 1932–35 when Beckett carried out his survey. Roads have been extended and their quality improved. Army purchases during the war years and continuing growth in the food requirements of urban areas in the postwar period have led to marked expansion of demand, which has made itself felt in areas that would have been virtually untouched by such outside influences two decades ago.

Broadening the "economic radius" through improvements in the local transportation system is not the only possibility to be considered. Enlarged food imports are, of course, another source of additional food supplies. The United Nations report on the enlargement of the exchange economy in tropical Africa rejects this possibility in summary fashion by asserting that this would mean importation of consumer goods "at the expense of capital goods, and the rate of possible development would be correspondingly reduced" (53, p. 48). There are territories in which a shortage of foreign exchange is a major bottleneck to development, but it is certainly not a universal condition. Taking a sufficiently long period to allow for shifts in the use of land and other factors of production, it seems quite possible that exchange of tropical crops such as cocoa and oil-palm products for wheat and certain other agricultural commodities from temperate regions will be increasingly advantageous (45, pp. 54, 216). Moreover, there seems to be no valid reason why consumer preference for bread should not be allowed to express itself, particularly since there is an appreciable nutritional advantage in substituting bread for root crops such as manioc. But in any event the possibility of importing foodstuffs certainly increases the short-run elasticity of supply. It is well to recall that special problems, which no longer apply, restricted the availability of food imports in 1948/49 and 1950/51. Postwar food shortages were still limiting export availabilities in 1948/49, and in 1950/51 there was a sharp upsurge in demand for food imports following the outbreak of hostilities in Korea. Furthermore, shortages of shipping and port facilities were a limiting factor that has now been eased considerably. And finally, in this current era of agricultural surpluses, even a shortage of foreign exchange may not be crucial in view of the possibility of obtaining imports on favorable terms from regions with large surplus stocks. At a recent committee session of the United Nations General Assembly the United States representative observed "that U.S. surplus stocks could be made available for the establishment in other countries of reserve stocks to meet crop failures or other emergencies, or to mitigate excessive price effects of increased demand due to development programs" (*13*, p. 17).

LONG-TERM EXPANSIBILITY OF STAPLE FOOD SUPPLIES

After the detailed discussion of the staple food crops, which has occupied the larger part of this book, it is appropriate to look at the prospects of long-run expansion of food production to satisfy the growth of demand resulting from population increase, urbanization, industrial and mining development, and rising incomes. Particularly does this seem pertinent since concern has often been expressed on this point. Reference was made in Chapter 1 to Pedler's statement that West Africa does not have "a system of agriculture which can provide surpluses to support large urban populations" (*45*, p. 44). And Dalton's statement that African food supplies would remain inelastic "until fundamental agricultural research can prescribe a secure substitute for the system of shifting cultivation" seems more relevant to this question of long-term expansibility of food supplies than to elasticity in the short-run sense.

In recent years the lack of fundamental knowledge applicable to tropical agriculture has been frequently stressed. This has been particularly true of the problems related to the rapid decline in soil fertility under tropical conditions of heavy rainfall and high soil temperatures and of the disadvantages inherent in the system of shifting cultivation. The FAO has recently appointed a consultant on shifting cultivation and has addressed an appeal to "governments, research centres, associations, and private persons" to aid in "the campaign to overcome shifting cultivation," described as "the greatest obstacle not only to the immediate increase of agricultural production, but also to the conservation of the production potential for the future, in the form of soils and forests" (*14*, pp. 159, 164).

Among the unfavorable consequences that are mentioned, the most important seem to be related to the fact that with shifting cultivation African farmers are not induced to intensify their agriculture or to undertake long-term improvements of the land. The periodic moves to a new village site also have the effect of discouraging the accumulation of material wealth and of making professional differentiation and specialization more difficult. A further charge is that soils may be degraded as a result of a reduction in fallow periods due to increased population pressure or the introduction of cash crops (*14*, p. 160).

The present keen awareness of unsolved problems and unanswered questions is scarcely surprising considering that serious attention to the general problem of agricultural improvement in tropical Africa is a fairly recent development. For most of the area considered here it seems true that "the contribution of the temperate world to the tropical world, whether in capital or in knowledge, has in the main been confined to the commercial crops for export, where the benefit mainly accrues to the temperate world in lower prices" (*34*, p. 183). A particularly clear example of well-nigh exclusive preoccupation with export crops is afforded by R. Guillemin's account of the "evolution of agriculture" in the savanna region of Ubangi-Shari in French Equatorial Africa. In concluding his monograph, Guillemin observes that "since some ten years the Department of Agriculture has been investigating solutions to the problems which resulted from the introduction and rapid extension of the cultivation of cotton in virtually all of the administrative regions"; and he suggests that these recent efforts have for the first time given adequate recognition to the importance of increasing the productivity of the native farmer and enlarging the output of food crops (*26*, p. 304).

Improved technology.—Among the territories of western tropical Africa, it is in the Belgian Congo that the problems of food crop production appear to have received substantial and sustained attention for the longest period. At least since the establishment of L'Institut National pour l'Étude Agronomique du Congo Belge (INÉAC) in 1934 as the organization responsible for "the scientific progress of agriculture in the Belgian Congo," substantial efforts have been devoted to developing improved techniques for the production of food crops as well as cash crops for export (*32*, pp. 5, 8).

After early failures resulting from the attempt to transfer temperate-zone techniques of "clean cultivation" to the Congo, the emphasis has turned toward measures to develop an improved and more stable version of "Bantu agriculture," retaining a long fallow of natural regrowth. The rotation of fields under cultivation and under fallow is systematized, usually according to a "corridor system" in which land is divided into long strips about 100 meters wide. Forest strips are left on each side of the cultivated area to facilitate regrowth when the land is returned to fallow, and the corridors are oriented in an east-west direction to reduce the unfavorable effect of shade on crop yields. The special problems that arise when tropical forests are cleared for the cultivation of crops have been well summarized by Richards (47, pp. 401–02):

The removal of the forest cover at once changes the illumination at ground-level from a small fraction to full daylight. The temperature range greatly increases and the average and minimum humidity of the air become much lower . . . Exposure to sun and rain very quickly alters the properties of the soil. Where the slope is sufficient, erosion will begin to remove the surface layers of their finer fractions. The rise in soil temperature leads to a rapid disappearance of humus. . . . Associated with the loss of humus is a very considerable loss of soil nitrogen, mainly in the form of gas.

Richards further emphasizes that where

there is a long period of cultivation after clearing, particularly if the crop does not provide an adequate ground-cover, the long exposure of the soil together with the losses of plant nutrients in the harvested crops, leads to such large changes in the structure, humus-content and nutrient status of the soils that the time needed to restore the equilibrium between soil and vegetation, even when there is no large-scale erosion, becomes much greater.

Agricultural research in the Congo and the native agricultural settlement schemes — the *paysannats indigènes* — have sought to evolve a system of agriculture that would provide a technically sound and economical solution to these problems. Emphasis has been placed on (*a*) using mixed and succession crops, including perennial as well as annual crops, to keep the soil shaded most of the time and to maximize extraction of nutrients from the deep soil; (*b*) adding organic matter and use of mulches; (*c*) avoiding unnecessary tillage; and (*d*) returning the cultivated land to forest with the soil shaded and before severe exhaustion of the soil nutrients (see 33, pp. 66–67). Within the range of these management practices dictated by the nature of tropical soils, experimental work has explored a wide range of agronomic problems. In the "first phase" of agricultural development in the Congo, stress has been placed on (18, p. 378; 1, pp. 916–17):

(1) breeding, selecting, and distributing improved varieties;
(2) perfecting cultural methods, e.g., the proper timing and spacing in planting crops;
(3) choosing the most suitable crop or rotation of crops; and
(4) controlling insects and plant disease.

During a "second phase" it is anticipated that a further increase in output and productivity of Congolese cultivators will be achieved through mechanization (initially of postcultural operations) and through changes in fallow practices. A number of experiments are in progress investigating the replacement of the natural fallow by a planted fallow with economic value as a forage crop and of reduced duration made possible by the application of fertilizers. Experimentation under savanna conditions at the paysannat at Gandajika indicates that crop yields and net farm incomes can be increased considerably through the use of commercial fertilizers and by plowing in a cover crop, such as Velvet bean, Mucuna, or Crotolaria (8, p. 629). A recent article in a bulletin of the Federation of Chemical Industries in Belgium expresses the view that fertilizer use will increase greatly in the near future, partly as a result of the favorable evidence being accumulated in the investigations at Gandajika (see 36, pp. 1051–54). Reference is made to an increase in cotton yield whose value at current prices is close to twice the cost of the chemical fertilizers used. Up to the present, chemical fertilizers in the Congo are entirely imported and are still of small importance—approximately 5,600 tons in 1955 and not quite 8,000 tons during the first eleven months of 1956. Studies are in progress looking toward local production of nitrogen fertilizers, either in the Katanga or in the Bas-Congo in conjunction with the projected Inga dam.

Promising experiments have also been carried out at the INÉAC station at Yangambi in which a grass such as *Brachiaria mutica* has been planted as a short-term fallow to replace natural forest regeneration. Grazing of cattle on the grass fallow to provide additional income is also under study and appears to offer considerable promise for the future. Although trypanosomiasis limits cattle raising in many forest and forest-transition zones, there is a large part of the closed forest of the Congo basin where tsetse is not a major problem and good success is being obtained in controlling ticks and other disease problems through the use of dips. The educational problem of introducing stock raising among people who are completely inexperienced in that domain is likely to be the major obstacle to the adoption of this more intensive type of agriculture. There is also some question whether periodic plowing under of a green cover crop will be widely adopted unless tractors are available for the operation. It seems likely that mechanical cultivation and application of chemical fertilizers will be introduced simultaneously and in conjunction with the use of a green manure crop to permit continuous cultivation (8, p. 629). In the Bas-Congo, favorably situated for the importation of fertilizers and equipment and within easy reach of the Leopoldville market, something over 1,600 hectares are now under mechanical cultivation with a rotation which embraces plowing in *Crotolaria* or other green manure crops. But elsewhere it is likely to be some years before there is widespread adoption of the "second phase" techniques. For mechanization and the use of fertilizers to be profitable, except under specially favorable conditions, there will no doubt have to be changes in the cost structure so that fertilizers become cheaper while labor becomes more costly.

Significant progress has already been achieved through application of the "first phase" techniques. G. Geortay, former Chief of the Division of Food Crops at Yangambi and now one of the research directors, asserts that efforts of this nature, which do not require "important structural changes," make possible yield increases of at least 50 per cent. And whereas it is frequently asserted that African cultivators cannot produce an appreciable surplus above their own food needs, Geortay notes that a farm family in the Paysannat des Turumbu consumes only about one-fourth of its output and can therefore supply the needs of three nonfarm families (*18*, pp. 377–78). A recent study of the increase in food production and quantities commercialized in the Congo between 1948 and 1955 suggests that the expansion in total output has been impressive. According to this study, the overall increase during this period was some 58 per cent, equivalent to an increase of 42 per cent on a per capita basis. The greatest increases were in meat and fish, milk and cheese, and sugar—all increasing from very low initial levels—but the increase in the staple foods was on the order of 50 per cent (*12*, p. 467). Clearly, these estimates are subject to important qualifications, and part of the indicated increase may be merely "statistical," reflecting more complete coverage. But it nevertheless seems clear that there has been substantial expansion of food supplies to meet the growth of demand in the Congo resulting from population increase and rapid economic growth.

Quickened activity is apparent in many other territories and some promising agricultural developments are on the horizon. In a brief but highly interesting paper presented to the West African Science Association, P. H. Nye called attention to several of these possibilities. He emphasizes that shifting cultivation is much less defensible in grassland regions than in the forest. The broad-leafed fallow of a forest region springs up rapidly from the stumps left in the ground, and its litter "decomposes to a type of humus which provides subsequent crops with abundant nitrate" (*43*, p. 92). For these areas, Nye regards the system of shifting cultivation as "perfectly satisfactory provided there is sufficient land available for fallows of the necessary length" (*43*, p. 92). Under such conditions, and he believes that land scarcity is at present a problem "only in a few areas such as parts of Sierra Leone and the eastern Region of Nigeria and . . . the maize belt north of Accra," satisfactory restoration of fertility is indicated by the fact that immediate responses to applications of fertilizers are never obtained. Although considerable research has been devoted to replacing the natural regrowth by frequent resting with planted fallows such as Mucuna or other leguminous cover crops, there seems to be a question whether this is really an economical practice; in any event, "no native farmer has adopted the practice" (*43*, p. 93). More promising, in Nye's opinion, is the use of a shrub (*Acioa barteri*) now being investigated at Benin by the West African Institute for Oil Palm Research. This shrub, which is planted in rows six feet apart, is cut back so that food crops can be grown between the lines for a two-year period, by which time new branches of the shrub are beginning to form a solid cover again. After a time the *Acioa* can be cut back again, and the cycle repeated, the cut branches being useful as firewood.

In the grassland regions, however, there is much greater need to modify the natural fallow of shifting cultivation (*43*, p. 93):

The grass colonizes the abandoned land only slowly, and has a shallow root system. It is liable to be burned every year, thus exposing the land to severe erosion by the storms of the early rains. And the high carbon to nitrogen ratio of the grass leads to a type of humus which maintains an exceedingly low level of available nitrogen in the soil.

Nye points out that planting a leguminous cover crop—mainly the pigeon pea in the Guinea savanna zone of Ghana—as a substitute for the grass fallow is an obvious improvement, although this is not feasible farther north where moisture is insufficient for a worthwhile planted fallow. Another promising practice in the savanna regions of West Africa, noted by Nye and many others, is the good response obtained with the application of phosphates. Farmers in the northern regions of Ghana and Nigeria are slowly beginning to purchase fertilizer, but Nye believes that means for securing more rapid and widespread application of phosphates should be explored, possibly even the spreading of superphosphate by air as has been done in parts of New Zealand and South Africa (*43*, pp. 93–94). Nye believes that with certain improvements in cultivation practices and with contributions from the plant breeder, the entomologist, and the plant pathologist yields of subsistence crops in northern Ghana and similar regions in other territories could be doubled (*43*, p. 94). But because of the unsatisfactory moisture regime, yields would still be low: some 1,200 to 1,400 pounds of grain per acre except for areas with double rainfall maxima where approximately a ton of grain per acre can be produced by growing two crops a year.

Most promising of all, however, in Nye's opinion, is the potential for developing production of irrigated rice by constructing small, inexpensive earth dams in the tributaries of large rivers. This approach has already been described in Chapter 9, but it is worth emphasizing here that this potential increase in output is from lands that have been largely unexploited in the past since in the absence of water control they are "alternately bone dry and inundated by uncontrolled floods" (*43*, pp. 94–95).

A recent report by M. Gaide on experimental work in the Chad Territory of French Equatorial Africa calls attention to a relatively simple modification of traditional practice which holds considerable promise. It has been found that the fallow regrowth is improved considerably when, at the time of clearing, trees and bushes are cut off level with the ground instead of a yard above, and if the cuttings are heaped up for burning in between the roots instead of on top. These indications come from a series of experiments begun in 1951/52 for the purpose of evaluating various crop sequences and fallows, but because of the long fallow period and the need to follow through at least one full cycle, this type of research is necessarily of a long-term character (*17*, p. 716 and *passim*).

In addition to the possibilities for enhancing productivity in the strictly agricultural operations, significant opportunities exist to reduce labor costs through mechanizing various processing operations. The information on labor requirements for various crops reviewed in Chapter 6 clearly revealed the high proportion of the labor time of food production in tropical Africa which is devoted to post-cultural operations such as shelling, cleaning, and grinding corn; threshing, winnowing, and milling rice; or processing manioc roots into products such as gari or manioc flour.

The results of a study by P. de Schlippe, already noted in Chapter 6, underscore the importance of these operations in producing cereal crops in northern Ituri in the Belgian Congo (*49*, pp. 388–93). As an average for four crops—finger millet, sorghum, maize, and rice—he found that only 28 per cent of the total labor time was devoted to field operations prior to harvest, whereas 34 per cent of the total was required for harvesting, transporting the crop from the field into storage, and the drying, threshing, and winnowing that are carried out immediately after harvest. But the most time-consuming of all were the final operations of threshing, grinding, winnowing, and screening carried out shortly before the grain is to be consumed, which claimed some 38 per cent of the total labor time of production and processing of these cereals.

With respect to manioc W. O. Jones has affirmed that (*31*, Ch. 6):

the greatest opportunities for cutting labor costs, and possibly for cutting total costs, lie in fairly simple machines for converting fresh roots into products that will stand storage and transportation. Traditional processing methods require many hours of labor for a relatively small yield. *Gari* producers in Nigeria turn out between 1.5 and 2.5 pounds of meal per hour; at the higher figure it takes 44 man-days to transform one ton of fresh roots into meal.

Jones stresses that the labor cost of producing manioc meal could be reduced substantially by the use of either foot-pedal rotary graters or power graters. He calls attention to the development of mechanized production of manioc meal and flour in Brazil, using power graters, presses, and rotating ovens or driers. A pilot plant for mechanical production of manioc flour is in operation at Yangambi in the Belgian Congo, and steps toward mechanical processing have also been taken in Togo and other parts of French Africa. Simple power grinders used to produce maize meal and manioc flour, which are found in many villages of Ghana and to a lesser extent in other territories of West Africa, save much labor.

Further gains in efficiency can be achieved at low cost through the introduction of simple but improved hand tools. The Division of Agricultural Mechanization and Engineering at Yangambi is doing interesting work in testing the performance of numerous types of machetes, hoes, axes, and other tools and making recommendations to manufacturers concerning optimum specifications relative to size, weight, and design. A beginning has also been made in encouraging the use of new and more efficient tools for particular operations. Scuffle hoes, weeders, and sickles are among the specialized tools which can effect considerable savings in labor time. Systematic study of the most efficient method of performing various standard operations may also lead to appreciable savings in labor time.

Economic environment and structural factors.—Many other possibilities of promising improvements in technology could be cited; and references have been made to a number of them in earlier chapters. It goes without saying that if improved technology is not widely applied, its practical effect in expanding staple food supplies and increasing productivity will be slight. Existence of an agricultural extension organization and other mechanisms for disseminating knowledge of improved techniques is thus of prime importance. But other aspects of the economic environment in which farmers operate are also vital in determining whether producers have the ability and the desire to step up their productivity.

In addition to the resistance of sheer inertia, there are often legal and customary restrictions on the use of land, which discourage innovation. According to Pedler, tenure arrangements in Africa applicable to land under food crops are often more restrictive than those applying to cash crops, so that "an individual may be in a position to act on economic motives in growing cash crops and to keep the reward for himself, while if he grows food he may have to do what the elders say and he may have to share the crop with others" (45, p. 52). Frequently, almost no credit facilities are available so that it is difficult for African farmers to secure even the modest amounts of working capital required for the purchase of fertilizers. The loose communal arrangements that generally govern land tenure preclude the use of land as collateral against loans and impede the adoption of improved farming methods in other ways as well. D. C. Igwe has observed that the work of the extension service of the Department of Agriculture in Nigeria has been rather limited: "but how can the department be blamed," he asks, "in the absence of clearly defined farms managed consistently by approved farmers, and when farm sites change hands like coins in the open market?" (29, pp. 67–68). Where such tenure arrangements prevail, efforts to secure improvement of the land by encouraging farmers to construct facilities for irrigation or drainage or through application of fertilizers will not achieve much.

The paysannats indigènes in the Belgian Congo are particularly interesting as an organizational device for creating an environment favorable to the introduction of improved practices.[2] Between 1944 and 1947 great hopes had been placed in school farms where young agriculturalists were given practical training. But these efforts failed because of the resistance the young graduates encountered in returning to their tradition-bound tribal societies; "and also because neither

---

[2] Four recent articles describing the paysannats indigènes are: P. Staner, "Les Paysannats indigènes du Congo Belge et du Ruanda-Urundi," *Bull. agr. du Congo Belge*, June 1955, pp. 467–551; F. Jurion, "L'évolution des méthodes culturales au Congo Belge," *Bull. inf. de l'INÉAC*, February 1955, pp. 1–12; R. de Coene, "Agricultural Settlement Schemes in the Belgian Congo," *Trop. Agr.*, January 1956, pp. 1–12; and "Agriculture congolaise," *Bull. agr. du Congo Belge*, August 1954, pp. 887–957.

the teachers nor the specialists who advised them had sufficiently valuable technical improvements to propose" (*25*, p. 1128).

The administrative arrangements, the systematic layout of the fields, and the technical guidance which are essential features of the paysannats facilitate the introduction of better crop rotations, improved varieties, and more efficient cultural practices with respect to such factors as the timing of planting, spacing, and use of compost. In short, the paysannat structure makes it possible to realize in some degree certain of the technical advantages commonly ascribed to plantations:

(1) Application of fertilizers, weed control, and use of pesticides and insecticides can be introduced more easily and executed more efficiently; the same is true of effecting a complete substitution of improved varieties of seed for the local varieties to avoid degrading the newly introduced seed.

(2) Harvesting can be carried out more systematically and more cheaply; gradual introduction of mechanization is facilitated.

(3) Processing facilities can be set up to serve a paysannat more efficiently than scattered, unorganized farming units.

(4) Roads and other transportation facilities can be developed on a more economical basis.

A further important aspect of the program is the establishment of schools, dispensaries, warehouses, permanent housing, a supply of potable water, and cooperative stores for buying and selling. It is because shifting cultivation becomes stabilized farming with the systematic pattern of assigning fields and rotations that these community services become possible, although an appreciable outlay of public funds is also a necessary ingredient. By 1955, approximately 120,000 families had already been settled in paysannats, and it is anticipated that by 1965 some 450,000 Congolese families (out of a total of 2.5 million) will be organized into paysannats indigènes (*28*, p. 68).

Interesting though it is, the paysannat device is probably not applicable to much of tropical Africa. In discussing the problems of improving the agriculture of Manilonde village in the Bas-Congo, Drachoussoff states that it would not be possible to establish a paysannat there, partly owing to certain unfavorable natural factors, but also because "individualism and cultural technique are already too highly developed" (*11*, pp. 96–97). Apparently, he has reference primarily to the fact that in this area, a source of supply for Leopold-

ville, the communal direction of agriculture has given way to individualism and an entrepreneurial approach to agriculture to such an
extent that the regimentation of a paysannat would not be acceptable.[3]
This would clearly be true of many parts of West Africa.

Elsewhere in western tropical Africa, the approach to these
problems of providing for the dissemination of knowledge of better
methods and the creation of an environment favorable to raising
agricultural productivity can be characterized as limited, experimental, and diverse. For some years emphasis in French West Africa was
placed on compulsory agricultural organizations known as *Sociétés
des prévoyances;* but in recent years the newly established legislative
bodies have been highly critical of these organizations as being too
heavily dominated by the administration and not sufficiently oriented
toward improving conditions of production at the village level.[4] The
Office du Niger and Richard Toll schemes for developing rice production, considered in Chapter 9, were based on a conception that
sought to minimize dependence on African farmers and that gave even
greater emphasis to centralized control and direction by a governmental or quasi-governmental agency. Subsequently, however, Richard Toll has been turned over to a private company to be operated
essentially as a mechanized plantation, whereas the transition at the
Office du Niger has been in the direction of increased use of native
settlers with the public corporation performing certain operations
with mechanical equipment on a fee basis.

Since about 1955 emphasis in the French territories has shifted
to a new approach based on an extension-type organization and program extending down to the village level. This policy was outlined
by a working party on rural development under the chairmanship
of M. Rossin, Director of Agriculture, Livestock, and Forestry of the
Ministry of Overseas Territories; the conclusions of this group were
summarized in a note published late in 1955 *(42).*[5] The "slow

---

[3] A few "paysannats" have been established in the Bas-Congo, but they appear to
have a markedly different character and are, in essence, arrangements for introducing
more intensive farming with mechanical cultivation on a contract basis.

[4] More recently emphasis has been placed upon developing *Sociétés mutuelles
de production rurale,* oriented more directly toward the needs and interests of the
rural populations. An interesting program initiated in 1955/56 for training African
specialists to assume administrative responsibilities in agricultural cooperatives has
been described by Gerard Cuny *(9).*

[5] See also an address by M. Rossin, "Le problème de l'education professionelle
agricole et de la modernisation rurale en Afrique noire et à Madagascar: Conditions
et modalités de la modernisation du paysannat outre-mer" *(48)* and a report on
Encadrement agricole et modernisation rurale en A.E.F. (15) which discusses the
need for and measures to implement an extension-type program in French Equatorial
Africa.

progress in agriculture and the lack of success of certain formulas for overseas development which have been tried" are attributed to two principal deficiencies: (a) reliance on an administrative structure that was too remote from the producer who was therefore unable to make known his real needs and concerns, and (b) failure to obtain intimate knowledge of farmers and farming at the village level and to come to grips with the over-all problems of a rural district (42, p. 794).

The policy advocated by the working party and which has guided agricultural programs in the French territories in the past few years emphasized direct and permanent contact between agents of the "organization for rural action" and the peasant, and the bringing of technical assistance down to the village level. The role of these "technical assistants" would be essentially that of a county agent or farm adviser. Increasingly these village-level workers are to be African graduates of agricultural schools, oriented toward practical agriculture and the "human problems" of working with people. As an interim measure considerable use is being made of graduates of regional and practical schools of agriculture in France who are being recruited and trained for this work, partly with the idea that as they gain experience they will be able to participate in the training of African technical assistants. An agricultural extension program emphasizing the work of agents at the village level will, of course, require a great increase in trained agriculturalists if the program is to be applied throughout the French territories of tropical Africa. This poses a difficult problem of expanding facilities for agricultural training as well as the problems related to financing such a program. At present this type of work is being undertaken only on a pilot basis in limited areas usually designated as "centres d'expansion rurale" or "centres d'encadrement rapproché."

Diversity in approach also characterizes the agricultural programs in the British territories of West Africa. Agricultural officers have carried on a certain amount of extension work, but they have been few in number and typically their work has not gone beyond organizing occasional demonstrations. In the years since World War II, heavy emphasis has been placed on agricultural development projects, several of which were reviewed in Chapter 9. Some of these have been organized as public corporations carrying on farming operations with mechanical equipment and hired labor. In others, for example the Shendam Resettlement Scheme in Nigeria, the government's role has been largely confined to the initial clearing, the construction of roads, and perhaps the sinking of wells. Many inter-

mediate arrangements are also to be found, such as the Bonthe Grassland Scheme in Sierra Leone, whereby mechanical plowing is performed by the Department of Agriculture on a contract basis while
all other operations are carried out by the individual operators.

Sharp differences of opinion exist concerning the pattern of land
tenure and farm organization which should be promoted.[6] H. A.
Oluwasanmi, an economist at the University College of Ibadan, has
advocated a land policy whereby the government would " 'enclose'
large areas of land for resettlement and other agricultural projects
without paying the heavy compensations now required under existing legislation" (44, p. 736). He is persuaded that "the state . . .
must continue to be the prime mover of projects of agricultural improvement," projects that will "increasingly become the instruments
for capitalizing tropical agriculture and introducing new and better
methods of cultivation" (44, p. 737). In this article, Oluwasanmi
gives equal indorsement to large-scale plantations operated directly
by public corporations and settlement projects in which the individual
tenants will have their tenure rights confirmed and holdings will be
heritable, though transfers will be subject to state control. While
indorsing "enclosure" by government, he is highly critical of "the
incipient growth in certain areas of capitalist landowners" in response
to new economic and social forces, notably "the growth of an exchange economy, pressure of population, foreign legal ideas and the
introduction of new types of crops . . ." (44, p. 733). The reasons
for his distaste for this type of individualization of tenure are not
entirely clear. He remarks that such private "enclosure" is "usually
in defiance of customary usage and authority" and states that "ava-
ricious chiefs, rich and educated individuals of landholding communities have been quick in grasping the changed economic conditions that are fast turning land into an economic good" (44, p. 733).
He asserts that "communal tenure acts as a strong cohesive force in
an agrarian society . . . [and] precludes the rise of a landed aris-
tocracy and thereby removes much of the source of social unrest
inherent in the landlord-tenant relations elsewhere" (44, p. 734).
There is also a suggestion that Oluwasanmi resents having an increase
in land value resulting from "the general progress of society" accrue
to individual proprietors, and he gives short shrift to the idea that
individualization of tenure will promote agricultural improvement
(44, p. 737):

---

[6] For a discussion of some of the faults that characterize unsatisfactory systems
of land tenure see G. B. Masefield's article, "Farming Systems and Land Tenure"
(37).

The impecunious peasant farmer with his three-acre holding and deeply ingrained habit of shifting cultivation appears a very unlikely vehicle for accomplishing the urgent changes desired in agricultural methods and agricultural productivity in tropical Africa.

A very different view is expressed by D. C. Igwe, an Assistant District Officer in Nigeria. "Clearly the time is now ripe for a general enclosure movement giving a free hand to any, in lawful and beneficial occupation of land, to develop the land resources to the benefit of himself and the country" (*29*, p. 63). He advances a number of the familiar arguments concerning the agricultural benefits to be expected as a result of enclosures on individualized holdings: the greater scope for individual initiative and increased incentive for measures of land improvement; opportunity for farmers with superior ability in managing their land to enlarge the scale of their operations; favorable conditions for the introduction of mechanization on holdings large enough for the economic use of tractors and equipment; the impetus to mixed farming; and a context in which advance planning and more rational management of a well-defined farm unit becomes possible (*29*, pp. 65–68). Igwe emphasizes, however, that such an enclosure movement should proceed slowly, that registration of titles should not be carried out until after perhaps 20 years, and that the movement should be subject to controls to avoid "the worst consequences of the English enclosure movement . . ." (*29*, p. 67).[7] His attitude toward the sort of group schemes advocated by Oluwasanmi is skeptical, even as a means of introducing mechanization under Nigerian conditions (*29*, p. 68):

Some of these schemes have proved disappointing because the peasant in Nigeria will not exert himself to the benefit of the many. He would prefer to reap the fruits of his own labor. Besides, these group schemes have often made one fatal mistake; that of inadequate screening of the participants so that the shiftless and lazy are lumped together with the energetic with the consequence that even the energetic soon lose interest. . . .

On the theoretical level, the arguments raised by Oluwasanmi and Igwe can be pursued interminably. Indeed, they have been continuing themes in economic analysis and controversy at least since the time of Adam Smith.

While it would be premature to draw conclusions concerning the relative merits of different systems of agricultural organization under

[7] Lord Hailey has offered some interesting suggestions on this problem which he characterizes as one of finding "a form of title which will, on the one hand, preserve the residual rights of the community in its lands, and on the other, provide the holder with the necessary economic incentive to the best use of land" (*27*, p. 7).

African conditions, the diversity of the approaches used can be of real value if serious efforts are made to evaluate the results achieved in various types of projects. Baldwin's objective critique of the Niger Agricultural Project at Mokwa in northern Nigeria represents a valuable contribution to this type of evaluation; and the Colonial Development Corporation is to be commended for recognizing that "the lessons learned at Mokwa should be set out for future guidance and warning" and for arranging for Mr. Baldwin to undertake the study (2, p. xiii). The different approaches that have been adopted seem to fall within the following general categories:

1. Mechanization schemes
    (a) Private or public corporations using hired laborers
    (b) Partnership schemes whereby crops are divided according to pre-scribed shares between an operating company (public or private) and participating peasant farmers
    (c) Contract schemes in which plowing and other operations are per-formed mechanically for individual operators who pay a per-acre fee
2. Plow schemes with animal draft power
3. Systematization and improvement of existing practices by native settle-ment schemes as with the paysannats indigènes in the Belgian Congo
4. Improvement of native agriculture by means of an agricultural exten-sion organization and other supporting services

It is perfectly obvious that local circumstances will largely de-termine the kind of scheme which is most promising for a particular area at a given time. Introduction of animal draft power, for example, is only feasible in regions where the problem of trypanosomiasis in-fection is not too severe. There are also substantial differences in the way a general type of program such as the introduction of plow-ing with animal draft power has been carried out. In the French Sudan there has been a comparatively rapid introduction of cattle for plowing, but there has been little success to date in securing a rational use of the animal manure. In the Northern Territories of Ghana, on the other hand, the introduction of plow farming has proceeded much more slowly, but there has been firm insistence on kraaling and use of litter so that the animal manure is being utilized effectively to maintain or enhance soil fertility.

It seems virtually certain that for many years to come small-scale production by peasant farmers will account for the great bulk of the staple food supplies in western tropical Africa. Measures that enhance the productivity of these peasant farmers will, therefore, be of great

importance; and this obviously underscores the need for strengthen-
ing agricultural extension activities. W. Arthur Lewis, economic
adviser to the Prime Minister in Ghana, has suggested that the number
of extension workers in that country should be increased fivefold;
and relative to many other areas in western tropical Africa, Ghana
already has a fairly sizable staff: an establishment of nearly 400 agricultural assistants of which close to half are primarily concerned with
cocoa farming (35, p. 4; 16, p. 11). Mere increase in the number of
extension workers is, of course, no guarantee that farming methods
will be improved. It was noted above that one of the reasons given
for the failure of extension efforts in the Belgian Congo in the period
before emphasis was shifted to the paysannats indigènes was that the
agricultural specialists did not have "sufficiently valuable technical
improvements to propose" (25, p. 1128). Clearly, agricultural research and field trials have a crucial role to play in developing and
testing improved varieties and farming methods and in providing
guidance concerning the use of fertilizers, insecticides, and pesticides
—and in terms of what is most profitable considering the additional
cost as well as the increase in yield that can be expected. Despite
the marked increase during the past decade in the attention given to
research bearing on African food crops, progress is limited by lack
of funds, shortage of qualified research workers, and insufficient continuity in the personnel at many stations. The handsome returns that
can be realized from investments in agricultural research and extension are beyond question. Particularly noteworthy for the immediate future are the increases in yield which can be attained through
the work of the plant breeders in developing higher-yielding varieties.
The Food Crop Division of INÉAC at Yangambi has developed varieties of rice capable of yielding 2,500 kgs per hectare as an upland
crop compared with 500–700 kgs obtainable from local varieties,
and in similar fashion manioc yields have been increased from 10
to 48 tons per hectare, and yields of peanuts from some 800 kgs to
two tons per hectare for improved varieties cultivated under favorable
conditions (4, p. 25). And there seems no reason to doubt the view
of R. H. Cammack, head of the West African Maize Research Unit
at Ibadan, that maize yields in much of West Africa can be doubled
by the introduction of improved varieties and without use of fertilizers.

A major problem in raising the level of productivity of large
numbers of African peasant farmers is the strength of tradition and
conservatism so characteristic of rural communities and especially

peasant societies which are not yet well integrated in a market economy and where literacy rates are exceedingly low. Pierre de Schlippe has stressed the need for agricultural programs in Africa to be based on a fuller knowledge of native farming methods and attitudes. He insists that such knowledge is needed not only as a basis for understanding the factors likely to cause resistance to innovations but also to suggest appropriate methods of overcoming resistance by utilizing, for example, local rites and symbols as one of the means of incorporating worthwhile innovations into the fabric of village customs and sanctions (*50*, p. 8). The need is not only for technical competence but also for skill and understanding in working with peasant farmers; and agricultural departments undoubtedly can benefit from the experience of the more successful community development organizations and some of the imaginative techniques that they have used to ascertain the "felt needs" of African villagers, to win their confidence, and to secure their cooperation.

CONCLUSION

What can be said about the general outlook for enlarging staple food supplies and increasing productivity in the area considered in this study? The increased attention now being given to such questions as plant breeding and selection, fertilizer use, crop rotations, insect and pest control, cultural practices, and techniques of water control will surely result in a significant growth of technical knowledge of the means of raising agricultural output and productivity. The presumption is strong indeed that impressive results will be achieved with the application of a scientific approach to agriculture in tropical Africa as they have wherever sustained and substantial efforts in that direction have been made.

Forecasting, always a precarious activity, seems especially uncertain in this situation since the growth of agricultural output and productivity will be determined so largely by the energy, intelligence, and resources that governments and individuals devote to the task. And, as emphasized above, the task is the twofold one of raising the level of technical knowledge and of developing extension work in order to promote wide application of improved technology. Efforts to find workable solutions to structural problems such as land tenure, credit, and agricultural organization will also be important. But there is nothing inherent in the situation which warrants a pessimistic appraisal of the prospects. Admittedly, the climatic and soil conditions of tropical Africa pose special problems. But this is probably less important than the fact that, even allowing for the land required to accommodate long fallows, agricultural land is abundant relative to population as compared with other regions, most notably the Far East. Indeed, sparseness of population is a handicap to development in some parts of tropical Africa, since it means that certain types of overhead investment, such as for roads and a communications network, are very costly. But on the other hand, agricultural mechanization, obviously a powerful means of increasing the productivity of labor, will undoubtedly become economic at an earlier stage in tropical Africa than in areas of dense population. The factors that determine whether mechanization is economic are complex. A number of them—soils and knowledge of how to handle them, levels of general education and mechanical skills, and climate—are unrelated to population density. But two of the most important determinants—scarcity or surplus of labor in the countryside and the rate of expansion of nonagricultural employment—are strongly influenced by the size of the population in relation to the land resources available (see *46*, p. 147).

On the basis of this somewhat rash attempt to weigh the many relevant considerations, there seem to be strong indications that the expansion of agricultural output in most if not all of western tropical Africa will keep pace with the growth of demand (that the food supply schedule will probably shift to the right at roughly the same rate as the demand curve). But this alone is not enough. There are good reasons to believe that the increase of productivity in agriculture should make a positive contribution to the process of economic growth. In Japan, to cite an interesting and pertinent example, agricultural output appears to have increased by nearly 80 per cent in 30 years (between the decades 1881–90 and 1911–20); and labor productivity—defined simply as gross output per person gainfully employed in agriculture—was doubled during the same period. These gains, mainly the result of increased use of fertilizers, development and widespread use of improved seed, and advances in farming techniques, made highly significant contributions to Japan's economic development. Especially noteworthy was its role in facilitating a high rate of capital formation, in releasing people from the land for employment in industry, and in providing ample and low-cost food for the urban population, thus counteracting to some extent the inflationary pressures generated by industrialization (*30*, pp. 498, 511–12). The potential contribution of measures to augment agricultural productivity in tropical Africa is certainly no less significant.

CITATIONS

1 "Agriculture congolaise," *Bull. agr. du Congo Belge* (Belg., Min. Col.), August 1954.

2 K. D. S. Baldwin, *The Niger Agricultural Project: An Experiment in African Development* (Oxford, 1957).

3 W. H. Beckett, *Akokoaso: A Survey of a Gold Coast Village* (London Sch. Econ. and Pol. Sci., Monograph on Soc. Anth., London, 1944).

4 Belg., INÉAC, *L'Institut National pour l' Étude Agronomique du Congo Belge (INÉAC): Son but, son programme, ses réalisations* (Brussels, 4th ed., 1957).

5 Robert Buron, "Le Développement des pays sous-développés. L'avenir de l'Afrique Noire," *Études et conjoncture* (France, Min. Fin. et des Affaires Econ., Inst. Natl. Stat. et des Études Econ.), November 1956.

6 R. H. Cammack, *A Study of* Puccinia Polysora *Underwood in West Africa* (unpublished doctoral dissertation submitted to the University of St. Andrews, 1958).

7 ———, "Observations on *Puccinia Polysora* Underw. in West Africa," in W. Afr. Maize Rust Res. Unit, *First Annual Report 1953* (London, 1954).

8 J. M. Clement, "Les Méthodes d'utilisation des sols agricoles et leurs perfectionnements," in Vol. I of *Proc. Second Inter-Afr. Soils Conf., Léopold-ville, 9-14 Aug. 1954* . . . (Commis. for Tech. Co-op in Africa, Belg., Min. Col., Brussels, n.d.), pp. 627–37.

9 Gerard Cuny, "Les Centres de formation coopérative en A.O.F.," *Marchés trop. du monde* (Paris), Aug. 10, 1957.

10 J. H. Dalton (in *Am. Econ. Rev.*, June 1955), review of P. T. Bauer, *West African Trade—A Study of Competition, Oligopoly, and Monopoly in a Changing Economy* (New York, 1954).

11 V. Drachoussoff, *Essai sur l'agriculture indigène au Bas-Congo* (Belg., Min. Col., 1947).

12 "Évolution de la consommation indigène au Congo Belge," *Bull. Banque Cen. du Congo Belge et du Ruanda-Urundi* (Brussels and Leopold-ville), December 1956.

13 Food and Agriculture Organization of the United Nations (FAO), Com. on Commod. Prob., *Functions of a World Food Reserve: Summary Survey of Discussions and Documentation* (Rome, CCP 57/7, Mar. 4, 1957).

14 FAO Staff, "Shifting Cultivation," *Trop. Agr.* (London), July 1957 (reprinted from UNASYLVA, Vol. 11, No. 1, 1957).

15 French Equatorial Africa, Gouvernement Général, Inspection Gen. de l'Agr., Comité de Coordination de la Rech. Agron. et de la Prod. Agr., *Encadrement agricole et modernisation rurale en A.E.F.: Doctrines et bilan* (Brazzaville, 1956).

16 Ghana, Dept. Agr., *Miscellaneous Information, 1957–58* (Accra, 1957, mimeo.).

17 M. Gaide, "Au Tchad les transformations subies par l'agriculture traditionnelle sous l'influence de la culture cotonnière," *Agronomie trop.* (France, Min. Outre-mer), Nov.–Dec. 1956.

18 G. Geortay, "Vers une amélioration économique de la culture vivrière

en région équatoriale forestière," *Bull. inf. de l'INÉAC* (Belg., Min. Col.), December 1956.

19 B. D. Giles, "Agriculture and the Price Mechanism," in Thomas Wilson and P. W. S. Andrews, eds., *Oxford Studies in the Price Mechanism* (Oxford, 1951).

20 Gold Coast, Dept. Agr., *Annual Report . . . 1949–50* (Accra, 1951).

21 ——, *Annual Report . . . 1951–52* (Accra, 1953).

22 ——, *Annual Report . . . 1st April, 1952, to 31st March, 1953* (Accra, 1954).

23 Gold Coast, Min. Fin., *Economic Survey, 1953* (Accra, 1954).

24 ——, *Economic Survey, 1954* (Accra, 1955).

25 Groupe d'Économie Rurale, "Evolution de l'agriculture indigène dans la zone de Léopoldville," *Bull. agr. du Congo Belge,* October 1954.

26 R. Guillemin, "Evolution de l'agriculture autochtone dans les savanes de l'Oubangui," *Agronomie trop.,* May–June 1956.

27 Lord Hailey, "The Land Tenure Problem in Africa," *J. Afr. Admin.,* Special Supp. on Land Tenure, October 1952.

28 J. Huge, "Economic Planning and Development in the Belgian Congo," *Ann. Am. Acad. Pol. and Soc. Sci.,* March 1955.

29 D. C. Igwe, "The Need for Enclosure and Land Resettlement in Nigerian Agriculture," *Trop. Agr.* (London), January 1954.

30 B. F. Johnston, "Agricultural Productivity and Economic Development in Japan," *J. Pol. Econ.,* December 1951.

31 W. O. Jones, *Manioc in Africa* (to be published in 1959).

32 F. Jurion, "Le Rôle de l'INÉAC dans le développement de l'agriculture congolaise," *Bull. inf. de l'INÉAC,* June 1952.

33 C. E. Kellogg and Fidelia D. Davol, *An Exploratory Study of Soil Groups in the Belgian Congo* (INÉAC Ser. Sci. 46, 1949).

34 W. A. Lewis, "Economic Development with Unlimited Supplies of Labour," *Manchester Sch. Econ. and Soc. Studies* (Manchester, Eng.), May 1954.

35 ——, *Diversifying Ghana's Agriculture* (Accra, M a r c h 1958, mimeo.).

36 "Le Marché des engrais au Congo Belge," *Bull. agr. du Congo Belge,* August 1957.

37 G. B. Masefield, "Farming Systems and Land Tenure," *J. Afr. Admin.,* Special Supp. on Land Tenure, October 1952.

38 Gunnar Myrdal, *An International Economy: Problems and Prospects* (New York, 1956).

39 S. D. Neumark, "Economic Development and Economic Incentives," *S. Afr. J. Econ.* (Johannesburg), March 1958.

40 B. M. Nicol, *A Report of the Nutritional Work Which Has Been Carried Out in Nigeria Since 1920, with a Summary of What Is Known of the Present Nutritional State of the Nigerian Peasants* [Kaduna?, 1956?, mimeo.].

41 Nigeria, Dept. Agr., *Annual Report . . . 1950–51* (Lagos, 1953).

42 "Note d'orientation sur l'action rurale dans les territoires d'outremer," *Agronomie trop.,* Nov.–Dec. 1955.

43 P. H. Nye, "Some Prospects for Subsistence Agriculture in West Africa," *J. W. Afr. Sci. Assn.* (Achimota), February 1957.

44 H. A. Oluwasanmi, "Land Tenure and Agricultural Improvement in Tropical Africa," *J. Farm Econ.*, August 1957.

45 F. J. Pedler, *Economic Geography of West Africa* (London, 1955).

46 J. R. Raeburn, "Agricultural Development in the Tropics and Sub-Tropics: Ways and Means," in *Proc. Eighth Internatl. Conf. Agr. Economists* (Oxford, 1953).

47 P. W. Richards, *The Tropical Rain Forest: An Ecological Study* (Cambridge, 1952).

48 M. Rossin, "Le Problème de l'éducation professionnelle agricole et de la modernisation rurale en Afrique noire et à Madagascar: Conditions et modalités de la modernisation du paysannat outre-mer," in *Agronomie trop.*, May–June 1957.

49 P. de Schlippe, "Sous-station d'essais de l'I.N.E.A.C. à Kurukwata (Extraits du premier rapport annuel)," *Bull. agr. du Congo Belge*, June 1948.

50 ———, "L'Agriculture nomade," *Bull. du Comité Natl. Belg. de la FAO* (Brussels), 11th Year, No. 1, 1957.

51 Dudley Seers and C. R. Ross, *Report on Financial and Physical Problems of Development in the Gold Coast* (Gold Coast, Off. Govt. Stat., Accra, 1952).

52 Uganda, Dept. Agr., *Annual Report . . . for the Year Ended 31st December 1952* (Entebbe, 1954).

53 United Nations, Dept. Econ. Affairs, *Enlargement of the Exchange Economy in Tropical Africa* (New York, 1954).

54 H. P. White, "Internal Exchange of Staple Foods in the Gold Coast," *Econ. Geog.*, April 1956.

APPENDIX TABLES

APPENDIX TABLES

TABLE I.—WEST AFRICA AND THE FRENCH CAMEROONS, RELATIVE AREA
OF STAPLE FOOD CROPS, ABOUT 1950*

(Staple with largest area in each locality = 100)

Territory and district	Maize	Millets and sorghums	Rice	Manioc	Yams	Coco-yams	Plan-tains	Sweet pota-toes	Area of crop taken as 100 (1,000 ha.)
French Sudan	88	100	17	1	—	...	...	1	1,270
Upper Volta									
Bobo-Dioulasso	22	100	4	...	...	...	...	...	140.5
Gaoua	15	100	1	...	...	...	...	...	136.4
Kaya	7	100	—	...	...	...	...	...	118.0
Koudougou-Yako	23	100	—	...	...	...	...	...	108.0
Ouagadougou	10	100	—	...	...	...	...	...	199.3
Tenkodogo	7	100	—	...	...	...	...	...	114.0
Fada-N'Gourma	9	100	—	...	...	...	...	...	94.8
Ouahigouya	15	100	—	...	...	...	...	...	120.0
Tougan	8	100	—	...	...	...	...	...	68.8
Dori	17	100	—	...	...	...	...	...	34.0
Dédougou	15	100	1	...	...	...	...	...	159.6
Total	14	100	1	...	...	...	...	...	1,293.4
Niger	—	100	—	—	...	...	...	...	1,342.0
Senegal									
Matam	3	100	—	—	...	...	...	—	70
Podor	4	100	1	—	...	...	...	—	50
Bas Sénégal	2	100	1	—	...	...	...	—	13
Linguère	—	100	—	—	...	...	...	—	20
Louga	—	100	—	18	...	...	...	—	60
Thiès	—	100	—	6	...	...	...	2	100
Dakar	—	100	—	8	...	...	...	18	4
Diourbel	—	100	—	4	...	...	...	1	125
Kaolack	—	100	2	2	...	...	...	—	230
Tambacounda	5	100	2	2	...	...	...	—	22
Kédougou	—	100	—	—	...	...	...	—	10
Ziguinchor	14	100	57	3	...	...	...	2	70
Total	2	100	6	4	...	...	...	1	774
French Guinea[a]									
Basse	4	33	100	11	...	6	...	11	96
Moyenne	24	100	15	8	...	24	...	12	125
Haute	13	100	74	32	...	11	...	18	62
Région Forestière	—	9	100	8	...	—	...	5	192
Total	12	67	100	16	...	12	...	13	353

TABLE I.—WEST AFRICA AND THE FRENCH CAMEROONS, RELATIVE AREA
OF STAPLE FOOD CROPS, ABOUT 1950*—(*Continued*)

(*Staple with largest area in each locality = 100*)

Territory and district	Maize	Millets and sorghums	Rice	Manioc	Yams	Cocoyams	Plantains	Sweet potatoes	Area of crop taken as 100 (*1,000 ha.*)
Ivory Coast									
Abidjan	15	—	12	62	31	8	100	1	13
Grand-Bassam	—	—	9	56	24	3	100	—	10.6
Agboville	25	—	12	83	12	4	100	2	12
Sassandra	23	—	100	18	9	18	52	—	6.5
Grand-Lahou	25	—	100	15	11	23	72	—	13.2
Gagnoa	35	—	100	13	10	17	51	—	18.6
Daloa	12	—	100	13	20	13	47	—	30.6
Abengourou	22	—	12	60	45	—	100	—	4
Bondoukou	36	20	3	73	100	11	100	—	5.5
Dimbokro	46	—	18	43	100	21	64	1	14
Man	9	—	100	46	2	—	7	1	56
Tabou	10	—	10	100	5	—	12	5	2
Bouaké	49	—	34	100	100	—	—	—	64
Katiola	100	19	22	25	62	—	—	—	16
Séguéla	77	28	100	31	51	—	—	6	32.5
Korhogo	—	100	34	3	21	—	—	—	72
Odienne	—	100	37	30	14	—	—	12	14
Total	49	45	100	72	67	8	43	2	220
Dahomey									
Porto Novo	100	—	—	60	14	—	...	5	116
Cotonou	100	—	—	90	—	—	...	8	10
Ouidah	100	—	—	97	—	—	...	—	61
Athiémé	100	—	—	14	—	—	...	—	84
Abomey	100	8	—	17	14	—	...	—	36
Savalou	40	20	—	100	30	—	...	—	20
Djougou	—	92	8	1	100	—	...	—	25
Parakou	59	100	1	12	100	—	...	—	17
Kandi	6	100	6	1	4	—	...	—	25
Natitingou	12	100	7	1	33	—	...	—	30
Total	100	33	2	57	26	—	...	2	311
French Togo									
Lomé	100	—	—	8	1	—	...	—	42
Anécho	100	—	—	67	1	—	...	—	45
Centre[b]	100	16	27	23	60	1	...	—	30
Skodé	4	100	1	1	22	—	...	1	97.5
Mango	6	100	1	—	5	—	...	1	66.5
Total	74	100	6	25	26	—	...	1	169
Gambia	2	100	20	2	—	...	...	—	52
Sierra Leone	3	6	100	4	1	...	...	—	316
Ghana									
Northern Territories	10	100	3	—	8	—	—	...	309.4
Ashanti	98	—	10	67	86	67	100	...	27.5
South Togo	100	—	79	39	47	19	30	...	8.5
Colony, forest	38	—	2	25	7	63	100	...	93
Colony, nonforested	100	—	—	92	6	5	9	...	40.5
Total	46	100	6	27	20	26	41	...	309.4

TABLE I.—WEST AFRICA AND THE FRENCH CAMEROONS, RELATIVE AREA
OF STAPLE FOOD CROPS, ABOUT 1950*—(*Concluded*)
(*Staple with largest area in each locality = 100*)

Territory and district	Maize	Millets and sorghums	Rice	Manioc	Yams	Cocoyams	Plantains	Sweet potatoes	Area of crop taken as 100 (*1,000 ha.*)
Nigeria-Stratum*c*									
1	23	—	—	100	86	19	...	—	367.4
2	100	—	—	45	76	24	...	—	324.6
3	57	1	4	51	100	28	...	4	136.4
3A	12	—	—	85	100	56	...	—	68.8
4	27	100	11	52	98	9	...	10	455.7
5	6	100	13	2	2	—	...	1	464.6
6	4	100	—	6	—	—	...	2	480.4
7	1	100	5	2	—	—	...	1	1,034.0
8	—	100	—	1	1	5	...	—	233.5
9	12	100	3	6	—	—	...	—	295.8
10	45	21	27	42	24	100	...	—	13.4
11	1	100	—	—	—	—	...	—	113.7
12	100	3	—	41	—	25	...	3	82.6
13	21	100	—	—	—	—	...	—	37.2
Total	26	100	5	32	40	10	...	2	3,121.0
Liberia	...	...	100	21	...	...	...	...	260
French Cameroons									
Nord ..../......	1	100	1	1	—	—	—	...	666.0
Centre	100	13	5	73	21	29	29	...	46.4
Est	100	—	1	23	—	3	25	...	36.1
Ouest	100	—	—	2	26	48	5	...	51.5
Maritime	36	—	—	46	19	100	55	...	14.8
Total	22	100	1	9	4	8	5	1	672.0

* Data from the following sources: For French Sudan, Upper Volta, Niger, Senegal, and French Guinea from L'Afrique Occidentale Française, Haut-Commissariat, *Annuaire statistique . . .* , *Edition 1951*, II (Paris 1951) ; for Ivory Coast direct from Jacques Miège, Off. de la Recherche Sci. et Technique Outre-mer, Inst. d'Enseignement et de Recherches Trop., Abidjan, July 8, 1955; for Dahomey direct from M. M. Thomas, Bur. Stat., Territoire du Dahomey, Porto Novo, July 27, 1955; for French Togo from France, Min. Outre-mer, *Annuaire statistique de l'Union Française Outre-mer, 1939–1949*, Tome Premier (1951), p. 355; for Gambia and Sierra Leone from FAO, *Report on the 1950 World Census of Agriculture, Vol. I: Census Results by Countries* (Rome, 1955) ; for Ghana from Gold Coast, Dept. Agr., *Annual Report . . . for the Period 1st April, 1952 to 31 March, 1953* (Accra, 1954), p. 21; for Nigeria from Nigeria, Dept. Stat., *Report on the Sample Census of Agriculture, 1950–51* (Lagos 1952), pp. 52, 55; for Liberia from FAO, *Yearbook of Food and Agricultural Statistics, 1954. Part I: Production*, VIII (Rome, 1955), pp. 37, 49 (comparable figures for 1956 and also figures for plantain area and production—2,000 hectares and 20,000 tons, respectively—are given in U.S. Dept. Agr., For. Agr. Serv., *Notes on the Agricultural Economy of Liberia*, May 1957) ; for French Cameroons approximated from France, Min. Outre-mer, *Annuaire statistique de l'Union Française Outre-mer, 1939–1949* (area of crops for the country as a whole—p. 343—subdivided by regions in the percentages reflected by the production figures shown—p. 357).

a The district groupings were as follows: Basse (Conakry, Dubreka, Forecariah, Kindia, Boffa, and Boké *cercles*) ; Moyenne (Mamou, Pita, Labé, and Gaoual *cercles*) ; Haute (Dabola, Kouroussa, Kankan, and Siguiri *cercles*) ; Région Forestière (N'zérékoré, Beyla, Macenta, Guekedou, and Kissidougou *cercles*).

b Assumed to include Klouto.

c The strata are identified on Map 4-1 and are described on pp. 79–83 of the *Report on the Sample Census of Agriculture, 1950–51*. Plantains were not included in the Nigerian sample census of agriculture and no area or production estimates are available; but they are of considerable importance in parts of southern Nigeria.

TABLE II.—AVERAGE PRICES OF STAPLE FOODS PER 1,000 CALORIES:
NIGERIA, GHANA, AND THE BELGIAN CONGO*

Market	Maize	Gari	Yams	Manioc	Coco-yams	Rice	Plan-tains	Guinea corn	Millet
NIGERIA (*Pence per 1,000 calories*)									
Western Region									
Delta*a*	3.27	2.08	6.70						
Ibadan*b*	1.79	1.92	3.93						
Ijebu-Ode	2.85	1.80	6.93						
Abeokuta	2.29	1.36	5.01						
Benin*c*	2.96	1.12	4.25						
Colony-Agege	2.56	1.75	8.47						
Ondo-Akure	2.41	1.31	4.72						
Oyo	1.78	1.04	3.18						
Composite	2.49	1.54	5.39						
Eastern Region									
Onitsha	2.44	1.37	7.33			4.54			
Calabar	3.33	1.86	6.10			5.37			
Ogoja	1.29	1.06	3.38			3.00			
Port Harcourt	1.87	1.40	5.87			3.95			
Ahoada	2.83	1.45	6.30			5.64			
Orlu	2.17	1.47	5.41			4.50			
Composite	2.32	1.43	5.73			4.50			
Northern Region									
Kabba-Okene	1.32		3.36	1.51		4.64		1.35	
Niger-Bida						3.24		1.51	1.26
Sokoto-Gusau						4.04		1.81	1.82
Composite	1.32		3.36	1.51		3.98		1.56	1.54
Nigeria composite	1.99	1.49	4.83	1.51		4.24		1.56	1.54
Nigerian Cocoa Farmers									
Abeokuta	2.79	2.39	3.70	1.19	3.46	2.36	3.14		
Ibadan	2.04	2.46	4.82	2.87	2.95		5.62		
Ife-Ilesha	1.99	2.03	3.97	2.34	2.72		2.39		
Ondo	1.63	1.88	3.65	1.27	2.59		1.65		
Composite	2.00	2.24	3.95	1.51	2.74	2.36	2.51		
GHANA (*Pence per 1,000 calories*)									
Accra	1.87	2.67	10.23	4.06	8.90	5.43		2.79	
Kumasi	1.92	2.30	5.67	...	4.38	5.88		2.49	
Sekondi	2.36	2.43	9.29	1.59	6.40	5.56		3.41	
Tamale	2.09	3.82	6.41	2.80	8.15	4.66		2.54	
Composite	2.06	2.81	7.90	2.81	6.95	5.38		2.81	
BELGIAN CONGO (*Francs per 1,000 calories*)									
Léopoldville	.48		1.57*d*	.58		1.71	2.87		.31
Équateur	.41		...	.57		.57	1.17		...
Orientale	.23		.33*d*	.41		.54	.76		.27
Kivu	.24		...	.98		.62	.83		.28
Katanga	.46		1.53*d*	1.36		1.44	3.68		.73
Kasai	.37		...	.97		.66	...		.33
Composite	.36		1.14*d*	.81		.92	1.86		.38

* Data for Nigeria based on averages of monthly "market prices" for the period June 1952 to July 1955, though with certain gaps in the series, for eight markets in the Western Region, six Eastern Region markets, and three markets in the Northern Region. For the "Nigerian Cocoa Farmers" unit prices calculated from quantity and value data for 1950/51 reported for four areas of the Western Region in R. Galletti, K. D. S. Baldwin, I. O. Dina, *Nigerian Cocoa Farmers* . . . (Nigeria Cocoa Mkt. Bd., London, 1956), p. 418 ff. have been used. For Ghana, monthly "wholesale market prices" for the period April 1953 to August 1955 were used whereas the Belgian Congo indices are based on yearly averages (1950–

TABLE III.—AVERAGE PRICES OF STAPLE FOODS PER 1,000 CALORIES: DAHOMEY, SENEGAL, FRENCH GUINEA, IVORY COAST, ANGOLA, AND BELGIAN CONGO*

Market	Maize flour	Manioc		Chick-wangue	Cos-settes	Rice	Millet	Plan-tains	Sweet pota-toes
		Flour	Fresh						
DAHOMEY, 1956 (*C.F.A. francs per 1,000 calories*)									
Cotonou	9.72	6.51				12.04[a]			
SENEGAL, 1956 (*C.F.A. francs per 1,000 calories*)									
Dakar	8.06	15.60				14.01[a]	6.76		
Saint-Louis	10.83	21.10				10.92[a]	6.18		
FRENCH GUINEA, 1957 (*C.F.A. francs per 1,000 calories*)									
Conakry	7.86[b]	11.01				11.76	12.35[c]		
IVORY COAST, Oct. 1957–Jan. 1958 (*C.F.A. francs per 1,000 calories*)									
Abidjan	5.90[bd]	10.09				13.45	8.52	15.49	13.40
ANGOLA, 1956 (*Escudos per 1,000 calories*)									
Luanda	.93	1.51				1.68[e]			
BELGIAN CONGO, July 1957 (*Belgian francs per 1,000 calories*)									
Léopoldville	1.64		1.69[f]	1.38		2.03		7.86	
Équateur			.94[f]			2.03		3.52	5.15
Katanga	1.19					2.52		10.56	5.15
Orientale	1.48		1.41[f]			3.22		4.62	5.62
Ruanda-Urundi	1.18		2.11[f]			3.22		3.52	2.06
Kivu	1.04					2.24		6.34	1.69

* Based on data in national currency per kilogram for Dahomey from *Bull. stat. du Dahomey* (Afrique Occidentale Française, Gouvernement du Dahomey), 1956, No. 4, p. 42, No. 7, p. 25, No. 8, p. 22, and No. 10, p. 16; for Senegal from *Bull. stat. bimestriel* (Territoires du Sénégal et de la Mauritanie, Serv. Stat.), June 1957, p. 32; for French Guinea and the Ivory Coast unpublished data made available by the Services des Statistiques at Conakry and Abidjan respectively; for Angola from *Boletim Mensal de Estatística* (Angola, Repartição Técnica de Estatística Geral), No. 6, June 1957, p. 18; for Belgian Congo direct from Belg., Min. Col., "Prix de vente de certaines produits alimentaires au chef-lieu de chaque province, Juillet 1957." Converted to price per 1,000 calories using factors in FAO, *Food Composition Tables—Minerals and Vitamins—for International Use* (Nutr. Studies 11, Rome, 1954), pp. 10–12, 18.

[a] Local rice.
[b] Maize.
[c] Fonio.
[d] January 1958.
[e] No. 1 rice; the price for No. 2 was 1.26.
[f] Converted at 2,130 calories per kilogram, as shown by B. Bergeret, R. Masseyeff, A. Cambon, *Tables alimentaires abrégées, provisoires pour le sud Cameroun* (Off. de la Recherche Sci. et Technique Outre-mer, Inst. de Recherches du Cameroun [Yaoundé], 1954), p. 3.

FOOTNOTES TO TABLE II—(*Concluded*)

52) of "average purchase prices of native products." The official sources are: Nigeria, Eastern Region, Agr. Dept., *Crop and Weather Report: Eastern Region*; Nigeria, Western Region, Dept. Agr., *Crop and Weather Report*; Nigeria, Northern Region, Agr. Dept., *The Crop and Weather Report* (all monthly reports); Ghana, Dept. Agr., *Monthly Report—Foodstuffs Supply Position* (various issues); Belgian Congo, Belg., Min. Col., *L'Agriculture au Congo Belge et au Ruanda-Urundi de 1948 à 1952* (1954), Table C following p. 155. Converted to price per 1,000 calories using factors in FAO, *Food Composition Tables—Minerals and Vitamins—for International Use* (Nutr. Studies 11, Rome, 1954), pp. 10–12, 18.

[a] Sapele 1952 and 1953, Effurun 1954 and 1955.
[b] Moor Plantation.
[c] Benin 1952 and 1953; Irrua 1954 and 1955.
[d] Sweet potatoes.

INDEXES

NAME INDEX

Abeele, Marcel van den, 87, 93, 101, 109, 114, 117, 118, 120, 236, 253
Abreu Velho, Homero de Liz, 85, 86, 87
Adam, Jean, 26, 87, 100, 120, 196, 212
Adandé, A., 175, 179, 188, 190, 209, 212
Adloff, Richard, 208, 214, 257
Adriaens, E. L., 169, 170
Adrian, Jean, 60, 87, 120
Ady, Peter, 6, 12
Ancien, M. G., 254
Anderson, Elna, 26
Ashby, D. G., 102, 120
Ashley, Sir William, 254
Aubréville, André, 51, 53
Autret, M., 203, 212

Bacon, Lois, 85
Baeyens, J., 105, 120
Baguena Corella, Luis, 87
Baldwin, K. D. S., 27, 88, 121, 131, 134, 170, 200, 212, 255, 280, 284
Barrett, O. T., 147, 169
Bascom, W. R., 190, 192, 212
Bascoulergue, Pierre, 163
Beckett, W. H., 16, 26, 209, 212, 261, 264–65, 284
Bennett, M. K., 12, 61, 90, 96, 123, 206–07, 212, 244–45, 248, 254
Bergeret, B., 256
Bernard, E. A., 33, 35, 47, 53
Bigwood, E. J., 169, 170
Bolhuis, G. G., 109, 120
Bonnefoy, C., 111, 129, 170
Bowden, J., 254
Brock, J. F., 161, 163, 170, 203, 212, 224, 254
Brown, D. H., 112, 113, 115, 120
Buchanan, K. M., 9, 12, 43, 52, 53, 87
Bultot, F., 40–41, 44–45, 53
Buron, Robert, 261, 284

Cabot, Jean, 83, 87, 235, 254
Cambon, A., 213, 256
Cammack, R. H., 120, 261–62, 281, 284
Carter, Douglas B., 30, 33, 34–35, 40–41
Cerighelli, R., 7, 12, 26, 92, 93, 110, 119, 120, 132, 170
Chateau, R., 254
Chauleur, Pierre, 83, 87
Chevalier, Aug., 26, 92, 120
Childs, H., 228

Church, R. J. Harrison, 62, 73, 87, 92, 120
Clark, W. M., 237–38, 239, 254
Clayton, E. S., 125, 141–42, 170
Clement, J. M., 284
Coene, R. de, 109, 120, 274
Colombani, J. A., 249, 254
Comhaire-Sylvain, Suzanne, 26, 206–07, 212
Cours, Gilbert, 110, 111–12, 121
Coyaud, Yves, 26, 231, 254
Cuny, Gerard, 276, 284

Dalton, J. H., 260, 266, 284
Dalziel, J. M., 21, 26, 61, 88, 112, 113, 115, 121
Danso, T. V., 27, 170
Davesne, A., 93, 103, 104, 111, 116, 121
Davol, Fidelia D., 10, 12, 285
Degras, M., 121
Delevoy, G., 51–52
Denis, Jean, 249, 254
Dina, I. O., 27, 88, 120, 131, 134, 170, 200, 212, 255
Douglas, Mary, 178, 188
Drachoussoff, V., 149, 199, 201–02, 212, 275, 284
Dresch, Jean, 88, 95, 121
Drogué, Aimé, 83, 88, 108, 121, 240, 254

Elvehjem, C. A., 166, 168, 170
Erhart, M. H., 83, 88

Figuères, Robert, 112, 121
Forde, C. Daryll, 89, 163, 170, 173, 188
Fortes, M. and S. L., 205–06, 207, 212
Fynes-Clinton, D. O., 23, 26, 85, 88

Gaide, M., 181, 182, 186–87, 188, 272, 284
Galletti, R., 27, 88, 115, 120, 131, 134, 141, 145, 153, 170, 200, 212, 225, 240, 255
Garnier, B. J., 41, 53
Geortay, G., 79, 88, 102, 121, 129–30, 131–32, 135–36, 170, 270, 284
Giles, B. D., 259, 287
Gillman, Clement, 12
Godard, Ch., 88, 143, 170, 243, 255
Gourou, Pierre, 23, 27, 75, 76, 78, 88, 111, 121, 145, 170, 187, 188, 208, 211, 212, 238, 255

297

SUBJECT INDEX

Acha (achcha), 21; *see also Digitaria exilis*

Agricultural: extension, 273–74, 276–77, 281–82; organization, 277–80; productivity, 3, 274, 280–83; research, 10, 267–69, 281–82; systems, 9–16; technology, 267–73

Akokoaso, 16, 264–65

Angola: climate, 48; distribution of staple crops (map), 86; maize exports, 21; maize production, 23; staple crops, 23, 85

Animal draft power, 10, 11, 24, 230, 232–33, 280

Animal feeding, 216, 218

Animal products, 196–97, 201–02, 218

Bananas, 68; *see also* Plantains

Beer, 193

Belgian Congo: agricultural research, 267–70; area and production relatives, 127; cereal imports, 19, 20; changes in staple food production, 223; climatic zones (map), 44; cost of production of staple crops, 135–39; imports and per capita consumption of flour, 245; index of calorie yield of staple crops, 127; introduction and spread of maize and manioc, 176–78; maize exports, 21; movement of food, 16, 18; *paysannats indigènes*, 267–68, 274–76; relative prices of staple foods, 146–51, 157; staple crop yields, 127, 132; staple food crop zones, 73–80; staple foods contrasted with West Africa, 22

Benguela Current, 46, 48

Bilharzia, 65

Brazilias, 179

Bread, *see* Wheat flour

Bulrush millet, 21; *see* Millet-Sorghum Group

Bush fallowing, *see* Shifting cultivation

Calories: calorie contribution of the staple crops, 8, 193–96; index of calorie yield of staple food crops, 126, 127; values for staple foods (table), 160

Cameroons, *see* French Cameroons

Cash crops and staple food supplies, 10, 183, 260–61, 267

Cassava, *see* Manioc

Cattail millet, 21; *see* Millet-Sorghum Group

CCTA (Commission de Coopération Technique en Afrique au Sud du Sahara / Commission for Technical Cooperation in Africa South of the Sahara), 54

Cereals: competitive position vs. root crops, 156–58, 216, 250–53; exports, 21; importance of, 21, 22; imports, 19, 20, 245; influence of day length and sunlight, 49; nutrient composition, 160–62; storage and transport characteristics, 251

Chad, 48, 82, 181

Chickwangue, 192

Child feeding, 203

Climate: climatic zones in Belgian Congo (map), 44; in Congo Region, 45–48; and distribution of staple crops, 28–48, 59; in West Africa, 42–45

Cocoyams: consumption trends, 253; distribution, 69–73, 80–82, 84; ecological characteristics, 116–18; in the Guinea Coast (map), 70; importance of, 22, 58, 126–27; introduction, 26; labor requirements, 142, 144; nutritional characteristics (table), 160; scientific and common names, 7; water requirements, 116–17; yields, 118; *see also* individual territories

Colocasia esculentum, Colocasia antiquorum, 7; *see also* Cocoyams

Commercial production: effect on cropping patterns, 11, 79, 240; extent of, 14, 15, 77, 79, 240–41

Compulsory acreage quotas, 79–80

Consumer preferences, 144–47, 217–18, 241

Corn, *see* Maize

Cosettes, 25

Costs of production of staple crops, 126–44

Couscous, 191

Cover crops, 269, 271

CSA (Conseil Scientifique pour l'Afrique au Sud du Sahara/Scientific Council for Africa South of the Sahara), 51

Japan, 98, 120, 222, 283

Kenkey, 191
Kokonte, 25

Labor requirements of staple crops, 135–44
Land tenure systems, 274, 278–79
Leaves, consumption of, 162–63, 191
Legumes, 167–69, 199, 202
Liberia: cereal imports, 20; expansion of rice, 235; staple food crops, 58
Light requirements, 48–49: cocoyams, 117; of maize, 102; of millets and sorghums, 92; of rice, 97

Maize: consumption trends, 219, 252–53; distribution, 65–67, 74, 78 (map), 84–86, 182; exports, 21; importance of, 22, 23, 58, 126–27; imports, 20; introduction and spread, 25, 26, 174–81; labor requirements and cost of production, 136–44; nutritional characteristics, 160, 166–67; power grinders, 166, 216; water requirements, 99–100; yields, 103–05; *see also* individual territories
Maize rust, 105, 261–62
Manioc: consumption trends, 219, 252–53; distribution, 69–72, 73–77, 80–82, 84–86; ecological characteristics, 106–12; expansion in areas of dense population and short fallows, 185, 186–87; as a famine reserve crop, 209–10; flour, 25; in the Guinea Coast (map), 70; importance of, 22, 58, 126–27; introduction and spread, 25, 26, 174–81; labor requirements and costs of production, 107–08, 136–42, 144; nutritional characteristics, 160–63; scientific and common names, 7; toxicity, 108–09; yields, 22, 110–11; *see also* individual territories
Manioc meal, *see* Gari
Mechanization, 11, 216, 227–34, 236–37, 241, 269–70, 272–73, 277–78, 283
Middle Congo, 48, 80
Millets, *see* Millet-Sorghum Group
Millet-Sorghum G r o u p : consumption trends, 253; distribution, 59–60, 74, 80–82, 86; ecological characteristics, 91–94; importance of, 21, 22, 58, 126–27; labor requirements and costs of production, 137–42, 144; nutritional char-

acteristics, 160–62, 164–65; water requirements, 91; yields, 22, 92–93, 103; *see also* individual territories
Mixed farming, *see* Animal draft power
Moisture conditions: Congo Region, 44–48; importance for crop distribution, 29; moisture regions (map), 32; West Africa, 36–39, 42–45

Natural vegetation, *see* Vegetation
Niger Agricultural Project, 280
Niger Office, *see* Office du Niger
Niger Territory, 58, 72
Nigeria: calorie and money value efficiency of staple crops, 134; cereal imports, 20; cost of production of staple crops, 141–42; dietary surveys, 193–96, 200–01; expansion of rice, 228–29; food prices, 5, 6, 146–56, 262–64; food purchases by cocoa farmers, 16–17; introduction and spread of manioc, 179–80; land tenure and agricultural organization, 274, 278–79; movement of food, 15–17; population density and expansion of manioc, 185, 186; population pressure, 9; soil classification, 50; specialization in f o o d production and processing, 17, 18; staple food crops, 58, 66
Nutrition: nutrient composition of the staple crops (table), 160; *see also* Protein, Enrichment
Nutrition surveys, *see* Dietary surveys

Office du Niger, 230–32
ORANA (Organisation de Recherches sur l'Alimentation et la Nutrition Africaines), 197
Oryza glaberrima, 94–95; *see also* Rice
Oryza sativa: indica and *japonica* varieties, 94; introduction, 26; *see also* Rice

Palm oil, 191, 193, 201
Parboiled rice, 164–65
Paysannats indigènes, 267–68, 274–76
Peanuts and peanut flour, 163–64, 199, 202
Pennisetum typhoidem, 21; *see also* Millet-Sorghum Group
Plant breeding, 281, 283
Plantains: consumption trends, 253; distinguished from bananas, 68; distribution, 67–69, 73–77, 80–82, 84; ecological characteristics, 69, 105–06; impor-

The Library of Congress has cataloged this book as follows:

Johnston, Bruce F   1919–
    The staple food economies of western tropical Africa.
Stanford, Calif., Stanford University Press, 1958.

    305 p. illus. 24 cm. (Stanford University. Food Research Institute. Studies in tropical development)

    1. Agriculture—Economic aspects—Africa, West. 2. Food supply—Africa, West. i. Title.

HD2119.W4J6   338.15   58–11697 ‡

Library of Congress

MARSTON SCIENCE LIBRARY

76

7

1977

WESTERN TROPICAL AFRICA

•

MILES

0   200   400   600